D1527281

THE WINGS OF ETHIOPIA

STUDIES IN AFRICAN-AMERICAN LIFE

The Wings of Ethiopia

AND LETTERS *by Wilson Jeremiah Moses*

IOWA STATE UNIVERSITY PRESS / AMES

Wilson Jeremiah Moses is the director of the Afro-American Studies Program at Boston University.

© 1990 Iowa State University Press, Ames, Iowa 50010

Manufactured in the United States of America

⊚ This book is printed on acid-free paper.

Authorization to photocopy items for internal or personal use, or the internal or personal use of specific clients, is granted by Iowa State University Press, provided that the base fee of $.10 per copy is paid directly to the Copyright Clearance Center, 27 Congress Street, Salem, MA 01970. For those organizations that have been granted a photocopy license by CCC, a separate system of payments has been arranged. The fee code for users of the Transactional Reporting Service is 0–8138–0019–6/90 $.10.

First edition, 1990

International Standard Book Number: 0–8138–0019–6

Library of Congress Cataloging-in-Publication Data

Moses, Wilson Jeremiah
    The wings of Ethiopia : studies in African-American life and letters / by Wilson Jeremiah Moses. — 1st ed.
      p. cm.
    ISBN 0–8138–0019–6 (alk. paper)
    1. Black nationalism — United States — History. 2. Afro-Americans — Race identity. 3. Afro-Americans — Religion. 4. American literature — Afro-American authors — History and criticism.
    I. Title.
E185.625.M68 1990
305.8′96073 — dc20   90–4020

For Ida Mae Moses

Riposa, o madre, Iddio conceda
Men tristi immagini al tuo sopor

CONTENTS

IV ■ Literature

PREFACE

These essays were written over a period of twenty years, from 1969 to 1989. Some of them underwent little refinement during that period, others have been substantially revised for inclusion in this volume, but most are presented in their original condition with respect to content. The first of them is an autobiographical sketch, which I wrote mainly for my own satisfaction, although it was delivered as a lecture at the Perkins School of Theology in 1977. I read it again to a gathering of Fulbright scholars and Austrian students from the University of Vienna in 1987. On that occasion it met with two criticisms. Some accused me of painting a rosy picture of black life in America and ignoring the problems of "the masses," while others accused me of laying a guilt trip on white liberals. In short, people seemed to impose upon it whatever they assumed to be "The Story of the Negro." Observing people's reactions to it led me to the horrifying conclusion that texts may indeed be created—as some literary theorists maintain—in the minds of those who receive them. Once an autobiography is published, the author becomes nothing more than the subjective creation of those who read it.

Chapter 2 represents my attempt to make some sense out of a question that probably cannot be answered in a way that will be satisfactory to any large number of people, because while it is possible to discuss race and ethnic relations systematically, it is probably not possible for students of race and ethnic relations to agree on a uniform terminology. Chapter 3 was written for the meetings of the New England Historical Association, but adapted from a review I once wrote for *Umoja,* the black studies journal of the University of Colorado. Chapter 4 represents some leftover material from my recently completed biography of Alexander Crummell. It is my hope that social historians will some day reconstruct the histories of additional antebellum back-to-Africa voyages. Perhaps I shall some day have the inclination to undertake more studies of the sort. For the present, I am more interested in interpretation of the written word than in historical detective work, but I shall be happy to suggest avenues of further inquiry to future investigators who may be interested in the problem. Chapter 5 was delivered as a paper at the meetings of the African Studies Association in 1982, and originally published in *The New England Journal of Black Studies* (1983). While I was learning to use the mainframe computer of Brown University, I printed it as an exercise, and I republished it privately with revisions. I have reprinted it here to allow it wider circulation.

Chapter 6 was written long ago, and published in *The Social Studies*. It was intended to introduce lay readers to some of the anomalies and paradoxes in the history of black nationalism. It was essentially a summary of ideas that dominated my first book, *The Golden Age of Black Nationalism, 1850–1925*. I include it here, because it may be useful to readers who are unacquainted with the argument of that book, on which all my subsequent work has been based. The origins of Chapters 7 and 8 are explained within the texts; they represent my free exercise of those curmudgeon's rights to which every middle-aged scholar is entitled.

Chapter 9, the paper on African Redemption, is based on an article that I published some years ago in *Radical Religion*. It no longer bears much resemblance to the original, either in form or in content. The first version of Chapter 10 was written during the summer of 1977, while I was associate professor of history at Southern Methodist University and head of the Afro-American Studies Program. It was delivered at a conference on the black church at the Perkins School of Theology at Southern Methodist University and originally included in the manuscript of my second book, *Black Messiahs and Uncle Toms*. I removed it from that volume for two reasons: the paper was written for a non-scholarly audience, and it simply repeated themes that were treated in greater detail elsewhere in the book. Looking over it again, more than a decade later, I decided to make substantial revisions and to include it in this collection. It makes some points about black religion that still seem important and which I have not otherwise made, either in the present volume or elsewhere. Although I have found it appropriate to save most of my reflections on black women's religion and religious writing for a forthcoming work, I did consider it useful to include some observations on Maria Stewart that were central to the theme of National Destiny.

Chapter 11 was originally a conference paper presented at the Drew University Theological School and subsequently published in *The Drew Gateway*. Participation in that conference led me to develop my ideas about the peculiar relationship of black Americans to the church/state controversy in this republic. It became increasingly clear to me that black Americans have always exploited the ambivalence of Americans towards the First Amendment. Aware that the separation of church and state in America is imperfect and that there is, after all, an American "civil religion," black Americans have attempted to cloak their quest for complete citizenship in a rhetoric of Christian morality.

It is a basic principle of my critical code that scholars should make an effort to read documents in the terms that their authors set for them. Religion should not be viewed as epiphenomenal to feminism, Pan-Africanism, or African-American nationalism. At the same time, it should be remembered that religious attitudes often reflected attitudes on these related social issues. I have devoted some efforts to defending the nineteenth-century A.M.E. Bishop, Daniel Alexander Payne, from the attacks to which he has recently been subjected by placing him within the context of Emancipation, Reconstruction, and the response to industrialism. The purpose of this essay is not to describe fully the nature of Reconstruction religion; that is the subject of another study in progress, which will detail the nature of black literary, intellectual, and religious experience on the eve of the industrial age.

With two exceptions, the literary chapters in this volume are reprinted from black studies journals, whose editors I very much thank for opening the pages of their journals to me. "The Lost World of the New Negro: Black Literary Life before the Renaissance" was published in *Black American Literature Forum*. "Literary Garveyism: The Novels of Rev. Sutton Griggs" first appeared in *Phylon*. "Sexual Anxieties of the Black Bourgeoisie" first appeared in *Western Journal of Black Studies*. "More Stately Mansions" was first published in *Langston Hughes Review*. The essay on Israel Zangwill and Sutton Griggs was presented as a paper at the International Conference on American Studies at Eotvos University in Budapest during the spring of 1980 and subsequently published in *New Hungarian Review*. While much of its contents will be familiar to American readers, I trust that there is sufficient original content to endow it with interest even for the *cognoscenti*.

The title essay is a slightly modified version of an essay that appeared in Susan Resnick Parr's casebook, *Approaches to Teaching Ralph Ellison's "Invisible Man."* I thank Dr. Parr for encouraging me to write on Ellison and for granting permission to reprint the essay in the present volume. It has not been my practice to write on living or very recent authors, and my interest in writing on Ellison on this and on one other occasion derives from my fascination with his hidden text on the history of ideas.

I must also acknowledge a debt to the many scholars who have influenced my work over the past twenty years. The observations on black nationalism of John H. Bracey, Howard Brotz, Harold Cruise,

August Meier, Alfred Moss, Otey Scruggs, and the late Elliott M. Rudwick were seminal influences. I have taken some candid exceptions to some opinions Bracey expressed twenty years ago, but my response to his discourse is an indication of my respect for his work and the importance that I attribute to it. I should also say that I much appreciate his gracious allusions to my own work.

I express, herewith, my gratitude to the numerous persons who assisted me along the way, particularly to Mr. Robert Schultz, who originally acquired the manuscript for Iowa State University Press, to Mr. Bill Silag, who is as helpful and supportive an editor as one might wish for, to Mr. Philip Beck, and to the other staff editors, who thoroughly "blue pencilled" the manuscript. My wife, Maureen, read through the galley and page proofs, saving me from many errors and inconsistencies. I also thank the administration of Boston University for its support and encouragement of my work and for allowing me the greatest flexibility in my teaching schedule during the final editing of these essays.

What Are Black Americans?

CHAPTER 1

Author's Declaration of Bias

**You Don't Have to Be White
to Be an Ethnic American:
Growing Up Black among
German and Italian Catholics**

*Despite their supposed "racial" distinctiveness,
black Americans constitute the very model of
"ethnic" assimilation in America. Speaking culturally, if not racially, it is difficult to say where
white leaves off and black begins in a civilization
that is so deeply influenced by charismatic and
evangelical religious movements, by jazz, blues,
and the rhythms of rap music. This essay was
written during the summer of 1977 and delivered
as an address to the Perkins School of Theology
at SMU in Dallas. I publish it here without revi-
sion, although I have added a second part, revealing some more mature reflections.*

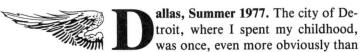

Dallas, Summer 1977. The city of Detroit, where I spent my childhood,
was once, even more obviously than
it is today, segmented into ethnic neighborhoods. Ethnic neighborhoods
encouraged marriages within one's own ethnic group. Urban renewal,
the construction of a metropolitan expressway system, a severe racial
insurrection, and the expansion of the black population outward from
the city's core encouraged massive suburban sprawl during the 1950s and
1960s. This led to a blurring of distinctions among the various white
ethnic groups in the metropolitan area and increased tendencies to intermarriage. White children intermingle promiscuously in the suburban
schools. A significant part of their activity constitutes a prelude to sexual
behavior, and this often leads to marriages across ethnic lines. But while
the patterns of dating and marital behavior have tended to erode the
ethnic consciousness of white Americans, they have not tended to erode

3

racial consciousness. The suburban schools that ring most American cities are melting pots for white ethnic groups; they are nonetheless havens of racial purity. The German-American and the Italian-American family are fading into one another, with the ecumenical movement among the American churches aiding in the process, but if the white American family is in danger of disappearing, it is not due to intermarriage with blacks. The ultimate test of whether Professor Glazer's ethnic model is applicable to black Americans is whether they are capable of vanishing into the suburbs, where other ethnic groups cease to be Polish-American or Italian-American and become Polish-Italian-German-Jewish-American, or just plain American.

I must confess that I am an unlikely person to be rejecting the currently fashionable "ethnicity" approach to Afro-American Studies. In many ways, my own life experiences seem to be a contradiction of the black nationalism to which I claim a sense of loyalty. I live in a white suburb of Dallas, Texas, an area of the city where black people entered only as gardeners and maids a decade ago. My older son attends a recently integrated middle school, where he is one of a handful of black children who are *not* "bussed in." To call him "black" is an extreme exaggeration. On his school records, he is identified as "Negro," although the Dallas Independent School District is "officially color blind." His mother is a blue-eyed Norwegian and Irish Catholic. His relationship to his blackness is different than mine was at his age. I wonder if his children will think of themselves as black, at all. I have skirted around the edges of this issue in conversations with several of my black American and West Indian colleagues. They are not married to white women, but some of them, especially those who reside in small isolated college towns have expressed similar concerns. Is our blackness vanishing? Is our intellectual black nationalism, our commitment to the black studies movement merely an academic ritual, a semi-religious experience by which we attempt to escape the doubts and fears of life in an anomic, disconnected civilization? Or do we have something to say regarding the black experience that no European or white American can say? Do we speak with an authority that no European or white American can muster?

Some years ago, I became aware of a painting by Roberto Ferruzzi, an often-reproduced example of holy-card-art called *The Madonna of the Street*. Its author does not appear in the standard reference works at my neighborhood library. The work's sentimentality and the author's obvious attempt at ambiguity would probably turn off the average first-year graduate student in art history. One cannot miss the implied statement that the slightly tarnished young girl with the sleeping child in her arms represents the abandoned women that one might have seen at any time in the streets of Rome. I have it as the first page of a calendar that one of my sisters gave me for Christmas one year, with an ironic expression that only I could have detected. It was an allusion to our background of Catholic education in Nativity of our Lord Parish on Detroit's east side, just south of the Harper-Gratiot streetcar terminal in an area that used to be called "Little Berlin." There was a German cornerstone on St. Thomas and Peter's Lutheran Church four blocks from us at Chapin and Fischer. We lived at 5458 Belvidere, just south of Chapin. If we walked north two blocks to Gratiot and Belvidere, we were at the German picture show. Two miles southwest from there on Gratiot was a bar with a neon-lit sign of a white horse rearing on its hind legs and the legend, *Zum Weissen Rossl*. I learned later that this was the title of an operetta. Hornung's meats and sausages, where you could buy *Landjäger* and *Brötchen*, was just northwest of the animated Pfeiffer's beer sign at Harper and Gratiot. Father Bernard N. Geller heard confessions in German and English, assisted by Fathers Baumgartner and Walling. Father Di Giulio heard confessions in English and Italian.

Italians had begun to move into the parish after World War I. We used to hear the music coming out of their houses and smell the odors of oregano and Parmesan cheese. My father said it smelled like old socks. "A whiff of ancient 'roma," he used to say, "they stowed their dirty togas back in fifty B.C." I guessed later that he gained his impression of malodorous Rome from the first act of *Julius Caesar*. There were two milk routes on our street. One milkman drove a horse, but we bought our milk from Joe Bomarito, who drove a truck. Once his son helped me push my car out of a snow drift. Mr. Cusimano was a vegetable peddler; Joe Tocco ran the corner grocery, paying his rent to Joe Kulchi's dad. There was an excellent Italian pastry shop, where we used to get lemon ice. It was destroyed so that the Edsel Ford Freeway could be dug. Jimmy Dinverno's dad's construction company made a lot of money hauling dirt out of the ditch, and they moved out of the neighborhood.

So there were German Catholics, and there were Italians (who are always Catholic), and there were black families. One family, the Harrisons, attended the Burns Avenue Baptist Church, which was white. Mr. Harrison was light enough to pass for white, and he attended church without his wife, who was considerably darker. His sons went to Burns Avenue Baptist without incident, however, and even persuaded me to attend daily vacation Bible school, but that was before my real conversion. I do not know where the Wrights attended church. Kinnard was a high school teacher, and I assume he was Episcopal—or something like that. The Yarboroughs went to a black Baptist church, farther downtown, and stayed there all day long on Sundays. The Weisses were mulattoes, and they went to some mulatto church. Mr. and Mrs. Daniels were very black and very old. They had lived on the street for a long time. I never knew their religion, nor that of the McIntoshes, who lived next door to us.

The houses of these eight families were the only black homes on our block of Belvidere when we moved there in 1950. Along the block there were some fifty houses, counting both sides of the street. We black folk were all working people. We kept our homes and lawns in good repair. I never saw anyone drinking anything stronger than beer. Card playing and listening to the blues on Sunday were definitely frowned on. We were perceived by the white ethnics as a threat, nonetheless. They began to sell their homes; property values declined, and this increased the rate of the white exodus. By 1960 the neighborhood was 50 percent black. By 1970 it was 95 percent black. Three-bedroom houses were selling for two thousand dollars in 1977, and perfectly good dwellings were often boarded up or bulldozed. In such manner does a racist society confront the problem of a housing shortage.

The Church of the Nativity of Our Lord is a mammoth structure, built during the twenties. It is a romanesque building, with its main doors opening to the West a sort of modified cathedral with a remote ceiling and a bell tower that was often lost in the mist on foggy mornings. The entire community, Catholic and Protestant alike, set their clocks by the ringing of the bells at six in the morning, noon, and six in the evening. The other parish buildings were a convent, a rectory, a high school, a grade school, and a recreation center. Four masses were said daily and six on Sundays by the four resident fathers. The schools were staffed by twenty-two nuns and two lay teachers. The nuns came from a motherhouse in Racine, Wisconsin. Some of them were German, and one or two spoke with accents. They were of the order of St. Dominic and wore a white habit with a black veil. Their presence was comforting. But when I visited them last, I found them disturbingly attired in civilian clothes.

I owed my Roman Catholicism to my mother's conversion during her late teens. She was educated by a German order, the Sisters of Saint Mary's at St. Mary's Infirmary, St. Louis, Missouri. She and my father were married in the Catholic Church. They were married in the rectory, because my father was Episcopalian, and in those days the Church would neither allow mixed marriages to be performed in the church, nor would it sanction them with a nuptial mass. Perhaps it was for this reason that my mother's attendance at mass was sporadic. My father grew up in Atlanta, in the Seventh Day Adventist Church. He once told me that he could remember the other children in the neighborhood throwing stones at his family because they went to church on Saturday. The true religious roots of my father's family were in the Colored Methodist Church. I once suspected that he had received his name, William Heard Moses, from the fifty-third bishop of the African Methodist Episcopal Church. William H. Heard (1850–1924) had been an Atlanta pastor before he was appointed American consul to Liberia. But my father believed that he had inherited his name from a friend and fellow union member of his father.

I was exposed to the Methodist Church as a child, on weekend visits to my great aunt Mary Traylor, who lived in an all black area of Ferndale, Michigan, a Detroit suburb. It had unpaved streets, and many people kept chickens. Across the street from Aunt Mary's cottage was a church that we did not attend; I can remember the rantings of the preacher from morning to night. Sometimes he would become possessed and repeat the same mystical word, hour after hour. Once he screamed the name of God for an entire afternoon – "YaaaaaWUH! AaaaaaWUH! AaaaaaWUH! AaaaaaWUH!" I can remember my elders being disgusted by his emotionalism and by what they perceived as the substitution of nonsense for religion. The first time I attended the Catholic Church I was perplexed by the priest's unintelligible chanting in Latin. I asked my mother why she had taken me to the "AaaaaaWUH! AaaaaaWUH!" church, but her answer was brief, indignant, and unsatisfying.

When I was around nine years old, my mother began earnest efforts to see to my Catholic education. The deterioration of the Detroit public schools, the mushrooming of juvenile gangs, and corresponding police brutality made it difficult for working class people to shield their children from the rougher aspects of life in Detroit without the assistance of such agencies as the parochial schools. Mother decided that I should attend instructions for a year before going to Catholic school so that I would know the Baltimore Catechism and receive the first sacraments before enrolling. Mom made certain that I memorized every question and answer in all the assigned lessons and that I was able to recite them with alacrity and verve. She also made certain that I could translate all the answers into my own words and tell what they meant. I was easily the best student in my second grade catechism class, although I was certainly not the oldest, and I was the only "colored kid." Just before Christmas, the nun who taught us announced that we would have a Catechism Bee, which would cover the first ten lessons in the book and the prayers we had been told to memorize. When the show was over, and I was the only one left standing – having answered the question that had stumped the only remaining contestant—the good sister turned to the back of the book, to a lesson for which our class was not responsible. Because Mother and I had covered just about all the concepts in the book, I knew the answer, but since I had not memorized it word for word, she would not be satisfied. The Catechism Bee had no winner that day. I was always a clown in school, despite my father's warnings and reprimands (A black boy must never be a clown.) I was never actually disruptive, but I liked to laugh and have fun. Also, I found religion class interesting. I would try to ask the sister questions that she could not answer. Before we made our first confession, we had to have a dry run in the classroom. We had to invent some sins and confess them to the entire group. Naturally, I told a fine fable of a life corrupt, an uninterrupted pattern of murders and thefts and blasphemies. The other catechists were delighted by my story, so much more colorful than their own dull catalogues of misdeeds, but the nun made a wry face and seemed to feel that I was showing a disrespect for holy things. As for the actual first confession, I took it very seriously, because I sincerely believed that I was sinful. Had I not kept impure thoughts in my mind and taken pleasure in the contemplation of sinful things? Had I not once looked at a picture of a naked woman, shown to me by a boy named Mario Fontana, who lived two blocks away on Rohns street? Had I not coveted? I was certain that if I were to die without the absolution of a priest, I would burn forever in the torment of hell. I did not particularly dread the loss of heaven, for we had at home an edition of *The Divine Comedy,* with engravings by Gustave Doré, and heaven seemed like a pretty dull place. Still, Doré left me with the impression that heaven was, compared to hell, decidedly the lesser of two evils. I made my first confession with real enthusiasm, therefore, and until I was fourteen, I was always certain to confess my sins on alternate Saturdays.

My Communion was actually more traumatic than my first confession. I wanted very desperately to accept the idea that the wafer of unleavened bread contained, in truth, the previous body and blood of our Lord and Savior, Jesus Christ—but I did not. I wanted to swallow along with the wafer the doctrine of transubstantiation, because I feared that not to believe would be a mortal sin. The first communicants from the after-school catechism class were for the most part older than the first communicants who attended the parish school. The two classes were brought together for the first Communion mass, however. If I remember correctly, it was May 4, 1952. We had learned a hymn to the Virgin for the occasion.

Mother all beautiful, hear us today,
Lead us thyself to the altar we pray.
Mother from birth, to his life's dark eclipse
Lay him, thyself, on our tremulous lips.

The younger children were instructed to march with their heads bowed and hands folded, palms together, pointing towards heaven in Albrecht Durer fashion. At home, I had been taught to fold my hands with the fingers interlocked. I felt that the communion procession, boys in dark suits, girls in white bridal veils, was somehow artificial. I was uncomfortable assuming the attitude of childish reverence that was part of the show. I found it impossible to get into character. I folded my hands in the way I had seen people fold their hands at home, when we said grace before meals, and I remember a few weeks later overhearing some older boys discussing my rebellion. "Look," one of them said with a sneer, "There's the guy who made his first Communion and didn't even fold his hands."

In the fall of 1952, I began the fifth grade in the parish school of Nativity of our Lord Church. My father accompanied me to the classroom of Sister Lydia. She was an interesting woman, over fifty, with a sardonic smile and a sense of humor. She spoke with a German accent and seemed to think that everything the German boys did was as cute as could be. She had one favorite named Julius, a nasty brat. We used to throw rocks at each other all the way home from school. Sister used to give us a certain amount of time for story hours, during which we were allowed a few minutes to entertain the rest of our class by reporting on our reading. I found during these periods ample opportunity to entertain the class and to satisfy my predilection for showing off by reciting the exploits of Pecos Bill, the legendary cowboy hero, who was raised by coyotes, drank boiling coffee straight from the fire, and used a rattlesnake for a necktie. I did not understand why the class was less captivated by my stories of Mowgli, the jungle boy, who was raised by wolves, but forced to live among men. I understand now that I identified with Kipling's *Jungle Book,* and later with much of Kipling's "adult fiction," because I had been forced to an early awareness of the problems of cross-cultural contacts. I understood how Mowgli felt, never certain of whether he was a man or a wolf. I understand now the story of the Indian girl, raised in a Western home, who could not find a place in the society of the English colonialists and went to live in a squalid village with a husband who beat her.

I also recall one other vivid experience with reading during the fifth grade. In the back of the room was a bookshelf from which we were allowed to select reading to occupy us during study hours or whenever we could find the time. At home we had been reading Howard Pyle's version of King Arthur, so the book that I selected — mainly because of the cover illustration, a knight on horseback — was called *Kings and Things.* I was disappointed, at first, to discover that it was history and not fiction, but I soon became engrossed — too engrossed. One morning, while I was bored by waiting for a group of other children to complete their recitations, I opened my book and began to read. Suddenly I felt the powerful slap of Sister Lydia's hand across the left side of my face. She had circled the room and approached from the rear, when I had not responded to the question she had asked me. Hurriedly I stood, went to the front of the room, gave my answer (which I had memorized) and returned to my seat. It has always seemed strange to me that a child should be punished for reading in school. In this era of the modern open classroom, we encourage children to work at their own pace. But the parochial schools in the Archdiocese of Detroit made little allowance for individual abilities or disabilities, in those days. I remember how much I hated reading class. Everyone had to sit still and wait while the slower children read aloud. One boy had a problem with stammering, but he was always forced to read aloud like everyone else. I felt sorry for Gene, until one day he called me a monkey, which I felt had a racial overtone. "No," I said, "You are the monkey; you must be a monkey, because you don't know how to talk." As early as the first grade, while still in public school, I realized that I read more quickly than most of the other students, and therefore I had to learn to play a little game. I would hold the place in the book with my finger, so I would know where the class was when the teacher called on me, and read ahead at my own pace. The teachers would try to catch me out, but I usually could find the place in time. Those of us who could read well would often compete when called on to see who could read the fastest, or would try reading with the book upside down, but this was emphatically discouraged.

As I passed through the fifth grade, I became increasingly religious. I found the orderliness of Catholic life appealing. My father was aware of my interest in English history, so he procured for me a copy of Charles Dickens's classic, *A Child's History of England,* but I eschewed the heretical text because of the author's irreverent attitude towards the Catholic clergy and the pope. I became increasingly and painfully aware of the difference between myself and the all-white fifth grade class at Nativity on the one hand, and the black youths with whom I associated after school hours, on the other. During the summer of 1953, and again in the summer of 1955, my religious feelings reached a peak of intensity. I spent those summers at Green Pastures Camp, which was operated by the Detroit Urban League for underprivileged black youth. Being black made you underprivileged. Provisions were made for Catholics to attend mass, but on one occasion we were not able to attend because a rainstorm had made the roads impassable. I felt a profound sense of betrayal and disappointment. Even worse, we were expected to take part in a non-Catholic service. The counsellors called it a nondenominational service. I was not fooled by this sophistry, and I hid in the lavatory until they had finished singing their heretical hymns and troubling heaven with their misguided prayers. I meditated on the sufferings of the mission children in Communist China, who were happy to die for their faith, and I felt that if they were willing to die, I should be willing to suffer embarrassment.

The pastor of Nativity of Our Lord Church was Father Bernard N. Geller; he was a stocky little guy, who reminded most people of Edward G. Robinson. There was a rumor that he had once fought for the Golden Gloves. Peter Waldmeir, a columnist for the *Detroit News* who had attended Nativity through the eighth grade, but many years ahead of me, recalls "where following a stern lecture he belted one kid and knocked him through a door and halfway down the stairs" (*Detroit News,* August 31, 1977). I remember an occasion when he kicked and slapped one of the Italian guys all around the classroom. There was no father in this boy's home. He had low self-esteem, smoked cigarettes, and did poorly in school. I may have imagined, but it seemed to me that Father Geller's victims were always the weak and underconfident, rather than those who were the worst behaved. As he grew older, his mind began to slip. He used to keep the entire school after mass for sometimes as long as half an hour to declaim against the long-dead Franklin D. Roosevelt and "that silly Mrs. Roosevelt." Some of us thought he sounded like Mr. Bluster on the Howdy Doody show. There was not a single boy from the sixth to the twelfth grade who did not think he could do a good imitation of Father Geller's distinctive speaking style.

> You're just a bluff, a bluff. I'll tell you what they should do with punks like you; they should get the chair, the chair! Call in a priest; get 'em in the state of grace; and turn on the juice!

In the seventh grade I became involved in Mariolatry. I shall not condemn out of hand the veneration of the Virgin, nor shall I ever deny the intensity with which I internalized the Catholic dogma on sex. I do not think it was right, however, for the sisters to create in our minds — the image of the mother of God in the likeness of a German nun. The girls at Nativity were told to idolize Saint Maria Goretti, a poor little

Italian girl, who was murdered by an insane half-wit. One sister told the class that if a girl were about to be raped, she should jump out of a twelfth-story window, rather than suffer violation. This would be the only sort of situation in which the end could justify the means—for impurity is a greater evil than suicide, and in any case the good of escaping defilement would be accomplished before the evil of hitting the ground below. I cannot say who I now consider more foolish—the sister who presented this sophistry, or myself for accepting it at the age of thirteen.

There are some historians who believe that the "cult of the Virgin" has had a humanizing effect on Catholic peoples. Gilberto Freyre has argued that as a result of the adoration of the Virgin, a high place consequently was assigned to women in Latin America. Motherhood was sanctified, and therefore female slaves in Brazil were less brutalized under slavery than were female slaves in the United States. Slave families—so the logic was extended—were less frequently broken up. Such assumptions, both as to the status of women in Iberian societies, and as to the security of family life among Spanish and Portuguese slaves, have not gone unchallenged. For my part, I find it difficult to believe that societies that put great emphasis on female chastity are truly concerned with exalting the dignity of womanhood. I believe they are more concerned with keeping women in their place and firmly under the control of men.

Of course I had no knowledge of such abstract historical and sociological issues during the years that I underwent my Catholic indoctrination. The power of the church over my mind derived from its incredible power as a symbol of wealth and stability. It wielded the symbols of two thousand years of history and philosophy, art and architecture, music and ritual. Nativity Parish and its impressive buildings represented not only a system of religion; it was a court, a museum, a library, an educational system—a Vatican in miniature. And I was a lone "colored guy" in the midst of a powerful European institution. My presence was suffered only because I was willing to take it all very seriously. The cult of the Virgin was my principal defense mechanism. It was a means of rationalizing the necessity for sexual repression, my unnatural relationship with the only members of the opposite sex with whom I came into daily contact. It was a means of preserving my self-respect in a situation where I could not allow myself to become involved in adolescent presexual activity.

As a black youth, living on Detroit's east side, in a neighborhood that was steadily changing from a multi-ethnic neighborhood into a black ghetto, I would have found it impossible not to realize the differences between the sexual morality of lower class blacks and working class whites. I was embarrassed by these differences, which I could perceive, but could not understand. At the same time I was envious of the earthier and more easygoing attitude towards sex that I witnessed among black youths my own age.

My Catholic education provided me with no tools for analyzing my feelings. The Catholic schools, as my father used to say, were strong in the humanities, but weak in the social sciences. The same could probably be said of all religious education throughout the Western world. Religion does not encourage the view that sexual morality is an outgrowth of social realities. I wish that at the age of sixteen I could have taken a course in black sociology, that someone could have introduced me to the works of E. Franklin Frazier, Charles S. Johnson, Alexander Crummell, and Lorenzo Turner. I wish that I could have read the following words of W. E. B. Du Bois:

> All womanhood is hampered today because the world on which it is emerging is a world that tries to worship both virgins and mothers and in the end despises motherhood and despoils virgins.
>
> The future woman must have a life work and economic independence. She must have knowledge. She must have the right of motherhood at her own discretion. The present mincing horror at free womanhood must pass if we are ever to be rid of the bestiality of free manhood; not by guarding the weak in weakness do we gain strength, but by making weakness free and strong.
>
> The world must choose the free woman or the white wraith of the prostitute. Today it wavers between the prostitute and the nun.

Wavering between the prostitute and the nun, there were boys at Nativity High School who were known to visit "black bottom." There, a woman could be purchased for the cost of a bottle of cheap wine. I would not have dreamed of visiting a prostitute at the age of seventeen. I was virginal and very smug about it. The recollection of the lynching of Emmett Till was still fresh in my mind, and I was filled with rage that black women could be available to white men on such contemptible terms, while I could not have decent, wholesome friendships with the girls at Nativity High School, who had known me since I was ten years old. Years later, when some of my black buddies began to tell me of their army experiences and their contacts with German women, I began to see the forces that created chastity and prostitution. A German Catholic after the war could sell herself to a Jewish American soldier for a

Hershey bar or a pair of nylons. Little Italian boys could pimp their sisters to Negroes for a loaf of bread. It is not only the threat of starvation that can corrupt a people, but the demoralization of being a conquered nation.

Providence, Summer 1987. Education under German Dominicans predisposes one to Thomistic rationalism, and can lead to a dispassionate perception of the religious experience. The nuns were very proud of Saint Thomas; and we therefore were emphatically taught that reason was never in conflict with Divine Revelation and that the basic truths necessary to salvation could be arrived at through the rational processes alone. Nativity was no world of high culture, but masses were still sung in Latin while I was there. The church had an excellent organist in Edward Person, and it was impossible to attend mass daily for eight years without learning some Latin. Ed Person had a lot to do with developing the interest in good music that I acquired at home. Catholicism has the potential to nurture the aesthetic sensibilities.

Fortunately, my Catholicism exposed me, not only to German Thomism, but to Mediterranean antinomianism. I shall never forget the Good Friday celebration during which I witnessed adoration of the cross. A life-size crucifix was placed in the nave of the church, and the women of the parish paraded past the exposed body of the Naked Man, kissing the wounds, some of them with tears in their eyes. Catholicism is more universal than Protestantism, because of its extreme eclecticism and syncretism. Philosophically, Thomism borders on Pelagian rationalism. Aesthetically, the veneration of statues and icons borders on idolatry. Catholicism has helped me to appreciate not only the idea of rational religion; it has given me an appreciation for the necessity of ritual and the irrational in human existence.

If I were not born a Catholic, I suspect the Divine Providence would have made me a Hindu. I feel that I could have loved the blue-faced Vishnu, or the dancing elephant god, Ganesa. Catholicism is like Hinduism with its love of incense, bells, and statuary. In every classroom that I can remember, there was a statue of the Virgin. She was always barefoot and stood with her foot on the body of a serpent. She was supposed to be crushing it beneath her heel, but the snake always seemed to be slithering sensuously between her toes. It occurred to me only recently that this image was similar to the idea of the serpent goddess of ancient Crete and the serpent goddess of India. I have always felt that churches that do not have statues are a travesty. In fact, I do not want anything modern in my churches. I consider it one of the great tragedies of modern life that the Catholic Church has lost its sensual, medieval character.

I believe that my constant oscillation between the white and the black world during my formative years did some good things for me. It taught me the principle of cultural relativism, for one thing. I experienced the dissonance between the world of Nativity Parish and the world of the adolescent black boy. The home of my parents was a refuge from both, as well as a halfway house between the two worlds. My experiences helped me to understand white people, not as a solid mass, but as a conglomerate of diverse interest groups, divided by class, region, and ethnicity. They made me understand that white people do not represent some sort of diabolical power. They can even, at times, be well-meaning and fair-minded, if painfully clumsy and condescending. They are no less superstitious than black folk, no less emotional, no less communalistic. Most of the clichés that one hears bandied about concerning the unique features of black culture may just as appropriately be applied to "white ethnics."

During the years I spent at Nativity, I never lacked for a sense of my black identity. The philosophy of Booker T. Washington was strong in my parents' house. My father had attended the Booker T. Washington High School in Atlanta, where he had spent his boyhood and had later attended Morehouse College. My father was not one to talk much of his youthful experiences. I only know that he was apprenticed to a plasterer, and that he paid for his college education by working in Atlanta. Shortly after graduating from college, he migrated to Detroit, where he worked in the auto plants. By the time I was old enough to be aware of such things, he was employed as a watchman at the Detroit Water Works. Later, he passed a civil service examination to become a filter attender and chlorinator operator at the Water Works Park in Detroit. He purchased our house at 5458 Belvidere in 1950, and he died there in bed on September 3, 1983. His favorite pastimes were "home improvements." He enjoyed carpentry, plumbing, finishing furniture, cooking, painting, and gardening. Occasionally he would go fishing on the Detroit River. I knew from an early age that I was fortunate to have a father who had a well-developed instinct of craftsmanship as well as a trained intellect. He never earned much money, and he was not materialistic, but when he died he left no debts, and his assets, though modest, were more solid than those of many professional men.

My mother's maiden name was Ida Mae Johnson. She was born in

Kansas City, Kansas, in 1918, and had a harder, more painful life than
she deserved, orphaned at the age of four, hospitalized with tuberculosis
in her mid-twenties, and dying of cancer after a long and painful illness
in December of 1983. Her earliest recollections were of her grand-
mother's bringing her to Tulsa, to the home of the woman she knew as
Aunt Lena, where she lived until she finished high school. She was proud
of her training as a nurse. This was not because she considered nursing
the ideal or even a very desirable profession. What she took pride in was
having lifted herself by her bootstraps from an impoverished condition.
She was largely self-educated, a woman who knew how to taste books
and magazines, and which ones to taste from. She was an able ironist,
with a well-developed cynicism respecting the ways of white folk, and yet
she was almost white herself. She read to her children a great deal,
everything from *Beowulf* (in translation) to Thoreau and Macbeth. She
liked decorative arts, papier maché, coloring books, Christmas tree or-
naments, centerpieces. She used to enter the annual hat making competition, which took place every Christmas at Women's Hospital, where she
worked. The hats had to be constructed from hospital supplies—gauze
bandages, adhesive tape, pill boxes, etc. Judging was anonymous, and
she gleefully took first prize several years in a row. My mother always
taught us to think of ourselves as ambassadors. We were made to believe
that if we were lazy or unclean, we would bring disgrace not only on
ourselves, but on the race. We would prejudice white folk against some
industrious and accommodating Negro, who would unfairly be made to
pay the price of our folly. In other words, we would be guilty of "holding
back the race."

   I never knew either of my grandfathers. My surrogate grandfather
was Jesse Burnett, a retired blacksmith, who lived only a short walk
away. As a nine-year-old, I would ride my bike over to his home on
Moffat St. where he had lived since 1925. That was the year of much
racial violence in Detroit, as black families began to move into white
neighborhoods on the east side. Du Bois editorialized on the most spectacular instance, the case of Dr. Ossian Sweet, the black physician, who

> shot into a mob which was threatening him, his family, his friends and his
> home in order to make him move out of the neighborhood. He killed one
> man and wounded another. . . . [The mob] came, cursed and threw stones
> and ordered him to move. He gathered his family and friends within and
> locked the door. Five or six thousand people lined the streets. The police set
> traffic officers to divert the traffic that could not get through. The mob
> invaded his yard and approached his doors. He shot and shot to kill. His
> wife and his friends are now in jail charged with *Murder in the first degree!*
> He was "colored."[1]

It was not a mob that attacked the home of Jesse Burnett, but a group of unruly boys. They threw a stone through his front window, injuring his infant son in his crib. Burnett did not possess any firearms, but he was a tough little man, and he went alone into the street, followed the boys and located the home of one of them. The grim-faced father came out to meet Burnett. He admitted the boy was wrong and said that he would be punished. Burnett lived in his house on Moffatt until his ninety-fifth year. One morning, he awoke to discover that someone had entered his bedroom and taken his pants from the chair next to his bed. The neighborhood was now entirely black but too unsafe for an old man, so in 1983 he moved out of the home that he had occupied for almost sixty years.

Mr. Burnett was one of the best teachers I ever had. He had been educated in one of the industrial colleges of the South, then he had set out travelling from town to town, looking for a place where he could practice his trade. After he was driven from one workplace by a mob armed with axe handles, his father urged him to leave the South, and he found a job in Detroit, replacing a drunken Englishman. Burnett was a shrewd old guy, who told me stories about his service with the Quartermaster's Corps as a mule driver during the First World War. He had visited the Hall of Mirrors at Versailles, and his usual greeting was "Comment ça va?" As I grew older, I came to appreciate what a remarkable thing it was that he could relate his own experiences to the larger currents of American social history. He could always tell you who was in Congress at the time of some important event in his life, who was Governor of Michigan at another, or how he felt the policy of a given Secretary of War had affected the black soldier. Old Burnett's knowledge was not limited to politics; he had an appreciation for the finer things. He was always quoting "old Plato" or "old Socrates," and he knew a pretty woman when he saw one. I can remember Old Burnett and my father sitting on our front porch after the Detroit "civil insurrection" of 1967. "It's not what I would call a race riot," was Burnett's comment. To his way of thinking, a race riot was the sort of thing that Dr. Sweet had experienced, or the sort of thing the entire city had experienced in 1943.

I had grown up knowing about the riot of 1943. I was only seven years old, and on my way home from school, when another little kid, a white boy not much older than I, and whom I had never seen before, related to me with wonder the startling information that there had once been a war between white and colored, in which "the colored lifted up and turned over cars." Of course, I was already aware of the fact of racial conflict. I was five years old when another little white boy had saluted me with the greeting, "Hi nigger." My mother had already told me that colored boys were not supposed to have white girlfriends. I asked my mother about this "war between white and colored," but she had little more to say than that it had happened, and that it had been unfortunate. My father thought so too. He described the state of emergency that ensued after the riot, saying that it was an ugly thing to see policemen carrying shotguns, patrolling the public parks, while families spread their picnic lunches.

My youth in Detroit was uneventful. It was a peaceful place in those days; nothing like New York or Chicago. I was aware of the changing nature of the neighborhood, of course; that was a constant fact of life. Things change; they don't *necessarily* get better or worse, but they do change, and the changes are inevitably traumatic. I was still relatively young when I began to think about a career as an intellectual. It started when my mother brought home that Doré edition of *The Divine Comedy*. By the time I was fourteen, I had come across two books by a person named Auslander—*The Winged Horse* and *The Winged Horse Anthology*, an introduction to the Western tradition in literature. I began contemplating a career as an intellectual long before I was exposed to Ivy League intellectualism, puritanism, or the Social Gospel. I began reading, writing, and thinking about literature, while I was still under the influences of Roman Catholic rationalism and aesthetic values.

My father listened to Milton Cross and the Texaco Opera every Saturday, so I grew up knowing at least the most popular arias. He also had an interesting collection of old 78 recordings, some of them printed only on one side, including the major symphonies: Mozart's 38th, Beethoven's 5th and 6th, Tchaikovsky's 6th, *Eine Kleine Nachtmusik,* and numerous singles of operatic arias. He had some of Bidu Sayão singing Violetta arias. I was fascinated by the title of *"Credo in un Dio crudel,"* and naturally I liked *"La donna è mobile"* and *"Vesti la giubba."* We used to listen to the "Voice of Firestone" and the "Bell Telephone Hour," and when Mario Lanza starred in *The Great Caruso,* we went as a family to see it in our neighborhood theater. I used to try to learn the more spectacular tenor arias, and would sing along with the records at the top of my voice, until my father had to make me go out and play, saying that it wasn't good for me to "sit up hollering in front of the record player all day."

My father had studied the violin during his youth in Atlanta, with Professor Kemper Harreld, and had played in the Morehouse College Orchestra. When it came time for music lessons, I wanted to "take up the trumpet," but my mother insisted that it would be violin. I had three violin teachers between the ages of eight and sixteen and never learned very much from any of them, but whether this resulted from insufficient talent, a lack of diligence, or poor teaching, I cannot say. My first teacher was named Miss Martin. She was my teacher in the public school, before I entered Nativity. She was a classic example of the musical snob, and claimed that she had been the teacher of Joe Louis, whom she had then known as Joseph Louis Barrow. Her excuse for not having been able to teach him was that "his hands were too big." I later learned that the size of the hands had nothing to do with ability to play the violin. Indeed I later heard it said that it was large hands that gave David Oistrakh his distinctive tone, but whether or not this was true, I do not know. Years later, when I saw photos of Joe Louis, standing outside Caeser's palace, I wondered if his life would have been happier as a violinist than it was as a prizefighter.

Black boys in America receive considerably more pressure to excel in athletics than in arts or intellectual activities. I had two significant failures in my first approaches to the humanities. These were in Latin and in music. It was difficult for a working class black boy to study the violin in Detroit in those days, and I imagine that it is even more difficult now. I still remember the fingering, and I can pick out a tune or two when I feel like it, but it doesn't sound very good. One of my greatest disappointments is my failure at making music. I failed to become a Latinist for the same reason that I failed to become a violinist. I was a relatively normal boy. I didn't like to sit still, and I didn't want to be a sissy. I liked to hang around the neighborhood with the other fellows, mostly black, and I liked to be out-of-doors. I had far less talent for football than for Latin, but I was always drawn in opposite directions — in the direction of the football field and in the direction of "the room where women come and go, talking of Michelangelo."

My best friend among the black boys in the neighborhood was Odie Hinton, who lived next door to me, and played on the trumpet, "Cherry Pink and Apple Blossom White," which he never could get quite right. He was a black giant — quiet, philosophical, and moody, who left the high school ROTC after hitting a sergeant, and left the football team after cursing out the coach. Bruce Hagen was jovial, a friendly bear, exceedingly strong, and quite intelligent. European history was his favorite school subject, and he had an admirable respect for facts, but he did not do well in school — too little encouragement. Marvis Lee Butts was a tall yellow Negro, and an expert on all matters having to do with sex, religion, or black folk. He had the bullying personality and gift of gab that make for a successful preacher, and it was he who first informed me that "the *Bible* says the Black man will rule the world some day." Marvis had two younger brothers. Ceolis claimed that he could "walk and talk with God." This was a line that he often used when trying to get into little girls' pants. The youngest brother was named Smudgie. No one asked where little, dark Smudgie got his name, and even as a five-year-old, he was becoming a very sulky kid.

During my high school years, I drifted away from the other black guys in the neighborhood. Of course, there were some other black fellows who were interested in things like science fiction and rocket ships. I knew two very "clean cut types," Conrad Harper and James Ellis, but I don't think they were acquainted with one another. In any case, I didn't spend much time with either of them. Each of them lived an hour's walk away, and in opposite directions. I occasionally ran into one or the other at the Mark Twain Library, but both seemed to be suspicious of me. They thought I was one of the hoods. My best friend in high school was Tom Murrell, whose father was Irish, and whose mother was German. We shared a lot of interests, and he was a good influence on me. He was interested in drawing, art history, and science fiction, but his musical taste never got beyond Ravel's *Bolero*.

Tom did not go on to college, and we drifted apart after I started to Wayne State University in September 1960. I took my B.A. and M.A. degrees at Wayne and worked on a Ph.D. in English until 1968. Wayne State U. was located in an area of Detroit known as the "Art Center," dominated by the Detroit Public Library's main building and the Detroit Institute of Arts. I worked summers and weekends at the Institute, in their workshop program for school children. It was during my years at Wayne State U. that I was befriended by Kurtz Myers, at that time a librarian at the Main Library and curator of the Azalea Hackley collection on blacks in the performing arts. He arranged for me to work with the Metropolitan Opera as a curtain walker for several years, when they visited Detroit on tour. My wife, Maureen Connor, was employed at the Main Library, and we met on a trip to the Shakespearean festival at Stratford, Ontario, which I visited annually with Kurtz Myers. My involvement in the Wayne State/Art Center complex provided me with a quality of life that I have never been able to duplicate. I am amazed that there were people who referred to Detroit in those days as a "cultural wasteland."

By the time of the second Detroit riot in 1967, I was sorting out the mechanics of shaping an academic career. That long hot summer was the dramatic turning point in the course of my intellectual development. 1967 was the year in which Harold Cruse published *The Crisis of the Negro Intellectual* and Stokely Carmichael published *Black Power*. Christopher Lasch reviewed the two books together in the *New York Review of Books,* and the Yale University symposium on "Black Studies in the University" took place the following November.

I was now married, and the father of a three-year-old, and thanks to the encouragement of Professor Jay McCormick, I was a graduate student in English at Wayne State University. Like many other young people of my background, I thought of the quest for a Black Studies curriculum as a timely godsend. I was still interested in Medieval and Renaissance Studies but was beginning to realize that I was not well prepared for either field. It was becoming obvious to me that people who became professors of British Renaissance literature mastered Latin at an early age, and usually took their degrees from places like Oxford, Cambridge, and Yale. They drew on a certain type of background that I did not have, and were able to bring their personal and intellectual lives into accord with their studies.

In February of 1968, I discussed my problems with Ralph Nash, a kindly and intelligent man with whom I had taken a seminar on Milton. He was certainly aware that I was having difficulty keeping my mind on Renaissance Studies. I told him that I was thinking of resigning my teaching assistantship, and switching to an American Studies program, perhaps at the University of Michigan, or possibly in the East. I planned, at that time, to write my dissertation on W. E. B. Du Bois. Professor Nash was far more understanding than I had expected. He found it quite reasonable, especially in those times, that I would be more interested in history, politics, and law than in Renaissance literature. I left the English Department in spring of 1968 and went to West Germany, where I walked into the University of Maryland offices, overseas division, in Heidelberg, was hired as a lecturer in English composition, and flown off to Samsun, Turkey, for my first overseas assignment.

When I returned to the States in the fall of 1968, the English Department at Wayne State took me back under its wing and gave me the opportunity to do some more teaching for them. I found an instructorship at Highland Park Community College, in a nearby suburb, and was able to support myself, while investigating the possibilities of pursuing an American Civilization degree. In the meantime, the students at Highland Park had gone on strike and put a picket line around the building. I was obviously torn between my sense of professional responsibility and my sympathy with the striking students, who were demanding a Black Studies curriculum. I continued to teach at Wayne State and Highland Park through the summer of 1969, while pursuing the idea of beginning American Studies at Brown University or the University of Michigan. I was admitted to both programs, but through the kind agency of Professor Daniel Hughes, the Shelley specialist who had directed my M.A. essay, I received a University Fellowship at Brown.

There was no question in my mind regarding the reality of why I had been admitted to Brown. The term Affirmative Action was not in general usage, but I took it as a matter of course that campus unrest and burning cities had something to do with my good fortune. But the fact that I had been admitted to Brown, largely because of my race, presented me with a moral difficulty. I wanted to change the direction of my studies, and I realized the importance of a degree from a "colonial university," for someone planning to pursue a career in academic life. At the same time, my home training and the values that had come from my parents and from the Burnetts were much opposed to accepting charity. My self-concept, at the point of receiving the University Fellowship, was not high. I have always enjoyed sketching cartoons, and I remember drawing a caricature of myself as a grinning Negro minstrel, sort of like Brother Todd in Ellison's *Invisible Man*. Finally, one of the older students in the Ph.D. program, a Jewish fellow, whom I really did not know very well, took me aside and offered the following advice: "I hear that you have been feeling uncertain about your admission to Brown, because you feel that you wouldn't have been admitted if you weren't black." And then his manner changed, and he said with obvious anger and passion, "Don't worry about what anyone else is saying. You've been admitted to Brown. Go on and enjoy it and do well." Those words made a lot of difference to me, because, as I thought it over, I realized that most of my colleagues at Wayne State would have been happy to go to Brown on any terms. In my situation, they would never have thought twice about accepting the opportunity. Daniel Hughes also took me aside and said: "Go to Brown. Think of it this way. You'll be that much closer to Europe."

On the more positive side, it now occurred to me that my intellectual interests and my academic pursuits would no longer have to be at variance. In American Studies, I could find ways of exploiting my own experiences as a source of academic strength, in much the way that graduates of Eton and Harrow made their youthful experiences work for them in Renaissance Studies. I still think of Black Studies as more than just another academic discipline. After all, the justifications for its existence were never purely academic. The universities and colleges did not institute Black Studies programs in an atmosphere of cool logic and restrained discourse. Black Studies departments grew up in a crisis situation, and were a response to demands on the part of black students that were made against the background of the Vietnam War and American cities in flames.

In the best of circumstances, universities like Brown and Yale set up Black Studies programs from a sense of justice, and as a result of a sincere commitment to introducing new perspectives and values into the curriculum. In other cases, responses have been cynical. Students and young faculty members were given just enough rope to hang themselves, and the result was often the establishment of Black Studies programs that were totally lacking in academic credibility. As one might expect, those programs that lacked credibility usually developed in universities that had weak programs in other areas.

At Brown I had the good fortune to come into contact with a number of professors and students who helped me make the transition from a rather broken-down and dispirited English major to a credible American Studies scholar. Rhett Jones, who possesses one of the most formidable intellects I have ever encountered, soon became a fast friend. He had been a graduate student in sociology at the University of Wisconsin, and had brought to his training in that field an excellent capacity for analysis and systematic debate. I learned a great deal from Rhett about clear thinking, and learned something else that many English majors never learn, that sociology should not be used as a pejorative term. There are any number of fiendishly clever sociologists, and good sociologists know far more about the humanities than mediocre humanists know about sociology.

A second influence was Professor William G. McLoughlin, who taught a demanding, but nonetheless popular Survey of American Social and Intellectual History. McLoughlin was particularly interested in the religious reform in the United States. He taught the history of American religion in terms of its perfectionist traditions before the Civil War, which flowered into a tradition of Social Gospel in the later nineteenth century. It was during my first semester that I realized that my long repressed interest in religion had been reawakened, and that I was going to be able to find myself, not only in the study of black history, but also in the study of American religion. McLoughlin really went out of his way to be supportive, but he was never patronizing, and he encouraged me to stand on my own feet. McLoughlin also taught me something that I had obviously not learned at Nativity High School. He taught me that American Protestantism had actually been responsible for something other than a few witch burnings, monkey trials, and segregationist statutes. He convinced me that Protestantism was not only a valid intellectual tradition, but a tradition that included a strain of progressive social reform.

A third influence on my intellectual development during my first year at Brown was my wife. Although she was still in Detroit at the time and working at the Detroit Public Library, she helped me get started in my new studies. She introduced me to the Arno/New York Times reprint series, forwarding to me the numerous publishers' catalogues, issued at that time by Arno and other houses. Many of these, especially the one from Arno, were actually annotated bibliographies. Up to that time, I had never learned to enjoy studying bibliographies, but this was something entirely different. I was encountering bibliographies that were fun to read, and the bibliographies led me to reprints of nineteenth century works that were suddenly appearing in libraries, drugstores, supermarkets and gas stations.

Admittedly, then, my approach to Black Studies is partially a result of my coming to Brown, but what has happened to me here was built on the foundations of my Catholic background. Both the strengths and weaknesses of my approach to Black Studies have roots in my Catholic education at Nativity, as well as in my black family background. There were also other influences, like the guys in the neighborhood, but I drifted away from the guys in the neighborhood by the time I was in high school. I have seen some of them grow up, some to become thugs or convicts, others to become "bogue rapologists." Some got themselves killed; others became honest hardworking stiffs with fancy cars and uncertain jobs. Two of them went to Harvard Law School, but they were fellows I knew from the Mark Twain Library. I never saw them "hanging out" on the streets. From early childhood, I became aware of the universe as a chaotic, relativistic place, unless one chose to impose some order on it. I accepted Catholicism, because of its ability to save the appearance of law, order, and authority, and I was a person who had to work very hard to keep my emotions under control. As a Catholic, I have a fondness for rituals and symbols of authority. I like Renaissance music and manuscripts illuminated in red, blue, and gold. Du Bois once noted that religion can often breed "the sensualist side by side with the martyr."

Du Bois's statement was made with specific reference to Afro-American Protestantism, but it could as easily have referred to Italo-American Catholicism. Sensuality and martyrdom, as Du Bois knew, were not cultural traits peculiar to black Americans. The black American religious experience must be understood not only in terms of its roots in Pentecostalism, African survivals, the frenzy of storefront preachers, or even the political sophistication of its educated ministry. Black religion is all of these things, but a good deal more. It is the symbol of interaction between several Afro-American religious traditions, but it may also represent a point of interaction with white hyphenated-Americans. Reflecting on my own interaction with German and Italian Catholics taught me that I was much closer than most of them to the American religious tradition, though I did not know it then. I now begin to understand something more of the role of black families as creators and sustainers of the American Protestant heritage. My parents taught me the meaning of the "bootstraps philosophy," of which my mother was a living example, and she also taught me the legend of Booker T. Washington. The German nuns could nurture and reinforce what I had learned at home about the values of cleanliness and hard work, but there was little new that they could teach me. As a black American, I came from one of the most experienced of American "ethnic groups" at the business of being American.

N O T E

1. W. E. B. Du Bois, *ABC of Color* (Berlin: Seven Seas Books, 1963), p.148.

More than an Ethnic Group, Less than a Nation

The pattern of Afro-American life in the United States has been one of gradually increasing acculturation, despite persistent segregation and despite the fact that separate institutions within black communities continue to spring up and to thrive. Acculturation is the process whereby two or more groups of people living in cultural proximity tend to become more similar with the passage of time. I would not use the term "cultural assimilation" as a synonym for acculturation, because assimilation implies changes of a rare and extreme nature to the extent that one of the groups becomes culturally absorbed by the dominant or assimilating culture, and indistinguishable from it.[1]

For black Americans, slavery was a melting-pot experience; members of numerous tribal and national groups were forced to assume a common identity. Ancient ethnic distinctions between the various imported peoples were destroyed at the same time that acculturation to European ways was occurring. Afro-Americans became a "new people," in the rhetoric of the nineteenth century. Genetically and culturally speaking, they were amalgamated into a composite of numerous African racial and ethnic groups. They were a new people in another sense, as well. Because of the acculturation they had undergone in two fundamental areas of life, language and religion, they were now no longer simply Africans; they were, like it or not, black Americans. Members of slave communities born in the United States differed from first-generation African slaves. By the end of the eighteenth century, the typical black

American spoke English reasonably well and had accumulated at least a veneer of Christian attitudes, although these were often superimposed on a body of spiritual beliefs and worship forms that were clearly African in origin. African religious vestiges were melded into an eclectic hodgepodge of old-world beliefs, mythologies, and conjure rites. They differed from pristine African religion, which is always identified with specific ethnic roots and with secret and exclusive community rites among people who share a common language and a common ancestry. Tribal exclusivism is characteristic of traditional religions in many parts of the world; it is not limited to West Africa, but it is a fundamental ingredient of West African religion.[2]

By the late eighteenth century, most black Americans had been stripped of their various African languages and their ethno-specific religiosity. They had also acquired the English language and various forms of Afro-Christianity. Two hundred years later, in the late twentieth century, those distinctive characteristics that separate black language and religion from the language and religion of white Americans have become subtle and elusive. Black Americans tend to resemble the various white groups with which they have the greatest amount of contact. The differences among American blacks resulting from class, religion, and other forms of diversity may be greater than those between individual white and black persons of similar education and class background. But while black Americans today are almost entirely acculturated linguistically, and while most of us who are religious have been religiously acculturated to some degree, the majority of Afro-Americans have not been and for the foreseeable future will not be integrated into American social life, despite their acculturation.

Integration usually refers only to the mechanical proximity of blacks and whites within the same social, political, educational, and economic institutions. Indeed, most black Americans, even in this final decade of the twentieth century, participate only mechanically in racially mixed institutions. After leaving the classroom or the workplace, they either voluntarily separate themselves or, more commonly, they are segregated away from those areas of life referred to as "purely social." Most Americans see this as perfectly natural and inevitable, and the reason is simple.

Although the word "integration" seems to imply only a mechanical proximity among blacks and whites, complete social integration cannot take place without integration of the family, because the family is society's basic unit. In other words, integration cannot occur without racial amalgamation, and that is something that few Americans, black or white, see as desirable. The fear of racial amalgamation makes impossible anything other than a very gradual rate of integration in any social institution. Black Americans have been slower to enter the middle class in America than other groups because racial separatism is the norm in this society. Racial separatism guarantees that social and economic knowledge will not be transmitted from sophisticated and highly organized white groups to unsophisticated and disorganized black masses.

Many people refer to black Americans as an ethnic group, but of course things are not quite so simple. In a brilliant work in progress, Professor Carl Senna of Providence College has noted that an ethnic group is united by communality of beliefs and by specific modes of behavior. It is possible to speak of certain groups of black people who possess U.S. citizenship or residency as American ethnic groups. For example, first-generation black immigrants, who still think of themselves as Puerto Rican–Americans or as West Indian–Americans or as Cape Verdean–Americans, may be spoken of as ethnic groups. These are subgroups within the Afro-American group and are distinguished by behaviors and beliefs from the amorphous black mass. Ethnicity, as Professor Carl Senna points out, is a category of behavior and belief. It has to do with learned behavior, rather than with racial characteristics.[3]

It is too much to expect, however, that Americans will ever utilize a systematic, consistent, or rational terminology to describe the patterns of black American life. Therefore, the purpose of these remarks is to clarify my own usage of some of the terms that are commonly used in discussions of American race relations. They are also aimed at identifying problems in popular terminology. Most discussions describe black Americans in terms of one of the following patterns: race, ethnic, or immigrant group, class, caste, minority, nation. Each of these modes of description will provide some insight into who and what we are.

Race is the category most often applied to black Americans. Most of us are physically identifiable as descended from "Negro stock" and are therefore racially distinct from the majority of North Americans, who are "Caucasian." However, many Afro-Americans are much closer in physical type to their European than to their African forebears. There is as much contrast of physical types within the Afro-American population as there is contrast between stereotypical Afro-Americans and stereotypical Euro-Americans. If we are to speak of Afro-Americans as a racial group, we should remember that many "black" Americans are more Caucasian than Negro in terms of the accepted criteria of racial classification developed by physical anthropologists a century ago.[4]

It may be useful at times to speak of Afro-Americans as an ethnic group, although to do so may be seriously misleading. Ethnicity is a confusing term because it is sometimes used to imply cultural traits and learned behaviors, as well as biogenetic features.[5] Many scholars, among them Sterling Stuckey and John Gwaltney, argue passionately that Afro-Americans possess distinctive cultural traits. If they are correct, this would seem to justify referring to black Americans as an ethnic group. On the other hand, "The Harvard Encyclopedia of American Ethnic Groups" and the works of Thomas Sowell offer compelling evidence that black Americans are a "racial group," displaying numerous signs of ethnic diversity within the group.[6] I place the term "racial group" within quotation marks because, as Ely Chinoy remarks in an eminently respectable sociology textbook, the physical differences among American Negroes are distinct enough to provide "evidence that in the United States 'race' refers primarily to social rather than to a biological race and ethnicity." Chinoy reduces "race" to a social category and equates "ethnicity" with "biological race," thereby illustrating the confusion and inconsistency of terminology that runs throughout all discussion of American race relations.[7]

Aside from the linguistic dangers arising from the problem of referring to black people as an ethnic group, there are serious implications for social policy. Scholars like Nathan Glazer have used the ethnicity model to argue that black Americans are like any other American ethnic group and that their position in America is no different from that of Irish Catholics or Russian Jews. There is no logic to such a position, which irrationally assumes that Irish Catholics and Russian Jews can be lumped together in one category called "ethnics" and that their assumed uniformity of experience can be employed as a model for what black Americans ought to do.

The ethnicity approach to race relations imposes the irrelevant model of European immigration on black Americans. In 1968 the Kerner Commission report outlined a number of similarities and differences between black Americans and the white "ethnics" who arrived in northern cities before World War 1. The Commission noted that black ghettoes of the 1960s, unlike immigrant ghettoes at the turn of the century, appeared to be dead ends, rather than stopping off places on the way to ultimate Americanization. The reasons for this difference in the experience of the two groups were given as follows: a decline in the importance of ethnic politics and political machines, and a lack of strong cultural, economic, and intellectual life among black Americans. The Kerner report concluded that "what the American economy of the late 19th and early 20th centuries was able to do to help the European immigrants escape from poverty is now largely impossible. New methods of escape must be found for the majority of today's poor."[8]

Nathan Glazer, a sociologist, expressed disagreement, along with the belief that the Commission's conclusions must be rejected. This was not so much because he found the arguments invalid as because of what he saw as the dire political consequences of accepting them. To accept the Kerner Commission's findings and to act on them might "divide the country to the disadvantage of all groups." But, argues Glazer, if we proceed on the assumption that the black experience will parallel the immigrant experience, then all we need to do is wait for time to improve the status of black Americans.[9]

Of course, neither the Kerner Commission nor any other group of informed people have ever rejected the analogy with the white immigrant experience, nor have they rejected the idea that time will be required to solve racial problems. What has been rejected is the tendency to stretch the ethnic immigration analogy too far.

White immigrants, organized around religious and economic institutions, often established charming ethnic neighborhoods within a generation. As time passed, however, most white ethnics abandoned their distinctive languages and many of their old-world religious practices. In subsequent generations, the grandchildren of immigrants often migrated to nonethnic suburbs, where traditional ethnic traits were almost impossible to maintain. In the meantime, old ethnic communities often dissipated before an influx of poor blacks, whose arrival accelerated the pace of suburban migration and converted ethnic neighborhoods into racial ghettoes. While time seems to have had the effect of breaking down white ethnic neighborhoods, it is uncertain whether the immigrant paradigm is applicable to black ghettoes. Fifty years was sufficient to do away with the stereotype of the white immigrant slum of the turn of the century. But the quality of life in black slums, which originated thirty or more years later, seems to deteriorate rather than to improve with the passage of time. It is indeed appropriate for scholars to understand the relationship between the black experience and the white immigrant group experience. And we should, as Glazer suggests, bear in mind the political consequences of all the possible interpretations of that relationship.

Another approach to black-white relations in the United States emphasizes class. At its most simplistic, the class analysis of racial problems is found wanting for the same reason that the immigration approach is found wanting. Proponents of the class model attempt to argue that since the overwhelming majority of black Americans are in the working class and since black Americans are more frequently represented at the lower levels than at the upper levels of society, they are just another lower-class group, who happen incidentally to be black. The principal difficulty of Afro-Americans, so the argument goes, is essentially one of economic deprivation, and the best way to do justice to black Americans is by improving their economic status.

This approach has both radical and conservative proponents. Among the conservatives, the most prominent was turn-of-the-century leader Booker T. Washington, who took a strongly materialist view of black life and culture. He argued that life-styles ought to be geared towards improving the economic welfare of the American Negro and worked out a theory of uplift based on cleanliness, thrift, and Puritan morality. A radical formulation of the economic-uplift theory came from Marxism, which began to attract a significant black following during the 1930s. In the Marxist view, black Americans were a special component of the working class, who should be assisted along somewhat independent lines to develop socialistic institutions. Like Washington, however, the Marxists tended to ignore the emotional basis of American racism, which seemed destined to perpetually override class issues. As Du Bois noted in 1940, "the split between white and black workers was greater than that between blacks and capitalists; and the split depended not simply on economic exploitation but on racial folklore grounded on centuries of instinct, habit, and thought. . . . This flat incontrovertible fact, imported Russian Communism ignored, would not discuss." The class approach to race relations was reformulated by William Julius Wilson, a black sociologist at the University of Chicago in 1976. He argued that in the second half of the twentieth century there has been significant erosion of the racial folklore and traditional bias that have kept black people a nation apart.[10]

Wilson argues that class distinctions within the black community are becoming more significant than racial distinctions between white and black. He presents controversial evidence that class is becoming more important than race in determining the life chances of black individuals, and argues that younger, more affluent blacks are becoming increasingly estranged from the urban ghetto poor. The central argument of his book will be welcomed by those who feel that any stick is good enough to beat the black middle class. It will likewise be appreciated by those conservatives who wish to undercut public and private-sector programs designed to correct racial imbalances in the higher levels of American life. The value of Wilson's renewed emphasis on class is that it has encouraged continued discussion of the alienation of the black middle class from the rest of the black population. If such analysis leads the middle class to dedicate itself to racial goals, then the effects of Wilson's study will be salutary. The danger is that many of the book's severest critics have read no further than its title. And the black bourgeoisie, perpetually ridden by guilt and confusion whenever race is discussed in connection with class, find it impossible to discuss the question with any objectivity.

Some scholars — notably John Dollard, Lloyd Warner, and Gunnar Myrdal — have suggested that the system of racial segregation in the United States is analogous to the caste system in India.[11] Negroes are assigned their status at birth, and although they may experience some vertical mobility within the group, they cannot move laterally across the caste boundary. Such an analysis is not without merit, so long as we bear in mind that all analogies are by definition imperfect. Caste is almost entirely a social rather than a biological category. It is based on the social phenomena of Hindu religion and culture. The caste system of India is maintained with the consent of the various castes affected. Each caste is tied to a traditional economic role as well as to a social status. Only recently have the lower castes of India launched anything approximating a civil rights movement, and this does not seem to have any militantly integrationist overtones. Nor have the lower castes impressed the outside world as having a national consciousness, a national mission, or a desire for a separate national identity or homeland. All of the foregoing attitudes have been present among the blacks of the United States. Furthermore, while the ethnic-group model has been appropriately applied to black Americans, there does not seem to be any way of applying it to the Indian castes.

If the black movement in the United States may be compared to the struggle of various Indian castes for greater social status and economic power, it is even more comparable to the struggle of the Indian people as a whole to free themselves from colonial rule. Under the leadership of Martin Luther King, the civil rights movement in the United States was deliberately patterned after Mahatma Gandhi's anticolonial struggle. Charles Silberman, in his once popular book *Crisis in Black and White,* viewed black Americans as colonial subjects of whites. Afro-Americans were linked to the rest of the country in a relationship of dependency by the vicious cycle of unemployment, poverty, and welfare. More sophisticated and imaginative applications of the colonial model began to appear in the late 1960s and early 1970s. Stokely Carmichael, Charles Hamilton, Robert Blauner, and Robert S. Allen viewed the black situation in terms of internal colonialism. Every aspect of black life, so the argument goes, is controlled from outside the black community. Whether in urban or in rural areas, the black community is a colony because it exists in a state of economic and administrative dependency, while ironically serving as a valuable repository of labor essential to the larger society.[12]

The approach that emphasizes the black population's "minority status" is perhaps the least useful for analysis of its social and economic condition. The prevailing definition of the "minority" concept has been expressed by Charles Wagley and Marvin Harris in their *Minorities in the New World*.[13] It refers simply to self-conscious, endogamous groups whose members are born into them and "which are subject to political, or economic, or social discrimination by a dominant segment of an environing political society." The term is laden with problems since, as Wagley and Harris are aware, "neither term, minority or majority, in this technical sense refers to a numerical minority or majority." Nonetheless, the use of the term carries with it the implication that the disadvantaged status of black Americans is mainly due to their numerical inferiority. It also has come to imply that the status of blacks can be compared to that of other "minorities," such as white males, hereditary millionaires, or homosexuals.[14] By lumping all such groups into the category of "minority," journalists and politicians have tended to obscure, rather than to clarify, issues. The problems of black people in white-dominated societies have nothing to do with their numerical minority status. Whites have been willing and able to treat blacks just as shabbily where blacks have been in the majority, as, for example, in eighteenth-century South Carolina and twentieth-century South Africa. The use of the term "minority" when speaking of the problems of black Americans confuses issues. German Catholics are a minority; so, too, are Jewish-American heiresses and Spanish-speaking aristocrats, but placement in these groups does not handicap members in the exercise of power or the enjoyment of privileges.

The popularity of the term "minority" in recent public discourse stems in part from its convenient vagueness. The term provides a semantical dodge for subverting affirmative action and equal opportunity programs. The hypothetical question that might be posed by persons hostile to programs for achieving racial justice is: "Why should blacks be treated any differently than anyone else? After all, aren't we all minorities? Shouldn't equality of opportunity be a principle applied equally to all of us?" When the question is posed in these limited terms, the answer can only be, "Yes." If the predominant sociological term used to describe black Americans were to become "minority," then Nathan Glazer's position would be given considerable undeserved validity on mere semantical grounds. At this point in time, it would be exceedingly cynical to pretend that black people should be treated no differently than "minorities" that occupy more advantaged positions in society or that, unlike black people, are represented broadly throughout the American class structure.

Black nationalism, the last of the models to be discussed here, represents one of the constant themes in this series of essays.[15] There is a difference between citizenship and nationality, and although Afro-Americans are, for the most part, loyal citizens of the United States of America, they tend to perceive themselves, and to be perceived by others, as a permanently distinct people in the land of their birth—in other words, as a "nation within a nation." The "Negro People of the United States," as they were once called, have a sense of identity as Americans, which coexists, somewhat uneasily, with feelings of identity with other black peoples throughout the world. While black Americans think of themselves as a part of the "American people," they nonetheless feel somewhat disassociated from them. It is difficult to feel a sense of common nationality with a dominant majority that does not wish to socialize with, to intermarry with, or to live in proximity with one's own group. Black nationalism is only partially a reaction to patterns of rejection. It also arises from a shared racial mythology and a shared sense of historical mission and destiny. The mystical, teleological element in American black nationalism has usually been related to religious tradition. In the nineteenth century, black nationalism was almost inseparable from religion. At present, this religious, mystical quality of black nationalism seems to be strongest among the lower classes.

Defining and describing black nationalism is a problem that has intrigued many scholars. Bracey, Meier, and Rudwick are agreed that the term has been used to indicate a broad variety of phenomena, "ranging from the simplest expressions of ethnocentrism and racial solidarity to the comprehensive and sophisticated ideologies of Pan-Negroism or Pan-Africanism."[16] For the present study, I shall adopt the inclusive approach. Black nationalism is the belief that all African peoples suffer to some degree from oppression by whites, and that a common heritage of oppression provides the basis for a system of universal cooperation among the Africans of the diaspora. American black nationalism involves the political belief that the Negro people of the United States are different from other ethnic groups in that they are historically separated from the rest of the citizenry. Chief Justice Taney stated in 1857 that they were brought to the Americas not as individual persons with expectations of individual rights and responsibilities but as a subject people.[17] The citizenship of black Americans is no longer disputable since the passage of the Fourteenth Amendment, but the black American is still perceived as a different sort of citizen. Although most white Americans would agree with the abstract proposition that black Americans are entitled to all the legal and political rights of citizens, there is widespread resistance to the idea of full inclusion for black Americans in all areas of American life. There is even greater hostility to the idea that the government should become an agency for bringing about such inclusion.[18]

Although black Americans are ethnically diverse, they have histori-cally thought of themselves as a people because of a shared history of racial oppression. They have developed a sense of common identity through the common experience of exclusion from the benefits of American nationality due to their racial distinctiveness. Black national-ism, like most nationalisms, is a reaction to outside pressures, and it represents an attempt to construct defenses against hostile practices and oppressive ideologies—in this case, the code of white supremacy. In its purest form, American black nationalism is concerned with territorial separatism and with the establishment of a separate government. In its more inclusive forms, it is broadly concerned with the codification and maintenance of culture and ideology to reflect realities of black Ameri-can history and to serve as a guide towards a happier future.[19]

The term "black nationalism" is sometimes used synonymously with "pan-Africanism," the idea that all peoples of African ancestry are united in the struggle against the code of white supremacy and that they therefore have had thrust upon them the same cultural and political goals. Imanuel Geiss and J. Ayodele Langley have noted that before World War 1 the term "pan-Africanism" was always used to denote spir-itual and political unity among African peoples, regardless of what con-tinent they lived on. Only in recent decades has it been confused with the movement to unite the continent of Africa into a federation of states. Pan-Africanism focuses on Africa as the center of concern for all people of the diaspora but does not require of all its supporters that they immi-grate.

Black nationalism early revealed a tendency to link cultural assimi-lation with political separatism. Early examples of proto-nationalistic literature written in English, like Ottobah Cugoano's *Thoughts and Sen-timents on the Evil of Slavery* (1787), reveal a tendency to utilize Chris-tianity for political purposes. Olaudah Equiano, in his *The Interesting Narrative of the Life of Olaudah Equiano, or Gustavus Vassa, the Afri-can, Written by Himself* (1789), recognized that the moral power of religion might be used to oppose the slave trade and the doctrine of African inferiority.[20] Abolitionist writers in the United States soon began to construct biblical arguments against slavery; these were offered as a counterbalance to the rationalistic arguments of pro-slavery Christians. Biblical arguments against slavery were by no means confined to black authors, but David Walker went a step beyond most of his white sympa-thizers with the assertion that God was on the side of the African race and that the Europeans, including those in the United States, were threatened with oblivion.[21] To be sure, much black Christianity has often been escapist, a subtle opiate placating its adherents with promises of a better life after death. On the other hand, a significant component of much black religion has been the belief that the God of history had promised deliverance for His long-suffering people, the African race. As Booker T. Washington noted, black religious music at the time of the Civil War expressed a hope for "freedom of the body, and in this world."[22]

Black nationalism in the nineteenth century was closely interwoven with religion and seemed, at times, a sort of pseudoreligion in its own right. In its origins, the Western tradition of nationalism is often buttressed with a religious justification—as, for example, in the Declaration of Independence. The supernatural element in the origins of proto-nationalistic thought are exceedingly ancient. Many primitive cultures have known the concept of divine kingship. The ancient Jews saw the Hebrew nation as enjoying a special relationship to God. The Athenians linked the destiny of their polis to the formidable Athena, Zeus's favorite daughter. Medieval and Renaissance statism accepted the divine right of kings and imbued the political structure with divine authority. Pan-Slavists spoke of the sacred destiny of holy Russia. German nationalists of the nineteenth century viewed every nation as representing some aspect of the divine personality. When black nationalism began to rise during the late eighteenth century, contemporaneously with Zionism and the classical expressions of European nationalism, it adopted the tradition of placing national destiny within religious frames of reference. Modern revolutionary nationalisms, especially in the Islamic world, clearly indicate the continuing relationship between religion and nationalism, as does anti-Soviet sentiment in Poland. Revolutionary nationalism has often developed with an intrinsic and essential element of what Vittorio Lanternari has identified as the religion of the oppressed.[23]

In the twentieth century, non-Christian forms of black nationalism, including Marxist and Islamic forms, began to appear among black Americans. Islam had long been present among Afro-Americans, but it was only in the years immediately before the First World War that Islamic black nationalism made its presence felt in the Moorish Science Temple.[24] Marxist black nationalism was evident in the African Blood Brotherhood during the 1920s and in the left wing of the Garvey movement, some of whose members defected to the Communist party during the 1920s and 1930s. Although W. E. B. Du Bois was still suspicious of communism in 1940, he advocated a variety of black nationalism based on the development of an independent economy but having no ambitions towards territorial separatism. Other black Marxists advocated a separate black territory in the Black Belt or a forty-ninth state, accepting elements of the communist definition of black Americans as a nation, after Joseph Stalin in *Marxism and the National Question.*[25] By the 1950s, both Marxist and Islamic forms of black nationalism emphasized the acquisition of land and the development of political self-determination as fundamental goals. Similarly, black Jewish sects have pursued nationalistic goals and have defined their objectives in terms of territorial separatism, statecraft, and economic independence.[26]

As I have said elsewhere, black Americans have combined the seemingly contradictory themes of political separatism and cultural assimilationism within a messianic myth. Black nationalism has ironically been the conduit through which assimilationist values have passed into black communities, and integrationist movements have often employed nationalistic rhetoric and have sometimes given birth to separatist activities. The fact that separatism so often seems to conceal assimilationist values, and integrationism so often asserts the exceptionalism of black American values and culture, indicates the ambivalence of black Americans with respect to aims and strategies, which is largely a result of the ambivalence of white Americans with respect to the destiny of black people in America.[27]

There can be no denying that the position of black people in the United States today is unstable and potentially tragic. Since the Second World War, the black upper classes have experienced tremendous upward mobility and rising expectations. This has created much jealousy and resentment among the white middle class. The experience of the lower classes, on the other hand, is much more difficult to categorize. While, on the one hand, the legal obstacles to their advancement have disappeared, economic and cultural barriers to their advancement seem to be as firmly in place as ever. The poverty, ignorance, and social disorganization that oppress lower-class black communities have made them breeding grounds for crime, violence, and disease.

The persistence of black-nationalist movements in the United States, especially among the lower classes, is in many respects a healthy sign. Black nationalism offers a counterbalance to the influence of narcotics traffickers and youth gangs. It is confrontational and offers channels for the articulation of rage in ways that are potentially constructive. Black nationalism offers a form of social organization within lower-class black ghettoes that is appealing to those who are suspicious of traditional, mainstream bourgeois ideals, but not completely cynical with respect to them. The subject of black nationalism will continue to be a topic of interest to social, literary, religious, and intellectual historians.

In the absence of catastrophic social upheaval in the United States, it is unlikely that extreme black nationalists will soon attract many supporters for their goal of territorial separatism. It is equally unlikely that black nationalism will disappear from Afro-American thinking in the immediate future. It will be eclipsed among the upper classes, however, for as long as upward economic mobility and access to mainstream institutions are available. At this moment, it seems clear that black nationalism is not on the decline among the lower classes and that it will persist in its religious forms as an important basis of community organization and cultural mythology. Among artists and intellectuals, cultural nationalism and ethnic chauvinism will continue to play an important part in rhetoric and ideology for as long as there is an identifiable black presence in North America.

N O T E S

1. The relationship between these concepts, as well as their occasional interchangeability, has been commented on by Milton M. Gordon in *Assimilation in American Life* (New York: Oxford University Press, 1964), p. 61. This is part of an extended discussion of the concepts and "a sample of the accumulated usages and meanings of the terms used to describe the processes and results of the meeting of peoples" (pp. 60–68). James H. Dormon and Robert R. Jones, *The Afro-American Experience: A Cultural History through Emancipation* (New York: John Wiley and Sons, 1974), pp. 1–26, contains a useful section on the distinctions between race and culture.

2. Works that discuss the early acculturation process among Afro-Americans and the retention of blending of African cultural forms in North America are too numerous to mention here. Among the most significant are Melville Herskovits, *The Myth of the Negro Past* (New York: Harper and Brothers, 1941); John Blassingame, *The Slave Community* (New York: Oxford University Press, 1972); Peter Wood, *Black Majority: Negroes in Colonial South Carolina* (New York: Norton, 1974); Sterling Stuckey, *Slave Culture: Nationalist Theory and the Foundations of Black America* (New York: Oxford University Press, 1987).

3. Carl Senna, "Being, Behavior, and Belief," typescript (1988).

4. Oliver Cromwell Cox, *Caste, Class, and Race* (New York: Doubleday, 1948), discusses black Americans with reference to all these terms. Winthrop Jordan, *White Over Black* (Chapel Hill: University of North Carolina Press, 1968), is the most influential study emphasizing race as the major determinant of the status of black Americans. For discussion of black Americans as a racial group, see Pierre L. van den Berghe, *Race and Racism* (New York: John Wiley and Sons, 1967); James J. Jones, *Prejudice and Racism* (Reading, Mass.: Addison Wesley, 1972); Richard A. Goldsby, *Race and Races* (New York: Macmillan, 1971).

5. The ethnicity approach is presented by Nathan Glazer and Daniel P. Moynihan in *Beyond the Melting Pot* (Cambridge: MIT Press, 1970), and Nathan Glazer, "Blacks and Ethnic Groups: The Difference and the Political Difference It Makes," in *Key Issues in the Afro-American Experience,* ed. Nathan Huggins et al. (New York: Harcourt Brace Jovanovich, 1971), pp. 193–211.

6. Stuckey, *Slave Culture*; John Gwaltney, *Drylongso: A Self Portrait of Black America* (New York: Vintage, 1980). Stephen Thernstrom, ed., *The Harvard Encyclopedia of American Ethnic Groups* (Cambridge: Harvard University Press, 1980). Thomas Sowell, *Civil Rights: Rhetoric or Reality* (New York: William Morrow, 1984), pp. 73–90.

7. Ely Chinoy, *Society: An Introduction to Sociology* (New York: Random House, 1967), pp. 209–38; see also illustrations and commentary on p. 61. Legal definitions of race are discussed in Thomas Stephenson, *Race Distinctions in American Law* (London: D. Appleton, 1910), pp. 12–20. Claude Brown, *Manchild in the Promised Land* (New York: Signet, 1965), seems less sanguine about the prospects of blacks conforming to the pattern of ethnic assimilation followed by European groups; cf. Glazer, "Blacks and Ethnic Groups."

8. "Comparing the Negro and Immigrant Experience," in *Report of the National Advisory Commission on Civil Disorders,* March 1, 1968 (Washington, D.C.: U. S. Government Printing Office, 1970), pp. 143–46.

9. Glazer, "Blacks and Ethnic Groups."

10. See W. E. B. Du Bois, *Dusk of Dawn: An Essay Toward an Autobiography of a Race Concept* (Harcourt Brace & World, 1940; reprint; New York: Schocken, 1968), p. 205. An opposing view, emphasizing Communist support for black nationalism and territorial separatism, is Wilson Record, *The Negro and the Communist Party* (Chapel Hill: University of North Carolina, 1951). William Julius Wilson, *The Declining Significance of Race* (Chicago: University of Chicago Press, 1978). William Julius Wilson reflects further on class and cultural issues in *The Truly Disadvantaged: The Inner City, The Underclass, and Public Policy* (Chicago: University of Chicago Press, 1987), pp. 127–28.

11. The emphasis on "caste" is associated with Lloyd Warner. See his introduction to Allison Davis et al., *Deep South* (Chicago: University of Chicago Press, 1941), which also utilizes the caste model. Other examples are John Dollard, *Caste and Class in a Southern Town* (New York: Harper and Brothers, 1937), and Gunnar Myrdal, *An American Dilemma* (New York: Harper and Brothers, 1947), 2:667–88, 1002–4. Dollard defines caste on p. 62 of *Caste and Class* without making a systematic comparison to the caste system of India. Lloyd Warner's introduction to *Deep South* is likewise devoid of detailed analysis. A critique of the caste theory is provided by Cox in *Caste, Class, and Race,* pp. 489–544. Gunnar Myrdal's section, "The Decay of the Caste Theory" in *An American Dilemma,* pp. 1002–4, is disappointing; it describes neither the theory nor its decay.

12. Stokely Carmichael and Charles V. Hamilton, *Black Power: The Politics of Liberation in America* (New York: Random House, 1967), pp. 2–32. Robert Blauner, "Internal Colonialism and Ghetto Revolt," *Social Problems* 16, no.4 (1969): 397. Robert S. Allen, *Black Awakening in Capitalist America* (Garden City, N.Y.: Doubleday, 1969), pp. 2–20. Charles Silberman, *Crisis in Black and White* (New York: Random House, 1964).

13. Charles Wagley and Marvin Harris, *Minorities in the New World: Six Case Studies* (New York: Columbia University Press, 1958), pp. 4–11.

14. Reference to the problems associated with the term "minority" is made in Alphonso Pinkney, *The Myth of Black Progress* (Cambridge: Cambridge University Press, 1984), p.27.

15. See Sterling Stuckey, *The Ideological Origins of Black Nationalism* (Boston: Beacon Press, 1972); Floyd J. Miller, *The Search for a Black Nationality* (Urbana: University of Illinois Press, 1975); Rodney Carlisle, *The Roots of Black Nationalism* (Port Washington, N.Y.: Kennikat Press, 1975); Alphonso Pinkney, *Red Black and Green: Black Nationalism in the United States* (Cambridge: Cambridge University Press, 1976); Wilson J. Moses, *The Golden Age of Black Nationalism, 1850–1925* (Hamden, Conn.: Archon Books, 1978). A variant on the national approach is the colonial approach developed by Stokely Carmichael and Charles V. Hamilton in *Black Power,* pp. 2–32; Robert S. Allen, *Black Awakening in Capitalist America,* pp. 1–20; John H. Bracey, "Black Nationalism Since Garvey," in Huggins et al., *Key Issues in the Afro-American Experience,* pp. 249–79.

16. John H. Bracey et al., eds., *Black Nationalism in America* (Indianapolis: Bobbs-Merrill, 1970), p. xxvi.

17. Taney's opinion in *Scott v. Sanford* is widely reprinted. Reactions of blacks to the Dred Scott decision are reported in *The Liberator,* 10 April 1857, where a meeting among black people in Philadelphia is described. There was apparently much bitter discussion concerning resolutions introduced by Robert Purvis and Charles L. Remond to the effect that black people were indeed not citizens and therefore owed no allegiance to the Constitution.

18. Nathan Glazer in *Affirmative Discrimination* (New York: Basic Books, 1970) argues that with the end of *de jure* segregation the responsibilities of the government to guarantee racial equality had been fully discharged. See also Barry R. Gross, *Discrimination in Reverse* (New York: New York University Press, 1977).

19. Definitions of cultural nationalism and other varieties of nationalism are in Bracey et al., *Black Nationalism in America,* pp. xxvi–xxx.

20. Selections from the writings of Cugoano are contained in Francis D. Adams and Barry Sanders, *Three Black Writers in Eighteenth Century England* (Belmont, Calif.: Wadsworth, 1971). *The Narrative of Gustavus Vassa* is reprinted in *Great Slave Narratives,* comp. Arna Bontemps (Boston: Beacon, 1969).

21. David Walker and Henry Highland Garnet, *Walker's Appeal in Four Articles and also Garnet's Address to the Slaves of the United States of America* (1848; reprint, New York: Arno Press, 1969), p. 22.

22. Booker T. Washington, *Up From Slavery* (1901), reprinted in *The Booker T. Washington Papers,* ed. Louis Harlan, (Urbana: University of Illinois Press, 1972), 1:224.

23. Vittorio Lanternari, *The Religions of the Oppressed* (New York: Knopf, 1963).

24. Allan D. Austin, *Muslims in Antebellum America: A Sourcebook* (New York: Garland, 1983). A description of the Moorish Science Temple is contained in Arthur Huff Fauset, *Black Gods of the Metropolis* (Philadelphia: University of Pennsylvania Press, 1944), The best introduction to the Nation of Islam is in E. U. Essien-Udom, *Black Nationalism: A Search for an Identity in America* (Chicago: University of Chicago Press, 1962).

25. For African Blood Brotherhood, see Robert A. Hill's introduction to Garland's reprint edition of *The Crusader,* which was the official organ of the African Blood Brotherhood and the Hamitic League of the World from 1918 to 1922. Joseph Stalin, *Marxism and the National Question* (1913), excerpted in *The Essential Stalin,* ed. Bruce Franklin, (Garden City, N.Y.: Doubleday, 1972), pp. 54–84. In that same volume, see "The National Question" from *Foundations of Leninism* (1924), pp. 145–54. A discussion of the Stalinist approach to black nationalsim in America can be found in Wilson Record, *The Negro and the Communist Party,* chapter 3. A Marxist exposition of the nationalist argument is William Z. Foster, *The Negro People in American History* (New York: International Publishers, 1954), pp. 555–56. Of course, some black nationalists reject Marxist analysis.

26. Howard Brotz, *The Black Jews of Harlem: Negro Nationalism and the Dilemmas of Negro Leadership* (New York: Schocken, 1970); Hoyt Fuller, "An Interview: The Original Hebrew Israelite Nation," *Black World* (May 1975): 62–85; Israel J. Gerber, *The Heritage Seekers: American Blacks in Search of a Jewish Identity* (Middle Village, N.Y.: Jonathan David Publishers, 1977).

27. Wilson J. Moses, *Black Messiahs and Uncle Toms: Social and Literary Manipulations of a Religious Myth* (University Park: Pennsylvania State University Press, 1982).

Black Nationalism
Then and Now

Inventing a Happier Past

National Myth and the Realities of Slavery

Black Americans have invented count-less measures for dealing with emo-tions evoked by the word "slavery." Some have understandably chosen to repress the racial memory of it, insofar as that is possible, simply refusing to think about it or to discuss it. Others have gone about in a state of rage, reduced to an often debili-tating anger by their shame. Still others have been obsessed with the cultural aspects of slavery in their search for "Roots," alluding to the heritage of folklore, religion, and community feeling, and attempting to emphasize slavery's less bitter aspects, to endow their history with some redeeming meaning and dignity. Since the 1960s, a number of studies, presently to be discussed, have stressed this last theme of cultural strug-gle and spiritual triumph. The most significant of these studies in recent years is Sterling Stuckey's *Slave Culture: Nationalist Theory and the Foundations of Black America*. He describes the work as largely "a study in irony." It is, indeed, and in more ways than he observes. His title implies, although it does not actually assert, that the political culture and ideology of black Americans have their foundations in slavery. Stuckey insists that much of what we value in black American culture was pro-duced by the ugly, oppressive condition that never fully dehumanized its victims.[1]

There is indeed irony in the fact that many of the ethnic values, to which a large number of Afro-Americans so obstinately and proudly cling, must have been shaped by the seemingly endless ordeal of slavery and the century of humiliation that continued after its abolition. Few scholars have been willing to concede this point, however. The more conventional, more acceptable way of putting things is to assert that the slaves had a culture, that it consisted of something other than a heritage of pathological reactions to oppression, and that it represented, largely, the survival of African culture. If there is any criticism to be made of Stuckey, and others who have taken this position, it is that they place far more emphasis on the African roots of slave culture than they do on the nature of the American experience in the shaping of slave ethnicity, slave mentality, and slave society. For, if a study of slave culture is meant to suggest that "slave culture" is what formed "nationalist theory and the foundations of black America," then its author has an obligation to demonstrate just that. We may legitimately expect him to show us how that grinding, three-hundred-year ordeal made black Americans what we are today.

Here at the outset, I am compelled to acknowledge that the African influences on Afro-American life, and on American culture in general, are just as undeniable as is the oppressive nature of the slavery experience. Stuckey and many others have demonstrated far beyond any reasonable doubt that Afro-American folkways, language, and religion retained identifiable African qualities well into the twentieth century. But, as Stuckey shows, the fact that the West African roots of Afro-American culture are sometimes traceable to specific origins in no way negates the fact that the political culture of black Americans, insofar as such can be said to exist, derives from a shared slavery experience in America. It was in the crucible of slavery that the various African ethnic groups were melted down into one entity known as the "American Negro." If black Americans cannot be said to have a common culture, we certainly have a characteristic set of assumptions about life in America that makes us more than a mere amorphous aggregate, united by the coincidence of racial features. It was in America that we merged into one people, adopted a common speech and ethos, and became susceptible to the movement known as black nationalism.

The purpose of history is to control the perception of time, to nurture the sense that time's patterns, if properly understood, may produce benefits for oneself and catastrophes for one's enemies. That is why all societies are ruthlessly committed to controlling the telling of history. Since slavery is of fundamental importance to the consciousness of black Americans, we have always recognized our vested interest in attempting to monitor the ways in which this experience has been recorded and interpreted. But black Americans, like most other Americans, tend to overestimate their ability to control history and the writing of it. They are caught up in the currents of time that they are seeking to control. They are just as inclined as other Americans to sentimentalize the past or to convert it into pageantry. As E. Franklin Frazier observed long ago, the masses of black people, like other ordinary people, require silly fictions in order to make their daily lives bearable.[2]

Social change produces shifting perceptions of what constitutes a bearable life, however, and the patriotic histories and hagiographies of today may easily be perceived as treason and devil worship tomorrow. The history of slavery, when written by black people, is almost invariably written with the assumption that this retelling of the past can influence the condition of the black masses in the present and the future. The lessons drawn from history vary, however, according to the personal psychology of the author and the historical moment in which he or she writes. With changing times, we find that opinions have changed among historians as to what sorts of interpretation should be given to the facts of history as they have known them. The historiographic course of black writers and intellectuals is unavoidably affected by winds of doctrine in the larger American society, as well as by the tide of events on which they drift. In part, it is influenced by changing cultural and political attitudes within the black community itself. That changing fashions in the interpretation of the history of slavery have been politically motivated is too obvious a point to require demonstration. More interestingly, changes in interpretations of slavery seem to coincide with changes in the direction of American intellectual life in general and the struggle for black equality in particular. And they are also affected by changing ideas as to what constitutes human dignity.

The earliest attempts at social-scientific statements on slavery were produced during the late antebellum period. These were the numerous treaties influenced by the growth of social science as a fashion that appeared at the same time that the vogue of such writers as Thomas Robert Malthus and Auguste Comte was consciously and unconsciously being felt throughout the literate Western world. The rise of the discipline of political economy led to the earliest attempts, by Americans, at a sociology of slavery, most of it in defense of the system. Southern writers like Henry Hughes, Edmund Ruffin, and George Fitzhugh, whom Eugene Genovese calls "the Marx of the master class," utilized avant-garde, European-influenced discourses to justify the pro-slavery position. They argued that slavery was by nature a more benevolent institution than free enterprise and that it was more consistent with the basic realities of human nature. But, although such writers were accomplished in their ability to fashion texts after the manner of contemporary social theorists, they did not contribute much to the descriptive sociology of slavery. Nor were their opinions particularly humane, for all their "modernity" and sophistication. The closest thing to sociology in the sense of a systematic description of slavery was the abolitionist text by Frederick Law Olmstead, *A Journey in the Seaboard Slave States* (1856), the first volume of a trilogy, later condensed and revised as *The Cotton Kingdom* (1861).[3]

There were few black Americans during the antebellum period capable of writing scholarly treatises on slavery. Not only were the educational opportunities that would have given them access to current social theories closed, but black Americans did not enjoy the freedom to move around in the slave states gathering data for systematic studies. It may have been possible for an educated black American like Martin Delany to make a tour of the South, but this was clearly a dangerous and exceptional undertaking. Delany traveled from Pittsburgh to Texas in 1839 to investigate the possibilities of establishing a black colony in that state. His report of the journey appeared years later, serialized and fictionalized in the novel *Blake* (1859). For the most part, however, the observations of black writers were confined to slave narratives, which were reports based on the experiences of individuals, not systematic studies.[4]

The first treatments of slavery as a historical phenomenon appeared in the late nineteenth century, and tended to view the institution as a cause of social discord. Historians of the period, like John Bach McMaster and James Ford Rhodes, were convinced that slavery had been the cause of the Civil War, but they were more interested in the effects of slavery on political and constitutional history than in its effects on the slaves themselves. It was Ulrich Bonnell Phillips, a Southern apologist and white supremacist who constructed the first postbellum social history of slavery written from the perspective of a professional historian. Phillips was committed to the idea that slavery was a benign, paternalistic form of social organization, the form of government best suited to the needs and aptitudes of the black population. In a period when most Americans were inclined to be conciliatory to the South, Phillips's interpretation had much appeal. His approach made use of carefully assembled data, but there was a bias in his method of collecting it. He felt no obligation whatever to approach the history of slavery from the slave's point of view and relied exclusively on plantation records and other documents that reflected the slaveholder's impressions of black people's mentality and emotions.[5]

William Wells Brown, himself a former slave, wrote the first histories of the South that focused on the lives of the slaves themselves and that looked at slavery from a black cultural perspective. Brown had published several versions of his autobiography before the war. In these he had used folklore and slave humor as means of demonstrating the wit, wisdom, and sense of personal worth that many of the slaves had been able to preserve. After the war, he published two historical volumes, *The Rising Son* (1874) and *My Southern Home* (1880). The first of these was a conventional historical work, but the second was far more interesting. Partly journalistic, partly anecdotal in form, it was a significant, if often overlooked, work that provided insight into the lives of the slaves. While it falls short of being a cultural history of slavery, it comes closer to depicting the world the slaves made than anything attempted by a trained historian for another ninety years. Brown was concerned with showing not only the evils of the system but the attempts of black people to cope with it and to preserve their dignity under it, despite its oppressive nature.[6]

A new phase in the attempts by black people to manipulate perceptions of slavery coincided with the rise of Booker T. Washington. The years following Reconstruction witnessed a dramatic escalation of violence committed against black people. The commonly offered justification for the crime of lynching was that it was simply the righteous retribution of the white community against the Negro rapist. Several black leaders—including Ida B. Wells, Frederick Douglass, and Booker T. Washington—countered with the argument that black males had been left on the plantations to guard the virtue of their masters' wives and daughters during the Civil War. The myth of the faithful slave, who remained on the plantation to protect his mistress from the Yankees and hid the family silver in the woods, was nurtured, not only by Joel Chandler Harris, but even by militant social activists, as a countermyth to that of the treacherous, libidinous savage. In this way, the slaveholder's old cliché of the contented slave was skillfully reintroduced but given a novel twist by black leaders of the nineteenth century, who simply cannot be dismissed as fawning sycophants. Even militant leaders encouraged a sentimental perception of slavery, which they felt would help to win the sympathy of a society in which Christian sentimentalism was an important element of bourgeois culture.[7]

A given historical myth gains legitimacy because of its ability to impress people as a useful vision of the past. At a later date, however, it may be perceived as useless, or downright harmful. This was the case with the myth of slave loyalty during the Civil War, which had never been universally admired and came to be utterly rejected by the early twentieth century. Rapid urbanization of the black population from 1915 to 1945 led to rising material expectations on the part of black people and their leaders. This was accompanied by a decline of otherworldly rhetoric that pointed to Christian patience and humility as proofs of black humanity. The new descriptions tended to view resistance, rather than patient endurance, as the proof of the slave's humanity. Thus, during the 1940s and 1950s, there was a shifting process under way. The historiography of slavery was moving in a direction that would reflect the civil rights militancy of the period.

By the late 1960s, when Black Studies programs began to appear — largely in response to traumatic social forces, including urban insurrections and campus violence — the standard work on slavery was Kenneth M. Stampp's *The Peculiar Institution*. This impressive study began with the assumption that black and white people are equally sensitive to injustice and vulnerable to oppression, and that black people reacted to American slavery in much the same way that white people might have been expected to react. Stampp viewed slavery as a burdensome, degrading, humiliating experience. He saw it not simply as an economic institution but as a social system designed to brand black people as an inferior order of humanity. Stampp thought it only natural that black Americans would resent their status as slaves, and he argued forcefully that the characteristic mode of adjustment was one of resistance. Granted, this resistance seldom took the form of out-and-out revolt, but slaves made themselves a "troublesome property" by developing habits of non-cooperation, malingering, and insubordination. The general pattern of resentment and day-to-day covert resistance to slavery was seen as evidence of both the uniform oppressiveness of slavery and the constant awareness on the part of the slaves that they were being victimized.[8]

Kenneth Stampp's work was a product of post-McCarthy liberalism and a timely corrective to the views of Samuel Eliot Morrison and Henry Steele Commager, who had been overly tolerant of the southern view that slavery was a benign institution and that black slaves had been contented "Sambos," who reflected little on their condition. At a time when scholarly paperbacks were beginning to replace textbooks as teaching tools, Stampp's book became a preferred alternative to the leaden tomes of Morrison and Commager. Stampp was, of course, not the first to insist that slavery was a brutal institution. Herbert Aptheker had long viewed the antebellum South as an oppressive police state that depended on a heavy-handed machinery of intimidation for its continued existence. John Hope Franklin advanced a similar argument throughout the bulk of his work and especially in *The Militant South*. E. Franklin Frazier had seen the slavery system as almost (but not quite) dehumanizing, so that even such a universal trait as a mother's devotion to her children was threatened.[9]

No one argued more strongly than did Stanley M. Elkins, however, for the thesis that slavery was unremittingly traumatic, degrading, and brutalizing. Influenced by the work of Erich Fromm and T. W. Adorno on the nature of authoritarian societies, particularly Nazi Germany, Elkins argued that slavery was an efficient authoritarian system that brainwashed its victims, making them dull, apathetic, and infantile. He agreed with Morrison and Commager that slavery was capable of inducing a *Sambo personality,* creating a dependent, infantile automation, but he saw "Samboism" as a pathological state. Its existence was seen as proof of the oppressiveness of slavery, not as a sign of natural tendencies to subservience in the African personality. Although there were many who took offense, E. Franklin Frazier hailed Elkins's work as proof, once and for all, that slavery was not benign. He saw it as support for his own contention that many aspects of black American institutional life were pathological as a result of the trauma of slavery, which had left its stamp on the behavior of successive generations. Frazier thought the heritage of slavery had left a lingering imprint on the black mentality, and he was convinced that Elkins had accurately described the heritage of slavery.[10]

Frazier's celebration of Stanley Elkins's work was not surprising to anyone who had followed the former's development over the preceding two decades. Frazier's unequivocal position that slavery had been culturally debilitating had placed him in conflict with Melville Herskovits, a product of Franz Boas's anthropology department at Columbia University and a proponent of the "cultural relativism" associated with that school. Herskovits believed that the principal factor in forming the culture of black Americans was their African background. Frazier, on the other hand, had been a student of Robert E. Park, the originator of the theory of social disorganization. Frazier accepted the idea that black communal life was disorganized as a result of poverty, ignorance, oppression, and the heritage of slavery. Herskovits viewed the behavior of black Americans as legitimate cultural difference resulting from their African background. Frazier saw it as deviance, the result of imperfect assimilation of American social norms.[11]

Much of the controversy over social policy in American race relations has been a reenactment of the disagreements between Herskovits and Frazier. During the Kennedy and Johnson administrations, when some of the principles of the civil rights movement were being transformed into social policy, governmental agencies often accepted the view that the contemporary status of black Americans derived from the heritage of slavery. Daniel Patrick Moynihan popularized the view that various pathologies of the ghetto, such as ignorance, poverty, marital instability, and crime, could be traced to the patterns of maladjustment that slavery had induced. He quoted E. Franklin Frazier as his principal source, advancing what many were inclined to view as a pejorative doctrine. Moynihan insisted, however, that his purpose was not to malign that black community but to set forth the case for national action, a massive program of social engineering in the areas of health, education, and welfare.[12]

As late as the Kerner Commission report of 1967, it was standard practice for white liberals and black radicals alike to accept the idea that discrepancies between white and black standards of living in America were attributable to the heritage of slavery. This approach to black history, so influential in determining public policy during the 1960s, was referred to by Charles Valentine as a "pejorative tradition." Pejorative it may have been — or, as some have suggested, ethnocentric — but it was not racist. It attributed American racial problems to historical and social forces rather than to biogenetic inferiority on the part of black people. Orlando Patterson has referred to this position, from which black American history was viewed as no more than a series of bitter traumas, as catastrophism, the view of Afro-American history as one prolonged catastrophe. Patterson cited as one of the foremost proponents of catastrophism the radical spokesman Malcolm X, who felt that black people since the slave trade had no history worth celebrating. Malcolm had proclaimed that black Americans had been robbed by slavery of all the history and culture they had possessed in Africa. Black people, according to Malcolm, had "left their minds in Africa." In America they'd been nothing but raped, driven, and brainwashed slaves, shameless eaters of hog bowels.[13]

That was where the historiography of slavery stood in 1970. Stampp had held that slavery damaged the attitudes of black people towards work, that it had made them slothful, destructive, improvident, and unwilling to follow directions. This had obvious consequences, social theorists were quick to argue, for the attitudes of twentieth-century Afro-Americans. Black unemployment could be at least partially explained by the hostility to labor inculcated in the plantation school. Frazier had demonstrated, at least to the satisfaction of Pat Moynihan, that marital and family instability among black people could be explained in terms of the catastrophic experience of the slave family. Slavery had obliterated the ancient family, left in its place only a distorted caricature of the white middle-class family. Stanley Elkins had shown, at least to the satisfaction of Frazier, that slavery produced a kind of mental illness among its victims, so that significant numbers of slaves were almost psychotic or at least subject to severe personality disorders. The implications of this for the descendants of slaves were quickly seized on by those who saw the slave background as providing an excuse for supposed pathologies in contemporary black society.

Those who attacked this pejorative view focused on undermining the premises of the argument. There was no need to explain away black social pathology by means of the Elkins thesis, because black society was not pathological. Black American slaves had never been stripped of culture as the Frazier school had argued. They had constructed counter-cultural systems from the remnants of African culture that they had brought with them to the New World. Slavery was an economically efficient system; slaves did not forget how to work in the antebellum South. They were a productive labor force, neither the inefficient Sambos described by Phillips nor the vindictive saboteurs described by Stampp.

The trend-setting study of slavery that appeared in response to the psychological need for an endurable past was John Blassingame's *The Slave Community* (1972). There had been other such attempts in the past, of course: B. A. Botkin's *Lay My Burden Down: A Folk History of Slavery* (1945), for example, and Marion Starling's New York University dissertation, "The Slave Narrative: Its Place in American Literary History" (1946). Charles Harold Nichols's *Many Thousand Gone: The Ex Slaves' Account of Their Bondage and Freedom* was published in Holland in 1963. Sterling Stuckey had published an attack on Elkins's thesis in 1968, "Through the Prism of Folklore," in which he attempted to "get 'inside' slaves, to discover what bondsmen thought about their condition." Stanley Feldstein had published a work based on slave narratives, *Once a Slave* (1970), in hopes "that through the description of the slave's heroic resistance to a system of dehumanization, the reader will gain a greater respect for his fellow man, regardless of color." It was Blassingame's study, however, that captured the imagination of a generation and led to widespread acceptance of the thesis that "the slave held onto many remnants of his African culture, gained a sense of worth in the quarters, spent most of his time free from surveillance by whites, controlled important aspects of his life, and did some personally meaningful things on his own volition."[14]

It is interesting to compare Blassingame's work to a similar study that appeared in the same year, George Rawick's *From Sundown to Sunup*. While Blassingame and Feldstein had worked primarily with antebellum narratives, published as abolitionist literature, Rawick had focused on narratives collected by the Works Progress Administration (WPA) during the 1930s. Some of this literature had been used by B. A. Botkin in *Lay My Burden Down,* but Rawick, as the editor of a project to make the original WPA typescripts available to scholars, offered us a nineteen-volume composite autobiography. Like Blassingame, Rawick made use of current social science and read the history through the lenses of anthropological studies that attempted to trace the African roots of black culture. He gave special acknowledgement to the work of Harold Courlander, William R. Bascom, and Sidney Mintz, whose efforts had been much concerned with establishing direct connections between African and Afro-American patterns of work, religion, and recreation.[15]

After Blassingame and Rawick, there was a plethora of studies attempting to understand slavery from the slave's perspective or to describe various aspects of the slave community. Among the more influential were Eugene Genovese's *Roll Jordan Roll,* Peter Wood's *Black Majority,* and Lawrence Levine's *Black Culture and Black Consciousness.* Perfectly respectable studies based on careful reading and serious work, their principal importance is in their demonstration of a consensus among historians that slave narratives, folklore, songs, and other expressions of mass culture were now considered a legitimate means of approaching the history of slavery. More important, they showed that it had now become respectable to accentuate the positive when writing about slavery. Now black Americans had the sort of history they demanded, a history they could live with and be proud of, a history that spoke of slavery not in terms of dehumanization and exploitation but in terms of community, consciousness, and culture.[16]

In 1974 Robert William Fogel and Stanley L. Engerman produced *Time on the Cross,* a two-volume work that like most studies of the period emphasized the stability and efficiency of slave communities. It differed from other approaches in that it was essentially an econometric study. With the aid of a substantial grant from the Ford Foundation, substantial quantities of computer time, and a staff of research assistants, Fogel and Engerman constructed a quantitative picture of slavery that seemed to complement much of what had been said by students of slave narratives. Fogel and Engerman's conclusions were more extreme than the others, however, arguing that in almost every material respect, emancipation led to a worsening of the former slave's condition. Rhetorically, they raised the question, "How could pecuniary income, diet, health, skill, acquisition, and other aspects of the material conditions of life have been worse for blacks during so many years after emancipation than it had been under slavery?" The answer they provided was that the severity of slavery had been exaggerated. Fogel and Engerman were roundly denounced by the academy during the ensuing two years, but *Newsweek* reported, nonetheless, that Fogel, "whose wife is black, remains supremely confident of his data, his methods and his results."[17]

Thomas L. Webber in *Deep Like the Rivers* views Engerman and

Fogel as perpetuators of an idea developed by Booker T. Washington and Ulrich Bonnell Phillips, "the idea of the plantation as a vocational school." Webber, who subtitles his book "Education in the Slave Quarter Community," endorses the views of Engerman and Fogel and joins with them and with Eugene Genovese in giving fresh impetus to the Phillips thesis that slavery provided African Americans with a worthwhile educational experience. Collaterally, all have contributed to the consensus in recent scholarship that "slave communities" supported, rather than undermined, work habits, human dignity, and family life. That was, after all, how slavery came to be the incubation period for the robust Afro-American culture that somehow manifests itself today in terms of gang warfare, teenage pregnancies, drug addiction, alcoholism, and a tragic vulnerability to AIDS, and assumes that somehow slaves were characteristically able to protect their psyches to a degree that is beyond the reach of large numbers of free black people today. Webber, Genovese, Engerman, and Fogel have all been guilty of revitalizing the views of Ulrich Bonnell Phillips, thereby minimizing the hideousness of slavery and the loathsomeness of its residue.[18]

There is a danger in the patterns of black historiography over the past twenty years. It is with considerable validity that Kenneth S. Lynn has referred to the current generation of writers on slavery as "regressive historians." For with all the emphasis for almost two decades on the cultural healthiness of the slave community, there seems to be some possibility that we may forget (or allow others to forget) what a horrendous experience slavery was. More significantly, as we respond to the charge of the Black Studies movement to rewrite the history of slavery in a way that can give us strength and self-respect, we seem to run the risk of underestimating those aspects of slavery that, while unpleasant to recall, constitute the basis for any claims to reparations, affirmative action, or equal opportunity programs, on which policies of racial justice must be founded. Thus, while the more extreme views and methodological shortcomings of the catastrophists may have been demolished, the most important aspect of their contribution still has to be taken seriously. The idea that slavery was a traumatic experience that scarred the black American psyche and damaged the moral code of America persists naggingly into the present. It is dangerous to discard the idea that the current status of black Americans derives from the heritage of the slavery experience, and from the laws and customs that supported it.[19]

For this reason, the appearance of A. Leon Higgenbotham's *In The Matter of Color* seemed a timely occurrence in 1978. Higgenbotham, a U.S. district judge who had taught in the law schools of several prestigious universities, wrote from a conviction that "there is a nexus between the brutal centuries of colonial slavery and the racial polarization and anxieties of today." Although he did not respond directly to the questions concerning slave culture and psychology that dominated almost all the writing of the 1970s, he approached from a different angle the central question that at least some historians of slavery had been attempting to solve. That is to say, he focused on the nature of slavery as an oppressive institution, and he came up with answers that provided a healthy corrective to current trends. His work emphasized the onerous legal code and seemed to have the potential of swinging the pendulum back in the direction of the hard line established by Frazier and Elkins, but without indulging in any of their excesses.[20]

In the Matter of Color was announced as the first of a multivolume treatment of race and the American legal process. One hopes that the projected volumes will eventually appear, for there is considerable need for reminders that slavery was a brutal, degrading, and humiliating experience, that its heritage is still with us, and that "the poisonous legacy of legalized oppression based upon the matter of color can never be adequately purged from our society if we act as if slave laws had never existed." Thurgood Marshall made a similar point in his dissenting opinion on the Bakke decision. The relevance of realistic, as opposed to sentimental, interpretations to socio-historical jurisprudence and its potential effect upon public policy should not be underestimated. But in the years since the publication of Higgenbotham's work, there has been no tendency towards realism. Slavery history continues to be written in such a way as to provide black Americans with an acceptable past. One simply cannot escape the implications of painting so positive a history of slave culture. If slavery produced, or allowed the retention of, a wealth of positive cultural practices and ideals, then where was the evil of slavery? The new historians of slavery seem to find this question uninteresting, preferring to follow the footsteps of Genovese—no longer as fresh as they were in the early 1970s.

Historian Jacqueline Jones's *Labor of Love, Labor of Sorrow* (1985) adds a new dimension to the recent historiography of slavery, in that it is a feminist work, but in other respects, it is a restatement of themes that have already been well developed. To her credit, Jones does not overlook the innate brutality of the system, but she is nonetheless concerned with the areas in which slaves were able to shape their own living space and take control of their own day-to-day existence. Her feminist perspective provides the insight that slavery, for all its evils, had at least the positive effect of preventing the economic dominance of females by black males. Her point of view is similar to that of Angela Davis, who has observed that slavery prevented black males from developing patriarchalist attitudes.[21] All of this is, of course, a variation on the theme stated by W. E. B. Du Bois, Martin Luther King, and others, who believed that the suffering of black people had given them an attitude to life that placed them in the vanguard of social reform. Black women had long experienced many of the problems now being encountered by middle-class white women in large numbers, and would have much to offer all women in working towards solutions. This is a work of advocacy scholarship, written for the purpose of justifying present-day reforms, but no less for the purpose of creating a past that blacks and other Americans can live with. As does Angela Davis in *Women, Race and Class,* Jones cites, with obvious relish, the description of a group of black working women provided by Frederick Law Olmstead, who on a journey through Mississippi observed:

> forty of the largest and strongest women I ever saw together; they were all in a simple uniform dress of a bluish check stuff, the skirts reaching a little below the knee; their legs and feet were bare; they carried themselves loftily, each having a hoe over the shoulder, and walking with a free, powerful swing, like *chasseurs* on the march.[22]

Of course, it does not make us happy to recall that these women were "led by an old driver carrying a whip," and that a "lean and vigilant white overseer on a brisk pony brought up the rear." It is far more gratifying to dwell on images of freedom, power, and lofty bearing.

Today, just about every guild member in good standing who writes on the history of slavery is identified with the idea that slaves had some degree of power not only over their own space but even over that of their masters. Paul D. Escott asserts this in *Slavery Remembered: A Record of Twentieth-Century Slave Narratives* (1979), saying that the slaves were able to win "significant ground in their contest with the master, ground on which they could build more firmly the foundations of a black community." One of the means of achieving this power for community formation was the religious experience, argued Escott, echoing a point that had been made some years earlier by Leslie Owens in *This Species of Property.* Eugene Genovese asserted in *Roll Jordan Roll* that community feeling arising out of slave religion eventually laid "the foundations of the black nation." Sterling Stuckey's claim that slave culture is related to nationalist theory and the foundations of black America is, therefore, not without precedent. *Slave Culture* does, however, make an important original point, and it is with this that the remainder of this essay is concerned.[23]

In his preface, Stuckey asks the questions: "How was a single people formed out of the many African ethnic groups on the plantations of the

South?" "How was a single culture formed out of the interaction of African ethnic groups in North American slavery?" (p. viii). He finds the answers in religious ritual, particularly in the tradition of the "ring shout," a widespread West African practice, in which the participants form a ring and move in a counterclockwise circle, until they are possessed by frenzy and shouting as the spirit moves among them. Stuckey presents massive documentation to buttress his contention that the "ring shout" was a widespread cultural phenomenon among black Americans, not only during slavery but throughout the nineteenth century. His research has led him "to the inescapable conclusion that the nationalism of the slave community was essentially African nationalism" (p. ix). He argues that the culture and the political consciousness of black Americans in the nineteenth century, and probably in the twentieth century as well, have been essentially African. He asserts that the retention of African culture traits was a weapon of supreme importance in the arsenal of slave resistance, and he suggests that those slaves who were most likely to question and resist white supremacy were those who clung most avidly to African cultural traits.

Stuckey meets up with a problem, however, when he is forced to admit that the ring shout was often condemned by black leaders of the nineteenth century, among whom nationalists were no exception. This leads him to describe his book as largely "a study in irony because the depths of African culture in America had been underestimated by most nationalist theorists in America." It is good to recognize such ironies, and even better to reflect on them. Stuckey does not satisfactorily confront the question of why so many of the free black leaders were hostile to the mass culture and failed to view it as a means of creating a true cultural nationalism. Contemporary white American and European nationalists were eager to develop a theory of culture, rising up from the grass roots as a complement to political nationalism. Black nationalists, by contrast, rejected mass culture, preferring a theory of civilization that would trickle down from the top and eventually penetrate to the lower levels of society.[24]

Stuckey repeats with some distaste Bishop Daniel A. Payne's well-known autobiographical account of his attempt to stamp out Africanisms from the A.M.E. Church and his crusade against the ring shout. Stuckey sees Payne's crusade against Africanisms as a mistake that damaged Payne's effectiveness and cost him converts. If indeed Payne made a mistake, he never admitted to feeling so, for he told the story without remorse. He wanted to stamp out the ring shout for two reasons, first because he considered it a backward practice, and second because he felt that it had nothing to do with true conversion. In every ethnic group, there are numerous varieties of religion, some for the more exuberant and some for the more sedate. Payne's opposition to folk worship probably did cost him a large number of converts, but perhaps he felt that he could accomplish more with a Gideon's band, who were prepared to worship in what he considered "a rational manner."[25]

Stuckey argues convincingly that most black leaders, nationalist or otherwise, must have been aware of Africanisms in black mass culture. This position is hardly contestable, for almost every antebellum observer who recorded impressions of American slave culture was impressed by the universal retention of Africanisms. The WPA narratives also provide ample evidence of Africanisms in slave religion. As Rawick observes, "West African meanings re-emerged in North America in totally different contexts." Rawick cites the example of slave documents that speak of utilizing an iron pot, overturned in the middle of the floor "to keep the white folks from hearing them pray and testify." Some anthropologists hold the view that the pot had a symbolic function, taking the place of the forbidden drum in religious rituals. That may well be, for while an iron pot may have a meaningful cultural significance, it certainly cannot magically prevent white folk from overhearing the shouts of enthusiastic worship.[26]

But do the examples cited by Stuckey, Rawick, and others really prove that black religious ritual was a significant indication of nationalism or a spirit of resistance? The slaves' midnight meetings in the forests were no secret. Planters were well aware of the ring shouts, midnight revival meetings, and even of what Leslie Owens calls "hushharbor" ceremonies. It stands to reason that they would have had some informers in the group, and that their best informers would have been among those who shouted the loudest and danced with the most frenzy. Persons who behaved in this way would have made the best spies, because they would have been trusted by the other slaves. A wily slaveholder would recognize the sound policy of encouraging his slaves to blow off steam with their energetic rituals, perhaps even providing them with liquor and pretending not to hear the revelry conducted in the presence of an upturned pot.[27]

There is no denying that folk music and magical practices had their usefulness in the process of resistance. Frederick Douglass, who had been a slave himself, showed considerable respect for the uses of folk practices in his autobiographical writings. He described his use of the magic root given to him by another slave, Sandy, and how it gave him the confidence to resist a whipping at the hands of the slave breaker, Covey. Martin Delany was apparently aware of this when, in a humorous scene from the novel *Blake,* he had Mammy Judy make use of a religious demonstration to temporize and avoid her master's questioning about the escape of a valued slave. Black abolitionists were never tempted to romanticize slave culture, however; they believed that any positive depictions of slavery or any of its trappings would be grist for the mills of pro-slavery propaganda. Their concern was to paint slavery in all its horror, and this led to extremely painful depictions of the degradation of the slaves.

Descanting on the theme of "our wretchedness in consequence of ignorance," David Walker claimed that in the South, one might witness slaves becoming accomplices to the dehumanizing practices of white folk.[28]

> He may there see a son take his mother, who bore almost the pains of death to give him birth, and by the command of a tyrant, strip her as naked as she came into the world, and apply a cow-hide to her, until she falls a victim to death in the road! He may see a husband take his dear wife, not unfrequently in a pregnant state, and perhaps far advanced, and beat her for an unmerciful wretch, until his infant falls a lifeless lump at her feet![29]

This was an extreme view, probably no more accurate than it was typical, but it demonstrates splendidly what Stuckey observed in an earlier work, "a black nationalist tendency to exaggerate the degree of acquiescence to oppression by the masses of black people." Black nationalists seemed more inclined than other black people to present "gloomy . . . devastating . . . stereotypical portraits of black humanity.[30] Nowhere was this attitude more obvious than in the *Ethiopian Manifesto* of Alexander Young, who claimed to be writing with the loving regard of "a fostering parent," "for the express benefit" of the "poor untaught and degraded African slave."[31]

Stuckey's willing confrontation of the ironies and contradictions of the black-nationalist position and his concern for the areas of overlap between nationalist ideology and slave culture are the striking justification for this highly informed and adventurous theoretical work. He has opened a new series of questions, different than those posed by Ulrich Bonnell Phillips, Stanley Elkins, John Blassingame, or Eugene Genovese. He does not solve all the problems that he identifies, and it may not be possible for anyone to solve them, but in this magisterial work, Stuckey has gone farther than any other historian in exploring the linkages between the bourgeois culture and the mass culture of black Americans. He is emotionally biased in favor of the mass culture, but he is too fine a historian to reject the literate culture of David Walker, Alexander Crummell, W. E. B. Du Bois, and Paul Robeson. Stuckey is to be commended for attacking the problem of a unified theory that will tie together all the known forces of black American life in one neat package. The problem is yet to be solved, but he is one of the few with the courage to tackle it.

There is also another problem, one that is not Stuckey's alone. It is shared by many historians of the black experience, including the present author, for we find ourselves in the difficult position of wanting to have our cake and eat it, too. We must somehow find a way out of the dilemma of celebrating the slavery experience as the womb of a wholesome Afro-American history, and in the same breath condemning slavery as a degrading and brutalizing institution. It is only human to desire a history that is in every respect honorable, but if we are honest, we must accept the fact that there is no people on earth that has such a history. If we try to create such a history for black Americans, we shall be indulging in an endeavor that is perhaps heroic but foolish, nonetheless, and inevitably doomed to failure.

NOTES

1. Sterling Stuckey, *Slave Culture: Nationalist Theory and the Foundations of Black America* (New York: Oxford, 1987).

2. E. Franklin Frazier, "Garvey: A Mass Leader," *Nation* (18 August, 1926), 147–48.

3. Eugene Genovese, *The World the Slaveholders Made: Two Essays in Interpretation* (New York: Vintage, 1969). The writings of Hughes, Ruffin, and Fitzhugh may be sampled in Eric L. McKitrick, ed., *Slavery Defended: Two Views of the Old South* (Englewood Cliffs, N.J.: Prentice-Hall, 1963). Frederick Law Olmstead, *A Journey in the Seaboard Slave States* (New York: Dix & Edwards, 1856), condensed and revised as *The Cotton Kingdom* (New York: Mason Brothers, 1861).

4. Martin R. Delany, *Blake: or The Huts of America* (1859; reprint, Boston: Beacon Press, 1970).

5. James Ford Rhodes, *History of the United States from the Compromise of 1850* (1893–1906); John Bach McMaster, *A History of the People of the United States from the Revolution to the Civil War* (1883–1913). William Henry Smith, *A Political History of Slavery* (1903; reprint, New York: Ungar, 1966). Ulrich B. Phillips, *American Negro Slavery* (New York, 1918).

6. William Wells Brown, *The Rising Son* (Boston: A. G. Brown, 1874), and *My Southern Home* (Boston: A.G. Brown, 1880).

7. Ida B. Wells, *Southern Horrors* (1892; reprint, New York: Arno Press/New York Times, 1969). Frederick Douglass, *The Lesson of the Hour: Why is the Negro Lynched* (1894), reprinted in *The Life and Writings of Frederick Douglass,* ed. Philip S. Foner (New York: International Publishers, 1955). Booker T. Washington's mythologizing of the faithful servant occurs in his "Atlanta Exposition Address," in *The Booker T. Washington Papers,* ed. Louis Harlan (Urbana: University of Illinois Press, 1972–89), 3:332. Joel Chandler Harris, *Uncle Remus: His Songs and His Sayings* (New York, 1908), pp. 201–14.

8. Kenneth M. Stampp, *The Peculiar Institution* (New York: Random House, 1966).

9. Samuel Eliot Morrison and Henry Steele Commager, *The Growth of the American Republic* (New York: Oxford, 1950). In a similar vein, see James G. Randall and David

Donald, *The Civil War and Reconstruction* (Boston: D. C. Heath, 1961); Herbert Aptheker, *American Negro Slave Revolts* (New York: Columbia University Press, 1943); John Hope Franklin, *The Militant South, 1800–1860* (Cambridge: Harvard University Press, 1970) and *The Free Negro in North Carolina* (1943; reprint, New York: W. W. Norton, 1971).

10. Stanley M. Elkins, *Slavery: A Problem in American Institutional and Intellectual Life* (Chicago: University of Chicago Press, 1959). On p. 86, n.6, Elkins cites Erich Fromm, *Man for Himself* (New York: Rinehart, 1947), and Theodore Adorno et al., *The Authoritarian Personality* (New York: Harper, 1950). E. Franklin Frazier, *Black Bourgeoisie* (New York: Macmillan, 1962).

11. Melville Herskovits, *The New World Negro* (Bloomington: Indiana University Press, 1966), and *The Myth of the Negro Past* (New York, 1941; reprint, Boston: Beacon Press, 1958).

12. Daniel Patrick Moynihan, "The Negro Family: The Case for National Action" is reprinted in *The Moynihan Report and the Politics of Controversy,* ed. Lee Rainwater and William Yancy (Cambridge: MIT Press, 1967).

13. The official name of the "Kerner Report" is *Report of the National Advisory Commission on Civil Disorders,* 1 March, 1968 (Washington, D.C.: U.S. Government Printing Office, 1970). Charles Valentine, *Culture and Poverty: Critique and Counter-Proposals* (Chicago: University of Chicago Press, 1968). Orlando Patterson expresses his views on the varieties of black history and the relationship of Malcolm X and others to catastrophism in *Harvard Educational Review* 41 (August 1971).

14. John Blassingame, *The Slave Community* (New York: Oxford, 1972). B. A. Botkin, *Lay My Burden Down: A Folk History of Slavery* (Chicago: University of Chicago Press, 1945). Marion Starling, "The Slave Narrative: Its Place in American Literary History," (Ph.D. diss., New York University, 1946). Charles Harold Nichols, *Many Thousand Gone: The Ex Slaves' Account of Their Bondage and Freedom* (Leiden: E. J. Brill, 1963). Sterling Stuckey, "Through the Prism of Folklore, " *The Massachusetts Review* 9 (Summer 1986), reprinted in Jules Chametzkey and Sidney Kaplan, *Black and White in American Culture: An Anthology from the Massachusetts Review* (New York: Viking Press, 1971), pp. 172–94. Stanley Feldstein, *Once a Slave* (New York: William Morrow, 1971).

15. George Rawick, *From Sundown to Sunup: The Making of a Black Community* (Westport, Conn.: Greenwood Press, 1972). The works credited by Rawick as particularly influential are Harold Courlander, *The Drum and the Hoe: Life and Lore of the Haitian People* (Berkeley: University of California Press, 1960); William R. Bascom, "Acculturation Among the Gullah Negroes," *American Anthropologist* 43 (1941): 43–50; Sidney Mintz, comments on George Rawick's paper, "West African Culture and North American Slavery," in *Migration and Anthropology Proceedings of the 1970 Annual Spring Meeting of the American Ethnological Society* (Seattle: University of Washington Press, 1970), pp. 149ff.

16. Eugene Genovese, *Roll Jordan Roll: The World the Slaves Made* (New York: Pantheon, 1974). Peter Wood, *Black Majority: Negroes in Colonial South Carolina from 1670 through the Stono Rebellion* (New York: W. W. Norton, 1974). Lawrence Levine *Black Culture and Black Consciousness* (New York: Oxford, 1975).

17. Robert William Fogel and Stanley L. Engerman, *Time on the Cross: The Economics of American Negro Slavery* (Boston: Little, Brown, 1974). The overwhelming response of the scholarly community to this volume was negative. See, for example, Herbert Aptheker, "Heavenly Days in Dixie: Or the Time of Their Lives," *Political Affairs* (June/July 1974); Herbert Gutman, *Slavery and the Numbers Game: A Critique of Time on the Cross* (Urbana: University of Illinois Press, 1975); Herbert G. Gutman et al. *Reck-*

oning with Slavery: Critical Essays in the Quantitative History of American Negro Slavery (New York: Oxford University Press, 1975); Constance Holden, "Cliometrics: Book on Slavery Stirs up a Scholarly Storm," *Science,* 13 December 1984; R. D. Rucker, *"Time on the Cross*: A Fascist Revisionism," *The Daily Iowan,* 25 March 1975; Fred Siegel, *"Time on the Cross*: A First Appraisal," *Historical Methods Newsletter* (September 1974): 299–303; Gary M. Walton, ed., "A Symposium on *Time on the Cross,*" *Explorations in Economic History* 12 (Fall 1974); C. Vann Woodward, "The Jolly Institution," *New York Review of Books,* 2 May 1974; Thomas L. Haskell, "The True and Tragical History of *Time on the Cross,*" *New York Review of Books,* 2 October 1975. Kenneth L. Woodward "History of Numbers," *Newsweek,* 20 October 1975.

18. Thomas L. Webber, *Deep Like the Rivers: Education in the Slave Quarter Community* (New York: W. W. Norton, 1978), p. 281, n.1.

19. Kenneth S. Lynn, "Regressive Historians," *The American Scholar* (Autumn 1978): 489–500.

20. A. Leon Higgenbotham, *In the Matter of Color: Race and the American Legal Process: The Colonial Period* (New York: Oxford University Press, 1978).

21. Jacqueline Jones, *Labor of Love, Labor of Sorrow: Black Women, Work, and the Family from Slavery to the Present* (New York: Basic Books, 1985), p. 14. Angela Davis, *Women, Race and Class* (New York: Vintage, 1983), pp. 12–18.

22. Cited in Jones, *Labor of Love, Labor of Sorrow,* p. 17. Cited in Davis, *Women, Race and Class,* p. 11.

23. Paul D. Escott, *Slavery Remembered: A Record of Twentieth-Century Slave Narratives* (Chapel Hill: University of North Carolina Press, 1979), p. 94. Leslie Howard Owens, *This Species of Property: Slave Life and Culture South* (New York: Oxford, 1977).

24. Wilson J. Moses, *The Golden Age of Black Nationalism, 1850–1925* (1978; reprint, New York: Oxford, 1988), pp. 10–11, 20–21.

25. Daniel Alexander Payne, *Recollections of Seventy Years* (1888; reprint, New York: Arno Press, 1969), pp. 233–38, 253–55.

26. Rawick, *From Sundown to Sunup,* p. 39.

27. Owens, *This Species of Property,* pp. 155–56.

28. Frederick Douglass, *The Narrative of Frederick Douglass, An American Slave: Written by Himself* (1845; reprint, New York: Doubleday, 1963), p. 71. Delany, *Blake,* p. 45. David Walker, *David Walker's Appeal, in Four Articles; Together with a Preamble, to the Coloured Citizens of the World, But in Particular, and Very Expressly, to Those of the United States of America* (Boston, 1830), reprinted in Sterling Stuckey, *The Ideological Origins of Black Nationalism* (Boston: Beacon, 1972), p. 11.

29. Walker, *David Walker's Appeal,* p. 60.

30. Stuckey, *Ideological Origins of Black Nationalism,* p. 60.

31. Robert Alexander Young, *The Ethiopian Manifesto* (New York, 1829), reprinted in Stuckey, *Ideological Origins of Black Nationalism,* p. 38.

The Voyage of the *Isla de Cuba*

Records of an African Return

The era of classical black nationalism began in response to a traumatic event, the passage of the Fugitive Slave Law of 1850. It was marked by an upsurge of Back to Africa and other emigrationist movements and ebbed and flowed for the next seventy-five years, culminating with the Garvey movement and ending with Garvey's imprisonment in 1925. During those years, almost every recognized spokesman, from the separatist Martin Delany to the assimilationist Frederick Douglass, threw something into the seething cauldron of African-American nationalism. These were years during which some of the best educated and most gifted black men and women were associated with institutional separatism. It was a period during which the most heated debates over the nature and functions of black nationalism occurred, including that between Frederick Douglass and Martin Delany and that between Marcus Garvey and W. E. B. Du Bois.

During the 1850s, Frederick Douglass, a former slave and the unacknowledged son of his master, became the most visible spokesman for black Americans. Douglass was entirely self-educated, and his independence of mind derived partly from that fact. He placed great value on individualism and was a militant abolitionist. He was also opposed to the Back to Africa movement and to all forms of racial separatism. He argued that black Americans must insist on all the rights of American citizenship, and argued that the first obligation of black political activists was to work for immediate and universal emancipation. Arguing that all black Americans were in a sense "slaves of the community," he saw the first obligation of the "nationalist" as fighting for the liberation of what he called "the nation in bondage."

Martin Delany differed from Douglass in many ways, of course, but two of the more significant differences in his and Douglass's backgrounds had to do with his parentage and his childhood. He was born free, and he was proud of his unadulterated black ancestry. Delany nonetheless "emulated the white society of his day," as Victor Ullman observes, and by the time he was a young man he had established a reputation among white and black folk in his home town of Pittsburgh as a vigorous and enterprising citizen. Delany—who had been educated in a church-related school run by the black nationalist Rev. Louis Woodson in the basement of the Bethel African Methodist Episcopal (A.M.E.) Church—was admitted to the Harvard medical school in 1850 under a program that was intended to train doctors for service in Liberia. Along with two other black students, he was denied permission to register for a second semester, and around this time he became a vocal emigrationist.

It is difficult to understand the direct route whereby Delany became interested in African emigration. He must have had some interest in the movement even as early as 1850 in order to have participated in good faith in the Harvard program. On the other hand, he expressed the most virulent hostility towards Liberia in 1852, when he published *The Condition, Elevation, Emigration and Destiny of the Colored People of the United States,* where he did include a chapter on the possibilities of migration to East Africa. The fact that he was willing to consider emigration at all put him in conflict with Frederick Douglass. He was in total agreement with Douglass when it came to Liberia, however; his position was, if anything, more hostile. In 1852 Delany described the republic as

> a poor *miserable mockery—a burlesque* on a government—a pitiful dependency on the American Colonizationists, the Colonization Board at Washington city, in the District of Columbia, being the Executive and Government, and the principal man, called President, in Liberia, being the echo—a mere parrot of Rev. Robert R. Gurley, Elliot Cresson, Esq., Governor Pinney, and other leaders of the Colonization scheme—to do as they bid and say what they tell him. This we see in all his doings.[1]

It is well known that Delany eventually made a tour of West Africa, where he entered into a treaty with some Nigerian chiefs for the acquisition of lands where he hoped to establish a colony. At the time of his visit to Liberia in 1859, he sent a letter to President Roberts asking for an audience and met and dined with a number of Liberian leaders. In a letter to several of the citizens, he wrote, "You are mistaken, gentlemen, that I have ever spoken directly against Liberia." But, of course, he had, and in more instances than the one previously cited. In 1853, despite the fact that he at the time knew nothing whatever of Liberia from firsthand experience, he unabashedly endorsed a controversial book on the subject written by William Nesbit.

Nesbit's book, *Four Months in Liberia, or African Colonization Exposed,* was a cheap diatribe, calculated to gratify steadfast opponents of Liberian colonization but offering little in the way of judicious fact-finding or calm persuasion. This is not to say that the book was entirely lacking in value, for indeed it must have been a useful remedy for the more feverishly optimistic cases of nineteenth-century black nationalism. Such alleged misdeeds of the settlers as oppression of the indigenous population, dealing in rum, and buying and selling slaves were roundly condemned by Nesbit, who also duly noted the problem of adjusting to the African climate.

Of course, Nesbit's limited knowledge of medicine did not allow for intelligent discussion of this subject. When it came to such topics as parasitism or yellow fever, West African native medicine was not much inferior to what was being taught in the medical schools of Europe and America. Fortunately, native medicine did not include such "cures" for "the fever" as the ubiquitous nineteenth-century practice of "bleeding." As Nesbit reported, "They [the natives] have few diseases among them, and the most common remedy is to grease themselves with palm oil and lay in the sun."[2]

Nesbit mercilessly ridiculed the Liberian military services, but he was accurate in his observation that they were totally incompetent to in any way hinder the transatlantic slave trade. He was equally correct in his judgement that methods of keeping European livestock healthy in most parts of Liberia were beyond the reach of nineteenth-century animal husbandry. On the other hand, his claim that the streets of towns were stalked by dangerous beasts was not only unfair but revealed a ludicrous disregard for scientific credibility. If there were no tigers in Africa, they were easily enough invented:

The Animal kingdom combines with the elements to render it the most detestable spot on earth. Elephants, leopards and tiger-cats are numerous, often coming into the settlements. Of amphibious animals, they have the hippopotamus and the crocodile. . . . Of reptiles they have the mammoth boa-constrictor thirty feet in length; the cobra de cabello, the most venomous of all snakes and every species that has any affinity to that family finds there its legitimate home. Lizards and centipedes, a foot in length, and the tarantula or hairy spider, very poisonous, are numerous. . . . The bug-a-bug, or termite, a white ant eats up all their houses, furniture, fences, and everything that is manufactured of wood.[3]

Nesbit's ship, the *Isla de Cuba,* arrived in Monrovia on December 18, 1853, five months after the arrival of Alexander Crummell, an Episcopal priest, who having been denied a college education in the United States had been able to procure one at Cambridge University in England. Crummell had come to Liberia under the auspices of his own church in order to become a missionary and soon discovered that the climate created problems for black emigrants, especially the very old and the very young. Crummell suffered from the indigenous diseases constantly throughout the sixteen years of his two sojourns in Liberia, between 1853 and 1872. Shortly after his arrival on the west coast, he lost a child to one of the many "fevers" that so often confronted the Americo-Liberian settler. His wife was almost continuously an invalid, if his letters are to be believed, and in the end Crummell became disillusioned with Liberia, writing to his ecclesiastical superiors in the United States that the settler community was doomed to extinction.

Nesbit did not require sixteen years to become disillusioned; he made his escape from Liberia after fifteen months, convinced that as soon as the Americans and the British withdrew their support the natives would fall upon the colonists, "driving them into the sea." Then the territory would "irresistibly fall back to its native heathenism." All things that the colonization agents had said with regard to "the thrift and prosperity of the country [were] most egregious falsehoods. Everything [was] exaggerated." It was a "region of darkness and desolation for which there [was] no hope." The streets of Monrovia were overgrown with bramble and bushes. "I know places in the streets of Monrovia, in which elephants might hide in perfect safety."[4]

In 1857 the Reverend Samuel Williams, who had also sailed with the *Isla de Cuba* on its voyage to Liberia in November 1853, fashioned a response to Nesbit's attack. Williams, a Methodist missionary, had been born in Pennsylvania, where he claimed to have had a stable working-class existence in the small community of Johnstown. In 1838 he was much aggrieved when he was not allowed to vote in the election, and although he claims to have continued to enjoy the friendship and respect of local townsmen, he was further discouraged by the passage of the Fugitive Slave Bill in 1850. Having made inquiries about Canada and deducing that racial prejudice was also present there, he began to reflect on Africa and came to the conclusion that he could support colonization without violating his abolitionist principles. He migrated with some financial help from the citizens of his town and arrived in Liberia along with William Nesbit.[5]

Williams found conditions in Liberia difficult but hardly so infernal as Nesbit had maintained. Admittedly, horses, oxen, and other livestock not native to that part of the world did not thrive, and Williams conceded the truth of another of Nesbit's charges—"the naked condition of the natives." Why the government did not pass laws against public nudity in town, he found incomprehensible, but he denied having seen any acts of indecency. Williams was much impressed by the natives, particularly by the Vey nation, whom he called "a remarkably good looking people," and admired their crafts, especially their spinning and weaving.[6] He came to believe that the so-called slash-and-burn agriculture, common to West Africa and other societies at similar levels of development, might be the best possible under existing conditions. In any case, he found it necessary to make use of the slash-and-burn technique himself. Far more thorough than Nesbit in his examination of native life, Williams described native dancing, warfare, engineering, hunting, and magical beliefs with remarkable objectivity, a fact that lends credibility to his report in other respects. Williams blamed Delany, "a most inveterate hater of colonization," for having conceived the idea of the book purely as a means of assisting Nesbit out of financial difficulties. Its contents were almost pure concoction, and "what Mr. Nesbit did not think of Mr. Delany could." The appraisal was fairly accurate.[7]

Another voyager arriving on the *Isla de Cuba* with Nesbit and Williams in 1853 was Daniel H. Peterson. Like most of his fellow travellers, Peterson lacked the education and the basic intellectual powers of a Crummell or a Delany. He practically idolized the American Colonization Society and was downright slavish in his admiration for the white churchmen whom he identified as his benefactors. "For I declare," wrote Peterson, "that from a child to this day I have found all my best friends among the white people." With his fellow Afro-Americans, things did not always go well for Peterson. He was quick to criticize, color-conscious, intolerant, and convinced of black inferiority. Memories of some old grudge had left him with a thinly veiled hostility towards the A.M.E. Church of Philadelphia. A considerable portion of his pamphlet is devoted to criticism of that church, the "backsliding and rebellious sister . . . who was guilty of oppression, and violated the disciplines of the church and rules of government from motives of malice and revenge."[8] Peterson had left the African Methodists, railing against them for their striving after fine churches, large congregations, and high learning. The fact that the African Methodists had installed a second and a third bishop, one of them the mildly anticolonizationist Daniel A. Payne, was particularly irritating to him. He accused the church of aping the white Methodists, who also had three bishops, employing language that was most inappropriate for a man who was supposedly committed to the idea of black independence and equality.

> The question may arise, Why do they want three bishops? I answer, Why does the ape attempt to imitate the human family? It is because he lacks understanding, and does not perceive that Nature has never bestowed upon him the proper facilities for doing the works or performing the part of a human being.[9]

Did Peterson mean to imply that the natural endowments of whites and blacks were as widely removed as those of man and ape? If he really meant to point up differences in training and experience, why did he speak of them as if they were actually differences in natural endowment? Whatever he meant to say, he clearly saw a difference between white and black Methodists as great as "that between the Hudson river and the Atlantic Ocean." The white church was known for her missions to the heathen. The African Methodists, poor and miseducated, had given bad advice to their members, "raising evil reports against a humane, benevolent, and Christian institution," namely the American Colonization Society. The essence of Peterson's hostility seems to have derived from two things: his frustrated ambitions within the African Methodist Church, and his recognition of an opportunity to attack an institution that had opposed the aims of his white colonizationist friends.

Peterson sailed for Liberia with a song of praise on his lips for the Reverend J. B. Penny, a white representative of the New York Colonization Society who had seen some years of service as a missionary in West Africa, and who on the eve of departure brought bedding and warm clothing for a family of destitute emigrants. During the thirty-eight days passage, Peterson kept a diary filled with praise for his benevolent white folks and contumely for the blacks, who were carrying vice into Africa.

> Violins and other trifling kinds of music should be left behind, — they only engender idleness and folly . . . for there were some that wanted to play the fiddle, with other vain amusements. I am very glad that the captain spoke against such proceedings. There were two fiddles. Augustus Washington from Hartford had one and a man named Kelly from the West had the other. It was not well to take them on board.[10]

The superstitious Peterson made a note in his journal that Washington broke his looking glass on the evening of the twenty-third day at sea, but no evil seems to have befallen him as a result. Peterson spent less time in Liberia than Nesbit or Williams, arriving on December 19 and departing on January 18. He dined with the president, met a few other dignitaries, preached in a church or two, and left for New York after stopovers in Sierra Leone and the Gambia. That was long enough to nurture his prejudices against British colonial administration. He remarked that many of the people were "Mahometans," others were idolaters, who might be seen "sitting or lying in the sand, in large gangs, worshipping their false gods. They wear long robes and sandals, but are half naked." Although the town of Gambia looked well from the sea, the people were mostly "wild and uncultivated. The greater part are the blackest persons I ever saw." He expressed nothing but contempt for native customs; his pride, narrow-heartedness, and ignorance occluded his vision almost entirely. Possibly reacting to the well-known tendency of many black Americans to admire English institutions, Peterson made some invidious comparisons of the penal codes of British West Africa and Liberia, arguing that the British system was much harsher. That Peterson found the British colonies in every way inferior to Liberia is not startling, since in his mind England was so vastly more hostile to blacks than was the United States. The English were responsible for Negro slavery in the United States, he reasoned, and this made them hypocrites, false friends of the Negro.[11]

Peterson sought to convince his readers that it was not the Americans but the British alone who "in an age of darkness made slaves of the colored people." White Americans were "kind, humane, and benevolent," but surely black people could not expect them to accept them as equals. He advised black people to observe themselves in the looking glass and realize that they could never be Americans. At the same time, the Americans were a wise nation, a Christian nation, "our best friends" to whom we should be "willing and obedient." It was a strange and twisted logic that argued that white Americans proved their friendship by advising black people that they had no rights in the land of their birth. Peterson's support of the American Colonization Society was born of a defeatist attitude and an acceptance of his inferiority. Although he recognized that slavery was an evil, he did not forcefully denounce it. It is difficult to think of him as a black nationalist, for he held to the philosophy of religious fatalism and escapism that Delany had denounced. Peterson apparently did not resent the patronizing attitudes of condescending whites. He seems to have been the very stereotype of the servile, self-hating accomodationist to racism that Douglass opposed. His collaboration with the forces of white supremacy was in no way compatible with the militant nationalism of Crummell or Delany.

Augustus Washington, one of the violin players on board the *Isla de Cuba,* provided the most detailed and systematic exposition of his reasons for migrating. The unusually articulate Washington had once been a schoolmate of Crummell's at Oneida Institute before going on to study at Dartmouth College, and had worked for several years in Hartford, Connecticut, as a daguerreotypist. The *African Repository* reported that he was an "unmixed representative of the African race," that he brought with him the "material and instruments for his profession, but we trust is destined to fill a higher position in the footnote republic." Washington's thoughts on colonization had appeared in the *African Repository* several months before he sailed. Like Martin Delany, Washington had entertained hopes of founding "a separate State in America," and was planning "with the aid of a few colored young men of superior talent and ability . . . to negotiate for a tract of land in Mexico, when the war and its consequences blasted our hopes, and drove us from our purpose." Finally, he was convinced that Liberia was the only place in the world suitable for the development of a society in which black people could enjoy human rights. He used arguments that by that time had become commonplace, namely that Providence had provided signs indicating that the destiny of black Americans must be to migrate. Universal emancipation would be achieved as would the development of the continent "larger than North America . . . lying waste for want of the hand of science and industry." Providence would certainly not "permit a land so rich in all the elements of wealth and greatness to remain longer without civilized inhabitants." And it was equally clear that colored people were "peculiarly adapted [to] civilizing, redeeming, and saving that continent if ever it is to be done at all."[12]

Aware that his declaration of support for African colonization would be startling to those who had hitherto regarded him as "intelligent and sound in faith," Washington insisted that the goals of emancipationists and colonizationists complemented one another. He admitted that the colonization movement contained both friend and foe, but he was willing to join with both "in moving the wheel of a great enterprise." In any case, he thought it was no inconsistency to work directly for emancipation in America and simultaneously for the development of a West African state. He was prepared to endure the "slanders and anathemas" which he felt certain would be his. Regrettably, loss of friendship and support among free blacks would certainly be the result of his change of position, but he looked forward to joining forces with the citizens of Liberia. He would follow in the tradition of the Pilgrims, who had settled America. Those who drove them from their mother country by persecution and oppression had unintentionally created a higher form of Christian republic in the New World. History would repeat itself; America's "oppression and injustice to one class of this people" would bring about the establishment of "a religion and morality more pure, and liberty more universal," at least so far as the blacks were concerned.

Washington professed great respect for both colonizationists and immediate abolitionists, calling attention to the great courage of the latter, both moral and physical. Despite occasional mistakes, the immediatists had "divested themselves of personal prejudices, aroused the nation to a sense of its injustice, and wrongs." They had defended the claims of the free blacks to education and political rights. They had consistently maintained that black Americans were entitled to full equality, even in America—an idea that had been rejected by many colonizationists. The colonizationists, however, had the virtue of realism. They recognized that black people would never be considered equal until they had proven their capacities for independent achievement. With the founding of Liberia, they had provided black Americans with a means for offering such proof. Abolitionists and colonizationists alike were doing some good, each in their own way, and both "might have accomplished more good, if they had wasted less ammunition in firing at each other." Although he admitted that colonizationists largely considered black people morally and intellectually inferior to whites, he did not believe that they were motivated solely by "hatred to the race and love of slavery." Like the abolitionists, they had their role to play in the designs of Providence, and he claimed not to see "why any hostility should exist between those who are true Abolitionists and that class of Colonizationists who are such for just and benevolent motives." Washington thus made a distinction—as even Frederick Douglass did—between philanthropic colonizationists, like the antislavery Pennsylvania Quaker Benjamin Coates, and misanthropic deportationists, like the slaveholding Henry Clay. Washington argued that most free blacks, by stressing only the hostile attitudes of some Colonization Society members, had done much to hinder any possible good that the Society might have accomplished. They were rightly repelled by the obviously vicious motives of some colonizationists, but some immediate abolitionists were also selfishly motivated and hostile to blacks. It was rare, however—observed Washington—to find any association, regardless of how sacred its mission, whose members were uniformly free of profane self-interest.

Washington believed that abolitionists should rigorously pursue their civil rights activities, especially in the realm of educational opportunity. This present experience of the free blacks often consisted of a lifelong education in servility, and some become "so accustomed to this degraded condition that they seem[ed] to love it." If colleges and academies were finally beginning to admit blacks, it seemed almost an empty gesture, since the black graduates were in no position to take advantage of the proffered opportunity. The effects of occupying a low social status were often so demoralizing that all motivation for self-betterment was destroyed. The teachers and ministers with whom the majority had contact educated them "only for the positions to which the American people . . . assigned them." As a result many of them aspired "no higher than the gratification of their passions and appetites." If black Americans were able to anticipate a future of opportunity in all the arts and sciences, they would be inspired to intellectual achievement. But even if the doors of opportunity were to open in America—which seemed unlikely—how could the black people be expected to compete with "the superior energy and cultivated intellect of long civilized and Christian Saxons"? Thus it was likely that liberally educated people might be particularly inclined to migrate.

Perhaps Washington was thinking of John Russwurm's case or Alexander Crummell's, as well as his own, when he challenged the colonizationists to give black people "such education as white men receive" so as to "entirely unfit them for the debased position they must here occupy" and it would be impossible to keep them in America. Washington expressed his thanks to the abolitionists, who had helped him to achieve his education, and insisted that it was their efforts that had made him a colonizationist. He had learned that regardless of natural capacity, as soon as a colored man "leaves the academic halls to mingle in the open society he can find in the United States, unless he be a minister or a lecturer, he must and will retrograde . . . just in proportion as he increases in knowledge, will he become miserable."[13]

Washington sailed as a cabin passenger on the *Isla de Cuba,* along with his wife and two children, and became a farmer and trader after teaching for a while in Monrovia's Alexander High School. His report on conditions in his new home was positive, if not glowing. He was sometimes criticized for the measured quality of his enthusiasm, and the *African Repository* disagreed with his statement that emigrés ought to come provided with their own capital to supplement the maintenance provisions of the Colonization Society. Of the several published reports from the *Isla de Cuba*'s November 1853 mission, Washington's offered the best justification for emigrating, and Williams's the most objective and detailed treatment of the colony and its environs. Nesbit's and Peterson's reports seem to have been purely self-serving.

Sources of insight into the minds of most migrants to Liberia are rare, since colonists were seldom as literate as cabin passengers on the *Isla de Cuba,* but limited observations are possible, based on an examination of letters written to former masters in the United States or to the American Colonization Society.[14] In such writings we should not expect to discover the passionate messianism or racial chauvinism that is present in the writings of nationalistic emigrants and emigrationists. In far too many instances, we observe a lingering dependency and a need to seek the approval of masters who had long ago abandoned any sense of seigneurial bond. Many of the letters are pathetically subservient pleas for provisions or money. Not that the settlers should be blamed for needing help or requesting it. They came down with tropical illnesses as soon as they arrived and often had no resources other than the subsistence funds provided by the Colonization Society. They soon realized, to their dismay, that prices of familiar foodstuffs were much inflated. They fell into violent conflict with the very natives whom they were supposed to convert — which must have troubled the soul of many a sincere Christian. They suffered from a lack of skills necessary to farming in an unfamiliar tropical environment. But most importantly, settlers were held back by lack of education and by habits of subordination and dependency, which left them with a severely damaged self-esteem. The typical former slave who was deposited in Liberia did not possess the robust virtues associated with the North American pioneer myth.

"There are many out here who are getting on poorly because they have no one to act for them, and they are totally unable to act for themselves," opined William C. Burke, a former slave of Robert E. Lee, who, showing unusual literacy and resourcefulness, established himself as a shoemaker and a farmer after migrating to Liberia in the mid-fifties. Even those who came with considerable reserves of determination and ability found the going difficult. James Skipworth was able to purchase ten acres of land but found that farm implements were hard to come by. He advised future emigrants to bring tools with them, "for they are few and very dear in this country." Farmers also discovered that vegetables they were accustomed to growing in the United States — with such important exceptions as sweet potatoes — did not grow well in Africa. Poor health could demoralize the bravest hearts, and if the situation was bad for the strong, it was unendurable for the weak. Mortality was high among small children and the elderly. Mid-nineteenth-century medicine often prescribed cures more injurious than the diseases themselves. One can easily imagine the effects that "bleeding" would have on an eighty-year-old suffering from malaria and homesickness. Adjustments were difficult for persons unaccustomed to independence and lacking enterprising habits. William Burke advised that "everyone that comes to

Africa should be a volunteer, determined to take everything just as they find it, and be satisfied."

Alexander Crummell was not impressed with the quality of the immigrants. He found many of them ignorant, many of them immoral, and many of them too old for the pioneer's life. Although he attributed at least some of the colonists' deficiencies to the crippling effects of slavery, that did not alter his judgement of their fitness for the work to be done. And yet, the settlers represented a wide variety of types and were blessed with varying levels of ability. Many were enterprising, able, and industrious, although they may not have compared with an Augustus Washington in terms of intellectual attainments. Washington McDonough, a former slave and ostensibly prepared for missionary work, was only marginally educated, but he labored to found a mission school for the natives.[15] Grandville B. Woodson, another former slave, was inspired by the rhetoric of African redemption and black nationalism but poorly equipped to carry out the grand design, as the following demonstrates:

> In my estimation, this is a good Country, taking all things in consideration, especially for the colored Man or the Suns of Ham Who have been So Long bound Down beneath the penetration of the Gospel light . . . Liberia is now spreading her rich perfume round and about the big valleys of the World and introducing and calling out her sons and Daughters to rise and come up out of the Valley of ignorance and Hethenism.[16]

Although the author had not attained the literacy of Delany, Washington, or Crummell, it is clear that he had somewhere acquired a feel for the rhetoric of African Redemptionism. The nationalist strain in Afro-American thought seemed to be permeating every level of society and to be having its impact on individuals, both lettered and rude. It would be misleading to force a distinction between nationalist and nonnationalist at this point in Afro-American history. It has been adequately demonstrated by fifteen years of scholarship that just about everyone threw something into the superheated cauldron in which the ideology seethed. The African civilizationists subscribed to a variety of nationalism that was interwoven with religious mysticism. It was elitist voiced territorial aspirations, and strove towards the formation of a nation-state. The civilizationists were, for the most part, better educated than the typical African-American and were committed to a doctrine of uplift. As their constitution demonstrated, they were dedicated to "the civilization and christianization of Africa and of the descendents of African ancestors everywhere." They believed, however, that before the

African-American people could be uplifted, the redemption of Africa must be achieved.

The more common variety of black nationalism was that articulated by Frederick Douglass; it was Whitmanesque in its earthy, democratic rhetoric, pragmatic, and egalitarian. Douglass's brand of black nationalism eventually evolved into mainstream American nationalism, and Douglass soon made clear his belief that the destiny of the black nation was in no way separate or distinct from that of the rest of America. Douglass's flirtation with the racial mysticism and separatism to which Crummell and Delany subscribed was brief and half-hearted and his advocacy of territorial separatism was extremely ephemeral. In his mind, the black nation was not a misty vision to be realized in another land; the historical tragedy of the slave trade had already brought the nation into being. The black nation must now determine its own destiny, here in the country where it had been raped into existence and where the mass of its population still suffered in slavery.[17]

N O T E S

1. Martin R. Delany, *The Condition, Elevation, Emigration and Destiny of the Colored People of the United States* (Philadelphia, 1852), pp. 169–70.

2. William Nesbit, *Four Months in Liberia, or African Colonization Exposed* (Pittsburgh: J. T. Shryock, 1855), p. 59. For descriptions of medical practice, both Western and native, see J. W. Lugenbeel, *Sketches of Liberia: Comprising a Brief Account of the Geography, Climate, Productions, and Diseases, of the Republic of Liberia* (Washington: C. Alexander, 1850). See also Martin R. Delany, *Official Report of the Niger Valley Exploring Party* (New York: Thomas Hamilton, 1861), especially pp. 64–66.

3. Nesbit, *Four Months in Liberia*, pp. 36–37.

4. Nesbit, *Four Months in Liberia*. See p. 13 for places where elephants may hide, pp. 51 and 53 for references to driving colonists into the sea.

5. Samuel Williams, *Four Years in Liberia: A Sketch of the Life of Samuel Williams* (Philadelphia: King & Baird, 1857).

6. Williams, *Four Years in Liberia*, p. 32. The Veys, like the Mandingos, are tall, slender, and very dark. They often possess aquiline features.

7. Williams, *Four Years in Liberia*, p. 65.

8. Daniel H. Peterson, *The Looking Glass: Being a True Report and Narrative of the Life, Travels, and Labors of the Rev. Daniel H. Peterson* (New York, 1854), pp. 61, 55–69.

9. Peterson, *Looking Glass*, p. 60.

10. Peterson, *Looking Glass*, pp. 75, 76, 85, 87.

11. Peterson, *Looking Glass*, pp. 109–11.

12. Letter of Augustus Washington, *African Repository* 27:259-65, reprinted in *The Mind of the Negro as Reflected in Letters Written during the Crisis, 1800–1860*, ed. Carter G. Woodson (Washington, D.C.: Association for the Study of Negro Life and History, 1926), pp. 133–44.

13. Ibid.

14. Bell I. Wiley issues some common sense warnings concerning the use of these documents in Bell I. Wiley, ed., *Slaves No More: Letters From Liberia, 1833–1869* (Lexington: University of Kentucky Press, 1980).

15. Wiley, *Slaves No More,* pp. 116–54.

16. Wiley, *Slaves No More,* p. 162.

17. The linking of black Americans to this Whitmanesque variety of American subnationalisms was first articulated in Leonard I. Sweet, *Black Images of America* (New York: Norton, 1976), p. 170.

"Cambridge Platonism" in the Republic of Liberia

Alexander Crummell's Theory of Development and Culture Transfer 1853–1872

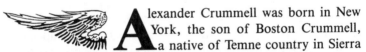lexander Crummell was born in New York, the son of Boston Crummell, a native of Temne country in Sierra Leone. He earned a B.A. degree in the University of Cambridge in England (1853), where he did well in classics and moral philosophy, but poorly in mathematics. Crummell was the author of three books, numerous published articles, a substantial correspondence, and over three hundred unpublished sermons that survive in manuscript. He was a missionary and political philosopher in Liberia (1853–1872), and after his return to the United States he resided in Washington, D.C., where he pastored St. Luke's Episcopal Church and assumed a leading role in black cultural life. In 1897 he founded the American Negro Academy and preached anti-mulatto doctrines to the young J. E. Bruce, later a contributor to Marcus Garvey's *Negro World*. Another of Crummell's protégés, William H. Ferris, became a vice president of Garvey's Universal Negro Improvement Association. The young W. E. B. Du Bois was much impressed by Crummell and devoted a chapter to him in *The Souls of Black Folk*. Students of Edward Wilmot Blyden have, of course, long noted the importance of Crummell, who was Blyden's comrade in the

passionate struggle against mulatto domination in nineteenth century Liberia.

During his years in Africa, Crummell was obsessed with the problem of making Liberia into the sort of economic and political power that would be taken seriously by European nations. Africans were not a highly respected people in 1850. The slave trade was still in existence, and many blacks in the New World were still in bondage. As Martin Delany, another prominent black nationalist, remarked with disgust, "Wherever there is one white person, that one rules and governs two colored persons" (Delany 1852:37). Crummell believed, as did Blyden and all other known black nationalists of that period, that the indigenous cultures were incapable of supporting the technological innovation that it would be necessary for Africa to undergo in order to rise politically, economically, and militarily (Blyden 1887:vi; Moses 1978:15–55).

When reading Crummell, it occasionally becomes necessary to remind oneself that his approach to social change was not a twentieth-century approach. The concept of cultural relativism had not yet come into fashion. Late nineteenth-century thinkers were not at all timid about thinking or speaking in absolutist terms. The metaphysical basis of their social theory was in absolutist conceptions of progress and evolution that ultimately found their most famous expression in the writings of Marx and the social Darwinists. Thus Crummell, Blyden, and other black leaders of the period tended to define civilization in terms of progress, as a process of improvement, but improvement based on certain eternal truths that had served as the basis for all higher human society since the dawn of history. Lacking a relativistic conception of culture, they would have dismissed as sheer nonsense the idea that all cultures are more or less equal. It is difficult to know what they meant when they occasionally maintained that each nation might be destined to realize civilization in its own way. They certainly were not born late enough to rejoice in the questioning of the very concept of civilization, a tendency in the writings of Oswald Spengler and Robert E. Park in the twentieth century. They would never use "civilization" as a term of ironic contempt, as Du Bois occasionally did. As one of my graduate students laconically put it, "Alexander Crummell had not read John Blassingame." Just so, nor had he any other basis for celebrating African and Afro-American culture. Finally, Blyden and Crummell had not read Chancellor Williams, Molefi Kete Asante, or any of the other theorists who have since questioned the relevance of Christianity and Islam as ideologies on which an African identity could be based. As nineteenth-century scholars, they based their theories of social change on the nineteenth century myth of "civilization."

This paper presents new data on Crummell's Cambridge education and its relationship to his theory of African development. He had gone to England in 1848 ostensibly for the purpose of assisting his church in New York with their building fund. Shortly after his arrival, however, he began to write to his American supporters of the encouragement he had received from English friends to remain in England long enough to complete the Cambridge or Oxford course of studies. There is good reason to believe that the idea had occurred to him somewhat earlier. In any case, he soon began preparations while living at Bath in the house of Thomas Fry, a venerable English scholar and cleric. During the months of waiting to commence his studies at Cambridge, he refreshed his knowledge of the classics by reading privately with Fry and delivered numerous antislavery addresses. In the autumn term, joined by his wife and children, and already twenty-nine years old, he moved to Cambridge and began his formal studies in classics, biblical studies, and moral philosophy.

Moral philosophy, as taught in mid-nineteenth century Cambridge, was still undergoing a reaction to the utilitarianism of Hobbes and Locke. The so-called "higher criticism" of the German theologian J. G. Eichhorn had found only one defender in Cambridge, H. Lloyd, regius Professor of Hebrew, who tried in vain to secure university and church patronage for a translation of his *Introduction to the Old Testament* (Cheyne 1893); and the works of David Friedrich Strauss were confuted in a four-year series of lectures by W. H. Mill (Chadwick 1966). In the lectures that Crummell attended, the Cambridge Platonism of the seventeenth century was highly regarded. One of the reasons for the retardation of theological scholarship was, no doubt, the fact that lectures on theology were delivered by mathematicians and natural scientists like William Whewell, who saw himself as maintaining the Cambridge Platonist tradition, or at least its anti-materialistic essentials. Hobbes's doctrines presented to the Cambridge Platonists and their nineteenth-century successors a number of unacceptable ideas: that morality was a matter of convention and practical necessity, that the natural state of man was a state of "Warre," that human instincts were base, and that virtue was an artificial and purely utilitarian mechanism for survival, grudgingly adopted by the species from such ignoble motives as fear and convenience. The Cambridge Platonists rejoined that the natural instincts of man were good, that the laws of nature were universal and absolute, that morality was imprinted in the human bosom, and that intuition as well as reason could provide for moral guidance in human affairs.

This hostility to the utilitarian philosophers persisted into the time of Crummell's sojourn at Cambridge, even though the brutal vision of Hobbes had given way to the more humane utilitarianism of Locke, Bentham, and Mill. It was widely held, rightly or wrongly, that these latter three attempted to base morality solely on reason. The most likely opponent of utilitarianism to have influenced Crummell while he was at Cambridge was William Whewell, Professor of casuistry and, ironically enough, a distinguished empiricist in his own right. Professor Whewell, whose lectures Crummell attended, believed that the Cambridge Platonists had proven "the groundlessness" of Hobbes's moral philosophy. He argued that moral truth was absolute, and that it was made known by means of the moral faculty—that is, by means of the conscience. This was an intellectual position to which Crummell showed an obvious commitment, even at the time of his arrival. He was, after all, an Episcopal priest, with a belief that moral goodness must originate in the supernatural agency of grace. Cambridge reinforced his ideas, however, and provided him with an intellectual framework for what once had been purely a matter of temperament and belief. Crummell followed Whewell's practice when, in drawing up a list of books for youthful Liberian readers in 1861, he included William Paley's *Natural Theology* but juxtaposed it to Joseph Butler's *Analogy of Religion, Natural and Revealed* as a corrective to fashionable moral empiricism.

Another professor who seems to have influenced Crummell during his Cambridge years was John Grote, who like Whewell attacked the utilitarianism of Hobbes, Locke, Bentham, and Mill. Grote also argued for the existence of a moral faculty and, as that suggests, for the importance of innate ideas as guideposts to righteousness. Grote insisted, however, that neither reason nor conscience were capable of functioning accurately without accurate information. Although this might seem to place him in the empiricist camp, it did not, for like Whewell he had great respect for the casuistry of Bishop Butler. A number of ideas that appear in Grote are consistent with themes in Crummell's mature writing: for example, the idea that the best arguments against slavery were founded in direct appeals to the conscience rather than in self-interest or practical considerations.

All this should not be taken to imply that Crummell's approach to religion was other-worldly. As he made clear in his address, "God and the Nation," he had no patience with that "loftiness and elevation that . . . cannot attend to the affairs of the earth." He believed that religion and philosophy must properly have a bearing on the material, legal, and political advancement of Liberia. National greatness could spring only from the grasping of "large, noble, and majestic ideas," which were inextricably bound up with religion (Crummell 1898:5).

During his African years and later, after his return to the United States, Crummell railed against those men who were, as he put it, "constantly dogmatizing theories of sense and matter as the salvable hope of the race" (Crummell 1898:4). Throughout his life, he insisted that the uplift of Africa could not be effected without "the influence and control of broad principles and superior ideas." In twentieth-century terminology, we might say that Crummell believed that cultural ideas were the determinants of socioeconomic realities.

Crummell had been in Liberia for only a year when—on July 30, 1854—he delivered his sermon "God and the Nation" in Trinity Church of Monrovia. He had completed his studies in the University of Cambridge some fifteen months earlier, and he was incurably an Anglophile, impressed with the intrinsic merit of English language, dogmatic on the benefits of tea drinking, persuaded of the British reverence for facts, and swept along by the tide of Victorian taste. But the fact of his infatuation with English culture had not made him blind to the indecency of London street life. It had not led him to forget his general distrust of white folk, nor to forgive the numerous slights and embarrassments that he had suffered at their hands. For this reason he had come to Liberia, a committed African nationalist, rigorous and unbending in the righteousness of his nationalism and yet a perfect example of the type who would one day be described by his as-yet-unborn protégé, W. E. B. Du Bois, as a man of "two souls, two thoughts, two unreconciled strivings, two warring ideals in one dark body."

The address, "God and the Nation," contained many of the themes that would be recurrent in his later writing, not only while he was in Liberia but during his later years in America. For Crummell's African years were instrumental in casting the shape of his later Afro-American program (Meier 1963:43), and his thinking had significance for the development of twentieth-century pan-African ideology, both directly and indirectly, in the United States and in Africa. It reflected tendencies that Karl Popper has identified as characteristic of the Platonist tradition, and that William Montgomerey McGovern has seen as its heritage in a revival of absolutism in the nineteenth century. These consisted of a sense of God-given duty, accompanied by an accusatory rhetoric of treason or betrayal. Those who did not share Crummell's ideas would be frowned on by God for their "base apostasy." It included a sense of historicism, the idea that history was moving towards some providential purpose. In Crummell's system, the ideal Christian state should be more important than the individuals who comprised it, and the individual ought to subordinate his personal desires to the national destiny.

Ideals must be the source of all national greatness; if Liberia could not learn this lesson of history, which was so obvious to Crummell, she would fail as had the great empires of antiquity, "for there is no inherent life in commerce, letters, laws, or luxury." Crummell was consistently impatient with the theory that the African race could be elevated purely by means of economic programs. Such national greatness as the black race was destined to experience would spring from the "ability to grasp the grand conceptions of being." And all such ideas were based in true religion. Africa could not be uplifted except under what he called "intelligence . . . the clear induction of world wide facts, and the perception of their application to new circumstances." He called the Greek idealists the progenitors of civilization, and, as he was aware of the German idealists, his writings make reference to them (Forbes n.d.; Crummell 1862). Plato was, however, his first love, and even as an elderly man he could quote lengthy passages from the Greek classics by heart. George W. Forbes recalled an all-night symposium in which "he actually stumped the house" orating on the "mighty masters of the ancient forum." The same author observed that Crummell still held the ancient writers to be preeminent:

> Not even the German absolutists could take precedence over them with him. To Plato he was so passionately devoted that he jokingly claimed to be a lineal descendant of the bee which tradition asserts lighted on the infant philosopher's lips to taste of that latent sweetness everywhere since so manifest in the writings of that philosopher. He greatly preferred the master idealist to his materialist junior, Aristotle, holding that no amount of the latter's minute observations could compensate one moment with him for the poetic vision and generalizations of Plato (Forbes, n.d.).

But Crummell's admiration of Plato was founded in something deeper than enjoyment of his poetic qualities. He was an admirer of that Plato who had conceived a rigidly ordered utopian society to be governed by reason and administered by an elite corps of the superiorly educated. His Platonism was of that sinister sort identified by philosopher Karl Popper in his treatise on *The Open Society and its Enemies*. Crummell, like Plato, advocated a political philosophy that may be termed "social engineering." People's daily lives and thoughts were to be brought into a prescribed framework before society could be improved. The technological and economic improvement of Africa would be at best incomplete if ideas and values were not first transformed.

Culture transfer was conceived as an indispensable companion to technology transfer. Christianity and civilization would be collateral agents in the uplift of Africa. One was inconceivable without the other. All race-conscious and race-loyal black people must be made to understand that the uplift of Africa would be impossible without the agency of Christianity. For, as Crummell proclaimed, a nation that worships "birds, and beasts, and creeping things" or that venerates "ugly idols" is doomed to grovel in the dust. On the other hand, if they "think that God is a spirit, that idea raises, or will raise them among the first of nations." Crummell believed that he could find evidence for this theory in ancient and modern history. Adopting a classical conception of a Golden Age and a Christian conception of natural religion, he asserted that the ancient civilizations of the Near East had been founded on natural and revealed ideas of true religion, but that idolatry had dragged them down. In like fashion, it was the modern idolatry of Romanism that was dragging the Italians and the Spaniards down. Even Haiti, the black republic, had no hopes for future greatness so long as her destiny was linked with decadent and idolatrous Catholicism.

Crummell's anti-Catholic bias was clearly a result of his Protestant education. He had embraced the prejudices of England and America with respect to Mediterranean Christianity and indigenous African religion and was unable to meet either on its own terms. He had no serious doctrinal quarrels with Catholicism, only a hostility to many of its outward forms, including the use of idols. He was equally impatient with the African's veneration of idols and failed to appreciate the abstract theological and philosophical content of West African religion. Crummell never came up with the idea that Casely Hayford toyed with in *Ethiopia Unbound* (1911), that the customs and beliefs of West African peoples were curiously reminiscent of Homeric Greece. To Hayford, this was proof of the nascent grace and beauty in unspoiled African culture. Crummell, Blyden, and their contemporaries believed that Africa was barbarous and that it must receive an infusion of civilization from without, such as that which northern Europe had once received from the Roman Empire.

Thus, Crummell saw himself not only as an apostle of Christianity but as an evangelist for a supposed world culture. His attitude has been referred to elsewhere as "civilizationist" (Moses 1978:59–82; Moss 1981:299), a term which describes the attempt to effect universal African redemption through the uplifting agency of those black people who had already achieved freedom and enlightenment. Civilizationism implied that the African race was partially responsible for its degradation because Africans had allowed themselves to lag behind the rest of the world on the highway of human progress. This did not absolve the white race of its crimes against the African peoples; on the contrary, it was the very cruelty of the whites that served to remind African civilizationists of the necessity of self-help. The principles of "civilizationism" can be conveniently illustrated by reference to the *Constitution of the African Civilization Society* (New Haven, 1861), published as a pamphlet to represent the opinions of Henry Highland Garnet, Martin Delany, and other black nationalists. The second article of the *Constitution* described the object of the society as "the civilization and Christianization of Africa and of the descendants of African ancestors in any portion of the earth, wherever dispersed. Also the destruction of the slave trade into Africa . . . and generally the elevation of the condition of the colored population of our country, and of other lands." The article implied, as had Crummell's 1851 speech before the Anti-Slavery Society in England, that political agitation was not the only activity in which free Africans should be involved. A rigorous program of self-improvement must be undertaken if the African race was to realize its destiny.

Crummell was perhaps the African civilizationist *par excellence*; he was in any case a central figure, who linked together the generations of David Walker (1785–1830) and Marcus Garvey (1887–1940). Like Walker, he believed that our wretchedness was in consequence of ignorance, and that black people must themselves assume the responsibility for correcting their ignorance. Like Garvey, he saw African uplift as an essential ingredient of any program for black advancement. Free black people throughout the world had a duty to contribute to the fulfillment of Africa's mission. Following in the tradition of Bishop Butler, Crummell argued that states of probation are intended for moral discipline and improvement. Africans, although backward, were still a strong race, as Professor Grote had conceded. Surely, this indicated that the African people could be neither exterminated nor permanently held down. Surely, the chastening that Africa had suffered through the slave trade was really only a providential phase of preparation for some great work. Africa, and especially Liberia, had a message to give to the world's civilization. And more than that, Crummell came to believe that the African race was destined for superiority in God's good time (Crummell 1882:332–52).

Here was the basic paradox in Crummell's position, the contradiction that existed not only in his thinking but in that of nationalists on both sides of the Atlantic. He was committed to the development of an African nationality, but he could conceive of this nationalism only in European terms. Perhaps, in the case of Crummell, it would be better to say that he could conceive of it only in English terms. Consider his arguments in an address delivered in Monrovia in 1861, in which he celebrated the providence that had brought the English language to West Africa:

> This Anglo-Saxon language, which is the only language that ninety-five hundredths of us emigrants have ever known[,] is not the speech of our ancestors. . . . Our very speech is indicative of sorrowful history; the language we use tells of subjugation and of conquest. . . . But this fact of humiliation seems to have been one of those ordinances of Providence, designed as a means for the introduction of new ideas into the language of a people; or to serve as the transitional step from low degradation to a higher and nobler civilization (Crummell 1862:17).

In 1858, Crummell found himself in the settlement of Cape Palmas, where he served as principal of the high school for three years. According to one report, he attempted to create a bit of England in West Africa. A Mrs. M. B. Merriam, who visited his mission, described her meeting with the "eloquent and accomplished scholar," who "spoke of England with affection. . . . On a green knoll stands the little stone church. . . . It is comfortable and homelike, much like a rustic English church. . . . The service was the morning prayer; the responses were made audibly, and the music, chanting included, was very pleasing. . . . I have seldom heard Jackson's *Te Deum* more beautifully rendered than by these African children" (Merriam 1868:111, 113–14).

British culture, of course, amounted to more than the lifting of angelic voices in morning prayer. Crummell was also concerned with some of the sterner aspects of Europeanization. He delighted in describing the activities of a group of recaptives taken from the slave ship *Echo* around 1859, and now under his tutelage in Cape Palmas High School:

> They have now become citizens of the Republic. They have been enrolled among her soldiers, and they can perform their duties with as much precision as the others. There is nothing which does so much for civilizing a man as putting a gun into his hands. It makes a savage into a man directly (Blyden and Crummell 1861).

It was inconceivable to Crummell that the hoped-for African civilization could be built on indigenous West African institutions; he conceived of civilization as a process that must be duplicated in its results by any race or nation on its way to becoming civilized. There was only one road to progress, and that road had been successfully travelled by the English-speaking peoples. They had left behind trail markers, written in English, of course. The tools of Christianity and the English language would be of inestimable usefulness to any group that followed along the road. And what if the Africans should fail to understand the importance of casting off their old cultures in favor of Christianity and the English language? Why then, the settlers must force them to accept the benefits of civilization. Crummell justified his black colonialist position with a rhetoric similar to that of white imperialists. The repatriated citizens must dominate the indigenous peoples for their own good.

> Perhaps it may be said that we have no right to command, or press such regulation upon our native population. To this I reply that both our position and our circumstances make us the guardians, the protectors, and the teachers of our heathen tribes. And hence, it follows that all the legitimate means which may tend to preserve them, which anticipate bloody antagonisms, and which tend to their mental, moral, and social advancement, determine themselves as just and proper (Crummell 1891:184).

While the foregoing is merely patronizing, that which follows is brutal, intolerant, authoritarian, and characterized by an inflexibility of purpose that all too often accompanies nationalistic ideology in Africa and elsewhere.

> All historic fact shows that force, that is authority, must be used in the exercise of guardianship over heathen tribes. Mere theories of democracy are trivial in this case, and can never nullify this necessity. You cannot apply them to rude people, incapable of perceiving their place in the moral scale, nor of understanding the social and political obligations that belong to responsible humanity. "Force and right," says a brilliant writer, "are the governors of this world; force till right is ready.**** And till right is ready, force, the existing order of things, is justified, is the legitimate ruler" (Crummell 1891:184).

The quotation was from Joseph Joubert, cited by Matthew Arnold in his *Essays on Criticism*. The ideas on governing heathen tribes were akin to the well-known opinions of John Stuart Mill. Crummell, of course, believed that Africans were to be speedily brought into full participation in the affairs of citizens. Crummell's cultural elitism was by no means atypical of black nationalist sentiment. Marcus Garvey, writing several decades thereafter, in the April 1934 issue of *The Black Man,* said, "The Negro must learn to colonize, he must learn to settle where he wills and to hold his settlement."

Crummell hoped that the American colonists would eventually blend into the native population and create a new "civilized" race, an idea forwarded by the True Whig Party and its high-handed leader E. J. Roye, who was deposed in 1872 and lynched shortly thereafter. Crummell was convinced that Roye's tragic downfall resulted from his commitment to "native regeneration." "Mr. Roye," he wrote on January 31, 1872, "was just on the eve of undertaking such a work; and had sent for the means to commence it. He is now in jail and may not unlikely end his life on the gallows." Roye had indeed expressed a commitment to the "improvement and incorporation of the native tribes contiguous to us. . . . The Aborigines are our brethren, and should be entwined with our affections, and form as soon as possible an active part of our nationality."

Crummell repeated these ideas in a speech before the Common Council and Citizens of Monrovia on Independence Day, July 26, in the same year. "One great mistake of the people of Liberia," he said, "has been neglect of our native population." This was due to an exaggerated conception on the part of the colonists of their own capabilities and a tendency to forget their own "humbling antecedents." Too many of the colonists were inclined to "look upon the native as an inferior, placed at such a distance" that achieving a community of aims and interests was almost an impossibility.

But while Crummell preached to his fellow Monrovians that they should "have faith in the native," and "trust him as a man fitted to 'Move and act in all the correspondences of nature,'" he insisted on the necessity of force:

> Force is indeed our prerogative and our duty with respect to the native but I maintain that it should be the force which anticipates the insensate ferocity of the pagan by demonstrating the blessedness of permanent habitation and lasting peace; which forestalls a degrading ignorance and superstition, by the enlightenment of schools and training; which neutralizes the barrenness of a native rusticity by the creation of new wants and the stimulation of old ones; which nullifies and uproots a gross heathen domesticity by elevating woman and introducing the idea of family and home (Crummell 1891:186).

With the passage of years, Crummell became increasingly bitter and disgusted with what he called the "ignorant, benighted, and besotted" condition of the colonists and the venality of the ruling mulatto elite. "I have no hope of the vitality of the American emigrants," he wrote on January 31, 1872. "We shall pass away; I see every indication of it." Rather than developing into an enlightened elite, benevolent despots after the manner of Plato's philosopher kings, the colonists were sinking into a decadent barbarism. They were unwilling to undertake "native regeneration," and in any case pathetically unfit for the work. He continued in the same letter:

> They are always ready for war against the tribes, but on the other hand they will do nothing nor suffer anyone to do anything for the heathen. Their

whole policy tends to drive them further and further away into the interior. One of the leaders of this movement got up at a missionary meeting and boldly declared that the heathens could never be converted until we put them to the sword.

While Crummell may have been ethnocentric, he certainly rejected the racialism and genocide that some other Americo-Liberians shared with the European imperialists of the day.

Accepting the failure of enlightened despotism, Crummell returned to the United States in 1873. He never abandoned his commitment to "African Redemption," although he did alter his theory as to how this was to be accomplished. His experience in Liberia convinced him that Africa could be redeemed only through the efforts of an indigenous leadership class. This leadership class must be founded in a commitment to high ideals; in other words, they must be Christianized and committed to the development of "civilization" as defined by the educated elites of Europe. Crummell never abandoned his philosophical idealism. True, during the 1880s he supported the utilitarian movement in education, advocating the founding of trade schools for black American youth. Indeed, he had been praised for his successful heading of a trade school while he was in West Africa. With the rise of Booker T. Washington, however, he found it necessary to state his opposition to what he saw as shortsighted attacks on classical education. It was in the reciprocal hostility between Crummell and Washington that the debates between Niagara and Tuskegee had their origins. Needless to say, there was a spiritual kinship between Crummell and the young Du Bois, who "instinctively . . . bowed before this man" (Du Bois 1903:216). Du Bois, like Crummell, was a representative of the idealistic tradition that thrived during the late nineteenth century in Cambridge and the German universities.

CONCLUSION

It would be easy enough to dismiss the black nationalism of Crummell as idle intellectualism, effete imitation, useless obsession with impractical theory. However, if we can penetrate for a moment below the level of the obvious, we may be willing to ask ourselves if Crummell was not, after all, raising some of the right questions. Granted he seemingly came up with answers that we find unacceptable today. Nonetheless, he was absolutely correct in seeing that there is a relationship between technology transfer and culture transfer. He would never have used those terms, for the same reason that he could not question the validity of the concept of "civilization." But Crummell knew that no nation or people could incorporate the economic structures of another without incorporating some of its alien customs, ethics, and values. This point is just now being grasped by those contemporary economists who recommend that American industry adopt Japanese management and production techniques.

Crummell's theory was obviously flawed in some respects, but sound in others. He was certainly not an idealist in the sense that implies impracticality or dreaminess. He understood, for example, that there is an organic relationship between culture and economics and that the belief systems of a culture are both a cause and an effect of what that culture accomplishes in material terms. Therefore, he saw nothing shameful in borrowing from British culture, just as the British had borrowed from the ancient Mediterranean civilizations. And since the British were the dominant political, economic, and military power of the nineteenth century, he considered them the ideal model for a nation aspiring to the ideal of world power, and this was just as true for Africans as for anyone else.

SOURCES CONSULTED

See Wilson J. Moses, *Alexander Crummell: A Study of Civilization and Discontent* (New York: Oxford, 1989). Luckson Ejofodomi has completed a dissertation at Boston University on Crummell's African years, and John Oldfield's dissertation is nearing completion at the University of Cambridge. Also nearing completion is a book-length study by C. R. Stockton, D. Phil., Oxon. Crummell's brief autobiography is *The Shades and the Lights of a Fifty Years' Ministry* (Washington, D.C., 1894). There are several early short accounts of Crummell's life, of which the most significant are George W. Forbes's unpublished typescript, "Alexander Crummell," Rare Books Room, Boston Public Library; William H. Ferris, *Alexander Crummell, An Apostle of Negro Culture,* published as American Negro Academy Occasional Papers, no. 20 (Washington, D.C., 1898); W. E. B. Du Bois, "Of Alexander Crummell," in Du Bois, *The Souls of Black Folk* (Chicago: McClurg, 1903). The following articles are generally considered the most important: Kathleen O'Mara Wahle, "Alexander Crummell: Black Evangelist and Pan Negro Patriot," in *Phylon* (Winter 1968); Otey M. Scruggs, "We the Children of Africa in this Land," in Lorraine A. Williams, ed., *Africa and the Afro-American Experience* (Washington, D.C.: Howard University Press, 1977); Wilson J. Moses, *The Golden Age of Black Nationalism, 1850–1925* (Hamden, Conn.: Archon, 1978) contains a chapter on Crummell, an earlier version of which appeared in *The Journal of Negro History* (April 1975); and M. B. Akpan, "Alexander Crummell and His African Race Work," *Historical Magazine of the Protestant Episcopal Church* (June 1976). Also see August Meier, *Negro Thought in America, 1880–1915* (Ann Arbor: University of Michigan Press, 1963), pp. 42–43; C. R. Stockton, "The Integration of Cambridge: Alexander Crummell as Undergraduate, 1849–

1853," in *Integrated Education* (Winter 1979); and Alfred A. Moss, Jr., *The American Negro Academy* (Baton Rouge: Louisiana State University Press, 1981).

Crummell manuscripts are widely scattered and we may be certain that a significant number remain to be discovered. The most important repository is the Schomburg Collection of the New York Public Library, which contains letters, pamphlets, and other materials published and unpublished. Three volumes of sermons and addresses were collected and published during his lifetime: *The Future of Africa* (New York: Scribner's, 1862); *The Greatness of Christ and other Sermons* (New York: T. Whittaker, 1882); *Africa and America* (Springfield, Mass.: Wiley and Company, 1891). Crummell published one volume jointly with Edward Wilmot Blyden, *Liberia: The Land of Promise to Free Colored Men* (Washington: American Colonization Society, 1861). The Schomburg materials, including some three hundred unpublished sermons and addresses, are readily available on microfilm. One should also be familiar with "Civilization, the Primal Need of the Race" in American Negro Academy Occasional Papers, no. 3 (Washington, D.C., 1898). Professor Richard Blackett graciously brought to my attention the fact that the Columbia University Library has a substantial collection of Crummell materials in the Jay Family Papers. Some of these have been microfilmed in *The Black Abolitionist Papers, 1830–1865,* edited by George E. Carter and Peter Ripley for the Microfilming Corporation of America. The Episcopal Seminary of the Southwest in Austin, Texas, has an essential collection of Crummell correspondence covering the African years. There is a good collection of Crummell letters in the American Colonization Society Papers at the Library of Congress.

Martin Delany's statement of disgust is in *The Condition of the Colored People* (1852; Arno reprint, 1969). Mary Bates Merriam's observations are in *Home Life in Africa: A New Glimpse into an Old Corner of the World, Written for the Young People, By One of Their Friends Who Went There* (Boston: A. Williams, 1868). Blyden's horror of "paganism" is explicitly stated in *Christianity, Islam, and the Negro Race* (1887; reprint Edinburgh: Edinburgh University Press, 1967), p. vi; Blyden elaborates on the idea that Islam "civilizes" Africa on pages 186–87. The idea that every culture must be evaluated on its own terms is one of the apparent assumptions of modern anthropology. See, for example, Franz Boas, *The Mind of Primitive Man* (1911) and *Race, Language, and Culture* (1940), or Melville Herskovits, *The New World Negro* (1966). See also Russell J. Linneman, ed., *Alain Locke* (Baton Rouge: Louisiana State University Press, 1982). The definitions of civilization by Spengler and Park occur in Oswald Spengler, *The Decline of the West* (1918), and Robert E. Park, *Race and Culture* (1950). Blassingame's *The Slave Community* (1972) — as well as George Rawick's *From Sundown to Sunup* (1972) and the restatement of their theories by Gutman, Levine, and Genovese — did much to create a respect for slave culture that would have been incomprehensible to Crummell during his African years. Current black-nationalist critiques of Islam are in Chancellor Williams, *The Destruction of Black Civilization* (Chicago: Third World Press, 1974), and Molefi Kete Asante, *Afrocentricity: The Theory of Social Change* (Washington, D.C.: Amulefi Publishing Co., 1980).

Professor John Oldfield kindly brought to my attention the material in the Cambridge University Archives and in the Caius College Archives, Cambridge. The Cambridge Platonists are treated in C. A. Patrides, ed., *The Cambridge Platonists* (1969). The development of British theology in the nineteenth century is discussed in T. K. Cheyne, *Founders of Old Testament Criticism* (New York: Charles Scribner's Sons, 1893). Also see Owen Chadwick, *The Victorian Church* (London: Adam and Charles Black, 1966). William Whewell's indebtedness to the Cambridge Platonists is acknowledged in his *Lectures on the History of Moral Philosophy* (London: Bell and Daldy, 1862). Paley's *Evidences* and Butler's *Analogy* are available in major university libraries. Matthew Arnold's *Essays in Criticism* and John Stuart Mill's *On Liberty* are the sources of the opinions on the governance of the unenlightened. John Grote's critique of utilitarianism is in his *An Examination of the Utilitarian Philosophy* (London: Bell and Daldy, 1870).

The relationship between idealism and absolutism is discussed in K. R. Popper, *The Open Society and its Enemies* (London, 1945), and in William M. McGovern, *From Luther to Hitler* (1941). The bibliography on the idea of Progress is immense. The four volumes that I have found most useful are: J. B. Bury, *The Idea of Progress* (1920); Georges Sorel, *The Illusion of Progress* (1908; reprint, 1969); Sidney Pollard, *The Idea of Progress: History and Society* (1968); and Robert Nisbet, *History of the Idea of Progress* (New York: Basic Books, 1980). For the relationship between culture and technology transfer as it applies to American industry, see William Ouchi, *Theory Z: How American Business Can Meet the Japanese Challenge* (Reading, Mass.: Addison Wesley, 1981).

Assimilationist
Black Nationalism, 1890–1925

It mattered little whether black leaders thought of themselves as integrationists or separatists during the early years of this century, since the extremists in neither camp were to see their visions materialize, and the moderates, being moderates, were influenced more by practical considerations than by ideological values. Both the integrationists and the separatists often accepted without question many of the Protestant, middle-class prejudices of the Anglo-American bourgeoisie. Afro-American leaders as different as Booker T. Washington, Marcus Garvey, and Mary Church Terrell agreed upon one point—the need for "Negro Improvement." Not only should the conditions under which the masses lived be improved, the people themselves should be improved. Both radical integrationism and black nationalism pursued their dissimilar goals by means of the rhetoric of uplift and "Negro Improvement" and through the formation of institutions to effect the "civilization" of all the sons and daughters of Africa. The idea was common to separatists and integrationists that the prime responsibility for the improvement of the status of black people rested with black people themselves; that if they intended to survive in the modern world and to command the respect of other peoples, they would have to dedicate themselves to self-improvement.

The black bourgeoisie usually were committed to this doctrine of uplift for at least the following reasons:

1. The petite bourgeoisie were embarrassed by the masses' lack of "civilization." In one of his perceptive sociological novels, Sutton Griggs describes a scene in which an educated black man stands at his front gate and observes an unkempt group of Negroes following a street parade, "walking along in boldness and with good cheer." As his eye scans "the unsightly mass," Griggs's protagonist muses, "Now those Negroes are moulding sentiment against the entire race." But both Griggs and his hero are committed to the idea that "the classes must love the masses." The race must encourage a spirit of unity and altruism, for justly or unjustly, "the polished Negro is told to return and bring his people with him, before coming into possession of that to which his attainments would seem to entitle him."[1]

2. The petite bourgeoisie believed that their own position would become more secure only as their race as a whole became more powerful, sophisticated and secure. Thinking along this line led to the philosophy of the National Association of Colored Women, "lifting as we climb." Alexander Crummell, founder of the American Negro Academy, opposed the idea that progressive individuals should be concerned only with their own attainments. He felt that progress was made by groups and asserted that he felt "urged by the feeling of kinship, to bind myself as "with hooks of steel" to the most degraded class in the land . . . ," and to take up the burden of "the regeneration and enlightenment of the colored race in these United States."[2]

3. Finally, there was a genuine feeling of sympathy on the part of the petite bourgeoisie for the struggling masses of black people. This was clearly conveyed in the writings of Paul Laurence Dunbar, which celebrated the homely joys of courtship, family life, honest labor, and simple faith. In *The Souls of Black Folk,* W. E. B. Du Bois wrote of the struggles of the common people with a love and sympathy that went beyond mere sociological description. Like Booker T. Washington, he spoke of the obligation of the educated black people to aid in the uplifting of the masses.[3]

The impulse toward the uplifting of the black American masses was never too far removed from the vision of African regeneration. During the decade before the Civil War, numerous black leaders had subscribed to the idea that no one part of the black race could be elevated without the rest. The "barbarism" of Africa was a principal argument used to justify the enslavement of black Americans. The universal debasement of the Negro race — whether in slavery or in savagery — was seen as proof of black inferiority. Only through a universal program of uplift, such as that proposed by the African Civilization Society, could the claims of the free blacks to full membership in the human family be vindicated. Marcus Garvey's revitalization of the African Civilization movement with his Universal Negro Improvement Association represented the twentieth-century expression of an old idea. His goal was "the general uplift of the Negro peoples of the world." This was to include "civilizing the backward tribes of Africa" and assisting in the industrial and economic development of Negroes of the diaspora.[4]

This commitment to uplift was noble, but the "Negro Improvement" and "African Civilization" rhetoric tended towards elitism. Black leaders of the period from the 1850s to the Harlem Renaissance were rarely concerned with the celebration of black culture. They were concerned with "civilizing" the masses, and since by "civilization" what most of them meant was Western European bourgeois culture, I must call them cultural assimilationists, regardless of their views on emigration or black nationalism. Ironic though it may seem, some of the foremost geographical separatists and political nationalists were cultural assimilationists. Several writers on the subject have had difficulty seeing this point. Howard Brotz divided black American social and political thought into categories that seemed too neatly discrete, and sometimes downright false. Was Henry Highland Garnet an assimilationist as Brotz implied, or did he simply express assimilationist views on some occasions? Could Booker T. Washington be more accurately described as a separatist or as an integrationist?[5]

Harold Cruse and Theodore Draper dichotomized black thinking even more rigidly. They recognized correctly that not all black people have agreed on the goals towards which their people ought to be striving; they did not recognize the patterns of cultural assimilationism in the pronouncements of major nineteenth-century spokespersons that transcended the integration controversy. The excessively rigid definitions of Brotz, Cruse, and Draper ignored such documents as *David Walker's Appeal,* which had employed in 1829 the rhetoric of black messianic nationalism in a diatribe against African repatriation. These early treatments of black nationalism tended to oversimplify the complexities of the doctrine and the personalities that created it. Cruse and Draper failed to see that attitudes on black nationalism were often reflections of how the various spokespersons felt on larger philosophical questions. Brotz was more sophisticated on this score and was able to see that black social and political thought was influenced by the personalities, temperaments, and experiences of the various spokespersons, and by the intellectual environments in which it was produced.[6]

John H. Bracey, Jr., August Meier, and Elliott Rudwick—in the introduction to their anthology of black nationalist documents, *Black*

Nationalism in America (Indianapolis: Bobbs-Merrill, 1969) — have presented eight categories of black nationalism, including: racial solidarity, cultural nationalism, religious nationalism, economic nationalism, black ethnic politics, revolutionary nationalism, territorial separatism, and pan-Africanism. The authors recognize that the categories are not in reality "as sharply delineated as they are presented here, nor are they mutually exclusive." They have openly acknowledged "that the definitions offered here are tentative." In addition to this disclaimer, they might have added that the categories are not exhaustive. For indeed the authors have simply listed an arbitrary selection of categories, although defined well and in some detail. This listing of categories gives the impression of a more systematic approach than actually does exist.[7] Bracey, Meier, and Rudwick might have included in their listing *conservative black nationalism,* which is, to be sure, represented in their anthology by one of William Hooper Councill's essays. Although characterized by a rhetoric of racial responsibility and uplift, this is, in reality, only an accommodation to racism. It is a ludicrous mask that fools no one, an attempt to keep up a brave front in the face of forced exclusion from many important areas of American life. It is rooted in a fear of confrontation.[8]

Certainly they might have responded to Kenneth Clark's provocative assertion that some black nationalism is no more than a "sour grapes philosophy."[9] This approach assumes that the militant rhetoric of black power advocates is only a cry of pain at their exclusion from white America, for they semiconsciously desire acceptance but would never admit it, even in their most private thoughts. Or they might have mentioned the *pragmatic institutional separatism* grudgingly accepted by Frederick Douglass, who appears at one point in their anthology. Douglass admitted the temporary need for segregated schools, so long as the alternative was no schools at all.[10] A final suggestion is the *Negro improvement philosophy,* which strives to create a civilization parallel to that of Western European civilization. It is useful to recognize the existence of this ideology as opposed to cultural nationalism, which advocates radical counterculturalism rather than a parallel civilization.

The great achievement of Bracey, Meier, and Rudwick — in addition to having provided an excellent collection of documents — is that they greatly broadened the definition of black nationalism by including among the nationalists some names that Brotz would have excluded, such as Frederick Douglass and Booker T. Washington. They were more concerned with identifying any elements of black nationalist philosophy, wherever they found them, than with pigeonholing the various thinkers into the categories they proposed. There was a small problem with the writings of W. E. B. Du Bois, whom they characterized as ambivalent, which seemed to imply that Du Bois was atypical of black nationalists or that ambivalence could not be found in the writings of other black nationalists as well.[11]

Ambivalence seems to have been present in most black nationalist thought, but especially during the years 1895–1925, for black nationalism during those years was undergoing a great change from its older nineteenth-century, Christian-civilizationist pattern to its present-day twentieth-century, secular-culturalist pattern. Christian-civilizationist black nationalism, before World War I, glorified efficiency, uplift, industrial management, sexual restraint, temperance, and military efficiency. Secular-cultural black nationalism, during and after the twenties, would glorify ghetto life, hard drinking, fast dancing, primitivism, exotic fantasy, and erotic escapism. The inability of old-school African civilizationists, like Du Bois and Garvey, to understand new-school cultural nationalists like Claude McKay and Rudolph Fisher, resulted from the secularization and urbanization of Afro-American life as black people streamed into the cities in what has been called the great migration.[12]

But ambivalence characterized the pronouncements of black nationalists long before the generational conflict of the twenties. We observe a persistent uneasiness cropping up in black nationalistic pronouncements during the Progressive Era. It is present in the utterances of Booker T. Washington, who publicly said that the races should continue to exist as separate as the fingers of the hand in all things purely social, and privately wrote letters to radical Boston white women saying: "If anybody understood me as meaning that riding in the same railroad car or sitting in the same room at a railroad station is social intercourse, they certainly got a wrong idea of my position." This ambivalence had already appeared in the thought of Alexander Crummell, who claimed a great respect for the indigenous manners and morals of the native West Africans but never gave up his idea of endowing them with Christian religion, English language, and American constitutionalism. We recognize this ambivalence in the thought of Marcus Garvey, who spoke of civilizing Africa and, as he described them, "the backward tribes." And, of course, W. E. B. Du Bois displayed such ambivalence when he spoke of his "two souls, two thoughts, two unreconciled strivings; two warring ideals in one dark body."[13]

The black nationalist has always been pulled in two directions at once; wishing, on the one hand, to exalt everything that is black or African, but recognizing, on the other hand, the need for black people to acquire some of the values and skills of the white world. The pattern of ambivalence did not prevail in all areas of black bourgeois life, however.

It was not particularly evident in the pronouncements of organized women's groups, especially in the area of sexual morality, where attitudes were unequivocally conservative. The black community was extremely sensitive with respect to this issue, and with good reason. Black women were victims of Victorian civilization. In an age that demanded beauty and chastity of women — seeing these as the highest, indeed the only, virtues to which women might aspire — popular attitudes acknowledged neither the beauty nor the chastity of black women.

During the Progressive Era, Afro-American women's organizations tended to encourage acceptance of the values of American civilization wherever there seemed to be any conflict between those values and the values of the southern black culture. The concern of the National Association of Colored Women (NACW), during the 1890s, with the issue of social purity provides an illustration of this. The NACW was founded in 1895 in response to an attack by one Jonathan W. Jacks of Montgomery City, Missouri, who wrote a vicious diatribe attacking the sexual morality of black people. The NACW was formed as a result of this incident, ostensibly to defend black men and women from the kind of slander being circulated by Jacks. As one might expect, the NACW affiliates devoted a large part of their energies to temperance and social-purity activities in addition to attacking the racism, both institutional and petty, that lowered the quality of Afro-American life. Their obsession with social purity would seem to have been an informal acknowledgment of the possibility that the infamous Mr. Jacks was right and that the morality of the black population — of the black sharecropper women, in particular — was something less than it should have been. This suggests the extent to which black leaders internalized Euro-American racist and sexist values.[14]

The circumstances under which black people lived in America could hardly have produced lives characterized by Victorian ideals of genteel courtship and sexual morality. And yet, black peasant life was not totally devoid of gentility. The works of Charles W. Chesnutt, W. E. B. Du Bois, and Sutton Griggs treat sensitively social life among the black masses, who are often portrayed as possessing an unpretentious natural nobility. Generally speaking, however, there was little appreciation among turn-of-the-century bourgeois blacks of the idea that the sexual morality of a black sharecropper might be healthier and more natural than that of a middle-class Negro. The Reverend William H. Ferris, a Yale M.A. and a high-ranking officer in the Garvey movement during the twenties, was typical of black intellectuals when he wrote in his sprawling masterpiece, *The African Abroad:*

"I have come to the conclusion that the Anglo-Saxon ideal of manhood and womanhood is the highest the world has yet seen, the highest that will ever be evolved in the history of the world. . . . God has given the Anglo-Saxon the dominion of the earth, only because he has obeyed His moral laws, only because he has reverenced and held sacred the purity and virtue of woman, and has respected the sanctity of the marriage tie."[15]

A statement such as this reveals the essentially conservative character of traditional black nationalism in America, which lags behind liberal movements in the endorsement of truly revolutionary and reform-minded activism, especially in the area of women's rights. Conservatism in the areas of sexual liberation and women's rights has been characteristic of American black nationalism, especially among such extremely orthodox factions as the Black Muslims and the Black Jews. Only with the emergence of militant feminism in the 1960s, which occurred simultaneously with a widespread questioning of American values throughout society, did articulate black women begin to challenge the traditional puritanism of classical black nationalism. By that time, black social scientists and men and women of letters had begun to indulge in an orgy of glorification of the values of the urban ghetto masses, including their supposed sexual freedom.

The Afro-American clergy had always been a little closer to the grass roots, since they depended upon them for their livelihood. True, many of them—like Bishop Payne, Alexander Crummell, and Frank Grimke—had combined an ideological pan-Africanism with an undisguised contempt for "Africanisms" in the religious expression of the folk. But there were always a few preachers who could relate to the "down home" style of preaching and ritual and at the same time maintain credibility with the petit bourgeois leadership. With the migration of southern Negroes to the cities during the period of the world wars, a new style of black religious leadership represented by the senior Adam Clayton Powell began to preach a social gospel in a gutsy, earthy style reminiscent of the "old time religion," except that it rejected its otherworldliness.

The Afro-American church in the Progressive Era clearly saw its work as encompassing more than the saving of souls. A significant number of black clergymen demonstrated interest in applying religion to the here and now. It was, during the Progressive Era, and still is today, common for black clergymen to publicize biblical interpretations well suited to the problems of Afro-Americans. *The Kingdom Builder's Manual,* published by Sutton Griggs in the early twenties, had such a concern and was intended as a companion piece to his *Guide to Racial Greatness*

and Science of Collective Efficiency. Griggs's scientific Christianity was
a typically "progressive," if somewhat folksy, approach to social engineering.[16]

Scientific Christianity is paralleled by the development of Moorish
Science under the leadership of Noble Drew Ali, one of many mystic
holy men to appear during the years of the great migration. Why is it
that these holy men were able to compete so successfully with the Christian churches in attracting converts? Did they bring followers with them
from the South, or people predisposed to accept Islam? Is it possible that
some forms of Islam had survived in the South, along with obeah and
voodoo ritual? What conceptions of civilization must have existed in the
minds of the poor black migrants, who, coming north in 1915, were
appealed to by the words "Asiatic," "Science," and "Moorish"? Since
becoming a member of the Moorish Temple meant undergoing a change
in status from Negro to Asiatic, can we conjecture anything about the
attitudes of the masses and their leaders to Africa and blackness? Black
religion — whether of the Muslim, Hebrew, or Christian variety — tended
to assume that there was something wrong with being a black African.
The program for uplift even among these sects, however, usually involved a renunciation of certain values, historically associated with the
life-styles of the Afro-American masses. The cult leaders often attempted to stamp out those aspects of black mass culture that did not
conform to mainstream culture, justifying their position by incorrectly
attributing all Africanistic behaviors, of which traits they disapproved,
to the heritage of slavery.[17]

The transition from classical black nationalism of the nineteenth
century, with its emphasis on "civilization" and uplift, to the black counterculturalism of recent years was nowhere more apparent than in the
area of literature.[18] The basic modes of black literature before the Civil
War were the slave autobiography, the sermon, and the political tract.
This literature was "civilizationistic," concerned either with describing
the efforts of individuals to uplift themselves from the debasement of
slavery to the dignity and independence of freedom, or with proposals
for the elevation of the race to the high standards of Western civilization.
Poetry and fiction were "heroic" and tended to be declamatory in style.

Much of the writing was in the tradition that we have come to speak
of as "Ethiopianism." This tradition was as much political and religious
as literary. It arose contemporaneously with the American doctrine of
Manifest Destiny, which was an important influence upon it but not its
only source. Ethiopianism was concerned with the destiny of black people to create an exemplary civilization, usually in Africa, but not only
there. "It is evident," agreed many of the movement's proponents, "that

Ethiopia shall soon stretch out her hands unto God!" [Ps. lxviii:31] This prophecy was soon to be fulfilled in terms of "the civilization and Christianization of Africa," and the improvement of "the welfare of her children in all lands." Writers in the Ethiopian tradition included Martin Delany, author of political tracts and a novel; Alexander Crummell, who penned over four hundred sermons of strong literary merit; and Marcus Garvey, many of whose essays were in this classical nineteenth-century mode. A good deal of the writing was heroic, as for example were Phillis Wheatley's "heroic couplets" and Frederick Douglass's short story, "The Heroic Slave." Booker T. Washington's *Up From Slavery,* published in 1901, was in the heroic tradition of the antebellum slave narratives and certainly in the Negro Improvement tradition.

While protest has certainly been an important element of black writing, some of the best works of black literature have been outside the protest tradition. Most black literature before the Civil War was concerned primarily with protest and agitation, since it was directed mainly at an audience of sympathetic whites. During the Progressive Era, the best literature was directed at a racially mixed audience. In the novels of Sutton Griggs, for example, there are messages of protest directed to the white reader and messages of uplift directed to the black reader. As our knowledge and understanding of black intellectual and literary history increase, we are discovering that literary traditionalism is far more pronounced than some scholars have assumed. The theme of "Negro Improvement," whether moral or material, mystical or temporal, dominates early black writing.

Changes occurred during the "Harlem Renaissance," although the old traditions by no means died out. With the exception of W. E. B. Du Bois, Marcus Garvey, and J. A. Rogers, few black authors concentrated on the forging of a heroic tradition. Antiheroic tendencies began to predominate, especially in black novels, where the central figures were usually the sorts of characters who opposed the traditional values of Euro-American society. Black authors, like their white counterparts, had come to question the values of Christian civilization. This tendency continued as the century progressed, reaching its climax in the novels of Richard Wright and Ralph Ellison and the plays of LeRoi Jones. But the old pan-African and Negro Improvement message still played an important part in black writing, and even though Ralph Ellison denied any ties to a black literary tradition, he owed a debt to Marcus Garvey and a greater one to Booker T. Washington.

The following chapters will describe some of the debts of the recent Black Power movement to nineteenth-century traditions. The traditionalism of Afro-American behavior in recent years has not always been recognized because so much of it has been directed towards social change and identified with countercultural movements outside the black community. Thus, the assimilationist tradition takes new forms; it has been modified in accordance with changing values in American society at large. The message that black America delivered during the 1960s was a blending of the old and the new. Even the most radical of the youthful voices of the sixties owed much of their rhetoric and public style to traditional forms of leadership. And many of their values were less radical than they appear at first glance.

N O T E S

1. Sutton E. Griggs, *Unfettered* (Nashville: Orion, 1902), p. 160.

2. Alexander Crummell, "The Social Principle Among a People; and Its Bearing on Their Progress and Development." The essay written in 1875 was collected in Crummell, *The Greatness of Christ and Other Sermons* (New York: T. Whittaker, 1882), p. 310.

3. The theme is self-evident in the dialect poetry of Dunbar. It is most prominent in Chapter 4 of *The Souls of Black Folk* (Chicago: McClurg, 1903). For Booker T. Washington, see *My Larger Education: Being Chapters from My Experience* (Garden City, N.Y.: Doubleday, Page & Co., 1911).

4. For African Civilization Society, see Howard Brotz, *Negro Social and Political Thought, 1850–1920* (New York: Basic Books, 1966), pp. 191–96. Marcus Garvey, "Aims and Objects of Movement for Solution of Negro Problem," in *Philosophy and Opinions of Marcus Garvey*, ed. Amy Jacques Garvey (1925; reprint, New York: Atheneum, 1968), 2:37–43.

5. Brotz, *Negro Social and Political Thought*, pp. 1–32.

6. Harold Cruse, *The Crisis of the Negro Intellectual* (New York: William Morrow, 1967), pp. 4–5. Theodore Draper, *The Rediscovery of Black Nationalism* (New York: Viking Press, 1970).

7. In addition to the introduction to *Black Nationalism in America*, ed. John H. Bracey (Indianapolis: Bobbs-Merrill, 1970), one should consult John H. Bracey, "Black Nationalism since Garvey," in *Key Issues in the Afro-American Experience,* ed. Nathan Huggins et al. (New York: Harcourt Brace Jovanovich, 1971), pp. 259–79.

8. William Hooper Councill, "The Negro Can Grow Only . . . In His Own Sphere, as God Intended," *Voice of Missions,* 1 December 1900; reprinted in Bracey et al., *Black Nationalism in America,* pp. 224–32. Councill writes, "Every hotel which refuses the Negro a meal, every soda fountain which declines him are voices telling him to go and open these places and make himself rich."

9. Kenneth Clark, "Black Power is a Sour Grapes Phenomenon," *Journal of Negro History* 53 (January 1968): 1–11.

10. Frederick Douglass, "Lecture at Inauguration of Douglass Institute, Baltimore, October, 1865," reprinted in *The Life and Writings of Frederick Douglass,* ed. Philip S. Foner (New York: International Publishers, 1955), 4: 178. See also Douglass's letter to W. J. Wilson in the same volume pp. 171–74: "I am heartily in favor of all needful educational institutions for the present education of colored people, even though they be separated institutions. Present circumstances are the only apology for such institutions."

11. Bracey et al., *Black Nationalism in America,* singles out Du Bois as particularly

ambivalent on p. xlv, although he is seen as representing a more widespread ambivalence later in the book (p. xlii).

12. Du Bois accused Claude McKay of licentiousness in *Crisis* (June 1928): 367. Negative appraisal of the "Harlem Renaissance" can be found in Du Bois, "The Negro College," *Crisis* (August 1933): 175–77. Garvey's hostilities to the spirit of the Harlem Renaissance must be deduced indirectly from his religious conservatism; his hostility to Paul Robeson in *The Black Man* (Sept.–Oct. 1936): 12; and his poetic praxis. For "Great Migration" see Emmett J. Scott, *Negro Migration during the War* (New York: Oxford University Press, 1920); Arna Bontemps and Jack Conroy, *Anyplace But Here* (New York: Ill and Wang, 1966). For the "Harlem Renaissance," see Nathan Huggins, *Harlem Renaissance* (New York: Oxford University Press, 1971); Alain Locke, *The New Negro* (New York: Albert and Charles Boni, 1925). *Shuffle Along,* the black musical produced in 1920, is seen as the start of the Renaissance. Garvey reviewed it with hostility in *The Black Man* (Sept.–Oct. 1936): 7.

13. Du Bois, *Souls of Black Folk,* p. 3.

14. A discussion of the origins of the NACW appears elsewhere in this volume and in Wilson J. Moses, *The Golden Age of Black Nationalism, 1850–1925* (Hamden, Conn.: Archon Books, 1978), pp. 103–31.

15. William H. Ferris, *The African Abroad or His Evolution in Western Civilization: Tracing His Development under Caucasian Milieu* (New Haven, Conn.: Tuttle, Morehouse & Taylor Press, 1913), pp. 405, 416.

16. Sutton E. Griggs, *Guide to Racial Greatness, or The Science of Collective Efficiency* (Memphis: National Public Welfare League, 1924).

17. For urban cults, see Arthur Huff Fauset, *Black Gods of the Metropolis: Negro Religious Cults in the Urban North* (Philadelphia: University of Pennsylvania Press, 1944); Howard Brotz, *The Black Jews of Harlem: Negro Nationalism and the Dilemmas of Negro Leadership* (New York: Schocken Books, 1970); Joseph R. Washington, *Black Sects and Cults* (Garden City, N.Y.: Doubleday, 1973); and Leonard Barrett, *Soul Force: African Heritage in Afro-American Religion* (Garden City, N.Y.: Anchor Press, 1974).

18. The first attempts by specialists in Black Studies to define the elements of a distinct literary tradition in Afro-American writing are detectable in Benjamin Brawley, *The Negro Genius* (New York: Dodd, Mead, 1937), and Benjamin Mays, *The Negro's God, as Reflected in His Literature* (New York: Chapman & Grimes, 1938). An excellent recent treatment is Darwin Turner, "A Black American Literary Tradition," in *Selected Proceedings of the Third Annual Conference on Minority Studies,* ed. George E. Carter and James R. Parker (La Crosse, Wis.: Institute for Minority Studies, 1976), 2: 11–20. Ethiopianism began as a religious movement in South Africa around 1900, spreading rapidly over the continent and reaching the Americas in due course. Allusions to the Ethiopian prophecy had appeared in black writing since the eighteenth century, but these are not related to the millenial movement in Africa described by George Shepperson in "Ethiopianism and African Nationalism," *Phylon* 14 (1953): 9–18. Other discussions include Jomo Kenyatta, "The New Religion in East Africa," in his *Facing Mt. Kenya: The Tribal Life of the Kikuyu* (London: Secker and Warburg, 1938); St. Clair Drake, *The Redemption of Africa and Black Religion* (Chicago: Third World Press, 1970); Daniel Thwaite, *The Seething African Pot* (London: Constable, 1936). An early example is J. E. Casely Hayford, *Ethiopia Unbound: Studies in Race Emancipation* (London, 1911). The introduction to the second edition (London: Frank Cass, 1969) by F. Nnabuenyi Ugonna is useful. Finally, see Wilson J. Moses, "The Poetics of Ethiopianism: W. E. B. Du Bois and Literary Black Nationalism," *American Literature* 47 (November 1975): 411–25.

E. Franklin Frazier and Others

Religion, Assimilation, and Black Separatism

Frazier should be re-evaluated," wrote Raymond A. Hall, a black sociologist at Dartmouth College, in his *Black Separatism in the United States.*[1] Hall, whose views were obviously influenced by the black separatism and nationalism that flourished among the black middle class in the early 1970s, apparently rejected Frazier's thesis in *Black Bourgeoisie* that the black middle class lacked racial consciousness. I reviewed Hall's book in 1978, when it first appeared, for *The American Historical Review,* and therefore my evaluation centered on the historical, rather than the sociological, aspects of Hall's treatment of black separatist movements. For some time I have thus been nagged by the feeling that I may not have done justice to Professor Hall's work. The introduction to the volume and its analysis of recent movements were unusually perceptive, and its final pages offered a number of thoughtful reflections on black nationalism, pan-Africanism, black Zionism, and other forms of separatism. I did, however, object to Hall's excessively optimistic view of black middle-class ethnic consciousness. Hall felt that Frazier had failed to take note of what he considered healthily separatist and nationalist tendencies within the black bourgeoisie.

While the present essay responds to Professor Hall's demand for further reflection on Frazier's observations on bourgeois separatism, it

moves in quite a different ideological direction than Hall seems to anticipate. It is indisputable that black separatism and cultural nationalism
were everywhere evident within the black middle class during the 1960s
and 1970s, but these phenomena often amounted to little more than
"radical chic" and were seldom accompanied by economic progressivism.[2] E. Franklin Frazier observed, correctly, that black bourgeois
separatism is definitely not altruistic. It has been my belief, therefore,
that the works of Frazier offer us good insight into the essentially cynical
and self-serving attitudes of black elites with respect to black culture and
black consciousness.

Frazier revealed an early professional interest in black nationalism
with his treatments of Garveyism during the 1920s. Published in 1926,
the year following Marcus Garvey's conviction for using the mails to
defraud, the essays were frank, but by no means curmudgeonly or un-
generous, in their description of the forces behind Garvey's success as a
mass leader. Frazier held it as self-evident that the territorial aims of
Garveyism were not feasible. He treated Garveyism as a religious movement, noting the use of biblical diction and evangelical rhetoric that
Garvey utilized to promise his followers an apocalyptic moment of racial
triumph and a paradise on earth. Frazier noted Garvey's employment of
the slogans of martyrdom at the time of his imprisonment in Atlanta.
Frazier refused to dismiss Garvey as a "common swindler," recognizing
that Garvey in the mind of the average "crowd-minded" black man was a
Christlike figure, who had been betrayed by pharisaic black leaders to
the imperial power of a modern American "Rome."[3]

Not all of Frazier's observations on Garveyism have held up so well
as his observation on the movement's religious character. Frazier spoke
of Garveyite separatism as a lower-class phenomenon, an idea that has
been discredited by recent scholarship. Frazier could have found ample
evidence of Garveyism's links to the black bourgeoisie if he had looked
for it. Furthermore, he would have given depth to his studies of the
black bourgeoisie if he had not ignored the well-trained but threadbare
intellectuals that flocked to the Garvey movement. Garveyism and other
separatist ideologies were always prominent among the striving working
class, the puritanical elements among the ministry, and other elements of
black communities that aspired to middle-class status. When Frazier
contributed his 1925 article to Locke's *The New Negro,* he displayed
positive attitudes towards black economic self-reliance as a basis for
ethnic regeneration of black Americans. In his 1928 contribution to
Calverton's *Anthology of American Negro Literature,* he praised the
Garvey movement for uniting "nationalistic aims with an economic program." But Frazier never came to an understanding of the similarities

between Garveyism and the black bourgeois separatism that dominated much of his later writing.[4]

In a 1947 article, Frazier observed that middle-class blacks were inclined to oppose integration because integrationist policies would inevitably lead to the erosion of black controlled institutions. Frazier argued that the segregated black community was "essentially a pathological phenomenon in American life," but that it had "given certain Negroes a vested interest in segregation—involving more than dollars-and-cents considerations." He predicted that with the disappearance of segregation, "the Negro will lose all these petty advantages." It was clear, however, that Frazier considered the disadvantages of separate institutional life to far outweigh the benefits. Furthermore, he felt that within the black world, the chief beneficiaries of segregation were the middle classes. "It is the Negro professional, the business man, and to a less extent, the white collar worker who profit from segregation," he said. "These groups in the Negro population enjoy certain advantages because they do not have to compete with whites."[5]

With this statement, Frazier established the thesis that was to dominate *Black Bourgeoisie,* his best-known work. Some of the elements of *Black Bourgeoisie* had appeared in an article under the title "La Bourgeoisie Noire" in 1928. But that article had barely touched on the theme of voluntary segregation that dominated the extended study, published in France in 1955. *Black Bourgeoisie* was a diatribe on the inconsistencies inherent in black bourgeois separatism. Frazier revealed that the black middle class insisted on institutional separatism in every area of life. He argued, however, that the apparent racial pride that was represented by the maintenance of separate institutions in educational life, business and political life, and religious and familial life was contradicted by the fact that all black institutions seemed to be mindlessly imitative of white institutions. The institutional separatism in which bourgeois Negroes took such pride was, therefore, only a "gaudy world of make believe." The hostility to integration that characterized black institutional life was contradicted by the affinity for assimilation with which their cultural lives were obsessed.[6]

Frazier sometimes spoke of black America as "a nation within a nation," but not with kindly overtones.[7] As an opponent of de jure segregation, he attributed numerous social pathologies within black communities to the isolation of black institutions from the white models that they so imperfectly imitated. He showed little sympathy for black separatism and argued that it was, in part, a flight from reality and an escape from competition. He often spoke of black leaders as provincial, self-serving, and having a "vested interest in segregation." Throughout

Black Bourgeoisie, in which he used the phrase "nation within a nation," Frazier was concerned with segregation and with voluntary separatism. He recognized that racial isolation and ethnic chauvinism had historically characterized black middle-class attitudes. He recognized, however, that although the black bourgeoisie swaddled themselves in the protective fabric of racial institutions, their separate lives reflected their assimilation of American middle-class values, including conspicuous consumption and political conservatism. If Frazier did literally view the black bourgeoisie as a nation within a nation, he was ambivalent on the question of whether it had a distinct national culture.

No doubt because of the emotional content of most questions related to race relations in the United States, Frazier admitted he found it difficult to communicate what he considered the important distinction between integration and assimilation. He admitted to this difficulty in a conversation with the black sociologist, Nathan Hare, shortly before his death. According to Hare, Frazier said that he had spent the greater part of his career unsuccessfully attempting to teach students the distinction between the two.[8] Unfortunately, Hare does not tell us precisely how Frazier drew the distinction, but it is clear form his writings that Frazier believed in integration, which he saw as a healthy social movement. He was opposed, however, to the total and indiscriminate assimilation of blacks into the existing white American bourgeois culture. Integration, in Frazier's system, seems to refer to a legitimate participation by blacks in American institutional life. Assimilation refers to the cultural absorption of blacks into an America known for its crassness, vulgarity, and venality. Frazier did not seem to appreciate the ironic consequences of his position, which might be construed as implying the segregation had positive as well as negative consequences. While segregation's inevitable result is isolationism and provincialism, it is also a bulwark against the absorption of blacks into a society that is noted for its sanctimonious ethnocentrism, swaggering anti-intellectualism, and hypocritical self-righteousness. Although Frazier's position in *Black Bourgeoisie* seemed to imply that the consequences of assimilation might be negative as well as positive, he was unquestionably in favor of integration, as he repeatedly made clear.

Unlike Frazier, numerous other writers who have focused on black separatism and black nationalism have tended to romanticize both movements, ignoring their moral proximity to segregation. By concentrating on the Negro's vested interest in segregation, Frazier pointed out the practical similarities and the political and economic interdependency between the two. Frazier argued that one of the strongest barriers against desegregation was the black American's opposition to it. Segregated institutions functioned as a barricade against overt racial assaults. They were arenas in which black leaders could work for self-fulfillment and in which the rank and file could find channels of expression. He was not obsessed with the distinction that black separatists themselves often make between separation as voluntary and segregation as involuntary. He argued that segregation had become to some extent voluntary on the part of the blacks, or it could not have persisted. He thus recognized that many "separatist" movements amounted to little more than opportunistic collaboration with segregationists.

Although Frazier stated an unequivocal belief that integration would "cause Negroes generally to acquire a saner conception of themselves and of their role in American society," he was hostile to "an implied or unconscious assimilationist philosophy, holding that Negroes should enter the mainstream of American life as rapidly as possible leaving behind their social heritage and becoming invisible as soon as possible." This is the most difficult, and seemingly contradictory, part of Frazier's theory of black nationalism, but he attempted to clarify it in his 1962 essay on "The Failure of the Negro Intellectual." The black leadership class was expected to encourage pan-Africanism and integration simultaneously. Like the spokesmen for the Harlem Renaissance, he called for a cultural recognition of black Americans as a part of American life in general. If the Negro were to be assimilated, "his heritage should become a part of the American heritage, and it should be recognized as the contribution of the Negro as one recognizes the contributions of the English, Irish, Germans, and other people." The black bourgeoisie and its intelligentsia should continue to pursue integration, but they should at the same time continue to pursue a sense of identification with Africa and with their African heritage.

This may sound like black nationalism, but it also reflects Frazier's ambivalent and contradictory position on the question of whether black Americans really had a culture or anything resembling a positive cultural heritage. For if black people possessed only a spurious culture based on the imperfect imitation of corrupt white institutions, what then was this contribution that they were to make to American life? How was total assimilation to be avoided in a fully integrated society, and if integration was a positive movement, why then was assimilation to be feared? Frazier never worked out all these questions satisfactorily. He left us, in his final published essay, a statement that was at once pan-Africanistic and integrationistic. In *The Negro Church*, published the year before his death, he warned of the pitfalls of black nationalism and institutional separatism.

Frazier used the phrase "A Nation Within a Nation" as a chapter heading in *The Negro Church in America* (1961). He asserted that the church was the fundamental institution within the black American social order. Although Frazier disputed Du Bois's contention that the church preserved remnants of African institutional life, he accepted his assertion that in the absence of the family (which slavery presumably had destroyed) the church provided the most important basis for social cohesion.[8] In the years following the Civil War, the religion of the slaves was integrated into the established churches of the free blacks and became the principal agency of social control. But this new institution, according to Frazier, was not based so much on religious instruction as on dramatic preaching. The authority in these churches was exercised by "dominating personalities," and particularly in the Baptist churches, "individual preachers ruled their followers in an arbitrary manner."[9]

The church represented, in Frazier's view, the fundamental unit of political, economic, and social organization among black Americans. At least for the journalistic purpose of intriguing the reader, it could be called a nation. And yet here, too, as in *Black Bourgeoisie,* he stopped short of a fully developed discussion of black nationalism in either its middle-class or its lower-class manifestations. He failed to see the rising tide of political militancy that was springing up from the church leadership. The cases of Martin Luther King and Malcolm X should have led to a further exploration of the themes that he had first articulated in his essays on Marcus Garvey. Frazier had not been blind to the messianic and millenarian aspects of black nationalism, nor had he failed to see the incipient black nationalism in the black religious movements. Unfortunately, he was never able to pull together all of his observations into a unified theory, encompassing black nationalism, bourgeois assimilationism, and Afro-American religion.

Frazier was neither the first nor the last to note the religious parallels or the messianic and redemptionist qualities of black nationalism. As the black sociologist St. Clair Drake noted in *The Redemption of Africa and Black Religion,* religious expression has been fundamental to black nationalist movements since their origin. The ideas of Frazier and Drake that Garveyism and other varieties of black nationalism could be seen as religious movements have been given thorough scholarly exposition in the writings of Randall Burkett. But Frazier's work suggests to me an even more important conclusion. It has led me to think of religion as an ingredient of black nationalism so fundamental that it is almost redundant to speak of "religious black nationalism," as some students of the movement have been inclined to do. Almost all the important manifestations of black nationalism have been intrinsically religious. Rather than thinking of religious black nationalism as one of the varieties of black nationalism, one might almost say that black nationalism is a variety of religion, or that black nationalism in general, like Garveyism in particular, is a religious movement.[10]

St. Clair Drake's study of Christian black nationalism went a long way towards dismantling some of the conventional misconceptions that had developed out of the ambivalences and uncertainties in Frazier's works. Drake questioned the idea that the adoption of Christianity inevitably led to submission. Christianity, he asserted, involved a tradition of "energizing a myth in both the New World and in Africa itself for those prepolitical movements that arose while the powerless were gathering their strength for realistic and rewarding political activity." Drake also challenged the widely accepted but ahistorical view publicized by Malcolm X that house servants had identified their interests with those of the master class to such an extent that they characteristically became spies and informers. Drake observed that the house-servant class had produced "creative individuals like the Haitian leader Toussaint L'Ouverture."[11]

Drake gave considerable attention to the phenomenon of "Ethiopianism," which derives its name from the biblical and later European traditions of referring to all Africans as Ethiopians. The tradition was based on freewheeling interpretations of the verse of the psalmist, "Princes shall come out of Egypt; Ethiopia shall soon stretch forth her hands unto God." Probably because of an ambiguity that allows for unlimited exercise of exegetical powers, this passage has been a favorite with black preachers and other leaders, who, from the late eighteenth century to the present day, have never tired of explicating it. Usually, it was seen as meaning that God had some mighty destiny planned for the black race. Thus "Ethiopianism" involved a good deal more than mere allusions to Ethiopia in the songs, sermons, and folklore of the African peoples. It was a historical mythology, presenting an exalted view of the black race and its cosmic messianic mission.[12]

Drake summarized the ways in which black Christians, especially in the United States, began in the eighteenth century to detect the hand of God in black history. He showed how the free blacks of New York and Philadelphia developed a tradition of interpreting history as a process whereby God always sided with oppressed peoples, whose torment he allowed only as a means of toughening them up for some great mission. Realizing that the leaders of three great slave insurrections in the nineteenth century—Denmark Vesey, Gabriel Prosser, and Nat Turner—had been known to incite their followers with quotations from the Bible, he linked them to this tradition. He saw this tradition flourishing in the writings of Alexander Crummell, who spoke of "the forced and cruel migration of our race," which in "the wondrous providence of God" had fitted large numbers of Afro-Americans for the work of Christianizing and civilizing the fatherland. The hero of Drake's study was Edward W. Blyden, identified as an "Intellectual Ethiopianist," without whose efforts "Ethiopianism might have remained merely an escapist myth system." Drake credited Blyden with the "recasting of Ethiopianism" and making it into an independent and separatist movement. He saw the nineteenth-century leader as "the first of a long line of Caribbean intellectuals who, while living in the United States, Europe, or West Africa, contributed toward the development of ideology 'situationally congruous,' as Karl Mannheim would phrase it, with the status of black men in a world dominated by White Power."[13]

The reference to Mannheim clearly reveals the sociological training of its author. More revealing is Drake's tendency to use the term "myth" in its wider social scientific connotation, to signify an "intellectually respectable 'thought style' " rather than a mere untruth. He clearly has great respect for the process of "myth-making and symbol-building as an example of early 'black achievement.' " Drake's use of the concept of myth in his essay on *The Redemption of Africa and Black Religion* makes use of ideas that are more commonly associated with the anthropologist Claude Levi-Strauss than with the sort of sociology one finds in the pages of *American Sociological Review*. This, of course, is a proof of the man's versatility as a scholar. One finds similar evidence of his versatility in his essay, "Hide My Face," which deals with the Harlem literary renaissance. Drake's contributions to the history of black nationalism are more a reflection of his own perceptions and skills than the methodology of his discipline. And yet one does observe a similarity between his work and that of fellow sociologist E. Franklin Frazier with respect to one important insight.

Like Frazier, Drake recognizes that separatist activity does not necessarily demonstrate a freedom from assimilationist values. As early as *Black Metropolis,* a study which he coauthored with Horace Cayton in 1945, Drake can be assumed to have subscribed to the view that many independent, self-assertive, and race-proud individuals have obviously and unavoidably been influenced by values absorbed from the larger society. It should therefore come as no surprise to us that Drake was among the first to recognize the importance of Western Christianity to the development of black political consciousness. The seeming contradiction between cultural separatism and religious assimilation has confused many observers to such an extent that they have mistakenly seen the Christian church as exerting a counterpressure to nationalism. But Drake, like E. Franklin Frazier, recognized that the black church was an important source—if not the most important source—of black nationalism in America.

John H. Bracey, another historian trained in sociology, relegates religious nationalism to a coequal status with several other varieties of nationalism, including: racial solidarity, cultural nationalism, economic nationalism, revolutionary nationalism, territorial separatism, and pan-Africanism. Bracey thus breaks with the tradition that has seen black religion as fundamental to all other black institutions. Bracey's chief concern as a historian of black nationalism has been with the period since the decline of Marcus Garvey. His best-known work on the subject appeared in 1971 and seems from the present vantage point to have been naively millenarian. Bracey was too quick to assume that the black nationalism of the late 1960s was "at a higher level than ever before." Bracey thought that the black nationalism of the 1960s revealed several characteristics that set it apart from earlier manifestations in terms of depth, intensity, and pervasiveness. He was certain that "especially among the youth" there was a rejection of American values and institutions.[14]

Bracey failed to recognize the extent to which black nationalism in the sixties was dependent upon an electronic communications network that black people did not control. Nor did he take advantage of the writings of contemporary social scientists like Marshall McLuhan, who could have provided him with some insight into the implications of a movement's being controlled by the media. In a society such as ours there is a planned obsolescence of ideas, which means that intellectual and cultural movements must be turned over even more rapidly than automobiles. When Afro hairstyles and dashikis no longer possessed the allure of newness, they went the way of miniskirts and James Bond movies. The radical groups of the sixties flew at one another's throats— each claiming to be more legitimately black than all the rest. Their behavior was predictable, in view of their history of disorganization, their powerlessness, and their lack of sophistication. The responses of the "authorities" were equally predictable, consisting as they did of ruthless persecution, intimidation, and legalized murder. The youthful leaders of the period who have survived are now middle-aged, and the youth who replaced them have found their own ways of seeking social change. When questioned, they invariably state their intention of working to create black-owned businesses, which will presumably exist for the purpose of bringing wealth back into "the black community." The least fortunate class of black youth seem to be cynical, depressed, and at least for the moment, apolitical. One wonders whether in retrospect the black nationalism of the 1960s will not seem pale by comparison to that of the period Drake describes in *The Redemption of Africa and Black Religion.* Bracey's interpretation of the black nationalism he saw around him betrayed an alarming lack of historical consciousness, psychological insight, and media awareness. Still we cannot discount the possibility that the trends observed in the 1960s may be revitalized at some future date.

Unlike Bracey, James Turner, writing in the January 1971 issue of *Black World,* did not see the black nationalism of the period as representing anything exceptional in kind or intensity. In Turner's view, recent black nationalist expressions were no more impressive than those of earlier periods, and he asserted that the movement had reached "its highest level in this country with the rise of the Garvey movement." Turner saw the movement of the 1960s as part of a continuous tradition that dates back to the Free African Societies of the eighteenth century and the Back to Africa movement of Paul Cuffe in 1815. As do all sophisticated commentators on black nationalism, Turner relies to some extent on past ideologues of the movement when he defines its characteristics. He turned to a statement made by Martin Delany in 1853 — quoted by Bill McAdoo in his article "Pre–Civil War Black Nationalism" in 1966 — in order to support the historical validity of his own thinking and its orthodoxy within a black-nationalist tradition and scholarship. Delany had not only recognized the obvious, that black-nationalist sentiments derived from white oppression, he also recognized that the acceptance of what Turner called "white ideas" in no way prevented the development of black nationalism. Delany had observed that "being distinguished by complection, we are still singled out — although having merged in the habits and customs of our oppressors — as a distinct nation of people."[15]

Turner recognized the truth of Delany's statement, that black people had been "merged in the habits and customs" of white America. Present-day terminology might describe them as "culturally assimilated," or as "acculturated." Turner, like Delany, acknowledged the fact that black Americans had undergone intense acculturation. Although they occupied the anomalous position of a "nation within a nation," they were immersed in the ideology of the larger society. The realization led to Turner's astute observation that "an ironic aspect of black popular movements is the way in which white ideas act as catalysts of Nationalist feelings." Although black Americans have been segregated physically from whites, they have been acculturated to white ways of thinking, "especially in the areas of religion and social morality." Black nationalism arises out of the experience of slavery and oppression. It is also a result of the symbiotic relationship between whites and blacks in which blacks have become more like whites in the process of developing institutions to help them resist racism. Thus, black nationalism is a reactive movement much influenced by the forces against which it is reacting. Thus, for example, Turner does not see Christianity as a force working to soothe blacks into a state of passivity, but as an idea that comes to inspire nationalism by pointing up the contradictions in white behavior. In other words, the process of acculturation endows blacks with a theory of nationalism and a religious framework to support it.

Another historian trained in sociological methods, Earl Ofari, has shown similar respect for the complex origins of black nationalism and its historical continuity in America. Ofari recognizes that "many of the problems which plague the struggle today—such as leadership, organization, direction, and goals—were equally as complex" in the nineteenth century. Ofari felt that an essential part of understanding the black nationalism of the 1960s was an appreciation for the period that had gone before. Ofari treated the black nationalist movements of the sixties as Turner and Drake had, viewing them as interesting and valid, but by no means novel, expressions of black American political consciousness.[16]

When compared to treatments such as Bracey's, Raymond Hall's *Black Separatism in the United States* exhibits considerable sophistication. The author does not overestimate the importance of recent movements and covers the period from 1787 to the early 1970s. But the awareness of past movements is not paralleled by a knowledge of past research, for early in the book he makes the assertion that "there is a paucity of serious works on black separatism in the United States." Curious, for his book is based almost exclusively on secondary sources. The study was conducted between 1968 and 1972 and published in January 1978. Attempts to update it were unsystematic, and significant developments in scholarship and American life were ignored. This has diminished the value of what still could have been a "timely book." Raymond Hall attacks the subject with enthusiasm, however, and does provide a lively synthesis of published work on civil rights and black power organizations during the late 1960s and early 1970s.

Part one, the section that is devoted to historical backgrounds, makes up a third of the book. It is weakened not only by the failure to treat on primary sources, but by logical and conceptual flaws. For example, Hall insists that "black separatism is a sub-category of black nationalism." This is patently untrue. The simple fact that people of any color may separate themselves along racial, cultural, religious, or political lines does not make them nationalists. Black separatism is not always a subcategory of black nationalism, although it may be proper at times to view it in this way. Most black separatism exists only on the level of social intercourse and family life. The typical black American is a separatist in terms of most intimate interpersonal contacts but an integrationist when it comes to education, employment, housing. To call such a person a black nationalist is clearly thoughtless. Black separatism may be a matter of convenience, a pragmatic accommodation to reality, or the result of firmly held nationalistic sentiments. But just as a nationalist is not always a separatist, so too a separatist is not always a nationalist.

Hall has a tendency to repeat his points rather than demonstrate them. One example is his frequent overstatement of the continuity between Booker T. Washington and Marcus Garvey. Citing Harold Cruse's *The Crisis of the Negro Intellectual* as his source, Hall stretches Cruse's point to assert without further documentation that Garvey came to the United States "at Washington's behest." True, Garvey wrote to Washington, announcing that he hoped to visit Tuskegee, and Washington responded hospitably, but there is no evidence that he intended to encourage anything other than Garvey's early scheme to establish a trade school in Jamaica. Since Hall has based his treatment of Washington on secondary sources, he should have perused Louis Harlan, *Booker T. Washington,* published well within the time frame of his study. More to the point, he might have consulted Harlan's edition of the *Booker T. Washington Papers,* six volumes of which had appeared by 1977. At one point the author states that he "believes Washington would have ardently supported military service for blacks." Speculation is not in order. Washington's opinions at the time of the Spanish-American War are well recorded, even in publications of early vintage.[17]

Hall is similarly cavalier regarding recent work on Garvey, whom he calls "the star" of his study. The works of Tony Martin, Robert Hill, and John Henrik Clarke are completely ignored. In his treatment of the relationship between Edward Wilmot Blyden and Henry McNeal Turner, Hall is guilty of the grossest exaggeration. He attempts to give the impression that Blyden and Turner were close collaborators. True, Blyden did work along with Turner in support of the Butler repatriation bill. But this was apparently more at the behest of the American Colonization Society than at that of Turner. During the course of this work, Blyden travelled in the United States and took occasion to vent his fury on the hated mulattos, of whom Turner was one. Blyden once described Turner as "the embodiment of hyperbole." Although he showed a good-natured tolerance for Turner's emigrationism, he contrasted his philosophy with that of Booker T. Washington and encouraged blacks to cast down their bucket in the United States.

Part two of Hall's study, which emphasizes the late 1960s, is imaginative and informative, although misleadingly referred to as "The contemporary Period." The trends he describes had long passed out of fashion by the time the book went to press. Here, too, one finds a puzzling neglect of readily available information. Why does Hall question the sincerity of the Black Muslims' recent integrationism? It was apparently taken seriously by those whites who came into the movement and by the die-hard separatists who withdrew in horror.

Part three, which deals provocatively with the question of social change, is marred by similar difficulties. Hall provides little analysis of the eclipse of black nationalism during the late 1970s. Much worse, he doesn't even seem to be aware of it, although a fellow black sociologist, Thomas L. Blair, has treated on the problem in his gloomy study *Retreat to the Ghetto* (1977). As Blair remarks, the revolutionary nationalists of the sixties are all either "dead, jailed, coopted, or compromised." The movement has "moved inexorably toward cultural, economic, and political forms of bourgeois nationalism." Hall is strangely sanguine with respect to the nationalism of the black bourgeoisie, which he is inclined to accept at face value. But while seemingly supportive of bourgeois nationalism, he displays an unexplained hostility to one of its more significant manifestations. He is hostile to the Black Studies movement, although here too he ignores much of the readily available source material. His observations are based entirely on personal experiences at Dartmouth and a bias against nontechnical education. Strange attitude for a practitioner of soft sociology in a liberal arts college.

Hall is not the first black sociologist to attempt a general book-length treatment of black separatism. Alphonso Pinkney's *Red, Black, and Green* (1976) is superior and more current, although published earlier. Pinkney, like Hall, is mainly concerned with the period since the rise of Malcolm X. His work is more comprehensive and systematic, however, and he addresses literary and artistic concerns to which Hall seems oblivious. Pinkney, like Hall, avoids statistics and blurs the distinction between separatism and black nationalism. This is perhaps unavoidable, since both concepts are nebulous. One category of separatism that both authors unexplainably avoid is the almost complete separation of black from white marital and familial life. Marital separatism is so fundamental to American life that it is taken for granted and seldom discussed. But the subject of marital separatism might have presented a challenge to Hall, who asserts, "a separatist is always a nationalist."

At the conclusion of his study, Pinkney, like Hall, seems convinced that black nationalism in the pattern of the 1960s is to be a permanent fixture of Afro-American life. He prognosticates optimistically on the coming unity between the black bourgeoisie and the masses of urban ghetto blacks. Subsequent scholarship by William J. Wilson, a black sociologist at the University of Chicago, argues convincingly that no such unity seems imminent,' that, indeed, the class differences within the black community are becoming more pronounced and more divisive. Perhaps it was an awareness of the decreasing interest in black nationalism during the mid-1960s that led Pinkney to attach an epilogue to his work, in which he recognized a drifting away from "cultural nationalism" in the direction of "revolutionary nationalism." Pinkney borrowed these terms from John H. Bracey, who had identified cultural nationalism with an emphasis on ethnicity, life-styles, and aesthetics, and had associated revolutionary nationalism with Marxism-Leninism and the class struggle. But Bracey's categories are arbitrary and confusing, since cultural nationalism can be revolutionary, while Marxism-Leninism is at times doctrinaire and conservative. Indeed, one of the weaknesses of Pinkney's study is that he depends on Bracey's definitions and categories, rather than examining the works of other black sociologists whose writings have not been quite so millenarian.

Sociology is a present-oriented discipline, and for this reason sociologists—like Bracey, Hall, and Pinkney—have been more comfortable dealing with contemporary black nationalism than with the historical patterns that have contributed to its present configurations. Historians and sociologists who practice interdisciplinary methodologies are more inclined to understand the larger patterns of black-nationalist phenomena and are inclined to see religion as central to the movement. Those sociologists who are concerned with practical, problem-solving techniques, and with the study of social problems rather than social change or the sociology of knowledge, are unaccustomed to dealing with the processes whereby ideologies evolve. Sociologists who were absorbed in the here and now were caught off guard by the sudden and dramatic decline of popular black nationalism during the late 1970s. The weaknesses of Hall's and Bracey's studies cannot be attributed solely to the biases of their discipline. St. Clair Drake demonstrates that an imaginative sociologist can rival the historians at their own craft.

The essential importance of religion to the phenomenon of black nationalism has been acknowledged by the major sociologists and historians who have written on the subject. Major political scientists, like E. U. Essien-Udom, have also recognized that religion is not epiphenomenal nor is it a variety of black nationalism. Black nationalism is, in essence, a variety of religious experience. In the past, Christianity, Islam, and even Judaism have been central to black nationalist ideology. The Garvey movement, as Frazier and Burkett realized, showed many of the qualities of a religious movement. The black nationalism of the sixties, while ostensibly non-religious, was in reality a sort of Marxist belief system. Even the most antireligious forms could easily be described as secular religions or as pseudoreligions. Present-day black nationalism, as represented by the Ansaru Allah community or by the leadership of Louis Farrakhan, is clearly religious. If scholars of any disciplinary persuasion are to make contributions to the study of black nationalism, then they must survey the entire historical scope of the movement in the way that Drake has done. They must also be willing to seriously weigh the importance of religious and quasi-religious phenomena. This will assist in avoiding the errors of Pinkney, Bracey, and others, who assumed that the phenomena of the period 1968–73 represented a millennium, and believed themselves to be witnessing a great gettin' up mornin' and day of jubilee.

N O T E S

1. Raymond L. Hall, *Black Separatism in the United States* (Hanover, N.H.: University Press of New England, 1978).

2. Tom Wolfe, *Radical Chic & Mau-Mauing the Flak Catchers* (New York: Bantam, 1971).

3. E. Franklin Frazier, "Garvey: A Mass Leader," *Nation* (18 August 1926), 147–48. E. Franklin Frazier, "The Garvey Movement," *Opportunity* (November 1926): 346–48.

4. Recent studies emphasize the participation of the stable working class, the petite bourgeoisie, and disfranchised intellectuals in the movement. See Tony Martin, *Literary Garveyism: Garvey, Black Arts, and the Harlem Renaissance* (Dover, Mass.: The Majority Press, 1983); Robert A. Hill, *The Marcus Garvey and UNIA Papers* (Los Angeles: University of California Press, 1983).

5. E. Franklin Frazier, "Human, All Too Human: The Negro's Vested Interest in Segregation," *Survey Graphic* (1947): 74–100; reprint in *E. Franklin Frazier on Race Relations: Selected Writings,* ed. G. Franklin Edwards (Chicago: University Press, 1968), pp. 283–91.

6. E. Franklin Frazier, *Black Bourgeoisie* (New York: Collier, 1962).

7. Frazier asked whether black Americans were "a nation within a nation." The question, which appeared as the third subheading of the first chapter of *Black Bourgeoisie,* may have been more than purely rhetorical, but it was never systematically addressed.

8. Frazier quotes and takes issue with W. E. B. Du Bois's position on African cultural survivals in the church as he stated them in *Some Efforts of the American Negroes for Their Own Betterment* (Atlanta, 1898). See also Du Bois's chapter "The Function of the Negro Church" in *The Philadelphia Negro* (Philadelphia, 1899), pp. 201–6, and his chapter "Effect of Transplanting" in *The Negro Church,* Atlanta University Publications, no. 8, (Atlanta, 1903).

9. E. Franklin Frazier, *The Negro Church in America* (New York: Schocken, 1964), pp. 18, 31, 34, 43.

10. Randall Burkett, *Garveyism as a Religious Movement* (Metuchen, N.J.: Scarecrow Press, 1978). Wilson J. Moses, *Black Messiahs and Uncle Toms: Social and Literary Manipulations of a Religious Myth* (University Park: Pennsylvania State University Press, 1982).

11. St. Clair Drake, *The Redemption of Africa and Black Religion* (Chicago: Third World Press, 1970). Like many black scholars, Drake found it necessary to provide such implicit responses to commonly held misunderstandings among militant nationalists, even if they were not professional academics or conventional scholars.

12. Drake, *Redemption of Africa,* p. 11.

13. Drake, *Redemption of Africa,* p. 54.

14. John H. Bracey, Jr., "Black Nationalism since Garvey," in *Key Issues in the Afro-American Experience,* ed. Nathan Huggins et al. (New York: Harcourt Brace Jovanovich, 1971), pp. 259–79.

15. James Turner, "Black Nationalism: The Inevitable Response," *Black World* (January 1971): 10, derives the Delany quotation from Bill McAdoo, "Pre–Civil War Black Nationalism," *Progressive Labor* (June–July 1966): 40.

16. Earl Ofari, "The Emergence of Black National Consciousness in America," *Black World* (February 1971): 75.

17. Booker T. Washington, "Our New Citizen" (address delivered before the Hamilton Club, Chicago, Illinois, 31 January, 1896): reprinted in Howard Brotz, *Negro Social and Political Thought, 1850–1920* (New York: Basic Books, 1966). In this address, Washington speaks of the role of black soldiers in the Spanish-American War.

Rediscovering Black
Nationalism in the 1960s

The black power movement of the late 1960s represented a typically American happening. It was a drama acted out by a racially distinct, but culturally assimilated, group of Americans in response to social forces that predominated in the United States during the period. As James Turner has commented: "The Black man lives in a symbiotic relationship with the white man, held in subordinate position by the caste system. Furthermore, the black man is governed by the white dominant group, especially in the areas of religion and social morality. . . . Thus an ironic aspect of Black popular movements is the way in which white ideas act as catalysts of nationalist feelings." Turner is in accord with a recent trend in scholarship when he cites black Christianity as an example of this, observing that black Christians have been quick to recognize the contradiction between the preachments and the practice of white Christians. It was within the segregated institution of the black church that Christianity was adapted to the cause of abolition and black nationalism.[1]

Black thought has always responded ingeniously to the changing American environment from which it sprouted. The development of black nationalism in the nineteenth century must be described as reactive in the sense that it was primarily a reaction to the status conferred on blacks as a result of the slave trade. It involved an immediate reaction to the slave trade that had upset the economy and ecology of Africa and degraded the status of black people throughout the world. That black

nationalism is essentially a movement of reaction has been acknowledged by such legitimate spokespersons of the movement as James
Turner and Stokely Carmichael.[2] It is also generally conceded that major
black nationalists of the past have been caught up in certain values of the
culture that served to generate the need for their movement. Nineteenth-
century black nationalists, for example, were not only Christian, they
tended to think of the liberation of Africa as going hand in hand with
missionary work. Even Edward Wilmot Blyden, who studied African
religion and language and developed a great respect for Islam, still saw
Christianity as superior to indigenous West African religions.[3] Marcus
Garvey believed that Providence had intended for the diaspora blacks to
return to Africa and regenerate the continent by means of Christian
missionary work. For this reason, it may be said that political black
nationalism in the nineteenth century often went hand in hand with
cultural assimilationism. The very rhetoric with which black nationalists
exhorted their followers was fertilized by the messianic oratory of European and American nationalism, with its *Volksgeist* mythologies and
theories of manifest destiny. Ironically, black nationalism developed
among the class of people who were most acculturated. An important
indicator of the degree to which one had become assimilated was the
degree to which one became an ideological separatist, borrowing doctrines of "the Conservation of Races" from learned European and
American sources.

Few students of the black-nationalist movement would deny that
this was true in the past, but many would stubbornly maintain that black
nationalism and the Black Power movement of the 1960s represented a
distinct break with the past. The movement of the 1960s indicated, in the
words of John H. Bracey, that black America had "successfully completed the ideological shift from a belief in integration and individual
success to a belief in the importance of political and economic power and
in collective responsibility." Bracey concluded that "Black America, now
aware and confident, will no longer tolerate a colonial status." In Bracey's view, and that of many others, the Black Power revolt was a spon-
taneous upswelling of social and cultural consciousness. It represented a
clean break with a past in which faltering black nationalist movements
had willingly or unwillingly allowed themselves to be affected by white
ideals. The only historical antecedent to the current movement acknowledged by many of its observers was Garveyism, but even Garveyism had
not achieved such "depth and intensity of nationalist feeling." Black
Power was viewed as a declaration of independence from white
America. Henceforth, any interaction with whites would be on terms

defined by blacks and under conditions that would be primarily advantageous to blacks.[4]

Black nationalism of the 1960s, no less than earlier expressions of the movement, was a by-product of American culture. It is true that in many ways it was different than earlier forms of black nationalism, but this was in response to the ways that the culture of the United States was changing. Since the First World War, American culture had undergone numerous changes, some of them severely traumatic, albeit they were heralded by many as the dawn of a more enlightened era. The chaos and bloodshed of the First World War led to considerable disillusionment with the civilizational process in both the white and the black worlds. The period witnessed an anxious ambivalence concerning religion among white artists and intellectuals, offset by a fundamentalist revival among the white masses led by Billy Sunday. While ordinary Americans sought emotional fulfillment through enthusiastic religion, intellectuals developed a passion for other varieties of primitivism. The secular religion of the sophisticated classes involved a fascination with the cultures of pre-industrial societies, which were sentimentally depicted as Edens of cultural stability in contrast to the civilized wasteland of the contemporary West. America had gradually evolved during the nineteenth century from an agrarian empire to an urban industrial society. The erosion of traditional sexual morality, increased opportunities for the education of women as well as men, and the explosion of electronic communications media, all worked to alter the nature of the society into which black people were gradually being integrated. By the time Afro-Americans began to achieve significant integration into American life around World War II, the society was quite different from anything Booker T. Washington would have recognized. The formulae that had been laid out by black leaders at the turn of the century to promote cultural assimilation and social acceptance were rapidly becoming outmoded. It had been assumed by Booker T. Washington and W. E. B. Du Bois that the adoption of Victorian bourgeois morality would hasten the integration process. Neither of them could have possibly foreseen the decline of that value system nor its replacement by the mass marketing ethic and its chief proselytizing device, television.

Television has been as important to the cultural assimilation of black people since World War II as religion was in the nineteenth century. Not only did television provide the means whereby black Americans learned the folkways of white America, it became an important means of promoting the civil rights movement and the process of social integration. Students of the impact of television on American life often note that civil rights demonstrations "had their major impact not upon the angry white mobs or brutal police who reacted violently to the marchers, but upon television audiences in other parts of the country." Civil rights demonstrations were effective principally because they were media happenings. Television is particularly well suited to the presentation of spectacle, and the sight of beer-bellied policemen attacking fresh-faced schoolchildren with firehoses and vicious dogs did a great deal to mobilize people against segregation. But by exploiting the sensational aspects of an event, television depletes its power to hold our attention. Television not only has the power to legitimize events; it reduces them to commonplace, and to the level of "live entertainment". The search for new stories produced a new fascination, the Black Muslims, a militant black group who — startlingly, for most Americans — were opposed to the very integrationism with which black leadership had become identified.

In the summer of 1959, Louis Lomax and Mike Wallace collaborated on a television show called "The Hate that Hate Produced," which featured conversations with Elijah Muhammad and Malcolm X. C. Eric Lincoln believes that within a month of the telecast, membership in the Nation had doubled. Feature stories in *Time, Newsweek, U.S. News and World Report,* and *Readers Digest* soon followed. Although many of the magazines and newspapers sought to discredit the Black Muslims as a lunatic fringe group, soaring publicity had the opposite effect of legitimizing them. If the white man's media took the Nation seriously enough to grant them exposure, surely they must have something to say. Malcolm X was apparently among the first to realize the importance of media coverage to the Muslims. According to Louis Lomax, "Malcolm flew to Chicago and convinced Elijah that the interviews would be the best thing that ever happened to the Black Muslim Movement."[5]

At the time of his discovery by the electronic media, Malcolm X represented a traditional black messianism, based in a theological historicism and a doctrine that Africans are God's chosen people. The inflamed passion with which he spoke, and the colorful rhetoric with which his message was delivered, gave it the dramatically intense quality that T.V. audiences demand. The fact that Malcolm insisted on referring to the white man as a devil appealed to the masochistic semiconsciousness of white society and the black community's sense of the risqué. Television had provided a traditional black streetcorner orator with a platform superior to any soapbox or stepladder. Now, in prime time, free from threats, jeers, or the witty retorts of hecklers, a black man was being encouraged to name off the sins of white society. "I have heard you say that a thousand times," remarked Lomax when Malcolm referred to the white man's satanic nature, "it always jolts me." Malcolm X — apart from the serious content of his message—was entertaining.[6]

During the five years of his access to the national media, Malcolm X was as much influenced by the intellectual currents of white America as he influenced them. Lomax tells of a conversation in which he suggested to Malcolm that he read Oswald Spengler's *The Decline of the West.* The following afternoon he arrived at Lomax's home "bleary eyed and bursting with ideas. He had withdrawn the complete Spengler from the library and stayed up all night reading."[7] Alex Haley also records information on the literary influences felt by Malcolm X. While in prison, he read Will Durant's *Story of Civilization,* H. G. Wells' *Outline of History,* the works of Frederick Law Olmstead, Fannie Kimball, Harriet Beecher Stowe, Herodotus, and Mahatma Gandhi.[8] That Malcolm was appealed to by Marxian analysis increasingly during his last year is an undeniable fact. "It is incorrect to classify the revolt of the Negro as simply a racial conflict of black against white," he said in a speech at Columbia University three days before his death. "Rather we are today seeing a global rebellion of the oppressed against the oppressor, the exploited against the exploiter."[9] Shortly after his death, there emerged a sort of "keep Malcolm Black Movement," concerned with de-emphasizing the statements that he made during 1964 and especially those made at the Militant Labor Forum and in the pages of the *Young Socialist.* Apropos of this, Albert Cleage and George Breitman debated during February and March of 1967 the issue of whether Malcolm X had become an "integrationist" during his last year. Both speakers published their views in a pamphlet entitled *Myths about Malcolm X: Two Views,* and came out in agreement that Malcolm was never an integrationist. In the words of the Marxist, George Breitman, "Until the day of his death he remained an opponent of what is generally or popularly understood, or misunderstood, as 'integration.' " On the other hand, there can be no doubt about the fact that he was profoundly influenced by ideas that were entertained by white radicals among his contemporaries. Thus, the speeches of Malcolm X became one of the principal conduits whereby Marxist ideas were channelled into the black community.[10]

It would be incorrect to argue that Malcolm was politically assimilated into the radical American left. On the other hand, he did make an ideological shift away from a white demonology and in the direction of analysis based on the class struggle. This signalled a revival of Marxism among American black nationalists during the late 1960s and early 1970s. The first signs of this were in the Black Power movement, whose leader, Stokely Carmichael, began in 1966 to issue demands not only to white America, but to the black middle class. The style in which he delivered his message to black college graduates was none too gentle.

"Don't take any job for IBM or Wall Street because you aren't doing anything for us." He said that black doctors ought to be told, "You can't go to college and come back and charge us $5.00 and $10.00 a visit. You have to charge us $.50 and be thankful you get that." Class consciousness was clearly in evidence when Carmichael told black lawyers they should "be happy to take a case and plead it free of charge." It was even more obvious when he said, "The food Ralph Bunche eats doesn't fill our hungry stomachs." Of course, neither Stokely Carmichael nor his audience were wanting for food at the time.[11]

In 1967 Carmichael collaborated with Charles V. Hamilton in the writing of *Black Power* and advertised it as "a political framework and ideology which represents the last reasonable opportunity for this society to work out its racial problems short of prolonged destructive guerilla warfare." *Black Power* was in some respects a nationalistic analysis, for it was based on the idea that "black people in the United States have a colonial relationship to the larger society."[12] This would seem to imply that the solution to the problems besetting black America would be revolutionary. It would also seem to imply that the only reasonable goal for black Americans to work for would be full-fledged national status. But this was not what Hamilton and Carmichael were talking about. In fact, they called for "the inclusion of black people at all levels of decision making." Nationalists ought not to be calling for the "inclusion" of their colony in the decision-making process. This would imply integration or assimilation of the colony, rather than self-assertion and the independent decision making appropriate to a nation. At the same time, ironically, Carmichael and Hamilton invited a comparison between themselves and the integrationist, Martin Luther King. As King had done, they outlined a program for reform and adjustment, then insisted that it paralleled the nationalist, separatist goals of Mahatma Gandhi.[13]

Hamilton and Carmichael were decidedly opposed to cultural assimilation in the sense of "Anglo-conformity." From this followed their hostility to coalitions with white liberals, who were concerned with the progress only of "qualified Negroes"—those who had conformed to the cultural norms of middle-class white America. Throughout the book, the authors revealed a strong hostility to coalitions between white liberals and the black bourgeoisie, which they felt would inevitably operate to the disadvantage of the black masses. Their position on coalitions was very clearly stated but seldom remembered in the heated discussions of black power that proliferated during the late 1960s.

> It is hoped that eventually there will be a coalition of poor blacks and poor whites. This is the only coalition that seems acceptable to us, and we see such a coalition as the major internal instrument of change in American society.[14]

Of course, Hamilton and Carmichael were intelligent enough to caution the reader that any discussion of such a coalition was "purely academic." They were quite emphatic on the point that "poor white people are becoming more hostile—not less—toward black people, partly because they see the nation's attention focused on black poverty and few, if any, people coming to them." The importance that should be attached to this statement is limited. One should not assume that Hamilton and Carmichael were preaching naive proletarian unity that denied racial realities. On the other hand, anyone should be able to hear the echoes of traditional Marxist rhetoric. The conception of black power articulated in the most authoritative book on the subject was not one of extreme nationalism. What Hamilton and Carmichael were serving up was a form of ethnic politics, highly seasoned with homegrown Marxism.

As was to be expected, *Black Power* was more widely read in the white community than in the black. Christopher Lasch reviewed the book together with Harold Cruse's *The Crisis of the Negro Intellectual* in the *New York Review of Books*. This represented the attempt by the white liberal intelligentsia to beat an intellectually respectable retreat from the integrationist position. It mattered little that *Black Power* offered a Marxist-influenced analysis while *The Crisis of the Negro Intellectual* was anti-Marxist; both books had invited a comparison between black Americans and other ethnic groups. There were many people in America who were quick to accept the similarity while ignoring the many differences.[15] Thus it was that white liberals—along with conservative blacks—were soon interpreting Black Power as no more than ethnic politics. Christopher Lasch, like many others, was too quick to take up the argument that black Americans would solve their problem by following the example of white ethnics. In the meantime, however, Stokely Carmichael, along with other blacks who considered themselves disciples of Malcolm X, were moving in the direction of a Marxist black nationalism. The best known example of the attempt to assert nationalistic aims, while absorbing Marxist ideology, was to be found in the Black Panther Party.

Philip Foner has said that the Black Panthers, "while by no means the first Blacks in the United States to oppose the capitalist system and espouse the cause of Socialism, were the first to do so as a separate organization." He maintains that earlier black socialists "became members of parties made up mainly of whites." This may or may not be true, and further research is needed on the question. The history of such groups as the African Blood Brotherhood has not been fully recorded, but it is certain that not all of its members were affiliated with the Communist Party from the beginning.[16] Be that as it may, the nationalism of the Panthers was always somewhat problematic. In the party platform, they spoke of the black population as "black colonial subjects" who should be allowed to participate in a national plebiscite, under United Nations supervision, "for the purpose of determining the will of black people as to their national destiny." This was clearly a nationalistic program. And yet, over the course of the 1970s, the Black Panthers seemed to drift further and further away from a hard-line black nationalism, and in the direction of increased collaboration with other communities under the Marxist banner. Collaboration with other radicals in the name of intercommunalism was perhaps legitimate enough; attending a chic reception at the home of Leonard Bernstein was a dramatic departure from the Black Power philosophy outlined by Hamilton and Carmichael.[17]

One can perhaps understand the emotions that led anonymous ghetto revolutionaries to enjoy their moment of fashionability with the fashionable set. Indeed, one does not find it difficult to empathize with the cynical humour of a Julius Lester, who took full advantage of the white liberals' radical chic in producing a book entitled *Look Out Whitey! Black Power's Gon' Get Your Mama!* Such exploitation of the Black Power phenomenon was relatively harmless, and, who knows, it may have represented a sincere attempt to teach by shocking. More sinister, however, was the vogue of a figure like Eldridge Cleaver, who used his media access to promote images of black people that were not only dishonest but seriously damaging. A convicted rapist, Cleaver openly stated that he had acted out his sick fantasies because that was the only way in which he could achieve his black manhood. He attempted to make his own behavior a metaphor for all black male behavior, and in so doing did much to discredit conceptions of black power. Cleaver was a typical example of the person who under the guise of a black nationalist rhetoric was really participating in the intellectual fads of the white world. While joining the Black Panther Party and parading in the guise of a separatist, he was really demonstrating the most thorough assimilation into the trendy culture of the so-called "hippie philosophy." While clenching his fist and shouting "Power to the people," he was really in line with the stylish slogan, "Do your thing!" And Eldridge Cleaver's "thing" was setting all black males up for the accusations of Susan Brownmiller a decade later. By pandering to the desire of the masochistic white bourgeoisie for prurient titillation, he was reinforcing paranoid fantasies of white America. Cleaver was no doubt sincere, in one respect. He was simply demonstrating his thorough indoctrination with the contemporary American attitude that encourages lurid sexual confessions at cocktail parties and places pornography on the coffee table.[18]

Not all signs of assimilation and acculturation manifested by members of the Panthers were necessarily pathological. On the contrary, it was a sign of their creativity and resourcefulness that they participated in and made use of the cultural movements that swept white America during the 1960s. Much of the assimilationism encouraged by the Black Panthers was indeed healthy. In numerous useful ways, the Black Panthers were a vehicle for carrying positive values of mainstream America into the black community. For example, the widely reprinted "Black Panther Party Platform and Program" contained a lengthy extract from the Declaration of Independence. Their own declaration of independence from white America paid homage to the words of Jefferson, recognizing the universality of their truth, and disseminating them among high school dropouts who would never otherwise have realized their relevance to black America. Even on the level of popular culture, the Black Panthers opened up channels of communication between white and black America. Bobby Seale tells of being introduced to Bob Dylan's satirical lyrics while laying out the Black Panther paper. Huey Newton played one of Dylan's records repeatedly while they worked and explained the lyrics to Seale and the others. Bob Dylan's song "Ballad of a Thin Man," according to Seale, "became a very big part of that whole publishing operation of the Black Panther paper . . . Brother Stokely Carmichael also liked that record."[19]

Not only were the Panthers affected by the culture of rebellious young whites, they were influenced by fringe political movements in contemporary white America. Huey Newton spoke of the need to form coalitions with whites, giving very broad endorsement to groups and movements that would have been entirely unacceptable within the framework set down in *Black Power*. In 1970 he announced: "The women's liberation front and gay liberation front are our friends, they are potential allies, and *we need as many allies as possible*. . . . We should try to form a working coalition with the gay liberation and women's liberation groups. We must always handle social forces in the most appropriate manner." Just as nineteenth century black nationalists had responded to surrounding social forces by aligning their concerns with movements in the white community such as temperance and "social purity", so did the Panthers align themselves with movements such as women's and gay liberation. The Panthers became known for their opposition to the indiscriminate hatred of whites. Bobby Seale devoted a section of his *Seize the Time* to the subject of "Why We Are Not Racists." Huey Newton insisted that the Black Panthers had progressed beyond "black nationalism."[20]

Of all the figures associated with black nationalism in the 1960s, there is, perhaps, no one who symbolizes better than Amiri Baraka the movement's continuity with the assimilationist patterns of the nineteenth century. Half mad, half visionary, always erratically individualistic and egotistical, Baraka has faithfully acted out the traditional role expected of the artist in America. His erratic genius, emotional virility, naive zeal, and boundless energy make him the archetypal artist — as artists are conceived here in the West. In some societies, artists may be everyday, ordinary people — just like butchers, bakers, and candlestick makers, but not in America. We want to see "flashing eyes and floating hair," and we don't believe anyone is an artist until he gives us reason to "close our eyes with holy dread." In the early part of the decade, Baraka was living in Greenwich Village and writing poetry influenced by the beatniks. By 1968, Baraka had abandoned his slave name (Le Roi Jones), his downtown friends, and his white wife to become an advocate of extreme separatism and black cultural independence. By 1971, Baraka was back in the village, this time teaching at the New School for Social Research and advocating Marxist-Leninist solutions to black racial problems. Along the way, Baraka had vacillated from Black Islam to mainstream ethnic politics in Newark, all the time giving immensely successful lectures in predominantly white universities, where he advised black students to shun the humanities and major in business and technological fields. Thus, Baraka was joining the march during the mid-seventies, as black students — following white students — moved away from an emphasis on the liberal arts to pursue the current academic trend, "practical education" and all that it implies.

I have saved my observations on women in the recent black movement until last because the most interesting developments are only now beginning to occur. During the 1960s, as Michelle Wallace has argued, the black woman was placed under great pressure to see herself essentially as a support for the black man. She would provide him with emotional nourishment and moral sustenance after his day of fighting the devils, and, of course, she would have lots of babies for the revolution. Whether or not Michelle Wallace overstates her case, it is certainly true that such themes can be detected in the writings of cultural nationalists in the black movement. Such ideas are decidedly out of fashion in the 1980s. Black women are increasingly aligning themselves with white women in the women's liberation movement. The goals of Black Power have clearly become subordinated to those of feminism, and I know of no prominent spokeswoman to have taken issue with Shirley Chisholm when she said: "Of my two 'handicaps,' being female put many more obstacles in my path than being black."[21] If Shirley Chisholm's observation is accurate, then clearly black women ought to continue in the present direction. It will be—as Michelle Wallace, Bell Hooks, and Angela Davis suggest—necessary to completely rebuild our ideology of black consciousness from the ground up, so that it will contain from the beginning fundamental propositions of feminism. Black feminists are demanding a basic restructuring of black consciousness along lines that interface with ideologies of white feminist spokeswomen. The ideology of black politicians, artists, and intellectuals has always been influenced by movements in the society at large, and thus it should surprise no one that feminism is an important element in contemporary black intellectual and literary movements.

Concluding Reflections on Black Nationalism since the Late 1960s

A short retrospective essay of this type clearly cannot do justice to the decade 1967–1976, the period that we refer to as the Black Power movement. What has been attempted here is an identification of a hidden text, an ideology of assimilationism that seems to have been concealed behind the theories of black nationalism during the period. If Amiri Baraka was really a beatnik, if Stokely Carmichael was really a Marxist, if Shirley Chisholm was really a feminist, if Harold Cruse was only a spokesman for hyphenated Americanism, where was the true Black Power ideology? There are many indications that black nationalism and Black Power of the 1960s did not represent the revolutionary shifts in thought and practice that some scholars, notably John H. Bracey and Houston Baker, seemed to believe. Bracey's observations on the revival of black nationalism in the early 1970s reveal a remarkably millenarian spirit:

> This revival continues to manifest several characteristics that distinguish it from earlier periods when black nationalism was the dominant ideology: the depth and intensity of nationalist feeling, the pervasiveness of black-consciousness ideologies among all classes . . . the large number of blacks, especially among the youth, who reject the legitimacy of American values and institutions, and the acceptance of the right of armed self-defense and retaliation.
>
> These characteristics indicate that black America has successfully completed the ideological shift from a belief in integration and individual

success to a belief in the importance of political and economic power and in collective responsibility . . . The rallying cry for blacks from Jesse Jackson's operation Breadbasket to revolutionary nationalists and pan-Africanists is "It's Nation Time."[22]

Jesse Jackson has abandoned nationalist rhetoric and distanced himself from black-nationalist leaders. During his 1988 presidential campaign, he was kissing babies and milking cows in Iowa, while publicly distancing himself from Black Muslim leader Louis Farrakhan, who once was prominently involved in Jackson's dealings with the government of Syria for the release of a black American naval pilot, shot down in air combat. Jackson, for want of better things to do, now leads a campaign to replace the term "black" with "African American." We must no longer be called Afro-Americans either, because "Afro is a hairstyle," and whites, that is, European Americans, do not call themselves "Euro-American." They call themselves Polish-American or Irish-American. Well, regardless of what Italo-Americans or Franco-Americans or Anglo-Americans call themselves, we are supposed to insist on being called African Americans.[23]

Sadly, but predictably, we now read an article by Derrick Z. Jackson in the *Boston Globe* entitled "Please Don't Call Me Black: As History Will Show I'm African American." Derrick Jackson is aware of the work by the present author dealing with the naming controversy, from which he kindly quotes. Others, including Lerone Bennett and Sterling Stuckey, have also written on the subject of our constantly shifting preferences for ethno-racial signifiers. The point still needs to be driven home, however, that the unceasing obsession with what we are to call ourselves only reveals our pathetic powerlessness in dealing with the persistent issues of racism, colonialism, and the heritage of slavery. In a world as mad as our own — a world that is far more concerned with signs, symbols, Hollywood presidencies, and voodoo economics than with material realities — who knows? Our problems may eventually be solved on the level of rhetorical cosmetics and semantical games, rather than in economic or political reform.[24]

In the meantime, the pages of *Jet* and *Ebony* magazines, which are black publications, are filled with advertisements for hair straighteners and skin bleaches, produced by black-owned companies.[25] In the magazine *Africa Press Clips,* published in Vienna, Austria, one discovers an article by Jimoh Babalola, "Skin Bleaching An African Dilemma." Ironically, the article begins with a gross example of historical misinformation:

In the late 1960s and part of the early 1970s a light-skin culture swept Black America. Black college campuses bristled with Black women in white skin who, it appeared then, got on better with male students. Then came the *Black is Beautiful* movement which did a lot to promote Black pride and restore confidence to confused youth. If seems that in Africa, the youth are today still far away from this stage of Black consciousness.[26]

Mr. Babalola has his facts wrong; it was in the late sixties and early seventies that the "black is beautiful" movement thrived. Black Americans since that time, and contrary to the millenarian expectations of Bracey, have returned to the emulation of Euro-American norms of beauty. The most extreme forms of Eurocentrism are predictably most pronounced among the underclasses, that is to say, among the politically apathetic *lumpenproletariat*. Socialist presidential candidate Dr. Lenora Fulani, like most black women intellectuals of her age, still wears the "Afro" hairstyle. In fact, nowadays, we are almost willing to place bets that the typical black American woman who wears her hair in its "natural" state will be highly educated and probably over thirty-five.

One should not be excessively pessimistic, however. There will be new black movements, and black nationalism is not dying out. Black nationalism will continue to be an emotional force among the striving and entrepreneurial members of the working class and the middle class. It also has striking expressions of a utopian nature in its Hebraic and Islamic forms, which are most strongly manifested in the lower classes. Certain predictions can be made concerning black nationalism, based on the patterns of its past existence. Just as the black-nationalist movement of the period 1967–1976 was a by-product of trends in the larger society, so too will future black-nationalist movements continue to be influenced by trends in the larger American society that brings them into being. New movements that come into existence will be dominated by those who believe themselves to be discovering black consciousness for the first time. Just as many scholars and journalists during the sixties were inclined to overstress the "permanent" and "revolutionary" qualities of what was happening in our generation, we may expect a future generation of scholars and journalists to tell us how their movement represents a revolutionary break with the outmoded and regressive ideas of an irrelevant past.

N O T E S

1. James Turner, "Black Nationalism: The Inevitable Response," *Black World* (January 1971): 13.

2. Turner, "Black Nationalism," pp. 11–12. Stokely Carmichael and Charles V. Hamilton, *Black Power: The Politics of Liberation in America* (New York: Random House, 1967).

3. Edward Wilmot Blyden, *Christianity, Islam, and the Negro Race* (1887; reprint, Edinburgh: Edinburgh University Press, 1967), p. 24.

4. John H. Bracey, "Black Nationalism since Garvey," ed. Nathan Huggins et al. (New York: Harcourt Brace Jovanovich, 1971), pp. 259–79.

5. Louis Lomax, *To Kill a Black Man* (Los Angeles: Holloway House, 1968), p. 55. C. Eric Lincoln, *The Black Muslims in America* (Boston: Beacon Press, 1973), p. 112.

6. Louis Lomax, *When the Word is Given* (New York: Signet, 1964), p. 171.

7. Lomax, *To Kill a Black Man*, p. 63.

8. Malcolm X, *The Autobiography of Malcolm X*, ed. Alex Haley (New York: Grove Press, 1966), pp. 174–76.

9. Columbia *Daily Spectator*, 19 February 1965, quoted in *Malcolm X Speaks*, ed. George Breitman (New York: Grove Press, 1965), p. 17.

10. Malcolm X's socialist phase is well covered in George Breitman, ed., *By Any Means Necessary Speeches, Interviews, and a Letter, by Malcolm X* (New York: Pathfinder Press, 1970); George Breitman, *The Last Year of Malcolm X: The Evolution of a Revolutionary* (New York: Pathfinder Press, 1970); George Breitman et al., *The Assassination of Malcolm X.*, ed. Malik Miah (New York: Pathfinder Press, 1976); George Breitman and Albert Cleage, "Myths About Malcolm X," *International Socialist Review* (September–October 1967).

11. Stokely Carmichael, "Speech of July 28, 1966" in *Notes and Comment* (Chicago: Student Nonviolent Coordinating Committee, 1966, Mimeographed); reprinted in *Black Nationalism in America*, ed. John H. Bracey, Jr., et al. (Indianapolis: Bobbs-Merrill, 1970), pp. 470–76.

12. Carmichael and Hamilton, *Black Power*, p. 6.

13. Carmichael and Hamilton, *Black Power*, p. 183.

14. Carmichael and Hamilton, *Black Power*, pp. 82–83.

15. Christopher Lasch, *The Agony of the American Left* (New York: Vintage, 1969), contains a revised version of an essay review that originally appeared in the *New York Review of Books*. Harold Cruse, *The Crisis of the Negro Intellectual* (New York: Morrow, 1967).

16. Philip S. Foner, ed., *The Black Panthers Speak* (Philadelphia: Lippincott, 1970), p. xix. Recent republication of Cyril Briggs's radical journal *The Crusader* under the editorship of Robert Hill has opened up much of the history of the African Blood Brotherhood, an organization headed by Briggs in the 1920s.

17. Tom Wolfe, *Radical Chic & Mau-Mauing the Flak Catchers* (New York: Bantam, 1971), describes Leonard Bernstein's forty-eighth birthday party, to which Black Panthers were invited.

18. Julius Lester, *Look Out Whitey! Black Power's Gon' Get Your Mama* (New York: Grove Press, 1968). Eldridge Cleaver, *Soul on Ice* (New York: McGraw-Hill, 1968). Susan Brownmiller, *Against Our Will: Men, Women, and Rape* (New York: Simon and Schuster, 1975).

19. Bobby Seale, *Seize the Time: The Story of the Black Panther Party and Huey P. Newton* (New York: Vintage, 1970), pp. 181–87, 350, treats the Black Panther party's relationship to Bob Dylan, hippies, and Yippies.

20. Seale, *Seize the Time,* pp. 69–72; Huey Newton, *To Die for the People* (New York: Vintage, 1972), p. 31.

21. Shirley Chisholm, *Unbought and Unbossed* (New York: Avon, 1971), p. 12.

22. Bracey, "Black Nationalism since Garvey," p. 279. Houston Baker's position is stated in his *Black Literature in America* (New York: McGraw-Hill, 1971), p. 308.

23. For the observations of Jackson and others on the naming controversy, see *Boston Globe* (15 January 1989), p. A24.

24. Derrick Jackson cites Wilson J. Moses, *The Golden Age of Black Nationalism, 1850–1925* (Hamden, Conn.: Archon Books, 1978). See also Lerone Bennett, "What's in a Name," in *Americans From Africa: New Memories, New Moods,* ed. Peter Rose (New York: Atherton, 1970), pp. 373–84; and Sterling Stuckey, "Identity and Ideology: The Names Controversy," Chapter 4 of his *Slave Culture: Nationalist Theory and the Foundation of Black America* (New York: Oxford, 1987),pp. 193–244.

25. See, for example, *Jet,* 30 January 1989, full color advertisement on pp. 34–35 for Vanitex™ Skin Bleaching Creme. See also full color advertisement on pp. 25–26 announcing that "Smart Women Know How to Give Their Hair That Softer, Silkier, Sexier Look: *Raveen.*"

26. Jimoh Babalola, "Skin Bleaching: An African Dilemma," *Africa Press Clips* 1, 2 (1987–88).

PART III

Religion and the Afro-American Identity

CHAPTER 9

African Redemption and the Decline of the Fortunate Fall Doctrine

It has long been felt, and with good reason, that the most unfortunate idea to have developed among African-Americans during the eighteen and nineteenth centuries was the doctrine of the "Fortunate Fall." This was the belief that slavery, although a terrible affliction on the African people, would become, through the workings of divine providence, a blessing in the fullness of time. It is hardly surprising that a people subjected to universal and lifelong humiliation would find ways to rationalize their inescapable experience in ways that might save face. Historians and anthropologists have long been aware of so-called "revitalization movements" through which victims of colonization or other forms of subjugation have learned to transform the religion of their oppressors into means of controlling the oppressors themselves. In the confrontation with Christianity, Africans and Africans of the diaspora were able to utilize an adapted Christian rhetoric, not only to protect their own feelings of self-worth but also as a means of undermining the confidence of whites. Christian rhetoric could exploit any feelings of guilt that a Christian slaveholder might feel with respect to his own status as an oppressor; it could undermine his confidence and feelings of superiority. Christianity was a means whereby slaves exerted some influence over the behavior of slaveholders. It also provided rationalizations through which slaves could endure their position in the world as a subject race and at the same time maintain their self-respect.

The doctrine of the Fortunate Fall was therefore more than a justification for slavery; it was a view of life that allowed a racially oppressed people to come to grips with the unpleasant reality of their powerlessness, while at the same time maintaining a hope that their status was gradually improving.[1]

The Fortunate Fall doctrine appeared in the writings of Africans and African-Americans during the late eighteenth century and underwent various changes until the early twentieth century. At that point, the religious basis of black intellectual life was weakened by a confrontation with modernism and primitivism. Many writers and intellectuals had thoroughly rejected the doctrine by the time of the Harlem Renaissance. It is tempting to view the doctrine of the Fortunate Fall simply as a temporary, unfortunate, and misguided opinion of earlier generations of black Americans, who happened to be psychologically burdened with the unnecessary baggage of Christian mythology. I am inclined, however, to think that the problems of assimilation and self-concept that the doctrine illustrates are manifestations of patterns in African-American thought that have recurred in more recent ideology and that are still with us, albeit in disguised forms.

The idea of the Fortunate Fall goes back to an ancient paradox in Christian theology. The fundamental idea is that Adam's sin, while cataclysmically egregious, was nonetheless the source of history's greatest blessing. If he had not eaten of the forbidden fruit, he would have enjoyed preternatural bliss indefinitely, but the need for the Incarnation and Redemption would never have existed. The Son of God would never have exalted human flesh by taking on its substance; nor would He, by lying in the bonds of death, have made it possible for mankind to experience the joys of heaven. Thus, one sees repeatedly in Christian thought the theme of the Fortunate Fall, resulting from Adam's "happy fault," *felix culpa*; the phrase appears in the Roman liturgy, putatively an exclamation of Gregory the Great in the seventh century. All Christians believe that God in His providence allows evil to thwart His purposes, only so that He may in the process of His mysterious movements bring forth an even greater good than that originally ordained.[2]

Perfectionism is an equally ancient idea in Christian thought, sometimes seen as originating in the millenarianism of the fourth century. It is founded in the idea that the purpose of Christ and his New Covenant was to bring about a state of perfect world order, a social millennium, flowing naturally out of the spiritual rightness of the good Christian life. There are numerous possible explanations for the frequent occurrence of perfectionism in the writings of literate anglophone Africans in the late eighteenth century. The rise of Christian abolitionism was clearly one influence, as was the growth of enlightenment Christianity, with its doctrine of benevolence, that questioned the lingering, fatalistic pessimism of Calvinist orthodoxy. Most importantly, however, free Africans were a future-oriented people with rising expectations. Their marginal position as emancipated blacks was clearly an improvement over their earlier position as slaves. It should not be surprising that they welcomed change and were attracted to eighteenth-century liberalism with its cult of sensibility and its egalitarian doctrines. Hopes for the improvement of the African condition were based on the idea of the perfectibility of society through the triumph of reason, benevolence, and evangelical Christianity.

The social millenarianism that grew up among English-speaking Christianized Africans during the eighteenth century was sometimes combined with a black-nationalist ideology. This development was simultaneous with the rise of European and American nationalism, from which it borrowed much of its rhetoric. Black nationalism, like European and American nationalisms, attempted to link together a particularism and a universalism. The early black nationalists envisioned themselves as a chosen people working out an independent destiny but at the same time cooperating generously with the rest of the world, which they would lead by example in the direction of Christian progress. This idea was particularly prominent in North America, where it gave birth to the dream that black and white Americans would someday become a "united and happy people." The millennium was usually believed to be attainable by peaceful means. Strangely, there was little correspondence in the thinking of most writers between nationalism and revolution.

Not all the black writers of this period may rightly be called black nationalists, although as Bracey, Meier, Rudwick, and others have demonstrated, nationalistic themes appeared frequently in the writings of all of the most prominent black writers. This nationalism did not always imply the desire to emigrate to Africa or to seize a part of the New World as a national homeland, although such a yearning was always present for some. The element of nationalism present in early black writing was the chosen people doctrine, a belief that the providence of God singled out certain peoples for special suffering and tempered them in the process, so that they would be better fit to carry out world-historical missions. In the case of African-Americans, the missionary or messianic destiny was to advance the enlightenment of Africa and ultimately the elevation of all mankind.[3]

It has become commonplace to remark that Afro-Christianity on both sides of the Atlantic has drawn analogies between the sufferings of ancient Hebrews and modern African peoples. But the religious basis of black nationalism derives from more than this one simple analogy, for black Christians learned more than one lesson from the Bible. They believed that they were the woeful nation, Ethiopia, whose rising on mighty wings was foretold in Scripture. From extra-biblical sources, they absorbed the concept of divine providence, which seemed to suggest that good would always triumph over evil, despite some temporary setbacks.[4]

Westernized Africans in Europe and in America developed a theory of "African civilization," a doctrine that their continent should draw good out of evil by capitalizing on the effects of the slave trade. A bizarre example of this point of view was to be witnessed in the book written by Jacobus Elisa Johannes Capitein (1717–1747), a West African graduate of the University of Leiden, who had been kidnapped, enslaved, and Christianized as a boy. In 1742 he published in Dutch, *A Politico-Theological Investigation of Slavery as not Incompatible with Christian Liberty.*[5] This was an apology for the slave trade, which argued that the Dutch Company had brought the Africans "out of the land of bondage" to heathenism, and that the trade was to be praised as an agency for the saving of souls and the civilizing of savages. Such attitudes persisted among assimilated Anglo-Africans throughout the eighteenth century and can be witnessed in the well-known admonition of the North American slave poet Jupiter Hammon to a younger writer in 1778:

> O, come thou pious youth adore
>   The Wisdom of thy God
> In bringing thee from distant shore,
>   To learn His holy word.
>
> Thou mightst been left behind,
>   Amidst a dark abode;
> God's tender mercy still combined
>   Thou hast the holy word.[6]

The lines were addressed to Phillis Wheatley, but in her case the instruction was hardly needed. Wheatley had already recorded such sentiments in her reflections "On Being Brought From Africa to America."

> Twas mercy brought me from my Pagan land,
> Taught my benighted soul to understand
> That there's a God, that there's a Saviour too.
> Once I redemption neither sought nor knew.
> Some view our sable race with scornful eye;

"Their color is a diabolic dye."
Remember, Christians, Negroes, black as Cain,
May be refined, and join the angelic train.[7]

In another composition, the poetess described the land of her ancestors in wistful but contemptuous tones, as a sort of imperfect pseudo-Eden.

I, young in life, by seeming cruel fate,
Was snatched from Africa's fancied happy seat.[8]

The same contempt is present in the following lines, but without the mild nostalgic tones of the former.

'Twas not long since I left my native shore,
The land of errors and Egyptian gloom:
Father of mercy! 'Twas thy gracious hand
Brought me in safety from those dark abodes.[9]

Wheatley was typical of her generation of black writers in her preference for the English language, culture, and religion over the supposed "error and Egyptian gloom" of her "native land." Although Wheatley rejoiced in her deliverance from African heathenism, she nonetheless condemned slavery and the slave trade.

Steeled was the soul, and by no misery moved,
That from a father snatched his babe beloved.[10]

Wheatley's conception of the Fortunate Fall was a highly personalized one, a reflection on her own individual experience. Her poetry is not engaged in any definite way with exploring the macrocosmic implications of the slave trade, its meaning for Africa as a whole, or its meaning for the African race, either in the present or the future. Other Africans introduced a new strain into their thinking. This was the tendency to link together the slave trade with the spread of Christianity, commerce, and civilization into the black world. These elements would lead, so it was imagined, to the simultaneous achievement of desirable goals—the redemption of Africa and the abolition of slavery. Thus would the evil of slavery recoil upon itself to its own destruction, and thus from the temporary catastrophe of slavery would spring the providential blessings of African regeneration, both spiritual and temporal.

Early black writers, with the exception of Capitein, condemned slavery unequivocally, but they hoped to convert it into a providential instrument of African redemption. African redemption and civilization, used in the broadest sense, do not refer solely to the uplift of the mother continent. The words signify a complex of utopian expectations. They represent the aspiration of a small and perhaps atypical group of black people, who lived during the late eighteenth century. Those Africans who were capable of expressing their views in literary form showed certain characteristics. Although they had been born of African parents, they had been Christian English speakers since childhood, and while they identified with the African continent and its misfortunes, their ties to their original African ethnic heritages had been lost. Their conception of a future perfect society was based on the idea that Africans, whether in Africa or abroad, should adopt English religion, culture, and family structure. They foresaw the development of a modern Christian state on the African continent.

The three best known African Redemptionists of the eighteenth century were Ignatius Sancho, Ottabah Cugoano, and Gustavus Vassa, who provide us with some interesting angles on the Fortunate Fall controversy. Sancho, although perhaps the most thoroughly acculturated of the three, seemed to be guardedly skeptical with respect to the doctrine. His ambition, in any case, was to find acceptance in England as a Christian bourgeois gentleman. Cugoano, the writer who expressed the most anger, made it clear that the infinitesimal good that came to slaves could in no way justify slave trading. He hoped to witness the rise of a proud and powerful African state, as a vindication of the abilities of African people. Gustavus Vassa represented an ambivalent and vacillating course between these two sets of attitudes. Given the thoroughness of their commitment to English Protestantism, at least on the rhetorical level, one should not be surprised at the way in which some Englishmen came to interpret the African mind.

> My mother bore me in the southern wild
> And I am black, but O! my soul is white.[11]

William Blake, the author, may have accurately portrayed the emotions of some Christianized Africans with these lines. The writings of Ignatius Sancho would have little to disabuse him of such notions as the verse reveals. Sancho was born in the "southern wild" but on a slave ship a few days off the cost of Guinea in 1729. His parents died shortly after their arrival in the New World, his mother falling victim to some unknown disease, his father a suicide. He was christened Ignatius by the Roman Catholic bishop at Cartagena. At the age of two, he was brought by his master to England and given to three maiden sisters, who endowed him with the surname Sancho, fancying that he bore a resemblance to the squire of Don Quixote. Sancho learned to read as a result of the munificence of the Duke of Montague, and when the duke died, he prevailed upon the duchess — after a period of desperate entreaty and threats of suicide — to admit him into her household, where he served as a butler until her death. The duchess bequeathed the young African an annuity of thirty pounds, and he had savings amounting to seventy. But Sancho squandered his first fortune on women and gambling, lost his clothes in a game of cribbage, and spent his last shilling on a Shakespeare play.[12]

Sancho later returned to Montague House to enter the service of the chaplain and later that of the new duke. Having now reached an age of greater experience and stability, he forswore the dissipation of youth, settled his thoughts on marriage, and found a young woman of West Indian origins to share his lot. His biographer relates that towards the end of the year 1773, "repeated attacks of the gout, and a constitutional corpulence, rendered him incapable of further attendance in the Duke's family." Apparently, however, the Montagues were still kindly disposed, and thanks to their good agencies and his own newfound frugality, he was able to establish himself as a grocer at 20 Charles Street, Westminster. He settled down to a comfortable existence as a virtuous, jolly burgher, tending to his business, bringing up six children, keeping abreast of public affairs, and maintaining a good-natured and graceful correspondence with his numerous friends.

Sancho's abolitionism was inseparable from his concept of benevolent Christianity. He spoke only occasionally of slavery, although when he did so, it was in strong, unequivocal language. He denounced that "unchristian and most diabolical usage of my brother Negroes — the illegality — the horrid wickedness of the traffic — the cruel carnage and depopulation of the human species. . . . " He wrote to the novelist Laurence Sterne in July 1776, identifying himself as "one of those people whom the vulgar and illiberal call 'Negurs,' " to thank the author for a few words he had written to attack slavery. He asked Sterne to devote his talents to an antislavery tract directed particularly at the West Indies, which subject, said Sancho, "handled in your striking manner would ease the yoke (perhaps) of many — but if only of one — gracious God! — what a feast to a benevolent heart."[13]

His response to the celebrity of Phillis Wheatley in 1778 was in quite a different vein than that of Jupiter Hammon, whose Fortunate Fall doctrine led him to advise enduring slavery with patience and with Christian gratitude. Sancho reacted indignantly and had no kind words either for the master or for those who praised Wheatley's accomplishments without concern for her state of enslavement.

Phillis's poems do credit to nature—and put art—merely as art to the blush.—It reflects nothing either to the glory or generosity of her master—if she is still his slave—except he glories in the *low vanity* of having in his wanton power a mind animated by Heaven—a genius superior to himself.— The list of splendid—titled—learned names, in confirmation of her being the real authoress—alas! shows how very poor the acquisition of wealth and knowledge is without generosity—feeling—and humanity.—These good great folks—all know—and perhaps admire—nay, praised Genius in bondage—and then like the Priests and the Levites in the sacred writ, passed by—not one good Samaritan amongst them.[14]

Sancho was obviously not interested in praising the virtues of even the most benevolent slave-holders. He expressed indignation at even the mildest examples of slavery and seemed less convinced than Phillis was herself of the good fortune of her fall. With respect to his own fate, Sancho clearly considered himself fortunate to have been blessed with literacy and enlightened Christianity, but he was happy enough to utilize these gifts in pleading the cause of antislavery, although he recorded no interest in African redemption. When anti-Catholic rioting broke out in London in 1780, he pointed to the "worse than Negro barbarity of the populace," asserting "I am not sorry I was born in Africa." Clearly he was no champion of the claim that the slave trade had introduced a higher and nobler civilization into the world of Africans. He had seen enough examples of Christian civilization on the streets of London.

Sancho did not choose to examine such problems at length, however. He masked the painfulness of his condition with an easygoing sense of humor and saw his blackness as only one of his personal attributes. He saw his blackness as an aspect of himself rather than projecting his personality as an expression of his blackness. He tried to escape seeing himself as a manifestation of a color phenomenon. In other words, he portrayed himself as a man of many parts, who was, among other things, fat, black, literate, Christian, and philanthropic. His blackness did not make him beautiful, nor was it to be separated from the other realities of a persona that he presented as tragicomical. He once described himself as a "coal black jolly African, who wishes health and peace to every religion and country throughout the ample range of God's creation." On another occasion, he pictured himself "a man of convexity of belly exceeding Falstaff—and a black face into the bargain—waddling in the van of poor thieves and penniless prostitutes—with all the supercilious mock dignity of little office—what a banquet for wicked jest and wanton wit." One is led to believe that although he made light of his situation, he was painfully aware of the capacity of the English streets for crime, depravity, and petty cruelty.[15]

The letters of Sancho reveal a shrewd and diplomatic mind, which made use of the Christian rhetoric of his adopted culture while skillfully avoiding anything approximating an endorsement of the process whereby he had acquired it. He would not concede that Christianity had done anything for Africa. The Europeans had found the Africans poor, benighted savages and had proceeded to debase them even further by carrying them "strong liquors to enflame their natural madness — and powder and bad firearms, to furnish them with the hellish means of killing and kidnapping." Sancho seldom let drop the persona of the "good-natured man" and hastened to assure his friends that he mentioned the evils of the slave trade only to guard "against being too hasty in condemning the knavery of a people who bad as they may be — possibly were made worse by their Christian visitors."[16] His theory of African underdevelopment anticipated those of Walter Rodney and Chinweizu, two hundred years later.[17] The causes of African backwardness were largely attributable to the Christians' greed for "Money — money — money," for which Sancho did not unequivocally blame them.[18] He accepted the popular views of John Locke and Adam Smith that the making of money was a virtuous and benevolent activity.

> Commerce was meant by the goodness of the Deity to diffuse the various goods of the earth into every part — to unite mankind in the blessed chains of brotherly love, society, and mutual dependence. — the enlightened Christian should diffuse the riches of the Gospel of peace, with the commodities of his respective land — Commerce attended with strict honesty, and with Religion for its companion, would be a blessing to every sore it touched at.[19]

Christianity, commerce, and civilization would function as collateral agencies for the solution of the problems of Africa. Sancho clearly felt that he could mirror the affability and common sense of the English middle class, and by his personal representation of literary and intellectual skill, contribute to benevolent attitudes towards the African continent and the African race. Thus, by his fall into slavery, Sancho had become an agency of that providence that would redeem the continent of Africa through a refinement of the mercantile passions that had led to the slave trade.

Ottabah Cugoano, who was born in Fanti country in the Gold Coast around 1757, was less infatuated with English manners than Sancho; his writing was more political and more resentful. Cugoano was kidnapped while playing with a group of other children in the year 1770, marched to the sea, and taken on board a slave ship. "I must own," he later said, "to the shame of my countrymen, that I was first kid-napped and betrayed by some of my own complexion, who were the first cause of my exile and slavery; but if there were no buyers there would be no sellers." While the ship lay at anchor off the coast, the band of captives began to plot a rebellion, but "we were betrayed by one of our country-women, who slept with some of the head men of the ship, for it was common for the dirty filthy sailors to take the African women and lie upon their bodies." Cugoano spent some nine or ten months in a slave gang at Grenada, and another year travelling to various other places in the West Indies as the servant of Alexander Campbell, who brought him to England in 1772. The following year, having undertaken a course of study in matters both religious and secular, he was baptized under the name John Stewart.[20]

On the level of thankfulness for his own conversion and salvation, Cugoano shared Wheatley's Fortunate Fall doctrine. In 1787, the year of the founding of the British colony in Sierra Leone as a haven for free Europeanized Africans, he published *Thoughts and Sentiments on the Evil of Slavery,* in which he said it was God's mercy and providence that had brought him away from his native land, albeit in a "torrent of robbery and wickedness." He compared his fortunes to those of Joseph, that prophet of the Old Testament sold by his brothers into slavery so that he might be of benefit to them in God's good time. He adopted the work of abolitionism with a will, reading in the works of Thomas Clarkson and Granville Sharp. He befriended Gustavus Vassa, and like Vassa he expressed a desire to return to Africa and perhaps discover what had become of his family, "as soon as I can hear any proper security and safe conveyance can be found. For the present, he considered prospects for African regeneration to be unlikely. Sierra Leone existed in the shadow of slave fortresses and garrisons, symbols of the continuing traffic in slaves.

On another level, Cugoano's ideology was totally at odds with the Fortunate Fall doctrine. He had no patience with the position once taken by Jacobus Capitein that slavery was compatible with Christianity. Furthermore, he revealed bitterness and militancy totally foreign to the writings of Wheatley, Sancho, or Capitein, and this was accompanied by a nascent cultural nationalism. Although Cugoano had received a Christian name at baptism, he published the book under his African name because "no name, whether Christian or Pagan, has anything to do with baptism. . . . And Christianity does not require that we be deprived of our own personal name or the use of the name of our ancestors." The fact that Cugoano not only insisted on using his African rather than his Christian name, and the fact that he took pains to call attention to this fact and to justify it, indicates a symbolic rejection of the supposed fruits of anglicization. Cugoano accepted Christianity on one level because it offered rhetorical weapons in the struggle for self-assertion, allowing him to exploit the guilt of English Christians. At the same time, he rejected what he perceived as one of the less useful symbols of his Christianization, the name given to him at baptism, John Stewart.[21]

There can be no equivocation about the fact that Cugoano appreciated his own conversion; personal salvation was not, however, the only message that he found in the Bible. He took greater consolation from such theses as judgement of the wicked, and he pounced with enthusiasm on an idea he found in the writings of British abolitionists, that "though the world is not the place of final retribution, yet there is an evidence maintained in the course of Divine Providence, that verily there is a God that judgeth in the earth." Cugoano made his point repeatedly, finding support in biblical verses for his argument that England would be punished for her part in the slave trade. He quoted Deuteronomy: "The Lord shall bring a nation against thee, from the ends of the earth, as swift as the eagle flieth, a nation whose tongue thou shalt not understand. . . . " Cugoano stated a theme that was to be stated repeatedly in black literature during the ensuing century—the idea that Anglo-Saxon dominance could not endure forever and that the English-speaking civilization was doomed, like all the great civilizations of the past, to decline and decay, while other nations would rise with the revolutions of fortune's wheel.[22]

Another aspect of the Fortunate Fall doctrine can be observed in *The Interesting Narrative of the Life of Olaudah Equiano, or Gustavus Vassa, the African*. It tells the story of a young man of the Ibo people, kidnapped and enslaved at the age of eleven, taken to the Americas and converted to Christianity, eventually to become a proto-black nationalist in England. To the unsophisticated young African, the first whites he ever saw appeared to be superhumans, perhaps devils or sorcerers. He thought that he "had gotten into a world of bad spirits, and that they were going to kill me." His first experiences with such wonders as a wind-powered sailing vessel, a watch, and a portrait had the immediate effect of convincing him of the superiority of the whites and of their magic. After living for two or three years among the Europeans and learning something of their customs and language, his fear and astonishment were considerably diminished, and he eventually "relished their society and manners."

> I no longer looked upon them as spirits, but as men superior to us; and therefore I had the stronger desire to resemble them, to imbibe their spirit, and imitate their manners. I therefore embraced every occasion of improve-

ment, and every new thing that I observed I treasured up in my memory. I had long wished to be able to read and write; and for this purpose I took every opportunity to gain instruction. . . . When I went to London with my master, I had soon an opportunity of improving myself, which I gladly embraced.[23]

Vassa had come to look on whites not as spirits but as men who enjoyed a superficial superiority but were not superior by nature. Circumstances had endowed them with a temporary and assailable superiority, and he determined to emulate them and to compete with them. Furthermore, he was determined to work for the elevation of his fellow Africans.

Are there not causes enough to which the apparent inferiority of an African may be ascribed without limiting the goodness of God, and supposing he forebore to stamp understanding on certainly his own image because "carved in ebony." Might it not naturally be ascribed to their situation? When they come among Europeans, they are ignorant of their language, religion, manners, and customs. Are they treated as men? Does not slavery itself depress the mind, and extinguish all fire, and every noble sentiment?[24]

After his conversion and baptism in 1759, Vassa, at the urging of his employer, considered going to Sierra Leone as a missionary, and his writings have often been viewed as important documents of incipient pan-African nationalism. True enough, Vassa became disillusioned with the prospects of the Sierra Leone colony, but he never abandoned the idea that importation of free trade and Christian nationalism would provide the ingredients for a regeneration of the African continent. He was typical of his contemporaries in that he linked the concepts of Christianity, commerce, and civilization, which he saw as collateral agents for the uplift of Africa. Also, like his contemporaries, he felt that free trade between the white world and West Africa could undermine the slave trade, which would be unable to compete with legitimate commerce. Merchants and traders, especially in England, should unite in the causes of abolitionism and African uplift, since legitimate trade with Christianized and civilized Africans would provide a market for British industry.

Population, the bowels and surface of Africa, abound in valuable and useful returns; the hidden treasures of centuries will be brought to light and into circulation. Industry, enterprise, and mining will have their full scope, proportionally as they civilize. In a word, it lays open an endless field of commerce to the British manufacturers and merchant adventurer. The manufacturing interest and the general interest are synonymous. The abolition of slavery would be in reality an universal good.[25]

The universalist attitudes that Vassa expressed were perhaps proto-nationalistic, as Imanuel Geiss has suggested, but they differed considerably from the more militant expressions of black nationalism that evolved during the ensuing century. The Anglocentric mercantilism that he advocated would have been unacceptable to the economic black nationalists of the 1850s, who foresaw African-controlled economies as the basis of real African power. The idea of "Africa for the Africans," if it occurred to him at all, was never publicly advocated. He believed that European civilization could be advantageously absorbed by Africans, an idea that was rejected by many of his contemporaries, who believed that Africans were doomed to perpetual savagery. Vassa may therefore be viewed as a prophet of the "African Redemptionism" ideology that was to appear in the nineteenth century. At this stage, he argued that the civilization of Africa would have to be effected before the abolition of slavery could be accomplished, and Christianization was seen as a collateral, if not a prior, necessity to civilization.

Vassa had no intention of setting out as a missionary for Sierra Leone, however, or even for his native Iboland, and he soon adopted a more practical view on African redemption. Assuming a more immediatist position on abolition, he came to believe that so long as the slave trade persisted, it would be impossible to found an African civilization. There was inordinate risk involved in attempting to set up a city on a hill alongside a slave fortress. How would the inhabitants be able to maintain security while all along the coast, warfare for black cargoes was constant? One suspects that the most important reason for Vassa's lukewarm support of colonization was his persistent "relish" for the "society and manners" of the Europeans among whom he lived. The utopia of Gustavus Vassa was not to be a neo-African culture but an integrated world order, in which all Christians would dwell happily together under European customs and values. Like the speaker of Blake's poem "The Little Black Boy," his soul was white and in his heavenly destination, he was to be transfigured along with his English counterpart.

> And then I'll stand and stroke his silver hair
> And be like him and he will then love me

A paradox of eighteenth-century Christianity in the English speaking world was its frequent linkage of cultural assimilation to African political idealism. This pattern in the thinking of its exponents has been referred to as "civilization," the belief that Africans would be uplifted and redeemed in proportion to their acceptance of European civilization. Africans, Anglo-Africans, and African-Americans continued to manifest a concern for proving their capacity for civilization and their relish for European society and manners. When they were excluded from white institutions, they formed black versions of the same, usually preserving the names and rituals of the originals, as in the case of the Methodist Church and the Masonic Temple. They thus demonstrated a commitment to cultural parallelism, not counterculturalism.

By implication, early black nationalism and pan-Africanism continued to conceal the Fortunate Fall doctrine, even after opposition to that doctrine in its overt form had become repugnant. The career of Captain Paul Cuffe, the black shipping merchant, illustrates how African Redemptionist ideology was linked to concepts of European cultural superiority in the early decades of the nineteenth century. Cuffe hoped to get the cooperation of the British government in opening up Sierra Leone to African Americans, and he was eventually able to carry a group of thirty-eight to the colony in 1816. Like Cugoano and Vassa, he had a vision of the civilization and redemption of Africa through commerce. He hoped to render the chiefs "friendly towards civilization" and to persuade them to establish European style factories as a means of making them less dependent on the slave trade. Cuffe saw himself as providing the repatriated black Americans with an opportunity "to rise to their proper level." He hoped that his commercial activities might encourage a means of putting an end to the slave trade and bringing the Africans into "the true light of Christianity."[26]

The African Redemptionism favored by Paul Cuffe fell into disfavor with the majority of black Americans in 1817 with the founding of the American Society for Colonizing the Free People of Color of the United States. The fact that this society included among its membership a significant number of slaveholders, whose only goal was to get rid of the "free African" population, fueled the belief that the society's benevolent aims were sheer hypocrisy. The real aim was to deport, along with the free Negroes, any political activism that might breed unrest among the slaves. During the antebellum decades, most writers became aware of the dangers of asserting that the enslavement of the Africans had been permitted by God as a means of bringing about African Redemption. But African Redemptionism did not die out as a result, nor did the religious arguments used to support African emigration movements.[27]

The Liberian nationalist Edward Blyden toured the United States in 1862, preaching on "The Call of Providence to the Descendants of Africa in America." He was careful to disassociate his African Redemptionism from any apparent associations with the Fortunate Fall doctrine.

> It can not be denied that some very important advantages have accrued to the black man from his deportation to this land, but it has been at the

expense of his manhood. Our nature in this country is not the same as it appears among the lordly natives of the interior of Africa, who have never felt the trammels of a foreign yoke. We have been dragged into depths of degradation. We have been taught a cringing servility. We have been drilled into a contentment with the most undignified circumstances.[28]

Blyden spoke of the call of providence to Christianized blacks in America to return as cultural, religious, and economic missionaries to the fatherland. He phrased his words carefully, however, and never actually said that the slave trade was part of the divine plan for the Christianization and civilization of Africa. There were, however, those who felt he had associated himself with such a position. Frederick Douglass was one of those, and he attacked the position of those who larded their colonization rhetoric with references to the call of providence.

> The satanic spirit of colonization, craftily veiling itself in the livery of Heaven, and speaking in the name of Divine Providence, proceeds with more than usual vigor to unchain, and let loose upon us, all the malignant and satanic influences of the country. The Colonization Herald, whether intentionally or otherwise is cooperating with the infernal spirit of persecution.[29]

Surprisingly, the Liberian nationalist Alexander Crummell agreed with Douglass when it came to the Fortunate Fall doctrine. Although he was the African civilizationist and colonizationist par excellence, he emphatically denied that slavery had played a significant role in the Christianization of Africa. The typical colonist sent to Africa by the American Colonization Society was "ignorant, benighted and besotted," and showed few if any signs of exposure to the gospel. They were, therefore, not fit to be representatives of the gospel in Africa. The masses of the slaves had never experienced anything resembling an exposure to Christianity. Long after emancipation, he continued to dismiss arguments of those who insisted that slavery had been a Christianizing and civilizing agency. The southern black population had not been uplifted, civilized, or even Christianized by their experience in the United States.

> Their whole history for two hundred years has been a history of moral degradation deeper and more damning than their heathen status in Africa. I am speaking of aggregates. I grant the individual advantages to scores and hundreds which have sprung from contact with Christian people. I am speaking of the moral condition of the MASSES, who have been under the yoke; and I unhesitatingly affirm that they would have been more blessed and far superior as pagans in Africa than slaves on the plantations of the South.[30]

Booker T. Washington was a throwback representing the Fortunate Fall doctrine in its most extreme form; he made the following statements, which were widely circulated in his book *Black Belt Diamonds*:

We went into slavery in this Country pagans; we came out Christians.

We went into slavery without a language; we came out speaking the proud Anglo Saxon Tongue.

If in the providence of God the Negro got any good out of slavery, he got the habit of work.[31]

Washington believed that the slavery experience had endowed black Americans with a mission "to teach the white man a lesson of patience, forbearance, and forgiveness." It was in reaction to such rhetorical peccancies that militant cultural nationalists like W. E. B. Du Bois came to oppose the leadership of Booker T. Washington. His progressive views on industrial efficiency, thrift, and material progress were apposite, but Washington overlooked the strategic injudiciousness of praising white folk too hastily for their supposed cultural uplift of African-Americans. Du Bois, it must be admitted, also tended to view black people sentimentally, as he spoke of the Christlike suffering that black people had undergone, which had supposedly endowed them with a second sight, a messianic vision.

Many of the writers who dominated the New Negro renaissance of the 1920s demonstrated a flagrant disregard for the traditional redemptionist panaceas of Christianity, commerce, and civilization. W. E. B. Du Bois displayed a perverse inconsistency concerning Christian discourse in his *Darkwater,* where, for rhetorical purposes at least, he was willing to say, "I believe in God."[32] He also created his own Christian myth on the nativity of the black Christ, "Jesus Christ in Texas," and speculated on "The Prayers of God." A younger generation of bohemians, including Langston Hughes and Claude McKay, never particularly captivated by the Christian rhetoric of past generations, moved in the direction of Marxist materialist doctrines and showed no interest in revitalizing the old-fashioned redemptionist myths. Another young man, Marcus Garvey, clung to the ancient Christian civilizationist rhetoric, but there was absolutely no sentimentality concerning slavery in his speeches and writings. Non-Christian black sects and cults that came to prominence during and after the First World War were quite emphatic in their rejection of the long-suffering Christian image, and since they were often Muslim or Hebraic in their mythologies, they had no place for the Christian doctrine of the Fortunate Fall in their ideologies.

While most African-Americans seem to have outgrown the doctrine of the Fortunate Fall in its Christian forms, secularized cognates and analogues of the doctrine still persist. Much recent scholarship, with its sentimental treatment of slavery, seeks to flatter the egos of black bourgeois intellectuals by gratifying their desire for a respectable past, in which they can view themselves as just another ethnic group. It also updates the Fortunate Fall myth that has always asserted that slavery was a positive, healthy experience during which an admirable culture was formed. There are also Marxist formulations of a Fortunate Fall doctrine that view black people as particularly suited for martyrlike roles in subversive movements. Middle-aged New Leftists, living in gentrified communes on inherited wealth, are quick to lecture their black counterparts on the virtues of poverty and suffering. Like prior generations of American radicals, they have assigned a role of martyrdom and long-suffering to black Americans, whom they perceive as cannon fodder for the revolution. Civil libertarians close ranks with conservatives to attack affirmative action programs, designed to improve the material welfare of black Americans. They unite with the shrillest protesters against "reverse discrimination," clearly betraying their belief that African-Americans are somehow an advantaged group and that they are "fortunate" to be black and in the United States, where they can experience the pampered status of a chosen people.

N O T E S

1. A. F. C. Wallace, "Revitalization Movements," *American Anthropology* 58(April 1956): 264–81, and Peter Worsley, *The Trumpet Shall Sound* (London: McGibbon & Kee, 1968). For other discussions of the transformation of Christian religious ideals, see Vittorio Lanternari, *The Religions of the Oppressed* (New York: Knopf, 1963); George Shepperson, "Ethiopianism and African Nationalism," *Phylon* 14(1953): 9–18; St. Clair Drake, *The Redemption of Africa and Black Religion* (Chicago: Third World Press, 1970).

2. A. O. Lovejoy, *Essays in the History of Ideas* (Baltimore: Johns Hopkins Press, 1948).

3. John H. Bracey, Jr., et al., eds., *Black Nationalism in America* (Indianapolis: Bobbs-Merrill, 1970).

4. For commentary on "Ethiopianism" and the adaptation of Hebraic mythology by black Christians, see Shepperson, "Ethiopianism and African Nationalism"; Gayraud S. Wilmore, *Black Religion and Black Radicalism* (Garden City, N.Y.: Doubleday, 1972), pp. 51–53; Drake, *Redemption of Africa and Black Religion.*

5. The contributions of Capitein are discussed in Janheinz Jahn, *Neo African Literature: A History of Black Writing* (New York: Grove Press, 1968), p. 35.

6. Jupiter Hammon, "An Address to Miss Phillis Wheatley," *Early American Negro Poets,* ed. William H. Robinson (Dubuque, Iowa: Wm. C. Brown, 1969). In a similar vein, one should see *Hammon's Address to the Negroes of the State of New York* (New York, 1787).

7. *Life and Works of Phillis Wheatley,* ed. G. Herbert Renfro (Washington, D.C.: Leila Amos Pendleton, 1916), p. 48.

8. *Life and Works of Phillis Wheatley,* p. 80.

9. *Life and Works of Phillis Wheatley,* p. 46.

10. *Life and Works of Phillis Wheatley,* p. 80.

11. William Blake, "The Little Black Boy," universally anthologized.

12. Ignatius Sancho, *Letters of the Late Ignatius Sancho, an African,* 5th ed. (London, 1803). The photographic facsimile reprint (London, 1968) contains biographical material on Sancho by Paul Edwards to supplement the memoirs of Sancho's life by Joseph Jekyll prefixed to the edition of 1803.

13. Ignatius Sancho to Laurence Sterne, July 1776, in Sancho, *Letters,* pp. 70–72.

14. Ignatius Sancho to Mr. F——, 27 January 1778, in Sancho, *Letters,* pp. 125–27.

15. Sancho's observations on the riots of 1789 are in Sancho, *Letters,* pp. 269–84. He compares himself to Falstaff on p. 238 of same.

16. Sancho, *Letters,* p. 149.

17. Walter Rodney, *How Europe Underdeveloped Africa* (London: Bogle-L'Ouverture Publications, 1972). Chinweizu, *The West and the Rest of Us* (New York: Vintage Books, 1974).

18. Sancho, *Letters,* p. 149.

19. Ibid.

20. Ottabah Cugoano, *Thoughts and Sentiments on the Evil of Slavery* (London, 1787), pp. 10, 12.

21. Cugoano, *Thoughts and Sentiments,* p. 147.

22. Cugoano, *Thoughts and Sentiments,* p. 117.

23. *The Interesting Narrative of the Life of Olaudah Equiano, or Gustavus Vassa, the African* (London, 1789), reprinted in *Great Slave Narratives,* comp. Arna Bontemps (Boston: Beacon, 1969), pp. 48–49.

24. Vassa, *Narrative,* p. 17.

25. Vassa, *Narrative,* p. 190.

26. Paul Cuffe to John James and Alexander Wilson, 10 June 1909, *Paul Cuffe: Black America and the African Return,* ed. Sheldon Harris (New York: Simon and Schuster, 1972), p. 166.

27. P. J. Staudenraus, *The African Colonization Movement, 1816–1865* (New York: Columbia University Press, 1961). Floyd J. Miller, *The Search for a Black Nationality: Black Emigration and Colonization, 1787–1863* (Urbana: University of Illinois Press, 1975). Wilson J. Moses, *The Golden Age of Black Nationalism, 1850–1925* (Hamden, Conn.: Archon Books, 1978).

28. Edward Wilmot Blyden, "The Call of Providence to Descendants of Africa in America," from his *Liberia's Offering* (New York: John Gray, 1862), reprinted in Howard Brotz, *Negro Social and Political Thought, 1850–1920* (New York: Basic Books, 1966), p. 113.

29. Frederick Douglass, "The Spirit of Colonization," *Douglass Monthly* (September 1862).

30. Alexander Crummell, "A Defence of the Negro Race in America," in his *Africa and America: Addresses and Discourses* (Springfield, Mass.: Wiley & Co., 1891), p. 92.

31. Booker T. Washington, *Black Belt Diamonds: Gems from the Speeches, Addresses and Talks to Students,* ed. T. Thomas Fortune and Victoria Earle Matthews (New York: Fortune and Scott, 1898).

32. W. E. B. Du Bois, *Darkwater: Voices from Within the Veil* (New York: Harcourt, Brace, and Howe, 1920), p. 3.

National Destiny and the Black Bourgeois Ministry

hile not every black American religious leader of the nineteenth century was a black nationalist, most of the best known and most literate clergy occasionally revealed elements of nationalism in their writing. African-American nationalism, in its purest form, must include, among its other ingredients, the quest for a national homeland, and it is perhaps incorrect to refer to anyone as a black nationalist unless he or she favors territorial separatism. But black nationalism has other ingredients besides territorial separatism, and most black leaders have some of the other ingredients of nationalism in their thinking, such as marital or institutional separatism. They believe that black Americans are a "people" rather than a mere ethnic group, that they have a history that separates them in essential ways from other Americans, and that they have a destiny to remain permanently separate from the rest of America. Historically, black nationalism has almost invariably been accompanied by a religious rhetoric; in fact, it might almost be perceived as a variety of religion in itself. The work of E. Franklin Frazier and Randall Burkett on the Garvey movement, and E. U. Essien-Udom on the Nation of Islam, has directed our thinking along these lines.[1]

Black nationalism and religious teleology seemed invariably to overlap in the thinking of major black religious thinkers during the nineteenth century, and the fact that black religious leaders have long been interested in black nationalism and pan-Africanism has attracted the attention of a number of scholars over the past twenty years.[2] Commentary on the exact nature of this interest has been less frequent, however, than the mere observation that such interest has existed. It is important to note that the period in American history during which the black clergy were most interested in nationalism was a period during which American nationalism and "missionary zeal to transform the world" were in their earlier developmental stages.[3] Thus, the black nationalism of the period was influenced by the expansionist rhetoric of American Protestantism and by the views of American destiny that were current among white clergymen throughout the nineteenth and early twentieth centuries. Alexander Crummell actually used the term "manifest destiny" in his speeches, but the theme was implicit in most black-nationalist rhetoric of the period.[4]

American religion is militant, crusading, self-righteous, and violent, and black American religion inevitably absorbed, along with the idea of Manifest Destiny, the idea of the Christian soldier. Although doctrines related to chosen peoples, covenants with God, and righteous wrath were not a part of the slave catechism, it is obvious that the slaves were never insulated from such ideas. White preachers spoke of smiting their enemies all the time, and as the Nat Turner incident effectively illustrates, a few slaves learned, all too well, the unbendingly righteous lessons of American Christianity. Washerwomen, trusted family retainers, and little children who accompanied their mothers to the white folks' Sunday services absorbed the messages of American Christian militancy and nurtured them within their hearts.

But the simple fact that black Americans adopted the ideas of Manifest Destiny and "regeneration through violence" from white American Christianity does not make them black nationalists. What we mean by black nationalism is purely and simply the belief among African-Americans that they constitute a nation, due to their common history, common destiny, and unbridgeable distinctiveness. The idea that black Americans are a permanently distinct people was widespread among nineteenth-century black Americans and is still virtually unopposed today. A belief in African-American destiny did not mean that black Americans should leave for Africa; it did not mean that they should give up their rights under the American Constitution. In the mind of Francis J. Grimké, African-Americans constituted a people who had been separate in the past but might be assimilated in the future. In the minds of others, like Henry Highland Garnet, the Zionist model predominated, and a search for a homeland was at least of passing importance, although the struggle for rights in America must be unrelenting. Territorial separatism was not always present in the political ideology of black Americans, but almost invariably theories of the destiny of black Americans were present, mingled with civil religion and a teleological rhetoric.

The religious fervor of nineteenth-century black nationalism can be conveniently illustrated by the works of Maria Stewart, who, although she opposed the idea of territorial separatism, employed an Old-Testament "Zionist" rhetoric in describing the predicament of black Americans. She clearly perceived her people as a "nation" and compared them not only to Old Testament Hebrews but also to the "suffering Greeks," whose "proud souls revolted at serving a tyrannical nation"; to the Haitians, whose "firmness of character and independence of spirit have been greatly admired, and highly applauded"; and to the Poles, "who rose against three hundred thousand mighty men of Russia." She called on black Americans to exhibit the spirit of unity that had raised other nations in the esteem of the world, saying "even the wild Indians of the forest are more United than ourselves. . . . They also have contended for their rights and privileges, and are held in higher repute than we are."

> But God has said that, Ethiopia shall stretch forth her hands unto him. True, but God uses means to bring about his purposes; and unless the rising generation manifest a different temper and disposition towards each other from what we have manifested, the generation following will never be an enlightened people. We this day are considered as one of the most degraded races on the face of the earth. . . .
>
> And why is it, my friends, that we are despised above all nations upon the earth? Is it merely because our skins are tinged with a sable hue? No, nor will I ever believe that it is. What then is it; Oh, it is because that we and our fathers have dealt treacherously with one another, and because many of us now possess that envious and malicious disposition, that we had rather die than see each other rise an inch above a beggar. No gentle methods are used to promote love and friendship among us, but much is done to destroy it. Shall we be a hissing and a reproach among the nations of the earth any longer? Shall they laugh us to scorn forever?[5]

Stewart, like her contemporary, David Walker, possessed a religiously based black nationalism and saw African-Americans as a modern Israel in Babylon, but like Walker she opposed colonization and the Back to Africa movement. She was not prepared to take up the cry of "come out from among them" and therefore lacked the geopolitical ambitions of the true nationalist. Nonetheless, there was in her orations and meditations a nationalist spirit, as there was in *David Walker's Appeal,* and she clearly viewed black Americans as a nation, despite her lack of willingness to carry her nationalism to its ultimate logical expression of territorial separatism.[6]

Of course, there were plenty of territorial separatists among black Americans. They were sometimes uncomfortable bedfellows with the

American Colonization Society. In their Liberian nationalism, they inherited the rhetoric of John Winthrop, who had spoken of a "Citty upon a Hill," a shining example to the rest of the world of what a Christian republic should be. Robert Breckinridge, a Southern aristocrat, addressed the American Colonization Society in terms that were often reflected in the speeches of nineteenth-century black nationalists in the North:

> The moment one city, one single city of free civilized Christian blacks, is placed near the equator, on the western coast of Africa, then the mighty prize is won! From that instant, the whole problem in all its complexity and vastness as to the black race is solved. The slave trade dies, the civilization and conversion of Africa is fixed; the destiny of the race of Ham is redeemed; the equatorial region of the earth reclaimed; and the human race itself launched into a new and glorious career, of which all the triumphs of the past afford no parallel.[7]

Such ideas were not uncommon among sentimental abolitionists, who advocated sending black Americans to Africa. Harriet Beecher Stowe and the more conservative Hollis Read preached the prospects of African regeneration with unrestrained exuberance. They viewed the black race as congenitally predisposed to Christianity and saw them as fit bearers of a new civilization that was destined to be kinder and gentler than any that had gone before. Stowe's George Harris is a model of Christian charity; on setting sail for Liberia at the close of *Uncle Tom's Cabin,* he declares that his hopes for the African republic are based on the peculiarities of the black race. Although "full half the blood in [his] veins is hot and hasty Saxon," he hopes to modify the "stern inflexible, energetic elements" of his Anglo-Saxon ancestry, and place his faith in the "affectionate, magnanimous, and forgiving" traits of the African personality.[8]

Although most black nationalists endorsed such rhetoric on occasion, they paradoxically endorsed and emulated the ideal of Anglo-Saxon toughness with equal vigor. Christian black nationalists were influenced by the strident American nationalism that surrounded them, with its faith in Anglo-Saxon traditions as the source of American greatness. They were familiar with ideas like those expressed by Henry Ward Beecher, who proclaimed that white Americans were sprung from "a stock in which inheres the tendency to government and self government", in contrast to "that great and unfortunate nation," France. "Our people carry institutions which are to moral force what machinery is to physical force." This idea, which developed throughout the nineteenth century, found its fullest expression in the writings of Rev. Josiah

Strong. It was never absent from the writings of black-nationalist clergy-men, and at least one of them viewed Strong's rhetoric as inspirational.[9] In fact, some black-nationalist leaders were even given to making com-parisons between French and English traits similar to Beecher's, and believed that the English language and the Saxon character had been imprinted on the black American. The aggressive habits learned from the "hardy and enterprising Anglo-Saxon race" were the greatest gifts that black Americans had to offer to the rising Afro-Christian nations.[10]

The fact that literate, urbanized blacks and their institutions were "nationalistic" ironically provides evidence of the extent to which they had become acculturated in America. It was not until the First World War, and the disillusionment with "Western civilization" that accompa-nied it, that black intellectuals began to question the ideal of Anglo-African imperialism that had been present so consistently in the thought and writings of the Christian pan-Africanists of the nineteenth century.[11] In nineteenth-century documents, however, neither Christianity nor elitism, nor an identification with sedate and restrained religious denom-inations, worked as a counterpressure to black nationalism. On the con-trary, elitist, hierarchical, sedate denominations did quite well at attract-ing black nationalists and pan-Africanists, who apparently saw no contradiction between cultural assimilation and racial self-interest.

The development of a literate class of "free Africans," as they called themselves in the northern states, led to the formation of numerous voluntary societies and black-controlled church congregations by the late eighteenth century. The Free African Society of Philadelphia is of partic-ular interest, because from it originated the African Group of the Prot-estant Episcopal Church and the African Methodist Church (A.M.E.). Absalom Jones organized the first black congregation under black pas-torship in the Protestant Episcopal Church and became the first black man to be ordained a priest in that denomination. We are told that Jones and his following wished to isolate themselves from the evangelical ex-uberance often associated with the Methodism of the times. Richard Allen, the genteel and circumspect man who organized the Methodist body, was hardly dedicated to noisy worship forms. He was, nonethe-less, convinced that Methodism, with its blend of intellectual and emo-tional appeals, was best suited to "the capacity of the colored people." Both groups at the time of their formation were dedicated to a high standard of public decorum, development of an educated ministry, and maintenance of a sedate ritual.[12]

In recent scholarship, the person who has come to represent almost a caricature of sedate black Methodism is Bishop Daniel Alexander Payne. He is seen as sadly misguided because of his failure to recognize the importance of African cultural retention.[13] To me, the more interesting point is that Payne's activities demonstrate that pan-Africanism and black nationalism had absolutely nothing to do with an affinity to mass folk culture during the nineteenth century. Recent treatments of Payne's views have focused on his hostility to African cultural survivals on the folk level. He once attended a "bush meeting," where he went to please the pastor whose circuit he was visiting, and observed that after the sermon the congregation "formed a ring, and with coats off sang, clapped their hands and stamped their feet in a most ridiculous and heathenish way." Payne asked the pastor to restrain his members, telling him that this was "a heathenish way to worship" and that it was "disgraceful to themselves, the race, and the Christian name."[14]

At the same time that he rejected "Africanisms" in worship, Payne was dedicated to independent efforts for racial uplift. He purchased the grounds of Wilberforce University, founded the Bethel Literary and Historical Association in Washington, D.C., and before the Civil War he was a vice president of the African Civilization Society, founded by black nationalists Henry Highland Garnet and Martin Delany. The purpose of the society was to advance "the civilization and Christianization of Africa and the descendants of African ancestors in any portion of the earth, wherever dispersed. Also the destruction of the African Slave-trade, by the introduction of lawful commerce into Africa."[15]

Although Payne was an assimilationist, an Anglophiliac, and an elitist in terms of culture, he was a separatist in terms of church government. His values may be seen as nationalistic to the extent that he believed that African-Americans constituted a distinct people, who required a special set of institutions to represent their special set of interests. He felt that the maintenance of "a distinct branch of the Christian family" was important to black people in secular as well as in religious terms. The ability of the church to provide for itself financially and to develop its own leadership was a vindication of the black people's capacity for government. Like many of his contemporaries, Payne felt strongly that the church ought to be organizationally and administratively as independent of whites as possible. Methodism was as important to Payne as the air he breathed, but he looked upon those blacks who remained in the parent church of the white Methodists as "ecclesiastical vassals" of their white brethren.[16] This, however, did not mean the rejection of European rituals, beliefs, or ceremonies. Payne, like his contemporary, Alexander Crummell, admired the chanting and responses in London's St. Paul's Cathedral and referred to them as "sublime."[17]

Payne's younger contemporary, Bishop Henry McNeal Turner, was known as the robust epitome of pan-Africanism, and he heartily embraced a black nationalism that he preached with vigor, but Turner also epitomized the missionary spirit of the "Three C's." From the end of Reconstruction to the eve of the First World War, he was known as the foremost exponent of African emigration. Turner did not bother to mask his hostility towards the white race and declared that it would never be possible for black people to thrive in the United States. At the same time, he was a supporter of the American Colonization Society, which Payne, along with the more radically militant free blacks before the Civil War, had viewed as a vicious threat to black people. Turner made several trips to Africa, establishing A.M.E. churches in Sierra Leone and Liberia in 1891. He was responsible for organizing the A.M.E. Church in South Africa, and he was the first A.M.E. bishop of Africa. From all reports, Turner did not have the same pretensions to gentility that had been typical of Payne, although he was broadly self-educated, had a strong writing style, and published prolifically between 1886 and his death in 1915.[18]

Turner's commitment to the "civilization" and "redemption" of Africa revealed little in the way of an appreciation for traditional African customs. He conceived the Back to Africa movement as Christian politics. One did not return to Africa to become an African in the cultural sense; the purpose for the African return was to redeem the African continent from heathenism. As had nineteenth-century emigrationists, Turner viewed slavery as a "providence" whereby black Americans were prepared for the purpose of missionary work. In 1875, shortly before he was elected to a vice presidency of the American Colonization Society, he said: "The four millions of us in this country are at school, learning the doctrines of Christianity and the elements of civil government, and as soon as we are educated sufficiently to assume control of our vast ancestral domain, we will hear the voice of a mysterious Providence, saying '*Return to the land of your Fathers.*' "[19]

Turner was probably the most important spokesman for African repatriation until the advent of Marcus Garvey, who arrived in the United States ten months after Turner's death, but his enthusiasms did not win him the friendship of Bishop Payne, who later opposed his election to the episcopacy. In the view of Edwin S. Redkey, his most authoritative biographer, Turner's ideas represented the most important black political philosophy of his day and were attuned to the sentiments of the masses even more than those of Booker T. Washington or W. E. B. Du Bois.[20] He was a man of the people, a hearty backslapper, a middle brow intellectual, a scrappy politician, indeed, in the opinion of some, a rabble-rouser. His message of race pride and God-given national destiny apparently met with tremendous sympathy among the poor blacks of the South and Midwest, but he mixed freely and comfortably with the better-educated class of black leadership.

Other A.M.E. bishops who displayed pan-Africanist sympathies were William H. Heard and Richard R. Wright. Heard, who was appointed minister resident and consul general by Grover Cleveland, accompanied Turner on his voyage to Liberia in 1895 and spent four years there, from 1895 to 1899. Elected to the A.M.E. bishopric of West Africa, he returned to Liberia in 1909 and remained until 1916. He served on the executive board of the Liberia Development Association, and he encouraged the emigration of educated and skilled persons to Liberia.[21] One other A.M.E. bishop of interest in this connection is Richard Wright, Jr., who took a Ph.D. in sociology from the University of Pennsylvania and studied in Berlin and Leipzig. He also served as bishop of South Africa from 1936 to 1940. While Wright was never associated with strident pan-African rhetoric, his missionary activities showed an interest in Africa, and there can be no ignoring his ties to the pan-Africanist and black-nationalist traditions.

Around the time that the A.M.E. Church was formed in Philadelphia, a parallel group, the African Methodist Episcopal Zion Church (A.M.E.Z.), was organized in New York. The most important pan-Africanist bishop to come out of this church was Alexander Walters, who, in connection with Henry Sylvester Williams and W. E. B. Du Bois, organized the first pan-African conference. Walters did not advocate mass emigration, but he felt it was his "duty" to impress on the masses of black people that the United States is "the greatest country on earth." Besides, since the Negro had aided in the development of this country, "he should remain here to enjoy its splendid civilization."[22] The Gold Coast scholar, J. E. K. Aggrey, who taught for many years in Livingston College in North Carolina, was an ordained elder of the A.M.E.Z. Church. Randall Burkett has described the activities of James W. H. Eason, who served as chaplain of the Garvey movement from 1919 to 1922.[23] In short, A.M.E.Z. bishops, like bishops of the A.M.E. Church, have consistently been identified with black nationalism and pan-Africanism, although neither church can be described as a black-nationalist institution.

One of the most striking features of the history of African-American nationalism is the high visibility of Episcopalians in the movement. Although the Episcopal church in northern cities before the Civil War was associated with elitism and High Church, ritualistic worship, it attracted numerous black nationalists and pan-Africanists throughout the century. Of the twenty-five black Americans ordained in the Episcopal church before 1865, seven were sent to Liberia as missionaries, seven were ordained in Liberia, and two more were sent to the West Indies as missionaries.[24] This should not necessarily be interpreted as a sign that black Episcopalians were singularly zealous black nationalists. The ruling white Episcopalians were hostile to black ministers and seldom allowed them any rights within a diocese until after the Civil War. The infrequency of ordination and the frequency of migration would seem to indicate that there was little room for black Episcopalians in the United States. In the words of one black priest, the Episcopal church was "a cold and repulsive stepmother."[25] Nonetheless, it was the Episcopalians — despite their obsession with apostolic succession, stately edifices, and High Church rituals — who attracted such notable pan-Africanists as Alexander Crummell, James T. Holly, Joseph Robert Love, and George Alexander McGuire.

Rev. Peter Williams, Jr., was an example of the African-American leader who, while not a black nationalist, often showed elements of black nationalism in his thinking. There were hints of nationalist sympathy in his eulogy on the death of Captain Paul Cuffe in 1817. In that year, large numbers of black abolitionists soured on the African movement as a result of the founding of the American Society for Colonizing the Free People of Color in the United States, whose intentions most black people regarded as hostile and antiabolitionist. Williams invoked the name of Cuffe in calling on black Americans not to condemn the movement, until "after we have seen the whole arranged and carefully examined its parts." In 1829 he supported John Russwurm, erstwhile editor of *Freedom's Journal,* when he decided to emigrate to Liberia under the auspices of the American Colonization Society. In 1834, when he withdrew from the New York Antislavery Society and defended the American Colonization Society at the advice of his bishop, it was rightly felt that Williams had exhibited excessive meekness. On the other hand, as Williams explained, he had long felt it his duty to assist "any man of color [who] thought it best to emigrate to Africa."[26]

Williams was the teacher and ecclesiastical sponsor of Alexander Crummell, who between 1853 and 1872 spent sixteen years as an Episcopal missionary in Liberia. Crummell was rigidly authoritarian and elitist in his theory of African progress. He expressed considerable concern for decorum in religious services, the importance of "suitable edifices," and education for the ministry. He was a good black nationalist, however, who gave a great deal to Liberian nationalism at a time when others only talked of their commitments. After his return to the United States, he continued to think of black Americans as a nation within a nation, having a mission and destiny separate from that of other Americans. He continued to think in terms of a separate destiny for black Americans, long after he had given up on territorial separatism. Thus, while his essay "The Social Principle Among a People" was not an expression of classical black nationalism, it did call for continued maintenance of separate black institutions. His sermon on "The Destined Superiority of the Negro" revealed the spirit of racialistic chauvinism that had characterized his earlier nationalistic statements.

"The Destined Superiority of the Negro," delivered as a Thanksgiving sermon in 1877, was adapted from ideas that Crummell had been preaching for the past thirty years. He had always been certain that a study of biblical and modern history could reveal the role of God in history. There were prophecies in the biblical texts in light of which he believed he could "determine the destiny of the race with which we are connected." He believed, as had David Walker, that nations and empires rose and fell according to their obedience to covenants with God, and like Maria Stewart he drew parallels between the Babylonian captivity of the Jews and the American captivity of the Negroes. His reading of history led him to believe that nations and races fell into two categories—those who were to be destroyed for their sinfulness and those who, like the Jews, were to be tempered by suffering so that they might carry out some important providential destiny. Furthermore, Africans shared with the Jews, the Greeks, the Romans, and the British a quality of imitativeness that allowed them to adopt the best civilized traits from other people with whom they came into contact. The hardiness and adaptability of the African-American people "in the midst of all reverses" demonstrated that they were destined for superiority.

The fact that black people in the United States had not been destroyed by slavery demonstrated that the sufferings of the "captive exiles from Africa" were meant not as a judgement but as a discipline. Their tribulations were not intended to punish or destroy but to prepare the black race for a glorious destiny. It was obvious that the black race in America had "risen superior to the dread inflictions of a prolonged servitude." It was clear to Crummell that, due to the congenital traits of plasticity, receptivity, and the ability to adapt readily to new manners and customs, the African-American in the land of thralldom had risen "taller, more erect, more intelligent, and more aspiring than any of his ancestors for more than a thousand years." This seemed to indicate that black Americans were one of those peoples in whom Providence was "graciously interested."

> In a sense, not equal, indeed, to the case of the Jews, but parallel, in a lower degree, such a people are a "chosen people" of the Lord. There is, so

to speak, a *covenant* relation which God has established between Himself and them.[27]

With a typically American arrogance, like that of his white American counterparts — who, from their vantage point in their City on a Hill, were able not only to know the mind of God but practically to force Him into covenants — Crummell read the will of God and assured his congregation that they might "take it as a sure and undoubted fact" that their "destined superiority" was ordained by a sovereign providence.

James T. Holly, like Crummell, represented the adaptation of Manifest Destiny doctrine and racial Christianity by priests of the Episcopal denomination. In his *A Vindication of the Negro Race as Demonstrated by Historical Events of the Haitian Revolution,* he identified himself with both a belief in the unique destiny of black Americans and the idea of emigrationism. Along with several other prominent black nationalists of the antebellum decade, he felt that Haiti would be a more hospitable nation than Liberia for black emigrants from the United States. He took a providential view of history, founded in the belief that God would not have allowed the evil of slavery unless He had willed to bring some good out of it. Former slaves in the New World, taking upon themselves the duty of building a black civilization in their own part of the globe, would become the means to disenthrall blacks from oppression and ignorance throughout the world. He had little tolerance for back to Africa schemes, which would

> send us across the ocean to rummage the graves of our ancestors, in fruitless, and ill-directed efforts at the wrong end of human progress. Civilization and Christianity is passing from the East to the West; and its pristine splendor will only be rekindled in the ancient nations of the Old World, after it has belted the globe in its westward course, and revisited the Orient again. The serpentine trail of civilization and Christianity, like the ancient philosophic symbol of eternity, must coil backward to its fountain head.[28]

This cyclical view of history may be dismissed as mystical nonsense, but the metaphysic of circularity was a venerable tradition in Western Christianity, and Holly, like Crummell and Walker, was merely adapting a view of history that was well established in the rhetoric of American Manifest Destiny.[29] Theories of national destiny always tend to mysticism and irrationality. Black nationalists are motivated in part by clearly conceived economic and political concerns, but also by emotional needs that require only the flimsiest of irrational schemes to justify them.

In the early twentieth century, two Episcopal priests from the West Indies were to have an influence on pan-Africanism through the Garvey movement. One of these was Joseph Robert Love, a Jamaican, trained as a physician in the United States and well known to Alexander Crummell and his circle as an able pamphleteer. He served as a priest in Haiti under Bishop Holly, but after a clash with the bishop he devoted himself to medicine, serving as a doctor with the Haitian army. Love was also editor of the *Jamaica Advocate,* a newspaper that Garvey knew as a boy, and it is believed that Garvey may have been influenced directly by Love during his early manhood. It is known that Love interacted significantly with Henry Sylvester Williams, an Episcopal layman, who along with Du Bois and Bishop Walters organized the pan-African conference in London in 1900.[30]

Anther Episcopal priest who had a direct influence on Garvey was George Alexander McGuire, an Antiguan, who was ordained to the priesthood in 1896. When Marcus Garvey began to organize the United Negro Improvement Association (UNIA) in New York after the First World War, McGuire determined to join forces with him. He organized the Independent Episcopal Church, holding a series of meetings with other ministers and lay persons who wished to cast off white dominance. Since the consensus of the group was that "the necessary authority . . . should be obtained from some proper ecclesiastical source," he sought consecration as a bishop from various sources, until finally the American Catholic Church, a branch of Greek Orthodoxy, elevated him to the rank of an Orthodox bishop. So began the African Orthodox Church, which McGuire sought to align with various black-nationalist organizations, including the African Blood Brotherhood and the UNIA. McGuire set aside a day when all right-thinking Garveyites were to divest their homes of pictures that depicted Christ and the Virgin as Caucasians. The newspaper of the church, *The Negro Churchman,* declaimed bitterly against the Protestant Episcopalians for refusing to appoint a black bishop to Liberia. In writing an introduction to the second volume of Garvey's *Philosophy and Opinions,* McGuire tacitly gave his endorsement to such Garveyite beliefs as divine apportionment of earth and racial separatism as the will of God.

Of course, support for black nationalism has not come only from High Church, hierarchical denominations. Black Baptists contributed their share to the development of nationalist ideology during the late nineteenth and early twentieth centuries. As Sylvia Jacobs has shown, they figured prominently in the African missionary movement from 1821, when Lott Carey and Colin Teague went to Liberia under the auspices of the American Baptist Foreign Mission Society.[31] Domestic black nationalism had an articulate spokesman in William J. Simmons, president of the State University of Louisville and the author of *Men of Mark: Eminent, Progressive, and Rising,* a collection of 177 biographies of persons who had made significant contributions to the status of black people throughout the world. The introduction to the volume was written by Henry McNeal Turner, and Alexander Crummell assisted him in researching the work. Elements of black nationalism were present throughout, and sometimes an enthusiastic national chauvinism emerged:

> The warm blood of the Negro, that haunts the channels of his veins with ancient Egyptian and Ethiopian fires, has been tempered in the climate of the South and educed to that proportion which robs it of its sluggishness, subdues its wild passion, and holds it by reason, while the trials of the past have been the friction that brightens, the winds that toughen, and the frosts that ripen. . . . As the Indian faded in the North, before the white man, so the white man of the South must yield to us, without, however, a bloody conflict. . . . Here in this new South the Negro shall shine in the constellation of the nations.[32]

Baptist black nationalists had another interesting representative in Rev. Sutton E. Griggs, whose novels and sociological treatises revealed a belief in the separate destiny of black Americans. Blending social Darwinism and other evolutionary theories with Ethiopianist teleology, Griggs was able to present a colorful portrayal of black Americans as something more than an ethnic group. They were, in fact, a nation, albeit a nation without a government or a territory. In the first of his novels, *Imperium in Imperio,* he revealed a plan that black Americans might exercise as a last resort, to gain an actual landed empire, should the attempts to live in peace among white Americans continue to be frustrated.

The Presbyterian minister Henry Highland Garnet was one of the best-known black nationalists of the antebellum period. He founded the African Civilization Society in 1858 as an agency for the universal elevation of the black race as well as an institution designed to encourage migration to and development of Africa. He was an emotional man, known for his "Address to the Slaves" of 1843, in which he called on the slaves of the United States to rise up and abolish slavery by violent means. His allegiance to emigrationism seemed to be situational, for while he vociferously opposed emigration in 1848, he attacked Douglass in 1859 for his refusal to support the African Civilization Society.[33] On one occasion, he voiced the opinion that the United States was destined to be filled with a mixed race, but with the coming of the Fugitive Slave

Law and the Dred Scott decision, as hopes for the ultimate assimilation of black Americans seemed unrealistic, he adopted nationalism, separatism, and emigrationism.

The influential Edward Wilmot Blyden, who made his career in Liberia, was also a Presbyterian minister. Blyden rivals, if he does not exceed, Alexander Crummell as the most influential black nationalist of the nineteenth century.[34] The pan-Africanism of Blyden is more consistently expressed than that of most of his contemporaries, and it developed to the logical conclusion of searching within traditional, indigenous African societies for the basis of a true cultural nationalism. In its inception, however, Blyden's nationalism was typically linked to the belief in divine providence and the supposed historic mission of the African-American people. There were two ways, he argued, in which God spoke to peoples — one was by His word and the other by His providence. In the case of black Americans, He had not sent any Moses with signs and wonders, but He had spoken through providence. He had allowed black people to be brought to America and "placed in circumstances where they could receive a training fitting them for the work of civilizing and evangelizing the land whence they were born." He had allowed them to suffer a sense of estrangement from the people among whom they lived, "as was the case with the Jews in Egypt."[35]

Blyden eventually began to express doubts concerning the appropriateness of Christianity for the African races. Its truths had been too distorted by Europeans, and it had been too long abused as a means of degrading African-Americans' images of themselves. In *Christianity, Islam, and the Negro Race,* Blyden said "just as Ishmael came before Isaac," so too would Islam precede Christianity in Africa. Christian missionaries should rejoice at the spread of Islam, which at least brought traditional peoples away from heathenism and prepared them for the idea of monotheism. He felt that Islam had merit in its own right, and he had found African Muslims to be "tolerant and accessible, anxious for light and improvement from any quarter."[36] He attributed much of the success of Islam in Africa to the egalitarianism of Arab missionaries, who at times even intermarried with the Africans.[37]

Blyden's maintenance of contacts with such of his African-American clerical colleagues as Henry McNeal Turner and Francis J. Grimké is noteworthy. He actively supported Turner's African repatriation projects for some time, impressed, as was just about everyone but Alexander Crummell, by Turner's overwhelming personality. He found the bishop contagiously earnest, although "frightfully" pugnacious, and "beyond comparison, the most combative writer who controls a Negro journal or any journal in America." He attributed Turner's impetuous and intractable nature to his Ibo ancestry, the ethnic bloodline in which Blyden believed he shared himself. Although Turner was a light-skinned mulatto, and although Blyden had identified himself with anti-mulatto prejudice in Liberia, he managed to cooperate with the bishop. In fact, so long as he was in the United States, Blyden was able to put aside his anti-mulatto feelings and cooperate with the likes of Victoria Earle Matthews, T. Thomas Fortune, Richard T. Greener, Frederick Douglass, Booker T. Washington, and the Grimké brothers, Francis and Archibald.[38]

When Blyden visited Washington, D. C., in 1883, Turner hosted a banquet for him at which several prominent clergymen were present. Although Alexander Crummell was explainably and conspicuously absent, the Presbyterian minister Francis J. Grimké, who was one of the persons called on to speak at the alcohol-free toasting ceremony, spoke in glowing terms of Blyden's work in Africa, according to a report in Turner's newspaper, "and said that he would join the Doctor himself in his great African work at some future time, perhaps."[39]

Blyden's continuing ties with Grimké reveal the persistent linkage between the church life of at least some middle-class black Americans and the nationalism of continental Africans. On a visit to the United States in 1895, Blyden spoke, at Grimké's invitation, to the "Saturday Circle," a literary discussion group that met under the auspices of the Fifteenth Street Presbyterian Church, where Grimké was pastor. He asked Grimké to have his circle read in advance his article "The African Problem," just published in the *North American Review*. Later that week, he addressed the Bethel Literary and Historical Association in that same city, founded by Bishop Payne in 1881. His talk at the Bethel Literary was on the appropriately ministerial subject of "The Prophecy of Noah."[40] During his 1895 tour of the United States, however, Blyden refused to support Turner's proposal of wholesale migration to Liberia. Crummell, who like Blyden had always believed that repatriates should be a small, select group, was pleased by Blyden's rupture with the Turner camp. As for Blyden himself, he apparently bore no permanent ill will towards Turner.[41]

While Francis Grimké seems to have permanently delayed his promised trip to Africa, and while he never became a fully committed nationalist, nationalism is nonetheless present in his writings. One scholar has interpreted him as moving steadily in the direction of racial chauvinism during the later years of his career, but I see no evidence of this.[42] Grimké often expressed strong racial sentiments, however, and, like his antebellum predecessors, he was willing to make comparisons between black Americans and the Old Testament Hebrews. In 1902 he delivered an address on "A Resemblance and a Contrast Between the American Negro and the Children of Israel in Egypt, Or the Duty of the Negro to Contend Earnestly For His Rights Under the Constitution." Grimké felt that the two historical situations were different, for several reasons that he discussed in depth. The Israelites went into Egypt of their own accord, but black Americans had been "seized by slave hunters and against their will forced from the land of their birth." The black race in the United States had increased at a much more rapid rate than had the children of Israel in Egypt. The Americans were bent on getting rid of the black population, but the Egyptians had sought to prevent the children of Israel from leaving. He rejected the idea that providence had intended the sojourn of the black race in America to be temporary, as the sojourn of Israel in Egypt. He saw no evidence that providence had brought Africans to America so that they might be prepared for usefulness in the land of their origin. In his opinion, no one knew the will of God with respect to the destiny of the black race in America, and in the absence of any positive information, he stated his assumption that the divine purpose was "that we remain just where we are."[43]

The hidden text in Francis J. Grimké's comparison between black Americans and the Old Testament Hebrews is the assumption that it is necessary, useful, or even possible to make such a comparison. In setting out to define the ways in which African-Americans were and were not like the ancient Jews, he gave a certain dignity and credibility to the argument that black Americans were a "peculiar people." In the process, Grimké offered the classic expression of anti-emigrationist African-American nationalism. He set the pattern for other figures of the twentieth century, like W. E. B. Du Bois, to whom we refer as black nationalists and pan-Africanists, although they were steadfastly opposed to the recrudescence of Back to Africa movements. His writings provide us with a model according to which we can speak of black nationalism in people's writing without calling them nationalists. On a higher level, I think we should perceive Grimké as a tough-minded, commonsensical thinker, who recognized the silliness of trying to read the workings of providence in the recent history of black America or trying to force God into a covenant on the basis of them. Still, Grimké, like numerous other bourgeois ministers in elite congregations, was, for what it is worth, capable of experiencing what S. P. Fullinwider has called "racial Christianity," if not a fully developed black nationalism. It can be shown from their writings that middle-class religion was one of the forces in society that sustained black nationalism and its concept of racial destiny, rather than a force that worked to oppose it.

NOTES

1. E. Franklin Frazier, "Garvey, A Mass Leader," *Nation* 18 August 1926, 147–48. E. Franklin Frazier, "The Garvey Movement," *Opportunity* 4(November 1926): 346–48. Randall Burkett, *Garveyism as a Religious Movement* (Metuchen, N.J.: Scarecrow Press, 1978). E. U. Essien-Udom, *Black Nationalism: A Search for an Identity in America* (Chicago: University of Chicago Press, 1962).

2. James H. Cone, *Black Theology and Black Power* (New York: Seabury Press, 1969). Gayraud S. Wilmore, *Black Religion and Black Radicalism* (Garden City, N.Y.: Doubleday, 1972).

3. Conrad Cherry, *God's New Israel: Religious Interpretations of American Destiny* (Englewood Cliffs, N.J.: Prentice-Hall, 1971).

4. Alexander Crummell, "The Duty of a Rising Christian State," in his *The Future of Africa* (New York: Charles Scribner, 1862), p. 100.

5. Maria W. Stewart, *Productions of Mrs. Maria W. Stewart Presented to the First African Church and Society of the City of Boston* (Boston: Friends of Freedom and Virtue, 1835), pp. 60–61.

6. For the nationalist implications of *David Walker's Appeal,* see Sterling Stuckey, *The Ideological Origins of Black Nationalism* (Boston: Beacon Press, 1972), and Wilson J. Moses, *Black Messiahs and Uncle Toms: Social and Literary Manipulations of a Religious Myth* (University Park: Pennsylvania State University Press, 1982), pp. 30–49.

7. "Speech of Robert J. Breckinridge before the Maryland State Colonization Society, 2 February 1838," *African Repository* 14:141.

8. Harriet Beecher Stowe, *Uncle Tom's Cabin* (1852; reprint, New York: Dodd Mead, 1952), p. 428.

9. Henry Ward Beecher, *The Original Plymouth Pulpit* (Boston: Pilgrim Press, 1871), 5:203–19. Alexander Crummell cites Josiah Strong in *Africa and America* (Springfield, Mass.: Wiley, 1891), p. 46. See also Josiah Strong, *Our Country* (1891; reprint, Cambridge: Harvard University Press, 1963).

10. Alexander Crummell, "The English Language in Liberia" in *The Future of Africa,* pp. 47–54. James T. Holly, *A Vindication of the Capacity of the Negro Race for Self Government and Civilized Progress as Demonstrated by Historical Events of the Haitian Revolution and the Subsequent Acts of the People since their National Independence* (New Haven: Afric-American Publishing Company, 1857).

11. Wilson J. Moses, *The Golden Age of Black Nationalism, 1850–1925* (Hamden, Conn.: Archon, 1978), pp. 250–71.

12. Daniel A. Payne, *History of the African Methodist Episcopal Church* (Nashville: A.M.E. Sunday School Union, 1891), to be read along with George F. Bragg, *History of the Afro-American Group of the Episcopal Church* (Baltimore: Church Advocate Press, 1922), for origins of the two groups in the Free African Society. Allen's autobiography is *The Life Experiences and Gospel Labors of the Rt. Rev. Richard Allen* (Philadelphia: A.M.E. Book Concern, 1833). A recent biography is Carol V. George, *Segregated Sabbaths: Richard Allen and the Rise of Independent Black Churches, 1760–1840* (New York: Oxford, 1973). Charles Wesley's early biography is *Richard Allen, Apostle of Freedom* (Washington: Associated Publishers, 1935).

13. Sterling Stuckey, *Slave Culture: Nationalist Theory and the Foundations of Black America* (New York: Oxford, 1987), pp. 92–93.

14. Daniel Alexander Payne, *Recollections of Seventy Years* (Nashville: A.M.E. Sunday School Union, 1888), p. 253.

15. *Constitution of the African Civilization Society* (New Haven, 1861), originally

published as a pamphlet, is reprinted in Howard Brotz, *Negro Social and Political Thought, 1850–1920* (New York: Basic Books, 1966), pp. 191–96.

16. Payne, *African Methodist Episcopal Church,* p. 12.

17. Payne, *Recollections,* p. 173ff.

18. The best work on Turner is Edwin S. Redkey, *Black Exodus: Black Nationalist and Back-to-Africa Movements, 1890–1910* (New Haven: Yale University Press, 1969). See also Edwin S. Redkey, ed., *Respect Black: The Writings and Speeches of Henry McNeal Turner* (New York: Arno, 1971). "Three C's" in African missionary parlance have traditionally referred to "Christianity, commerce, and civilization."

19. Henry McNeal Turner, *African Repository* (April 1875): 39; reprinted in Redkey, *Respect Black,* p. 42.

20. See the introduction to Redkey, *Black Exodus.*

21. Redkey, *Black Exodus,* pp. 223–24, 283.

22. I. Garland Penn, *The United Negro: His Problems and Progress* (Atlanta: D. E. Luther, 1907), p. 593.

23. Randall K. Burkett, "James W. H. Eason," *A.M.E. Zion Quarterly Review* (Spring 1987).

24. Randall Burkett, "Afro-American Episcopal Clergymen to 1865" (August 1980, typescript).

25. Alexander Crummell to G. Frazier, 18 September 1894, Alexander Crummell Papers, Schomburg Collection, New York Public Library.

26. Peter Williams, Jr., "To the Citizens of New York," *African Repository* 10:186–88; reprinted in *The Mind of the Negro as Reflected in Letters Written during the Crisis, 1800–1860,* ed. Carter G. Woodson, (Washington, D.C.: Association for the Study of Negro Life and History, 1926), pp. 630–34.

27. Alexander Crummell, "The Destined Superiority of the Negro," in his *The Greatness of Christ and Other Sermons* (New York: Whittaker, 1882), p. 351.

28. Holly, *A Vindication of the Negro Race,* p. 65.

29. Henry Nash Smith, *Virgin Land: The American West as History and Myth* (Cambridge: Harvard University Press, 1950).

30. Williams worked as a lecturer for the Church of England Temperance Society in 1896. See Owen C. Mathurin, *Henry Sylvester Williams and the Origins of the Pan-African Movement, 1869–1911* (Westport, Conn.: Greenwood, 1976), p. 31.

31. Sylvia Jacobs, *Black Americans and the Missionary Movement in Africa* (Westport, Conn.: Greenwood, 1982).

32. William J. Simmons, *Men of Mark: Eminent, Progressive, and Rising* (Cleveland: Geo. M. Revell & Co., 1887), pp. 57–58.

33. Brotz, *Negro Social and Political Thought,* contains Garnet's charge and Douglass's response, pp. 262–66.

34. See Hollis R. Lynch, *Edward Wilmot Blyden: Pan-Negro Patriot, 1832–1912* (New York: Oxford University Press, 1967), and Hollis R. Lynch, ed., *Black Spokesman: Selected Published Writings of Edward Wilmot Blyden* (New York: Humanities Press, 1971).

35. Lynch, *Black Spokesman,* p. 26.

36. Edward Wilmot Blyden, "Mohammedanism and the Negro Race," in his *Christianity, Islam, and the Negro Race* (1887; reprint, Edinburgh: Edinburgh University Press, 1967), p. 24.

37. Blyden, *Christianity, Islam, and the Negro Race,* p. 20.

38. Edward Wilmot Blyden, "The Negro in the United States," *A.M.E. Church Review,* (January 1900): 308–15, contains Blyden's comments on Turner.

39. The banquet is described in Wilson J. Moses, *Alexander Crummell: A Study of Civilization and Discontent* (New York: Oxford, 1989), pp. 254–55. Crummell's conflicts with Turner and Blyden are discussed at several points.
40. John W. Cromwell, *History of the Bethel Literary and Historical Association* (Washington, D.C.: H.L. Pendleton, 1896), p. 29.
41. Redkey, *Black Exodus,* pp. 229–30.
42. S. P. Fullinwider, *The Mind and Mood of Black America* (Homewood, Ill.: Dorsey Press, 1969), pp. 14–18.
43. Francis J. Grimké, "A Resemblance and a Contrast between the American Negro and the Children of Israel in Egypt," in *Works of Francis J. Grimké,* ed. Carter G. Woodson (Washington, D.C.: Associated Publishers, 1942), 1:352

Civil Religion and the Crisis of Civil Rights

Biases and Generalizations

Black Americans have always done their best to exploit the fact that church and state in America are only imperfectly separated and have benefited from the liberal and progressive tendencies in American civil religion. But in postindustrial secular America—where religion is viewed with suspicion by liberals and has been appropriated by paranoid, reactionary elements—the capacity of American civil religion to bear the burden of progressive reform must seriously be questioned. We must ask ourselves if black Americans will be able to enlist the rhetoric of civil religion as an instrument of social change, as they have done in the past. Black Americans and civil religion have stood at the center of the two great industrial crises in American history. Civil religion played an important role in solving social and industrial problems at both junctures. The crisis of agrarian democracy, which led to the Civil War and emancipation, had racial causes and religious overtones. The same must be said of the crisis of industrial democracy, which led to the social gospel, the civil rights movement, and desegregation. The interweaving of religious doctrine with liberal attitudes towards rights and freedoms has significantly affected the position of black people in American life. The struggle of black people for their rights has significantly affected the nature of American civil religion.

To be sure, the Constitution expressly forbade the establishment of a national church, but its authors never intended to abet atheism, popishness, or infidelity. The framers of the Constitution held the truths of Enlightenment Christianity to be self-evident and God-given. The Founding Fathers did not conceive of themselves as establishing a religion, but if Montesquieu's Persian traveller had passed through the governmental assemblies of the early republic, he would have found Christian attitudes everywhere dominant, and he would have found the Protestant clergy exerting influence in every aspect of public life.

American Jews and Catholics were never so deluded as to believe that church and state were separate in America. Indeed, an important element of their ethno-religious consciousness in the United States has been their struggle to preserve the distinct religious traditions that they brought with them from the Old World. They have tended to view strong evangelical Protestantism as threatening to their interests and have fought to keep it from exerting too great an influence over their lives. Thus, the separation of church and state is a meaningful issue for Catholics and Jews in a way that it has not been for black Americans. Black Americans have historically perceived religiosity not only as a means of preserving distinctiveness, but paradoxically as a means of demonstrating assimilation. When confronted by antidemocratic or racist traditions in American religion, blacks have not traditionally called for the separation of church and state; they have been more inclined to appeal to the progressive tendencies in the Protestant tradition, and have called on the American people to renew their supposedly democratic and egalitarian covenant.

Eighteenth-century black Americans were aware of the church-and-state linkage because of the peculiarities of their own experiences. They had been dragged kicking and screaming away from their ancestral religions and violently plunged into the turbulent waters of evangelical Protestantism. They were, therefore, and still are for the most part a Protestant population, and thus in some respects in a relatively advantageous position for communicating their spiritual and material aspirations. They have based much of their political activity on the fact that much American political thought and behavior are grounded in religious assumptions. They have used this fact to their advantage whenever possible. From colonial times to the present, black Americans have attempted to utilize religious ammunition in their political battles. The struggles for the rights and freedoms of black people were based on the assumption that Americans share a civil religion. While other ethnic groups may have felt the need to fight for religious pluralism, black Americans have found it useful to exploit the fact of their religious assimilation.

I understand the term civil religion in America to signify the assumption that all Americans worship the same God and that they enjoy a special covenant with Him under which He will lead the nation towards an exalted and prosperous future, so long as Americans retain their devotion to principles of liberty and justice for all. The American civil religion is characteristically contradictory; it is tough-minded as well as soft-hearted. While it holds on the one hand that God is a god of the oppressed, it also holds that worldly success is pleasing to God and a sign of divine favor. It holds that every individual must work out his or her own salvation, but it also includes the idea of community and civil rights. Black American civil religion—which must be distinguished from the more emotional and escapist forms of folk worship—has not deviated significantly from the civil religion of the society at large. It was never enough for black Americans to argue that God watched over a long-suffering people simply because they were oppressed, for if God was in some special way on the side of the weak, He also seemed in some special way to be looking out for the interests of the strong. Black Americans hoped to become strong. They did not assume that the progression from weakness to strength must necessarily be accompanied by a diminution of favor in the sight of God. Thus, black religion does not always conform to Vittorio Lanternari's model of "the religions of the oppressed." It does not inevitably challenge mainstream American Protestant values; it seeks, on the contrary, to demonstrate that it is a legitimate part of the mainstream.[1]

The Crisis of Pre-Industrial Democracy: Civil Religion and Slavery

In the early days of the Republic, as several scholars have shown, the moral assumption that slavery was wrong was invariably the basis of abolitionist arguments.[2] This moral assumption was, in turn, based on the fundamental assumptions of Enlightenment Protestantism: that there was a God and that He spoke to mankind through common sense, through the sentiments of the heart, and through the *King James Bible*. Black abolitionists were always clever enough to base their arguments on the additional assumption that both the slave and the slaveholder were part of the same Christian commonwealth.

This led to a serious problem during the colonial period, when many slaveholders feared that Christianizing the slaves would lead to their automatic emancipation. In the state of Virginia, these fears were soon put to rest when a statute of 1667 declared that baptism would not alter the status of a slave. In this instance, the separation of church and state served to infringe, rather than to protect, the rights of black Christians. Ironically, the statute that weakened the power of the church to guarantee civil rights, made church and state co-partners in the enslavement of black Americans.[3] The collaboration between church and state, the undeniable reality that the American civil religion equivocated on the question of slavery's moral status, eventually evoked Thomas Jefferson's famous jeremiadic rhetoric in *Notes on the State of Virginia:*

> and can the liberties of a nation be thought secure when we have removed their only firm basis; a conviction in the minds of the people that these liberties are of the gift of god. that they are not to be violated but with his wrath? [the following was crossed out] when they cannot imagine a single argument in their support which their own daily practice does not deny. [the following was inserted in minute handwriting] indeed I tremble for my country, when I reflect that God is just: that his justice cannot sleep forever: that considering numbers, nature, and the natural means only, a revolution of the wheel of fortune, an exchange of situation, is among possible events that it may become probable by supernatural interference! The almighty has no attribute which can take side with us in such a contest.[4]

The classic expression of black civil religion in antebellum America was written largely as a response to Jefferson's *Notes on the State of Virginia,* albeit four decades later. It was written by David Walker, the proprietor of a secondhand clothing store in Boston, where he participated in antislavery meetings and served as an agent for *Freedom's Journal,* the nation's first black newspaper. In 1829 he published a pamphlet, *An Appeal in Four Articles, Together with a Preamble, to the Colored Citizens of the World, but in Particular and very Expressly to Those of the United States of America.* The pamphlet appears to have gotten him into a lot of trouble; that is, some of his contemporaries thought he was assassinated because of it.[5]

When Walker responded to Jefferson, the farthest thing from his mind was the separation of church and state. The fundamental Protestant assumptions on which he based his arguments were just as important to him as they were to the supposedly deistic Jefferson. And to the mind of David Walker, the words of Jefferson were as a revelation of hypocrisy on the part of a man who recognized evil but was incapable of following through on the convictions of his conscience. Walker really went no further than Jefferson when he predicted that the hand of God would bring about a terrible apocalyptic event that would free the slaves and punish Americans for the crime of having enslaved them.

Religion, my brethren, is a substance of deep consideration among all nations of the earth. The Pagans have a kind, as well as the Mahometans, the Jews and the Christians. But pure and undefiled religion, such as was preached by Jesus Christ and his apostles is hard to be found in all the earth. God, through his instrument, Moses, handed a dispensation of his divine will to the children of Israel after they had left Egypt for the land of Canaan, or of Promise, who through hypocrisy, oppression, and unbelief, departed from the faith. He then by his apostles handed a dispensation of his, together with the will of Jesus Christ to the Europeans in Europe, who in open violation of which have made *merchandise* of us, and it does appear they take this very dispensation to aid them in their infernal depredations upon us.[6]

Walker believed that the signs of God's judgements were already apparent in Europe, especially in the Catholic sections, because Catholics were the first to have perverted the dispensation and violated the Christian covenant with God. It was a fact that slavery had been introduced into the New World by Bartholomew Las Casas, "that very notoriously avaricious Catholic priest or preacher, and adventurer with Columbus in his second voyage. . . . This wretch succeeded so well in his plans of oppression, that in 1503, the first blacks had been imported into the new world." The great crime was now being punished by the inexorable workings of Providence. Walker observed:

I shall call your attention a few moments to that *Christian* nation, the Spaniards, while I shall leave almost unnoticed that avaricious and cruel people, the Portuguese, among whom all true hearted christians and lovers of Jesus Christ, must evidently see the judgments of God displayed. . . . I say all who are permitted to see and believe these things, can easily recognize the judgments of God among the Spaniards. Though others may lay the cause of the fierceness with which they cut each other's throats to some other circumstances, yet they who believe that God is a God of justice, will believe that SLAVERY *is the principal cause.* While the Spaniards are running about upon the field of battle cutting each other's throats, has not the Lord an afflicted and suffering people in the midst of them whose cries and groans in consequence of oppression are continually pouring into the ears of the God of justice.[7]

Although we know almost nothing about Walker's background, there is no reason to assume that his hostility to Spanish Catholics was in any way related to any suffering that he had experienced at their hands. Protestant America was responsible for the sufferings of Walker's people, but nonetheless he had great faith in them and in their religious tradition. A considerable portion of *Walker's Appeal* was addressed specifically to white Americans. Indeed one is led to question whether black people really were the target audience of *Walker's Appeal*. Much of his exhortation of the slaves seems to have been done for the benefit of whites, and he directly addressed white readers in such sections as the following:

> Perhaps you will laugh or make light of this; but I tell you Americans! that unless you speedily alter your course, *you* and *your Country are Gone!!!!!!* For God Almighty will tear up the very face of the earth!!!!
>
> * * *
>
> Remember Americans, that we must and shall be free, and enlightened as you are, will you wait until we shall, under God obtain our liberty by the crushing arm of power? Will it not be dreadful for you? I speak Americans for your good.[8]

Such passages force one to question Walker's claim that he was writing to a black audience. It is at least questionable whether this pamphlet was really an appeal to the slaves and a call for revolt. It is far more easily interpreted as an appeal to the conscience of white America, based on the commonly held values of the American civil religion. Walker hoped that white Americans would be capable of perfecting their Christianity so that black and white Americans could, in his own words, "live in peace and happiness together [and] become a united and happy people."[9]

During the antebellum decades, black religious leadership was divided into two camps—egalitarian radicals, who favored integration, and black nationalists, who believed that the races were destined to be perpetually separate. The integrationists, of course, advocated joining their fortunes with American destiny and appealed to the egalitarian elements in the democratic civil religion. Egalitarian radicals tended to emphasize the traditions of Jeffersonian democracy. For them, the *Declaration of Independence* and even the *Notes on the State of Virginia* were interpreted optimistically. These documents were seen as providing a fundamental set of moral guidelines that could be used as instruments of liberation. Black leaders in this tradition were not deaf to the hypocrisy of a national religion based on the idea of God-given rights, and they constantly hearkened back to the rhetoric of Jefferson to stir the conscience of the nation. Typical of those who manipulated civil religion in this way was Frederick Douglass, who said:

> You declare before the world, and are understood by the world to declare that you "hold these truths to be self-evident, that all men are created equal; and are endowed by their Creator with certain inalienable

rights; and that among these are, life, liberty, and the pursuit of happiness," and yet you hold securely in bondage which according to your own Thomas Jefferson "is worse than ages of that which your fathers rose in rebellion to oppose," a seventh part of the inhabitants of your country.[10]

Douglass obviously believed that a moral rhetoric based on the common civil religion could and should influence the political process. He was, in other words, attempting to exploit the fact that church and state were not separated in America.

The civil religion of black nationalists was ironically adapted from that of American conservatives. The civil religion of these persons was after the pattern that John R. Bodo describes in his *Protestant Clergy and Public Issues*. It was a civil religion that assumed that God had never intended for black people to share in the blessings of American nationality. They operated under the assumption that America's egalitarian claims were hypocritical. They felt that they must work out their own salvation in a land of their own, which would be a "city on a hill" and a beacon of liberty. They viewed America as a land of lawless mobocracy and tyranny of the majority. Their goal was to get away from the United States, because they believed that black Americans would never be full citizens. They felt that the destiny of black Americans was to found a nation of their own, and they employed a religious rhetoric to this end, which ironically reflected their exposure to the American doctrine of Manifest Destiny.[11]

They accepted a doctrine that had been popularized since the turn of the century by American clergymen like Samuel Hopkins and Robert Finley, who concurred with Jefferson's judgement that there was no place in America for a free black population. The doctrine came to be supported by an increasing number of clergymen and passed into secular circles. In 1816, Finley published his *Thoughts on Colonization,* a group of distinguished Americans met in the hall of the House of Representatives to establish the "American Society for Colonizing the Free People of Color of the United States." Although the society was never, strictly speaking, a government agency, it consistently made use of government resources and obtained the support of president Monroe in supporting colonization ventures. The rhetoric of colonization was invariably religious and tied to the prospect of African evangelization. In short, a plan to deport free black Americans was supported by the American president and the U.S. Navy, and partial justification for the government support was in the claim that the goals of the colonization society were missionary.[12]

With the coming of the Civil War, it seemed that the dire predictions of Thomas Jefferson and David Walker were coming to pass. James Moorhead in his *American Apocalypse,* a study of American social and intellectual history during the Civil War, has shown how Americans tended to interpret the war years in terms of Christian religious mythologies. In the minds of abolitionists, the war was the price the nation must pay for the sin of slavery. In Lincoln's second inaugural address, this was certainly the theme. Finally, Lincoln himself came to be seen as the sacrificial victim, whose death was demanded in expiation of the nation's guilt. If such attitudes were present in the minds of whites, they were just as present in the minds of the black population, who, rightly or wrongly, believed the war to be a struggle over Christian principles. The state was at war, in the name of the church militant. In a Christian nation, it was thoroughly appropriate for the state to do the bloody work of an avenging God.

> Murmer not against the Lord on account of the cruelty and injustice of man. His almighty arm is already stretched out against slavery—against every man, every constitution, and every union that upholds it. His avenging chariot is now moving over the bloody fields of the doomed south, crushing beneath its massive wheels the very foundations of the blasphemous system. Soon slavery shall sink like Pharaoh—even like that brazenhearted tyrant, it shall sink to rise no more, forever.[13]

Crisis of Industrial Democracy: Reconstructing Black Religion

The moralistic enthusiasm of the Civil War years did not last. There followed a period that was, in some dismal respects, similar to our own. It was accurately described by W. E. B. Du Bois as "the psychological moment when the nation was a little ashamed of having bestowed so much sentiment on Negroes, and was concentrating its energies on Dollars."[14] This gilded era, extending from 1876 to 1920, marked an age when America was becoming obsessed with power. It was a time when white Americans got tired of feeling guilty. It was a period during which land was being grabbed, fortunes being made, wars being fought, and hegemonies being defined. It was a period during which white religious leadership was much concerned with spreading the message of American dominance to the far corners of the world. One of America's most prominent preachers declared that the entire world was "our world," and repeated De Tocqueville's warning of an impending clash with Russian imperialism.[15] During this period, black religious leadership found itself in a confrontation with white backlash and discovered that moral suasion alone was not going to be effective in the fight, because the rhetoric of moralism had given way to the preachments of self-satisfied piety. American religion was safely in the hands of colorful and immensely popular evangelicals, who had decided that racial justice need not be among the concerns of the revivalist.

In post-Reconstruction Washington, the most prominent intellectual leader among the clergy was Alexander Crummell. Crummell was a freeborn Episcopal priest of unmixed African ancestry. He migrated to Liberia in 1853 and, like many of his contemporaries, soon began to speak of Liberia as a "city on a hill." Crummell had no real conception of the separation of church and state. Indeed, he practically advocated a theocracy:

> I call that a free system which recognizes the secondary as well as the primary ends of government; which not only subserves men's temporal interest, but also seeks their moral elevation, and aims to strengthen their souls.
>
> I call that a free system which inspires respect for authority; which reverences law in the person of rulers, which recognizes the authority of God in governors and magistrates.
>
> In fine, I call that a free system which acknowledges government an ordinance of God; which holds all human law as subject to the higher law of heaven; which regards a nation as a grand instrument for human blessedness and the divine honor.[16]

Like many of the blacks who went to Liberia during its first fifty years, he believed that the nation had a manifest destiny to Christianize the continent. He spoke with the utmost disparagement of "heathenism" and of Islam, and he eventually left Liberia in disgust, because he could not persuade the government to support his ideas of the intimate linkage between Christianity, commerce, and civilization. Separation of church and state was never very important to Crummell, who was an Anglophile and in no way put off by the established church in England. At one stage of his career in Liberia, he even drafted a bill for the establishment of an Episcopal bishopric in Liberia, which would have had the effect of banning the activities of any other Episcopalians not under the jurisdiction of the bishop in Monrovia.[17] On his return to the United States in 1873, Crummell became a leader among black writers and intellectuals and on numerous occasions voiced his hostility to Jeffersonian democracy, because he felt that it went too far in the direction of separation of church and state.

When Thomas Jefferson declared that "governments derive their just powers from the consent of the governed," and left his dogma crudely at that point, he shut out a limitation which the pride and self-assertion of degenerate humanity is always reluctant to yield, and tardy to supply.

The theory of the Declaration is incomplete and misleading. Governments, my brethren, derive their just authority *first* of all, from the will of God, and then *next* from the consent of the governed. . . . Your president is as much a ruler, he is as truly a potentate as the Emperor of Russia or the Queen of Great Britain. He is your ruler and great magistrate and mine.[18]

Crummell exemplified the spirit of "uplift" ideology that Edward L. Wheeler attributes to black churchmen of his generation. He believed that black religion should address the concerns of this world. It ought to promote self-love and enlightened self-interest, and in order to do this it must first become a rational religion.[19] But, as Crummell saw it, slavery had tended to support only the most emotional, self-indulgent, and antinomian tendencies. Crummell recognized a problem that many of his contemporaries also recognized, and he spoke the sentiments of more than a few of them when he characterized plantation religion in the following way:

Their religion, both of preachers and people, was a religion without the Bible—a crude medley of scraps of Scripture, fervid imaginations, dreams, and superstitions. So thorough was the legal interdict of letters and teaching, that the race as a whole, knew nothing of the Scriptures nor of the Catechisms of the churches. I state it as a strong conviction, the result of wide inquiry, that at the close of the civil war not five hundred blacks . . . knew, in its entirety, the CATECHISM of the Episcopal Church. The Ten Commandments were as foreign from their minds and memories as the Vedas of India or the moral precepts of Confucius. Ignorance of the MORAL LAW was the main characteristic of "PLANTATION RELIGION!"[20]

Crummell's attitudes on the ideal relationship between church and state can be efficiently summarized. The United States was a Christian commonwealth, and public policy ought to be determined in accordance with nonsectarian, but nonetheless Christian, principles. The religion of black people ought to be concerned with the affairs of this world and with the perfection of American society. The extreme enthusiasm of traditional black religion must be ruthlessly stamped out, because it is anti-intellectual and apolitical.

Daniel Alexander Payne, senior bishop of the African Methodist Episcopal Church, held similar views, and many others among the reform-minded black clergy of the time were committed to the idea that church leadership must be in the hands of politically sophisticated and educated men. They actively opposed traditional black religion, along with its music and chanting and its almost universal belief that one could be saved purely as a result of the conversion experience.[21]

It should not be surprising that Payne gave his full endorsement to Booker T. Washington, when the latter established a bible college at Tuskegee Institute. Washington's position was that the church ought to be brought under the control of "strong, well-trained leaders in the industrial walks of life." These ministers would teach, by the example of their own productive industry, as tradesmen, farmers, and merchants; they would demonstrate the responsibilities of citizens in an industrial democracy. Industrial concerns were to permeate every aspect of black reform ideology, including religious ideology. The role of the church was to create a Christianity that would equip black folk for the responsibilities of living in an industrial democracy. In accord with this, Washington never lost an opportunity to oppose enthusiastic religion.[22]

Some of the most extreme examples of this gospel of uplift appear in the statements of Rev. Theophilus Gould Steward, an army chaplain, who argued that

> Nothing will do for the Negro race in this land what the rifle will do for him. War will winnow out his chaff; war will steady his nerves; toughen his fibre; assure him his limitations; harden his virtue; and lay the foundation for his character. Civilization has its foundation on the battle field. If we could get fifty-thousand or one hundred thousand black Americans in arms and keep them in training for a quarter of a century, the race would be carried forward many centuries. The general Negro needs to be taught respect for law and order and authority. . . . There is no greater civilizing agency for the Negro . . . than the army.

Steward made these remarks in 1898, the era of gunboat diplomacy and the social gospel of Josiah Strong. Such statements anticipated the Moynihan Report's emphasis on military training as a means of inculcating progressive manly virtues.[23]

This tough-mindedness in black religious thought was present in the writings of Rev. Francis J. Grimké, who combined Booker T. Washington's self-help doctrines with militancy in the area of civil rights. Grimké was both the slave and the son of Henry Grimké, which made him the nephew of the famous abolitionists Sarah and Angelina Grimké, who assisted him in acquiring an education and publicly acknowledged him and his brother Archibald. From 1875 to 1878, Grimké studied at the Princeton Theological Seminary, and on graduation he accepted a call from the 15th Street Presbyterian Church in Washington, D.C. The years of Grimké's pastorate spanned the decades that one historian referred to as "The Nadir," the period following Reconstruction, when the legal system and the force of social custom interacted to erode the effects of human rights activism that had emancipated and enfranchised black Americans during the years from 1860 to 1875. Grimké belonged to a small set of black intellectuals and activists who based their approach to black advancement on the self-help doctrine. His Saturday Circle entertained prominent black leaders from the United States and Africa, and he participated in numerous ecumenical activities with other black churchmen, including the Colored Minister's Union and the Bethel Literary Society.[24]

Grimké's theology was a reaction to the otherworldly religion that he and other educated ministers knew to be widespread among blacks in the South. This enthusiastic religion, which placed exclusive emphasis on the conversion experience, was also attacked by Alexander Crummell and by other black leaders, who felt that plantation religion was almost as bad as no religion at all. Grimké said:

> Where emotionalism prevails, there will be little or no instruction from the pulpit. The minister whose sole aim is to get up a shout, to excite the animal spirits, will not give much time to the study of God's word, or to the instruction of the people in the practical duties of religion. . . . Most of the shouting that is done is when the pulpit is dealing in glittering generalities, in meaningless utterances, or is conjuring up pictures that appeal purely to the imagination. It is when the minister is speaking of golden streets, and pearly gates, and white robes and a land flowing with milk and honey, that the noise is greatest. Everything is quiet when the theme is practical Christianity.[25]

During the years of Grimké's pastorate, most black American social and political thought flourished in the pulpit. Blacks were more dependent upon the church than were whites in this regard. The most prestigious black congregations in Washington were under the guidance of stern, puritanical men, who saw religion as a serious business. These men had, in many cases, lived through the Civil War, and had actually seen the glory of the coming of the Lord. Apocalypse, Armageddon, the New Heaven, and the New Earth had earthly as well as spiritual meaning for them. Their religion was not otherworldly, and they had witnessed the power of righteous religiosity to reshape the destiny of the nation.

Grimké was typical of the first generation of social gospelers. Despite the Calvinist roots of his intellectual tradition, Grimké had little time for the fatalism that pervaded much black religious thought. He believed that individuals were responsible for their own salvation. But his emphasis on personal responsibility in no way implied a rejection of the social gospel that was emerging among his contemporaries. Black leaders, contrary to what has been claimed by S. P. Fullinwider, were not oblivious to the movement. Most black preachers believed that individuals were responsible for the perfection of society, and that the godly life involved the attempt to build a heavenly city on earth. Thus, while he rejected the implicit determinism of both Calvinism and the social gospel, he accepted the political activism that was central to both. Grimké used the term "practical Christianity" to denote an emphasis on personal responsibility and righteous living, but practical Christianity implied more than individual morality. It was concerned with the struggles of the church militant and the political activism of the black nation.[26]

Because Grimké saw race relations not only as a political but as a moral issue, he was not the least squeamish about using the pulpit to speak on civic matters. He used the church to drum up membership for the National Association for the Advancement of Colored People, in which he was an officer. Grimké read to his congregation from *Crisis,* which was the official organ of the NAACP. He advocated using the church as a means of influencing public policy and molding public sentiment. Among the specific issues that he advocated from his Washington pulpit were antilynching legislation, abolition of segregation in departmental offices in Washington, restoration of Haitian independence, abolition of Jim Crow cars in interstate commerce. Grimké also reminded the congregation that the NAACP needed money to carry on its lobbying efforts. This was worldly and political religion.

Grimké epitomized the so-called social gospel with his position that "the Christian church cannot address itself to the solution of any problem without bettering conditions." But he was among those who interpreted social gospel most broadly, for he believed that the churches should be actively involved in the setting of public policy, and his ideas were not confined to race relations. Grimké served on the board of trustees of Howard University, the federally supported university for blacks in Washington, D.C. His angry remarks on the failings of the white Christian churches, delivered in the Howard divinity school, occasioned an attempt by Rep. James F. Byrnes of South Carolina to cut the university's budget. Howard's president, in the words of one biographer, "hedged on the question of academic freedom by pointing out that the School of Religion received no federal appropriations."[27]

Crummell and Grimké represent the triumph of progressive social Christianity in the black community. Their hostility to otherworldly religion, and to what Gayraud Wilmore has called "excessive piety," was fully consistent with their late nineteenth-century conception of Victorian morality as the hallmark of superior civilization.[28] Their Victorian conception of progress was, after all, a secularized form of the Christian perfectionism that had permeated nineteenth-century teleology. History had a purpose, and this purpose was to bring about a triumph of righteousness on earth. The role of the church was to mold public policy and bring it into conformity with Christian conceptions of civilization.

Within the black community, the church should guide the black masses in meeting the requirements of life in modern, urban, industrial society. Booker T. Washington's worldview was less militant and more secular than that of the churchmen, but he too believed that black people must be modernized, Christianized, civilized. They were a new people, said Crummell and Washington. By the turn of the century, Washington was using the term "New Negro" frequently. This New Negro was well represented by the imposing Victorian portraits of black community leaders in Washington's book, *A New Negro for a New Century*. Booker T. Washington, the chief prophet of the New Industrial Negro, preached a doctrine of Christian modernism in Tuskegee Chapel and did all he could to oppose the emotional and otherworldly variety of black religion that was common at the South.

The economic events of the first half of this century brought about a shift in the demography of black America. In 1900, they had been a predominantly agrarian population, but the labor demands of two world wars had drawn large numbers from the South to the North and had converted masses of peasants into an urban working class. Their leadership still came largely from the churches, and in the 1950s two of the most important leaders were Adam Clayton Powell, a congressman from Harlem, in the North, and Martin Luther King in the South. These two Baptist preachers were certainly not the only significant black public figures during these years, but they were among the most visible, and they became the foremost symbols of black Christian militancy in the public sphere. The essence of the public policy with which they were identified was the principle that segregation was fundamentally injurious to black Americans and therefore immoral. The impact of Powell and King on American government cannot be seen as ethnic politics; it must be seen as moral policy, and thus, as a successful breaching of the wall between church and state.

The integration movement, led by Martin Luther King, was one of the most successful breaches of the separation of church and state for black Americans. The movement was revivalistic in quality. It was overtly Christian in its methods and in its message. King proposed a missionary role for black Americans; they were to function as God's humanizing agents, with a message for the reform of America and for the world. It was his ability to demonstrate in vivid terms the message of nonviolence before the modern media, especially television, that led to his success. Passive resistance and turning the other cheek, whatever their theoretical shortcomings, proved effective. Nonviolence had an appeal and led to the conversion of the masses of white Americans to the principle of desegregation. Without the overwhelming power of the media shaping a favorable moral consensus on its side, the civil rights movement could never have been successful.

But as the civil rights movement began to achieve its successes, it soon became obvious that American race relations could not be equated with desegregation. There were economic problems to be solved as well as community disorder and institutional pathologies that were the heritage of slavery and racial discrimination. In 1965, Daniel Patrick Moynihan published his controversial report, *The Negro Family: The Case for National Action*. The document was, in a manner of speaking, the last attempt of the social gospel to put its policies into practice. The "Moynihan Report" was based on the same principles that had motivated the NAACP and the Urban League at the time of their founding fifty years earlier. Its assumption was that the black population of America would be saved only if they could begin to practice the style of life that ideally was supposed to characterize the upper middle classes in white America. Moynihan assumed that what was normal for the middle classes would be best for the masses of black Americans. The federal government was to become involved in making the dreams of the social gospel a reality. Monies were to be appropriated for the purpose of making the black man a warrior and a provider. Government policy was to bend all its efforts to making the black woman a mother and a homemaker.

Needless to say, the Black Muslims had no quarrel with such a prescription. They too accepted the conservative definitions of family normalcy to which Moynihan subscribed. *The Autobiography of Malcom X* reveals the high premium that the Muslims placed on the very values that Moynihan hoped to encourage, and shortly after the report was issued the Muslim newspaper, *Muhammad Speaks,* acknowledged the Moynihan Report as having documented some of Elijah Muhammad's claims with respect to the catastrophic effects of American life on black social institutions. Muslims were also pleased by a statement in the report that read, "The only religious movement that appears to have enlisted a considerable number of lower class Negro males in northern cities of late is that of the Black Muslims: a movement based on total rejection of white society."[29]

Martin Luther King's response to the Moynihan Report was even more strikingly supportive:

A recent study offers the alarming conclusion that the Negro family in the urban ghettos is crumbling and disintegrating. It suggests that the progress in civil rights can be negated by the dissolving of family structure and therefore social justice and tranquility can be delayed for generations. . . .

The negro family for three hundred years has been on the tracks of the racing locomotives of American history and was dragged along mangled and crippled. . . .

Because the institution of marriage was not legal under slavery, and with indiscriminate sex relations often with masters, mothers could identify their children but frequently not their fathers; hence a matriarchy developed. After slavery it did not die out because in the cities there was more employment for women than for men. Though both were unskilled, the women could be used in domestic service for low wages. The woman became the support of the household, and the matriarchy was reinforced.

The Negro male existed in a larger society which was patriarchal while he was the subordinate in a matriarchy.[30]

The annual beatification of Martin Luther King that coincides with Black History Month is tragically antihistorical. King's social gospel, even at the height of his influence, was already out of step with developing conceptions of progressive reform. It was absolutely in conflict with the consensus morality that liberals embrace today—only twenty years later. We are living in a world of constantly shifting attitudes towards labor, leisure, and social biology.

The Crisis of Post-Industrial Democracy: Reform in a Moral Vacuum

The Moynihan Report was the last gasp of the Victorian progressive conception of social gospel and social engineering. The problem with the report was not that it was racist or sexist but that it was out of date. In the years following World War II, American racial reform still followed patterns that had evolved as aspects of Christian progressivism and industrial Christianity. Since that time, however, the relationship between church and state in American social reform has reflected the crisis in American civil religion and the inability of the American people to take solace in the consensus view of what constitutes its system of moral belief. Between 1945 and 1965, something of a national consensus evolved with respect to American social values, at least in the area of race relations, but that consensus is no longer with us.

The coalition between the progressive Church and the sympathetic media that we witnessed in the late fifties and early sixties is no longer extant. It is the conservatives who now control televised religion, and cable television impacts on race relations in ways undreamed of at the time of the civil rights movement. The "700 Club," now the most prominent and political arm of American electronic religion, includes blacks on a basis of almost total social equality. They are used to promote conservative foreign policy and to endorse religious leaders for political candidacy.

White liberals have changed course on black leadership, and as a result a black public figure like the Reverend Jesse Jackson seems to be trying to run in several directions at once. Through Operation Push, he endorses traditional social gospel values, insisting on the importance of strong family life based on traditional marital relationships between heterosexual couples. At the same time, he attempts to enlist the support of our "gay brothers and sisters." At the Democratic convention in San Francisco, he tries to wrap himself in the remnants of McGovernist liberalism, and yet demonstrates a mean-spirited jealousy regarding the candidacy of Geraldine Ferraro. Jesse Jackson represents the perplexity of many black Christians who cannot accept that the goals of Martin Luther King's revolution are no longer desired by the radical/liberal wing in American politics. He attempts to exploit the heritage of the social gospel, while at the same time courting the new liberals who reject its outmoded industrial-age values.

During the first half of this century, the major black organizations — including the Urban League, the NAACP, and the Southern Christian Leadership Conference — based their programs on progressive Christian teleologies, a kind of providential historicism that assumed that race relations must inevitably improve. But like most modern advocates of social change, whether Marxist or Christian, they believed that the inevitable historical processes must be assisted by the machinery of the state. Social gospel programs were to be institutionalized by the federal government, which did indeed seem to be the instrument of Providence under the presidencies of Roosevelt, Truman, Eisenhower, Kennedy, and Johnson. Lyndon Johnson's programs for racial reform were the political realization of the social gospel, and the program of Daniel Patrick Moynihan was nothing more than a restatement of clichés that had been voiced by organizations such as the National Association of Colored Women and by the progressive black clergy for several decades.

Black American religion in 1950 was concerned with such worldly goals as indoctrination of the masses with middle-class sexual morality.

Black religious leaders advocated the support of the patriarchal nuclear family through economic policy, and the inculcation of military virtues in young men. These goals are no longer advocated. Black Americans, and other reform-minded people, are confronted with the problem of finding new ways of shaping public policy in an age when the traditional goals of the industrial progressives can no longer be accepted by religious radicals. In the past, black civil religion provided the black community with a sense of righteousness and purpose, and helped to articulate goals for public policy and governmental action. But black religion must adjust to the shifting priorities of white liberals if it is to regain its ability to overcome the barrier between church and state.

In past generations, black civil religion was aided by the fact that liberals were committed to the tough-minded, self-denying variety of Christianity that taught that salvation was a painful process. Such allies made steadfast friends. Unfortunately, the traditional ties between puritanism and civil rights reform are no longer extant. The values that the black church and many black activists support are more likely to be found in the self-help philosophies of Jerry Falwell and Minister Farrakhan than in the editorials of *The Village Voice*. That is why Jesse Jackson sounds like Jerry Falwell one day and like Minister Farrakhan the next.

If it were possible for black Americans to isolate themselves from the hedonism, self-indulgence, and subjectivism that are fast becoming the American liberal creed, it might be possible for them to serve as the saving remnant of American values. Martin Luther King, in his *Stride Toward Freedom,* expressed the hope that the struggles of black Americans would become the conscience of America and the world. But I do not believe that it is fair to ask black Americans to be the guardians of America's cultural and moral health. Healthy living can be burdensome, as can all forms of righteousness. In any case, black Americans are no more righteous than any other ethnic or racial group, difficult though it may be to reject the myth of black moral exceptionalism. It does not seem likely that black people are willing to sacrifice the American dream in order to fulfill the prophetic role that Martin Luther King wished on them. What seems most likely is that black Americans will experience, along with the rest of America, a decline into the electronic antinomianism that preaches that salvation is a playful pastime. The only hope that I can see for reform in America is for liberals and radicals to somehow regain the tough-minded puritanism, sobriety, and ascetic spirit of the abolition movement and the social gospel, which have served so well in the past as the basis of civil religion, civil rights, and progressive movements in church and in state.

N O T E S

1. Vittorio Lanternari, *The Religions of the Oppressed* (New York: Knopf, 1963).

2. Arthur Zilversmit, *The First Emancipation: The Abolition of Slavery in the North* (Chicago: University of Chicago Press, 1967), treats the religious basis of eighteenth-century abolitionism.

3. A. Leon Higgenbotham, Jr., *In the Matter of Color* (New York: Oxford, 1978), p. 36, treats the legal questions concerning the status of baptized slaves. See also Albert J. Raboteau, *Slave Religion* (New York: Oxford, 1978), p. 99.

4. Quoted from the manuscript version, Massachusetts Historical Society.

5. Henry Highland Garnet, ed., *Walker's Appeal in Four Articles* (1848; reprint, Arno/New York Times, 1969).

6. *Walker's Appeal,* pp. 46–47.

7. *Walker's Appeal,* p. 15.

8. *Walker's Appeal,* pp. 51, 80.

9. *Walker's Appeal,* p. 81.

10. Frederick Douglass, "Oration Delivered in Corinthian Hall, Rochester, July 5, 1852," *The Life and Writings of Frederick Douglass,* ed. Philip S. Foner (New York: International, 1955).

11. John R. Bodo, *The Protestant Clergy and Public Issues, 1812–1848* (Princeton: Princeton University Press, 1954).

12. Dated, but nonetheless indispensable, P. J. Staudenraus, *The African Coloniza-tion Movement, 1816–1865* (New York: Columbia University Press, 1961), contains basic information on white colonizationists but must be supplemented by Floyd Miller, *The Search for a Black Nationality* (Urbana: University of Illinois Press, 1975) for an under-standing of black participation in the movement. There is also much useful information in John R. Bodo's *Protestant Clergy and Public Issues.*

13. Daniel Alexander Payne, "To the Colored People of the United States," extract in William Wells Brown, *The Black Man* (New York: Thomas Hamilton, 1863), pp. 209–10.

14. W. E. B. Du Bois, *The Souls of Black Folk* (Chicago: McClurg, 1903), pp. 41–42.

15. Josiah Strong, *Expansion Under New World-Conditions* (1900; reprint, New York: Garland, 1971).

16. Alexander Crummell, *Africa and America* (Springfield, Mass.: Wiley, 1891), p. 140.

17. Alexander Crummell, "An Act to Provide for the Incorporation of Religious Societies in the Republic of Liberia, which Societies are now Existing as a Mission of the Protestant Episcopal Church, U.S.A.," Alexander Crummell Papers, MS. C. 51, Schom-burg Collection, New York Public Library.

18. Alexander Crummell, *The Greatness of Christ and Other Sermons* (New York: Whittaker, 1882), pp. 325–26.

19. Gayraud S. Wilmore, *Black Religion and Black Radicalism* (Garden City, N.Y.: Doubleday, 1972), pp. 156–59.

20. Crummell, *Africa and America,* p. 94.

21. Daniel Alexander Payne, *Recollections of Seventy Years* (Nashville: A.M.E Sun-day School Union, 1888), pp. 233–38, 253–55.

22. Booker T. Washington, "The Colored Ministry: Its Defects and Its Needs," *Chris-tian Union* 42 (August 1890): 199–200; reprinted in *The Booker T. Washington Papers,* ed. Louis R. Harlan (Urbana: University of Illinois Press, 1974), 1:71–75. Daniel Alexander Payne to Booker T. Washington, 3 Nov. 1890, in Harlan, *Papers,* pp. 97–98.

23. T. G. Steward, "Washington and Crummell," unidentified clipping in John Wesley

Cromwell scrapbook, in possession of Dr. Adelaide Cromwell. Lee Rainwater and William L. Yancey, eds., *The Moynihan Report and the Politics of Controversy* (Cambridge: MIT, 1967), contains the text of the original report.

24. Rayford W. Logan entitled one chapter of his *The Betrayal of the Negro* (New York; Collier Books, 1965), "The Nadir under McKinley." The first edition appeared under the title *The Negro in American Life and Thought: The Nadir, 1877–1901.* Biographical data on Grimké taken from the article "Francis James Grimké" by Henry J. Ferry in *Dictionary of American Negro Biography,* ed. Rayford W. Logan and Michael Winston (New York: Norton, 1983). See also Carter G. Woodson, ed., *The Works of Francis J. Grimké,* 4 vols. (Washington, D.C.: Associated Publishers, 1942).

25. Woodson, *Works,* 1:2030–31.

26. S. P. Fullinwider, *The Mind and Mood of Black America* (Homewood, Ill.: Dorsey Press, 1969), p. 15.

27. Ferry, *Dictionary of American Negro Biography,* p. 275.

28. Wilmore, *Black Religion and Black Radicalism,* p. 158.

29. Rainwater and Yancey, *Moynihan Report,* pp. 267–68. See also *The Autobiography of Malcolm X* (New York: Grove Press, 1964), p. 193.

30. Martin Luther King, "Speech at Abbott House," in Rainwater and Yancey, *Moynihan Report,* pp. 402–49.

Literature

The Lost World of the New Negro, 1895–1919

Black Literary and Intellectual Life before the "Renaissance"

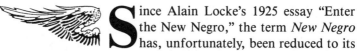 ince Alain Locke's 1925 essay "Enter the New Negro," the term *New Negro* has, unfortunately, been reduced to its linkage with the "Harlem Renaissance" of the 1920s. Due to the mistaken but still widely held belief that Alain Locke coined the term, Robert Bone once criticized Hugh Gloster for saying that the "New Negro Movement" began at the turn of the century.[1] Locke realized that the New Negro movement was not really new, and acknowledged that the term *New Negro* was problematic, but he proceeded to use it anyway. It was, after all, accurate to say that a new black proletarian culture had come into existence during and after the First World War. The interpretation of *New Negro* is of more than passing interest here, and it may be well to indicate something of its evolution in the decades before Alain Locke gave it its current meaning. In the Old South, the term *New Negro* referred to newly imported slaves. In the post-Reconstruction era, it referred to the new spirit of confidence and assertiveness among the recently freed masses of black Southerners. It began to appear in black publications during the mid-1890s. It was used as the title of a paper read by John M. Henderson at a meeting of the Bethel Literary Society in Washington in 1896. Booker T. Washington published a book called *A New Negro for a New Century* in 1900. Both Washington and Alexander

Crummell commonly spoke of the black American population as a "new people," referring to their emerging ethnic consciousness. Sutton Griggs used the term *New Negro* in his novel *Imperium in Imperio* in 1899.[2]

Locke's interpretation was by no means naive. The New Negro was viewed as the result of social and cultural change deriving from, but not limited to, the migration of masses of black peasants out of the South and into Harlem. This migration, argued Locke, led to the creation of a new material and economic base for black artists, politicians, and intellectuals. In New York, a substantial segment of the black population had relocated itself both physically and spiritually, and the professional classes — the doctors, lawyers, and school teachers associated with them — were forced to follow in both a practical and a symbolic sense. What was true of the stable bourgeois professionals was even more true for artists, novelists, journalists, and intellectuals. It is from Locke's interpretation that subsequent interpretations of the Harlem Renaissance and the New Negro phenomenon have been derived. Robert Hayden's definition of the period in the preface to the 1968 Atheneum reprint of *The New Negro* represents standard orthodox opinion:

> The New Negro movement, known also as the Harlem Renaissance and the Negro Renaissance, was less a movement, as we generally use the term, than a configuration of "new" racial attitudes and ideals and the upsurge of creativity inspired by them and by the iconoclastic spirit of the times. . . .
>
> The Negro Renaissance was a short duration, beginning in the Midtwenties and ending with the decade. Harlem was its acknowledged center. A Negro city within a city, bohemian, cosmopolitan, "fast"; vibrant locus of a variety of racial strains, nationalities, languages, dialects, folkways.[3]

This is the antihistorical, but largely unchallenged, prevailing view of the "New Negro Movement" that stresses "iconoclasm" and "bohemianism," and equates it with the Harlem Renaissance of the 1920s. Like most myths, this myth of the New Negro movement contains elements of truth despite its lack of conformity to fact. It reflects a common, albeit one-dimensional understanding.

Several scholars have observed that conflicting conceptions of the black ethos occurred in the consciousness of *soi disant* New Negroes during the 1920s. S. P. Fullinwider attributes the conflicting conceptions to a generation gap and to the replacement of "Racial Christianity" by the "sociological imagination."[4] It is important to remember, of course, that Racial Christianity was preserved in the Garvey movement, which included blacks, "old" and "new." Furthermore, not all members of the younger generation were fascinated by sociology. David Gordon Nielson attributes the conflict to class antagonism.[5] The small elite groups of blacks in Washington, Philadelphia, and Boston were color-conscious and obsessed with "superrespectability." And yet, an overlooked fact is that the elite upper classes also produced the American Negro Academy, whose members took active roles in the New Negro movement. Theodore Kornweibel has seen the New Negroes ethos as balancing two views of racial contributionism.[6] On the one hand, there was pride in distinct racial accomplishment, but this went hand in hand with a desire to have that accomplishment accepted as part of the American picture. Some were assimilationists, and some were separatists, and, as June Sochen has observed, while some pursued the generalized and hazy conception of the "American Dream," others sought to create a counterculture.[7] Individually, the observations of these scholars may tend to oversimplify, but taken together, they lead us to the conclusion that the New Negro was a composite of different types of persons. New Negroes were not only bohemian artists, but staid intellectuals, rugged labor leaders, tough-minded preachers, and conservative pan-Africanists. Most of them did not see themselves as breaking with past literary and intellectual traditions. During the twenties, they simply continued to engage in the same sorts of activities that had always interested them.

It is generally conceded that the concepts *New Negro* and *Harlem Renaissance* are problematic; so are the dates to which they refer. W. E. B. Du Bois, in a 1927 essay, dated the Renaissance from the turn of the century, and included Booker T. Washington's *Up From Slavery* among its masterworks.[8] It is probably for this reason that, since the time of Locke, scholars have attempted to avoid the term with such circumlocutions as *New Negro Movement* and *The Renaissance of the Twenties*. These terms, while safeguarding against the notion that the movement did not include Chicago and Atlanta, are just as unsatisfactory, hence the experimentation by Saunders Redding and Arthur P. Davis with the term *New Negro Renaissance* to refer to a period lasting from 1910 to 1940. While Robert Hayden would limit it to the half-decade from 1925 to 1930, Jervis Anderson seems to want to extend it from 1900 to 1950. The interesting thing, in my view, is that each of these definitions is perfectly intelligent and has its own internal logic.[9]

Dating the New Negro movement is not really important in this context; what is far more important is recognizing its continuity with the past, identifying the traditions that survived and thrived despite the clichés of the 1920s. Its cultural thrust was not always innovative; on the contrary, it was frequently preservationist. The "movement" was no more a *naissance* than it was a *renaissance*. There were traditional and conservative elements among the Harlem literati, and there were any number of persons who rejected the "happy-go-lucky," "iconoclastic," "bohemian" stereotype. In any case, there was nothing new about this stereotype, and even Sterling Brown, who enjoyed toying with it, correctly observed that the Harlem Renaissance stereotype was really the old plantation darky recreated with fashionable Jazz Age rhetoric. Nathan Huggins has reminded us that when Al Jolson blackened his face, he symbolized not only the Americanization of European Jews but the historical impulse that led many white Americans to Negrify themselves.[10] The desire of whites to chase the chocolate sweets of black bottom tells us less about blacks than it does about whites. The happy-go-lucky Negro became a fascinating symbol to white Americans seeking to free their personalities from the constraints of Victorian civilization. David Lewis has suggested that the reason for the ephemeral success and ultimate "failure" of the Harlem Renaissance is the fact that white Americans eventually lost interest in the stereotypes that had once been chic and ceased to nurture them with their financial support.[11]

Michael Peplow, Arthur P. Davis, and June Sochen observed, some years ago, that the literary and intellectual activity of the period was not confined to the iconoclastic and exotic. Unfortunately, the more traditional aspects of the period have been referred to pejoratively with such terms as "genteel school" and "best foot forward literature" and attached to the pathetic slogan "We are like you," presumably addressed to whites as if the alternative urban ghetto culture were any less concerned with impressing white folk. More recently, Gloria T. Hull has taken us a long way toward correcting the idea that the genteel, bourgeois tradition in black writing is "conservative, stiff, uptight, and accommodationist." I agree with Hull's observation, and I would add that the "bohemian/realistic" tradition may just as easily (and just as unfairly) be characterized as licking the boots of white cultural imperialists by conforming to minstrel show stereotypes of the black personality.[12]

Standard portrayals of the twenties are based on the questionable premise that black artistic and intellectual life benefited from the fashionable linkage between modernism and primitivism during the period. Perhaps fortunately, no term has yet been invented to describe the literary and intellectual life among black Americans that was centered in Washington, D.C., during the 1890s and had its roots in the traditions of abolitionist political rhetoric and evangelical Protestant reform. Bourgeois religion in its Victorian manifestations was a fundamental and indispensable ingredient of nineteenth-century American literature among blacks no less than among whites. It is generally well known that turn-of-the-century Washington was an important center of black social and political life, but this world is usually treated in a pejorative manner. The over-reactive condemnation by artists and intellectuals of the follies and foibles of the black bourgeoisie has obscured any interest in the more legitimate aspects of their cultural and intellectual life.

Even such a perceptive scholar as Constance McLaughlin Green, who handles Washington's black bourgeoisie objectively and respectfully, provides an illustration of the problem I describe. Her excellent volume *The Secret City* is so far the best general history of black Washington.[13] Perfectly commendable as social history, it reveals no interest on the part of its author in literary or intellectual history. One would almost be led to believe that black Washingtonians simply did not participate in the life of the mind in America. Mary Church Terrell, a woman of considerable literary talent, is mentioned purely in connection with her social and political activities. She is not mentioned as often as is her politically active husband Robert H. Terrell, a federal judge. Paul Laurence Dunbar is not mentioned, except as the inspiration of Dunbar High School. Alexander Crummell is represented by two passing sentences and a handsome photograph, but his literary significance is never acknowledged.

Black Washingtonians cannot be dismissed as "toney" mulatto snobs. The existence of an elite group of serious and educated black Americans in turn-of-the-century Washington made possible the existence of an E. Franklin Frazier and an Alain Locke, two of the more important figures of the Harlem Renaissance who, ironically, lived in Washington. There was a cultural movement in Washington, and much of the Harlem Renaissance did, in fact, take place there. Furthermore, a Washington Renaissance had predated the one in Harlem by at least twenty years. Harold Cruse seems close to acknowledging this very point when, with appropriate homage to Carter G. Woodson, he describes developments in Washington life between the Civil War and the First World War as a result of the "Migration of the Talented Tenth."[14] This migration included black politicians, who left the South with the collapse of Reconstruction; artisans and tradespeople, who were displaced by the rise of all-white labor movements; and schoolteachers and other educated persons, who refused to work under the degrading conditions that undermined the roles of intellectual leadership. Such persons found the centers of their intellectual life in the churches of Washington, particularly the Presbyterian, Episcopal, and African Methodist Episcopal.

One likely reason that the cultural movement in Washington at the turn of the century has not received more scholarly attention is that it does not conform to vulgar perceptions of black culture. Most scholars who concern themselves with nineteenth-century black culture are attracted by its rich and colorful folklore, its exuberant religiosity, and its earthy peasant traditions. Twentieth-century black culture is visible only so long as it conforms to the patterns of urbane exoticism found in jazz and the blues. Students of literature and culture for the past twenty years have evaluated black life and art almost solely in terms of their usefulness in undermining any vestiges of Victorian civilization that survive in the larger society. Black culture is valued for its undermining qualities. In the words of one of its admirers, it represents "one big syncopated Bronx cheer for the righteous squares everywhere."[15] Black culture is thus judged on the basis of how well it conforms to the iconoclastic, modernist criteria that white critics wish to impose. Judged by these criteria, black literature is interesting for its exotic quality rather than its more tough-minded traditions.[16]

The popular image of black American culture was recorded by Carl Van Vechten, a white aficionado of avant-garde culture, in his 1926 novel of the Harlem Renaissance, *Nigger Heaven*. Van Vechten seemed aware of the fact that there had been some sort of bourgeois cultural life before Harlem, and although he wasn't quite certain as to what it was, he depicted it unsympathetically through the character of Hester Albright:

> Hester, a spinster of thirty-eight, lived with her mother, a deaf, querulous, garrulous, tiresome, old lady, on the fourth floor of an apartment building on St. Nicholas Avenue. They had migrated from Washington to Harlem about five years previously. Why, nobody exactly understood, as Washington society, according to Hester, was immeasurably superior to the Harlem variety. . . . She particularly assumed an aggressive and antagonistic attitude towards the new literary group which was springing up in Harlem, albeit it was fostered by older intellectuals as one of the most promising indications of an eventual Negro supremacy. This antagonism . . . was inspired by the fact that this younger group was more inclined to write about the squalor and vice of Harlem life than about the respectable elegance of Washington society.[17]

Van Vechten's symbolic treatment of the relative places of Harlem and Washington in black culture did not lack validity, but it was based on an unfortunate bias. Like any number of observers during the first half of the century, he had an impression of Washington society as a shallow, artificial, spurious culture that attempted to imitate white gentility and failed embarrassingly.[18] But because Van Vechten did not understand the goals of Washington cultural and literary life, he provided only the most superficial allusion to the rivalry between Washington and New York. He did not probe the economic, demographic, and intellectual forces that were at work to make the public impressions of these two black Meccas so different. Van Vechten wrote from the perspective of a liberal white

bohemian whose interest in Harlem was a good illustration of the aforementioned "Bronx cheer" phenomenon. Harlem and the black bohemianism associated with it were the elements that attracted Van Vechten,
and while he acknowledged the existence of Washington society and
manners, he characterized them as, at best, spinsterish and stiff.

It is true that turn-of-the-century Washington, like any other community, had its fatuous and factitious elements. E. Franklin Frazier's
unacknowledged precursor, Booker T. Washington, wrote of Washington
society with contempt and hostility. The Tuskegeean described the nation's capital as a place where foolish young Negroes spent their time and
their money attempting to imitate the manners and lifestyles of wealthy
whites.[19] W. E. B. Du Bois agreed with him. In his first novel, *The Quest
of the Silver Fleece,* Du Bois presented black Washington as the focal
point of all black venality, artificiality, and cynicism. Alexander Crummell, an Episcopal priest, complained bitterly of the class of government
clerks and political hangers-on, the fashionable set, who cared nothing
for racial advancement.[20]

But there was another side to the black Washington elite; it contained a group of writers and thinkers who were racially responsible and
worthy of respect. Literate culture in Washington was dominated by
flinty old black nationalist preachers who had come of age before or
during the Civil War. They were Puritanical, committed to "practical
religion," and hostile to the characteristic expressions of the backwoods
revival and the storefront church. They took their politics seriously,
preached the necessity of adjusting to industrial democracy, and advocated temperance. Black literary activity in turn-of-the-century Washington was centered around literary societies that the churches sponsored.
These literary clubs were of great importance as the framework for some
of the important structures of the Harlem Renaissance. Black bourgeois
literary institutions prepared the way for Garveyism, the Association for
the Study of Negro Life and History, and the NAACP—all of which
eventually established journals that published black authors during the
Harlem Renaissance.

Black literary societies, whose activities dated from the late 1700s,
witnessed the origins of the pan-Africanist and Negro Improvement
rhetoric that became highly visible in the 1920s, but was hardly new.
Marcus Garvey and W. E. B. Du Bois, the chief pan-Africanists of the
1920s, represented the Spartan qualities of the Harlem Renaissance, elements that were not celebrated by the prophets of jazz and the blues.
Their philosophy of black leadership, with its emphasis on the uplift of
the masses, derived from a nineteenth-century tradition in leadership
that had sought to prepare black people for a new industrial age. The

black literary societies of Washington, D.C., had encouraged such notions by inviting Booker T. Washington to address them and by otherwise urging him to participate in their activities. Although black literary and intellectual figures were often critical of Washington, they did not disagree with his public pronouncements in favor of Puritan virtues.

The most important of the Washington literary societies was maintained by the African Methodist Episcopal Church, which also supported a major literary journal, *The AME Review*. The A.M.E.s were notably committed to education, and at the insistence of their senior bishop, Daniel Alexander Payne, the denomination purchased and began to operate Wilberforce University in Xenia, Ohio, during the Civil War. The bishop encouraged elitist notions of culture and literature and was known for his crusade to rid the church of "Africanisms." Although he did not settle in Washington, he was responsible, on one of his visits to the capital, for founding the Bethel Literary Society, which began to function in that city in 1881.[21]

Major leadership in the intellectual life of black Washington was provided by Francis James Grimké and his wife, Charlotte Forten.[22] The Grimkés maintained a position in the lives of literate black Washingtonians through their "Saturday Circle," where prominent blacks from all over the United States found the opportunity to share ideas with receptive audiences. Both of them left a legacy of interesting writings. Frank Grimké's sermons and addresses are clear, forceful, and direct; the style of Charlotte's *Journal* is subtle and sometimes ironic. The Grimkés were among the radical black leaders of their time. They found themselves among the critics of Booker T. Washington's so-called Tuskegee Machine. During the First World War, the widowed Frank Grimké was among the rising number of black intellectuals who attacked W. E. B. Du Bois for his "conservative" leadership and his temporary flirtation with the Democratic Party. To a mind such as Grimké, and because of his familial connections with both white and black abolitionists, the struggle for civil rights was inextricably linked with Puritanism, temperance, and sexual discipline. Frank Grimké was one of the founders of a short-lived association known as the Negro American Society. This group met during late December 1877 and the early months of 1878 in the home of John W. Cromwell. It was unsuccessful as an institution, but it formed the basis of a later organization, the American Negro Academy. The existence of the Negro American Society also demonstrates that Washington intellectuals were meeting and interacting during the late nineteenth century.[23]

Among the more notable black leaders who interacted with the

Grimkés was Edward Wilmot Blyden, a well-known pan-Africanist and Liberian nationalist of Ibo origin, who, born in the Danish West Indies, made a tour of the United States in the 1890s. He authored *Christianity, Islam, and the Negro Race.* Edwin S. Redkey has demonstrated that there was even a Blyden cult among the masses of black peasants in the deep South. Blyden spoke before the Bethel Literary Society and met with the Grimké's "Saturday Circle".[24]

The most impressive of the Washington-based organizations was the American Negro Academy, founded by the leading black man of letters in turn-of-the-century Washington, Alexander Crummell (1819–1898).[25] Crummell was born free in New York to parents of unadulterated African ancestry. He was brought up in the Episcopal church, where he came early under the influence of Peter Williams, an Episcopal priest with some sympathies for Back to Africa movements. The first black newspaper in the United States, *Freedom's Journal,* was founded in his father's home, and he was exposed early to the superheated dispute over black nationalism that rent the New York black community. He was old enough to be aware of the Nat Turner revolt at the time of its occurrence, and he spoke of his awareness in later years. As a youth, he could not have avoided coming into contact with the ideas of David Walker, who was a correspondent for *Freedom's Journal.* His teachers, his parents, his spiritual advisors, and his schoolmates were all aware of the publication of Walker's controversial *Appeal,* a heated response to Jefferson's *Notes on the State of Virginia.*[26]

At the age of fourteen, Crummell became aware of the claim of John C. Calhoun that if he could find a Negro who understood Greek syntax, he would accept the humanity of black people. Crummell in response had determined to become an intellectual and began to collect his papers in 1837, at the age of eighteen. Among those available on microfilm are some four hundred sermons and addresses written between 1840 and 1898. He studied at Cambridge University in England, where he earned an "ordinary degree" in 1853. Crummell served as an Episcopal missionary to West Africa between 1853 and 1872, but not for the total of twenty years commonly ascribed to him. When he returned to the United States in 1872, he settled in Washington, where his influence was strongly felt. He published three books, in which he outlined a philosophy that was conservative on every conceivable issue, save equal rights for black Americans. His writings are filled with allusions to classical and modern authors, his favorites being Tacitus, Burke, and St. Paul. In the last years of his life, Crummell founded the American Negro Academy, which was of considerable significance until the Harlem Renaissance, but which collapsed in the 1920s with the rise of the Jazz Age definition of black culture.[27]

Shortly after founding the American Negro Academy in 1897, Crummell visited England, where he made contact with West Indian and West African students, who later formed the African Association in London. The Academy inducted a number of corresponding members in Africa and in England, as well as Africans and West Indians in the United States. West Africans such as Orishatukeh Faduma and J. E. Casely Hayford, along with Edward Wilmot Blyden, attracted the attention of reading Afro-Americans. As William H. Ferris has demonstrated in *The African Abroad,* they wrote novels, published newspapers, and made speaking tours in the United States.[28] West Indians, like Orishatukeh Faduma and Sylvester Williams; East Africans like Duse Mohamed; and South Africans, like P. K. Isaka Seme, were also widely read and quoted wherever there were literate black populations. All of the above were reasonably well known among people of the Du Bois/Ferris ilk, and their pan-Africanism laid the groundwork for the Harlem Renaissance. Alfred Moss, in his first-rate volume *The American Negro Academy,* has addressed the problem of changing cultural values as a cause of the demise of the Academy during the 1920s.[29] The papers of the Academy allow only a few tantalizing glimpses at the question of shifting cultural values. Several prominent cultural figures of the twenties were members of the Academy, including Jesse Moorland, Carter G. Woodson, and Alain Locke. But these figures distanced themselves from the rhetoric of the blues and jazz, and their best-known activities were not centered in New York.[30]

Civilization was the watchword of this earlier New Negro movement in Washington, and the variety of literature that it produced, mostly essays and sermons, resulted directly from the material conditions under which its chief figures lived. Their literary awareness was still largely informed by the apocalyptic moral struggles of the Civil War and Reconstruction. They did not conceive of black Americans as one of a number of ethnic groups maneuvering for power in a system of national ward politics but viewed race relations as a moral struggle. The solution of racial problems was seen mainly as a matter of bringing moral influences to bear in the cause of making white Americans more democratic and more just and black people more civilized. In the words of Alexander Crummell's inaugural address before the American Negro Academy, "Civilization" was the "primal need of the Race." The idea was not new; it had dominated the rhetoric of racial uplift since the late 1850s. Black people were to assume the principal responsibility for "Negro Improvement." The educated class of black people, the "Talented Tenth," had the responsibility to become *servi servorum dei,* servants of

God's chosen people, the African race. When the task of civilizing had been accomplished in the time of God, the world would witness "The Destined Superiority of the Negro."[31]

Two of Crummell's protégés, who later joined the Garvey movement, were William H. Ferris and John E. Bruce. The career of Ferris reveals the continuity between the spirit of the American Negro Academy and that of the Harlem Renaissance. Ferris held master's degrees from Harvard and from Yale, and like many of the disfranchised intellectuals who joined the Garvey movement, he was committed to the preservation of genteel traditions. In the American Negro Academy, Ferris demonstrated a pronounced admiration for "that spirit which the Anglo-Saxon exhibits — that spirit of the age: the more obstacles you put before it, the more determined it is to overcome, to triumph".[32] In his extraordinary compilation of philosophical meanderings, *The African Abroad* (1913), Ferris defended genteel traditions, discoursing on "The Black Man's Spiritual Strivings," which he discussed in terms of Cicero's *Pro Archaea Poeta* and the works of Milton and Goethe.[33] Randall Burkett has correctly stressed the social Darwinist and Christian civilizationist elements in Ferris's thinking, to which Burkett attributes the influences of Social Darwinism on Garvey. In any case Garvey, like Ferris, had great admiration for the aggressive empire-building spirit of the Western powers, especially Great Britain.[34]

The career of Ferris reveals not only the reasons that we cannot associate "New Negroes" with bohemianism; it shows us that the Harlem Renaissance grew out of the conception of a New Negro that existed in black America during the counter-Reconstruction era. His cultural and literary ideology reflected a Christian black nationalism, with its roots in the African Civilization movement of the antebellum decade. His attitudes can be described as "civilizationist," meaning that he sought to "civilize" the black masses. His rhetoric was always chauvinistic, and he had a penchant for quoting European authors in support of his black teleological theories. Ferris and his fellow editor at the *Negro World,* John E. Bruce, provide illustrations of the fact that there is a continuity between turn-of-the-century "New Negroes" and those who appropriated that term during the Harlem Renaissance. Their sense of literary and intellectual tradition did not have to undergo a rebirth; it had never died out.

One would not wish to convey the impression that Washington was the only significant center of black literary and intellectual activity before the First World War. Atlanta, with its several black colleges and theological seminaries, was able to support a thriving intellectual community. There were, of course, disadvantages to being in Atlanta, as J.

Max Barber soon learned. When his literary magazine *The Voice of the Negro* protested against the Atlanta Riot of 1906, Barber was run out of Atlanta and the magazine eventually failed. There can be no question, however, of the quality represented by *Voice of the Negro,* which compares favorably with the best products of Harlem twenty years later. W. E. B. Du Bois also undertook literary publishing ventures during his Atlanta years, when he experimented with two publications, *Horizon* and *Moon.*[35]

Boston, too, produced a number of high quality literary publications. Charles Alexander published *Alexander's Magazine,* known for its pan-African sympathies. Pauline Hopkins was a prominent editor and contributor to *The Colored American Magazine.* Josephine Ruffin published *The Woman's Era.* All of these publications were in the genteel tradition, but they cannot be described as frivolous. They provided a window into the self help philosophies of their editors and authors, while at the same time assuming a militant stance on race relations. *The Colored American* soon moved to New York where, under the control of persons sympathetic to Booker T. Washington, it eventually failed. *Alexander's Magazine,* which remained in Boston, resisted Washington's control and eventually went out of business.[36]

The Woman's Era was a tasteful, attractive publication, and represented the "civilizationist" imperatives and domestic feminism of its founder, Josephine St. Pierre Ruffin. Ruffin, who is credited by some scholars with founding the national black women's club movement in the United States, was dedicated to a crusading brand of journalism. Her magazine supported the militant antilynching crusade of Ida B. Wells, which naturally put her into conflict with such black women as Mary Church Terrell, Fannie Barrier Williams, and Margaret Murray Washington. On one issue, however, all black women's leadership seemed united: the need to encourage respectability and uplift among the black masses. "Lifting as we climb" was their motto, and the development of new ideals of sexual morality was among the chief concerns of *The Woman's Era.*[37]

The Harlem Renaissance was, of course, a different sort of phenomenon than what had occurred earlier in the other eastern centers of culture. In some respects, however, the two intellectual movements were similar and closely related. There was overlapping leadership in the persons of such European-educated intellectuals as W. E. B. Du Bois, Alain Locke, and Carter G. Woodson. At least three Harlem Renaissance figures — William H. Ferris, John E. Bruce, and W. E. B. Du Bois — had been disciples of Alexander Crummell, or had at least worked with him in the American Negro Academy. Thus, there were two groups of New

Negroes associated with the Renaissance of the 1920s: the "old" New Negroes, mentioned above, and the "new" New Negroes, including the novelists Claude McKay and Rudolph Fisher and the poets Countee Cullen and Langston Hughes. The latter group celebrated the fast, jazzy life-style associated with the Harlem myth.

W. E. B. Du Bois, a cultural conservative, believed that the only legitimate black mass culture was that of the rural peasantry. He did not think much of the Jazz Age conception of black culture, as he made clear in his review of *Nigger Heaven,* with its celebration of the exotic and its superficial treatment of the Washington "civilizationist" tradition. He was equally hostile toward Claude McKay's novel *Home to Harlem.*

> McKay has set out to cater to that prurient demand on the part of white folk for a portrayal in Negroes of that utter licentiousness which conventional civilization holds white folk back from enjoying – if enjoyment it can be called. That which a certain decadent section of the white American world, centered particularly in New York, longs for with fierce and unrestrained passions, it wants to see written out in black and white and saddled on black Harlem.[38]

These attitudes reflect more than the desire of an "uptight" bourgeois Negro to suppress embarrassing depictions of the black "riff raff." No one believed more strongly than Garvey in "Negro Improvement." Largely because of his movement, it is impossible to dismiss the concern for black respectability as the confused twitchings of aging Washington mulattos. And, thanks to Garvey, the concern for genteel conceptions of black cultural destiny did not conveniently disappear when the Harlem Renaissance began. Garvey's critique of Van Vechten, like that of Du Bois, harkened back to the original conservative values of the American Negro Academy. Garvey's contacts with John E. Bruce, William H. Ferris, and Duse Mohamed had exposed him to the American Negro Academy philosophy and made him a part of its international network. He reacted negatively to white literary dictators like Van Vechten.[39] He also attacked McKay's *Home to Harlem:*

> "The white people have these Negroes to write [this] kind of stuff . . . so that the Negro can still be regarded as a monkey or some imbecile creature. Whenever authors of the Negro race write good literature for publication the white publishers refuse to publish it, but wherever the Negro is sufficiently known to attract attention he is advised to write in the way that the white man wants."[40]

Garvey and McKay were members of the same generation and came from the same Jamaican background, but the differences between them were profound. McKay embraced the bohemian/proletarian conception of black culture; Garvey belonged to a tradition, originating in the eighteenth century, known as "Ethiopianism." This involved a teleological view of history, based on the Biblical prophecy "Ethiopia shall soon stretch out her hands unto God."[41] This Ethiopian prophecy, which had informed the writings of such nineteenth-century authors as David Walker, Alexander Crummell, and Edward Wilmot Blyden, was known to black authors in both the United States and Africa. The Biblical mysticism of Ethiopianism was often blended with other teleological world views. There was a common tendency among black authors, for example, to refer to the observations of Tacitus on the virile barbarians of western Europe. Just as the western barbarians had risen to superiority over the decadent Romans, so too would the Africans rise to superiority over western Europe, if they could maintain the cold water regimen of Spartan Christianity.[42]

Until very recently, the Garvey movement was viewed as a movement of the unlettered masses. Scholarship of the past fifteen years has tended to stress the fact that university students, petty capitalists, and disfranchised intellectuals were also well represented among its followers. Garveyism attracted at least two members of the American Negro Academy—William H. Ferris, a Yale Divinity graduate, and John E. Bruce, a popular essayist. Garvey himself had been influenced as a boy by the journalist Dr. J. Robert Love, a physician as well as an Episcopal priest, much admired by Bruce and Crummell. Garvey had worked in the London offices of Duse Mohamed in the year that Mohamed was elevated to membership in the American Negro Academy, and an article on the Academy appeared in Mohamed's magazine *The African Times and Orient Review* during the time of Garvey's London sojourn. When Garvey set up his American program, he included Duse Mohamed, John E. Bruce, and William H. Ferris, all members of the Academy, in his movement. Du Bois was asked to join, but he was arrogant, independent, and stubborn. He was too proud to consider working with the extravagant, theatrical Garvey, although the spiritual values of the two men were not entirely divergent.

Treatments of the Harlem Renaissance are for the most part too concerned with the clash between Garvey and Bu Bois to take notice of the points on which their philosophies overlapped. They were agreed on the need for "Negro Improvement," black uplift, and African Civilization. Through the writings of Garvey and Du Bois, one can see that the old ideal of Negro Improvement had collided headlong with the cultural relativism and bohemianism of the Harlem New Negro movement. For Langston Hughes and Claude McKay, on the other hand, the Renaissance was associated with iconoclasm, dadaism, the blues, jazz, and cubism.[43]

By the late 1920s, Du Bois was convinced that the new definitions of black American culture were injurious. His novel *Dark Princess* attempted a panoramic view of the New Negro movement and was critical of its stereotypes. One recalls his hostile depiction of the cabaret in one of the novel's early chapters, and of what the omniscient narrator calls "vulgar blues":

> The cabaret was close, hot, and crowded. There was loud music and louder laughter and the clinking of glasses. More than half the patrons were white, and they had the furtive air of fugitives in a foreign land, out from under the eyes of their acquaintances. Some were drunk and noisy. Others seemed looking expectantly for things that did not happen, but which surely ought to happen in this bizarre outland! The colored patrons seemed more at home and natural. They were just laughing and dancing, although some looked bored.[44]

In 1933 Du Bois offered a more directly hostile appraisal, once again focusing on the idea that the Renaissance pandered to the prurient interests of whites:

> Why was it that the Renaissance of literature, which began among Negroes ten years ago, has never taken real and lasting root? It was because it was a transplanted and exotic thing. It was a literature written for the benefit of white people and at the behest of white readers, and started out privately from the white point of view. It never had a real Negro constituency, and it did not grow out of the inmost heart and frank experience of Negroes; on such an artificial bases, no real literature can grow.[45]

The legitimate roots of black American culture are not confined to plantation folklore, the blues style, and proletarian iconoclasm. As Langston Hughes observed, "there is a wealth of unexploited material to be discovered in the world of the black middle class."[46] A sound theory of black literature should heed the caveat of Lawrence Levine, who reminds us that "folk expression is only one part of a people's culture."[47] The study of black culture necessitates recognizing a multiplicity of traditions that existed in black American letters before the Jazz Age, including the abolitionist tradition in leadership and the heritage of the "social gospel." The language of the sermon is one of the most important elements in this tradition, because if flows naturally into the rhetoric of black nationalism. The missionary movement in Africa during the nineteenth century bears close examination as a source of pan-African literary and intellectual conventions such as "civilizationism" and "Ethiopianism." Black language and literature have been shaped not only by plantation laborers and the urban poor but by the more literate classes. We shall never really appreciate the nature of black American language and literature until we have reconstructed the cultural and intellectual life of literate, urban nineteenth-century black America. Likewise, the so-called Harlem Renaissance will not be understood until we have seen its relationship to the cultural life of black Washington in the late nineteenth century.

However, black intellectual and literary life before and during the Harlem Renaissance are usually presented as if the tough-minded Puritanical and Spartan tradition had never existed. Black cultural conservatives like Josephine Ruffin, Mary Church Terrell, Du Bois, Garvey, and the Grimkés are left out of literary history. We proclaim by fiat that they are not "literary" and restrict our attention to writers like Claude McKay, Jean Toomer, and Langston Hughes, who were sympathetic to the "Bronx Cheer" phenomenon. As modern students of literature, we know what to do with them. We have a critical vocabulary that is suited to the exaltation of both "modernism" and "primitivism." The two ideas are closely linked in the discourse of the present age. Contemporary discourse, like the artists it venerates, celebrates the decline of Victorian bourgeois morality, assuming that a relaxing of cultural norms will lead to a more hospitable environment for contemporary social and artistic aspirations. The cultural relativism and relaxed sexual morality that characterized the "bohemian/proletarian" conception of the "New Negro Renaissance" of the twenties was anathema to the values of the traditionalists. But their protests were futile in the face of neglect by those whites who were most interested in black culture. Du Bois, as we have seen, was convinced that the Harlem Renaissance was a failure because if was too dependent upon the taste of chic whites, who were interested in blacks only as symbols of the exotic. Langston Hughes eventually came to share that opinion, and David Lewis has correctly reminded us of the failings of the Harlem Renaissance in this regard.[48]

So thoroughly established is the myth of the Harlem Renaissance that no one has responded to the question Harold Cruse raised in 1971: "Why could not the Harlem Renaissance have taken place in Washington, D.C., even though Howard University, a major cultural institution is located there?"[49] The line of inquiry Cruse has introduced is by no means inconsequential, although he may be accused of begging the question. The intellectual life of post-Reconstruction Washington, rich though it was, has been all but ignored by literary and intellectual historians. Surely no one will contest the point that the typical first-year graduate student of Afro-American literature is unfamiliar with such names as Maria Stewart, Alexander Crummell, Francis J. Grimké, Anna J. Cooper, Pauline Hopkins, John Wesley Cromwell, and Mary Church Terrell. Some of these authors left substantial amounts of published and unpublished works, but their works are not available in accessibly priced editions and are, therefore, not assigned in undergraduate courses. There may be many reasons for their exclusion from the canon, but one of these is obviously the hostility of the critical establishment to the Victorian values that their writings represent. The "genteel tradition" among black writers is held in contempt by the proletarian/bohemian tradition in criticism. The critic who is likely to admire black literature often expresses stylistic objections to Du Bois's *The Quest of the Silver Fleece.* Most of us (myself included) harbor ideological objections to Du Bois's "The Conservation of Races" and Crummell's "Sermon on the Assassination of President Garfield."[50]

Cruse's question should not be dismissed as a rhetorical one. He was on the trail of something big, although I would suggest that the question could have been more precisely put. Cruse was certainly correct in his assumption that the Harlem Renaissance of the 1920s is celebrated as "the seedbed of modern black literature"[51] whereas Washington intellectual life of the 1890s is all but forgotten, except in the esoteric works of a handful of academia's "harmless drudges." Why is it that the tendency to equate the literature of the "New Negro" with the "Harlem Renaissance" has become the overwhelmingly dominant view?

Frederick Douglass anticipated one aspect of the answer when he observed in 1894 that the quaint, rustic aphorisms of Sojourner Truth were better known than the writings of Alexander Crummell.[52] It may be observed, in passing, that one of Douglass's quarrels with white abolitionist arose from his refusal to speak "black English."[53] He could not have chosen a better example of the lost tradition than Crummell, who remains unquoted, and generally unknown, mainly because his contributions to black literary history are not in conformity with the bohemian/proletarian aesthetic. He does not fit in with that view of black culture that arose in the antebellum era, was strengthened during the 1920s, and was reinforced during the 1960s.

Du Bois answered the question with characteristic bluntness in 1933. The literature of the Renaissance, he said, was "written for the benefit of white people and at the behest of white readers."[54] The culture brokers, with their erotic/exotic predilections, were interested in advancing only those authors who would nourish their perceptions of Negroes as frightening, or picturesque, or titillating. More recently, Kenneth Lynn has appropriately observed that the study of black life and culture has always been dominated by political mythmaking and the search for colorful literary anecdotes. Fair enough—these concerns are present in all cultural history.[55] I am only partially in agreement with Lynn, for I applaud the work of Genovese, as well as that of Levine and other culture historians. I would only argue for broadening the definition of black literature to include the products of late-nineteenth-century middle-class culture. The proletarian/bohemian interpretation, with its Jazz Age bias, has been granted a sort of moral superiority over any other framework of analysis in black literary and intellectual history. This has led to a distorted perception of the "New Negro Movement" that ignores the tough-minded, self-exacting, puritanical, meritocratic values that were nurtured in the American Negro Academy and preserved in Garvey's Universal Negro Imporvement Association.

NOTES

1. Alain Locke, "Enter the New Negro," *Survey Graphic* (March 1925): 631–39; reprinted as "The New Negro" in Alain Locke, ed. *The New Negro* (New York: Albert and Charles Boni, 1925), pp. 3–16. Robert Bone, *The Negro Novel in America* (New Haven: Yale University Press, 1958), pp. 33 and 35, is rash in his critique of the better informed Hugh Gloster, "Sutton Griggs: Novelist of the New Negro," *Phylon* 4 (1943): 335–45.

2. It would be irrelevant to the purposes of this essay to attempt a definitive genealogy of the term *New Negro*. A few cursory references should suffice to indicate something of its lineage. John W. Cromwell refers to Henderson's speech, "The New Negro," in his *History of the Bethel Literary and Historical Association, Being a Paper Read Before the Association on Founder's Day February 24, 1896* (Washington: Pendleton, 1896), p. 30. In 1916 William Pickens published a series of essays under the title *The New Negro: His Political, Civil, and Mental Status, and Related Essays* (New York: Neal, 1916), a book of sociological insight but no real literary significance. *The Cleveland Gazette* (28 June 1895) announced the arrival of a "New Negro," who had entered American life since the Civil War. For more on this, see the discussion of the term *New Negro* in August Meier, *Negro Thought in America, 1880–1915: Racial Ideologies in the Era of Booker T. Washington* (Ann Arbor: University of Michigan Press, 1963). The book is excellent as an introduction to the period but should be supplemented with Rayford W. Logan, *The Betrayal of the Negro: From Rutherford B. Hayes to Woodrow Wilson* (New York: Collier, 1965). The paperback edition of Logan is recommended over the hardcover, which appeared under the title *The Negro in American Life and Thought: The Nadir, 1877–1901*.

3. Robert Hayden, introduction to *The New Negro*, ed. Alain Locke (1925; reprint, Atheneum, 1968), pp. ix–xiv.

4. S. P. Fullinwider, *The Mind and Mood of Black America* (Homewood, Ill.: Dorsey Press, 1969), pp. 92–122.

5. David Gordon Nielson, *Black Ethos: Northern Urban Negro Life and Thought, 1890–1930* (Westport, Conn.: Greenwood Press, 1977), pp. 52–60.

6. Theodore Kornweibel, *No Crystal Stair: Black Life and The Messenger, 1917–1928* (Westport, Conn.: Greenwood Press, 1975), p. 116.

7. June Sochen, *The Unbridgeable Gap: Blacks and Their Quest for the American Dream, 1900–1930* (Chicago: Rand, 1972), pp. 41–44.

8. W. E. B. Du Bois expressed contradictory opinions on the Renaissance. In "Mencken," *Crisis* (October 1927): 276, he expressed positive feelings, but in a later essay, "The Negro College," *Crisis* (August 1933): 175–77, he deprecated the Renaissance as an "exotic" and "artificial" growth, having its origins in the early 1920s.

9. Arthur P. Davis and Saunders Redding, eds., *Cavalcade: Negro American Writing from 1760 to the Present* (Boston: Houghton, 1971), made use of the category "New Negro Renaissance," pp. 229–35. See also Michael W. Peplow and Arthur P. Davis, eds., *The New Negro Renaissance: An Anthology* (New York: Holt, 1975).

10. Nathan Huggins, "Afro-American Studies and American Studies," in *American Character and Culture in the 1980s: Pluralistic Perspectives,* University of Massachusetts – Boston Occasional Papers, no. 1 (Boston: University of Massachusetts – Boston, 1982), pp. 11–14.

11. David Lewis, *When Harlem Was in Vogue* (New York: Vintage, 1982), offers a good treatment of Harlem chic during the period in question. Nathan Huggins, *Harlem Renaissance* (New York: Oxford University Press, 1971), treats the fashionableness of black primitivism in terms of the white American's search for an alter ego. See also Jervis Anderson, *This Was Harlem* (New York: Farrar, 1982), and Chidi Ikonne, *From Du Bois to Van Vechten: The Early New Negro Literature* (Westport, Conn.: Greenwood Press, 1981).

12. Peplow and Davis, in their introduction to *The New Negro Renaissance,* identify the period 1910–40 as "the seedbed of modern black literature," p. xxxi. June Sochen, in *The Unbridgeable Gap,* stresses the assimilationist rather than the exotic quality of black cultural expression. Theodore Kornweibel, in *No Crystal Stair,* stresses the hardheaded economic and labor emphases of the New Negro movement. Gloria T. Hull, in the introduction to *Give Us Each Day: The Diary of Alice Dunbar-Nelson* (New York: Norton, 1984), analyzes the "best foot forward" phenomenon, p. 23.

13. Constance McLaughlin Green, *The Secret City* (Princeton: Princeton University Press, 1967).

14. Harold Cruse, "Black and White: Outlines of the Next Stage," *Black World* (March 1971): 4–31; Carter G. Woodson, *A Century of Negro Migration* (Washington: Associated, 1918). Both Cruse and Woodson were indebted to Du Bois for the concept "talented tenth." See Du Bois, "The Talented Tenth," in *The Negro Problem: A Series of Articles by Representative American Negroes,* ed. Booker T. Washington et al. (New York: James Pott, 1903), pp. 33–75.

15. Milton Mezzrow, quoted in Lawrence W. Levine, *Black Culture and Black Consciousness: Afro-American Folk Thought from Slavery to Freedom* (New York: Oxford University Press, 1977), pp. 294–95.

16. The German scholar Jahnheinz Jahn, *Geschichte der neoafrikanischen Literatur* (Dusseldorf-Koln: Eugen Diederichs Verlag, 1966), is much concerned with the exotic/iconoclastic elements of black art, but Imanuel Geiss, *Der Panafrikanismus* (n.p.: Europaische Verlagsanstalt, 1968), offers a more comprehensive and, therefore, more complex analysis. The French scholar Roger Bastide, *African Civilizations in the New World* (New York: Harper, 1971), is much influenced by literary and artistic interactions between French-, Portuguese-, and English-speaking blacks. Another treatment of the interaction between Francophone and Anglophone Africans is in A. James Arnold, *Modernism and Negritude: The Poetry and Poetics of Aimé Césaire* (Cambridge: Harvard University Press, 1981).

17. Carl Van Vechten, *Nigger Heaven* (New York: Harper, 1926), pp. 65–66. The 1971 Harper Colophon reprint edition is likely to be of greater usefulness to readers than the edition from which I have cited, since that edition contains valuable reviews by W. E. B. Du Bois, Claude McKay, and James Weldon Johnson.

18. E. Franklin Frazier, "La Bourgeoisie Noire," in *Anthology of American Negro Literature*, ed. V. F. Calverton (New York: Modern Library, 1929), pp. 379–88.

19. Booker T. Washington, *Up from Slavery,* vol. 1 of *The Booker T. Washington Papers*, ed. Louis Harlan (Urbana: University of Illinois Press, 1972–89), pp. 260–62.

20. Alexander Crummell to Bishop William Pincknew, 22 April 1882, Maryland Diocesan Archives, Maryland Historical Society. Crummell claimed that his support came from the poor working people of his parish and consistently denounced well-dressed, wine-sipping partygoers in his published sermons.

21. Cromwell, *History of the Bethel Literary and Historical Association,* p.3.

22. See Carter G. Woodson, ed., *The Works of Francis James Grimké,* 4 vols. (Washington: Associated, 1942), and Charlotte Forten Grimké, *The Journal of Charlotte Forten,* ed. Ray Allen Billington (New York: Collier, 1961).

23. Adelaide Cromwell Gulliver, "Minutes of the Meetings of the Negro American Society," *Journal of Negro History* (April 1983): 59–69. I am grateful to Dr. Adelaide Cromwell for allowing me to see the originals of these documents, which are in her possession. Dr. Cromwell was also good enough to allow me to work with the manuscript minutes of the meetings of the American Negro Academy in her possession.

24. Edwin S. Redkey, *Black Exodus: Black Nationalist and Back to Africa Movements, 1890–1910* (New Haven: Yale University Press, 1969), pp. 47–72. Redkey's concerns in this path-breaking study are focused elsewhere than on Washington's intellectual life. He does an excellent job, however, of documenting the impact of Blyden on politics and the masses. Blyden's interactions with lettered persons can be glimpsed in the following documents: Blyden's letter to Booker T. Washington in *The Booker T. Washington Papers* 4:26–28; Blyden's letters to Francis J. Grimké in vol. 4 of *The Works of Francis J. Grimké;* and letters to numerous Afro-American and American figures in *Selected Letters of Edward Wilmot Blyden,* ed. Hollis R. Lynch (Milkwood: KTO Press, 1978). Crummell, of course, knew Blyden well, having served with him on the faculty of Liberia College. For Crummell's later comments on Blyden, see *A Thanksgiving Sermon* (Washington, D.C., 1895), pp. 10–11.

25. In a letter to Charlotte Forten, John Greenleaf Whittier characterized Crummell and his writing with accuracy, although we today would find his tone rather patronizing. "I send thee a volume of A. Crummell's. Its author is a churchman and conservative, but his writings are a noble refutation of the charge of the black man's inferiority. They are model discourses, clear, classic, and chaste": *The Letters of John Greenleaf Whittier,* ed. John B. Pickard (Cambridge: Belknap Press, 1975), 3:35.

26. A full-length biography of Alexander Crummell has recently been completed. See Wilson J. Moses, *Alexander Crummell: A Study of Civilization and Discontent* (New York: Oxford University Press, 1989), and "Civilizing Missionary: A Study of Alexander Crummell," *Journal of Negro History* (April 1975): 229–51.

27. See Otey M. Scruggs, *"We the Children of Africa in This Land"* (Washington: Howard University, 1972); Alfred A. Moss, Jr., *The American Negro Academy: Voice of the Talented Tenth* (Baton Rouge: Louisiana State University Press, 1981); and Wilson J. Moses, "Cambridge Platonism in West Africa: Alexander Crummell's Theory of Development and Culture Transfer," *New England Journal of Black Studies* 3 (1983): 60–77.

28. William H. Ferris, *The African Abroad or His Evolution in Western Civilization: Tracing His Development under Caucasian Milieu,* 2 vols. (New Haven: Tuttle, 1913).

29. Moss, *American Negro Academy,* pp. 54, 127, 128–29.

30. Locke's hostility to popular music of the period and to the "Shylocks of Tin Pan Alley" may be seen in his *The Negro and His Music* (Washington: Associates in Negro Folk Education, 1936). Locke demonstrated this same coldness toward 1920s fashions in black culture and aesthetics in "The Legacy of the Ancestral Arts," in *The New Negro,* pp. 254–67.

31. Crummell's teleological view of history was stated often in his writings. A succinct statement is in "The Destined Superiority of the Negro," in Alexander Crummell, *The Greatness of Christ and Other Sermons* (New York: Whittaker, 1882), pp. 1–19.

32. Edward Beckham, "The Organization of the Academy for the Promotion of Intellectual Enterprises among American Negroes" (Afro-American Studies Center, Boston University, typescript), p. 12.

33. Ferris, *The African Abroad,* p. 209.

34. Ferris's admiration for the British and for social Darwinism is observed by Burkett in *Black Redemption: Churchmen Speak for the Garvey Movement* (Philadelphia: Temple University Press, 1978), pp. 69–70.

35. Abby Arthur Johnson and Ronald Mayberry Johnson, *Propaganda and Aesthetics* (Amherst: University of Massachusetts Press, 1979), pp. 24–29.

36. Johnson and Johnson, *Propaganda and Aesthetics,* pp. 1–29; Wilson J. Moses, *The Golden Age of Black Nationalism, 1850–1925* (Hamden, Conn.: Archon, 1978), pp. 205–19.

37. Moses, *Golden Age,* pp. 106–8, 110–15.

38. W. E. B. Du Bois, "Two Novels," *Crisis* (June 1928): 202.

39. Reactions to Van Vechten's *Nigger Heaven* are discussed in Wilson J. Moses, *Black Messiahs and Uncle Toms: Social and Literary Manipulations of a Religious Myth* (University Park: Pennsylvania State University Press, 1982), p. 121. A more thorough treatment of Du Bois on Van Vechten and related issues appears in Darwin T. Turner, "W. E. B. Du Bois and the Theory of a Black Aesthetic," *Studies in the Literary Imagination* 7, no.2 (1974): 1–21.

40. Marcus Garvey, "*Home to Harlem:* An Insult to the Race," *Negro World,* 29 Sept. 1928. Garvey was just as opposed to the novel as was Du Bois but argued his position differently. Cf. Du Bois, "Two Novels." Both reviews are reprinted in Theodore Vincent, ed., *Voices of a Black Nation: Political Journalism in the Harlem Renaissance* (San Francisco: Ramparts Press, 1973), pp. 357–60.

41. For a discussion of Ethiopianism and the missionary movement, see Wilson J. Moses, "The Poetics of Ethiopianism," *American Literature* 47 (1975): 411–26, and George Shepperson, "Ethiopianism and African Nationalism," *Phylon* 14 (1953): 9–18.

42. A discussion of the nineteenth-century origins of Garvey's philosophy would be far beyond the scope of this essay. The secondary literature on the subject is impressive. For example, see Robert Hill, "The First England Years and After, 1912–1916," and Edwin S. Redkey, "Henry McNeal Turner and Marcus Garvey," both in *Marcus Garvey and the Vision of Africa,* ed. John Henrik Clarke (New York: Vintage, 1974), pp. 38–70, 383–402. See also my own observations on the tradition in *Black Messiahs and Uncle Toms* and *The Golden Age of Black Nationalism.*

43. Langston Hughes, "My Early Days in Harlem," in *Harlem: A Community in Transition,* ed. John Henrik Clarke (New York: Citadel, 1969), p. 64.

44. W. E. B. Du Bois, *Dark Princess* (New York: Harcourt, 1928), pp. 66–67.

45. Du Bois, "The Negro College," p. 176.

46. Langston Hughes, "The Negro Artist and the Racial Mountain," *Nation,* 3 June 1926, 692–94.

47. Levine, *Black Culture and Black Consciousness*, p. xiv.

48. Lewis, *When Harlem Was in Vogue*, pp. 256–62. Langston Hughes's hostility is evident in his short story "Slave on the Block," in *The Ways of White Folks* (New York: Knopf, 1934), pp. 19–31.

49. Cruse, "Black and White," p. 31.

50. Crummell's sermon was printed in his *Greatness of Christ and Other Sermons*. It is a condemnation of egalitarianism and an argument in favor of authoritarian government, law, and order. A similar set of values is presented in Du Bois's "The Conservation of Races," American Negro Academy Occasional Papers, no. 2 (Washington: American Negro Academy, 1897).

51. Peplow and Davis, *New Negro Renaissance*, p. xxxi.

52. Frederick Douglas, "The Lesson of the Hour," in *The Life and Writings of Frederick Douglass*, ed. Philip S. Foner (New York: International, 1955), 4:507. Douglass was seventy-seven when he made the statement. There had been some friction between Douglass and Truth, because she had publicly called his religiosity into question.

53. For plantation English, see Frederick Douglass, *The Life and Times of Frederick Douglass* (New York: Collier, 1962), p. 180.

54. Du Bois, "The Negro College," p. 176.

55. Kenneth S. Lynn, "Regressive Historians," *American Scholar* (Autumn 1976): 471–500. See especially pp. 489–500. Lynn's position is an attack on the scholarship and ideological directions of Eugene Genovese in his *Roll Jordan Roll: The World the Slaves Made* (New York: Pantheon, 1974).

Literary Garveyism

The Novels of Reverend Sutton E. Griggs

he distinguished black American Scholar Arna Bontemps was once heard to express his objections to white critics making more of the novels of Sutton Griggs than Bontemps felt they deserved. Perhaps Bontemps suspected the motives of his white colleagues and intended to halt, at the outset, a subterfuge that would ultimately lead to the ridiculing of black literature by displaying unrepresentative and pathetically weak figures. Or perhaps Bontemps simply felt that he, along with all other black literary figures, was being patronized and resented it.[1] Sutton Elbert Griggs, like all artists, had weaknesses as well as strengths, and his writing, like even the greatest art, was sometimes flawed. The older generation of black critics have certainly not been guilty of overstating the strengths of Sutton Griggs. And if there has been any sinister conspiracy on the part of the white literary establishment to elevate his work, with all of its supposed inferiority, to public view, I am completely unaware of it. Griggs has been a prophet singularly without honor, either among his own people or in the larger society. With the exception of the noted Afro-American critic, Hugh M. Gloster, there have been few readers to treat Griggs with any serious appreciation. There is a bitter irony here, because Griggs was perhaps the first black writer to consciously attempt to create a distinctly Afro-American philosophy of literature and a body of writing to go with it.

From the 1930s to the 1950s, when black historical and literary

scholarship were understandably preoccupied with the fight against segregation, there was little concern for emphasizing the black American
separatist tradition. Literary black nationalism, as exemplified in the
novels of Sutton Griggs, was usually disparaged. Rayford Logan, the
distinguished historian and pioneering pan-Africanist, estimates that
Griggs "probably had more Negro readers than did Chesnutt and Dunbar." He nonetheless offers the stringent criticism that Griggs's novels
had "little literary merit and presaged the black chauvinism of Marcus
Garvey." Logan is correct in attributing to Griggs a proto-Garveyist nationalism, although he does not support his view that this amounted to a
stylistic shortcoming.[2]

Logan's appraisal was not atypically harsh. Sterling Brown, in *The
Negro in American Fiction,* speaks of Griggs's novels as "counter-propaganda." *Unfettered* (1902) is characterized as "trite and pompous."
Brown sees *The Hindered Hand* (1905) as "also a bad novel. . . . All of
the darker phases of the South appear in the book, but melodramati-
cally, unrealistically."[3] Hugh Gloster, who views Griggs as "a significant
pioneer in the history of American Negro fiction," admits nonetheless
"his failings as an artist."[4] Robert Bone, a white scholar, belittles Gloster's insight that Griggs was a political thinker of stature, and finds his
social philosophy confused and contradictory, vacillating between bla-
tantly fanatical "Negro nationalism" and conciliatory servility.[5] Bone's
attack on Gloster is supported by David M. Tucker, another white
scholar.[6] Arthur P. Davis and Saunders Redding see Griggs as sharing a
weakness "common to many other black authors of his era: he was too
much concerned with the Race Problem and too little with the art of
fiction."[7] S. P. Fullinwider, a white scholar, is fascinated by Griggs's
complexity and finds his "rugged intellectual honesty . . . astonishing."[8]

Griggs was not only concerned with writing about the "race problem"; he was concerned also with writing for black audiences. Rayford
Logan has speculated that Griggs was able to appeal to a significant
number of black readers. W. E. B. Du Bois also spoke to this issue and
noted that Griggs was unlike his contemporary, Charles Chesnutt, who,
as is well known, sought acceptance from the white reading public and
even went so far as to conceal his racial identity in his search for
publishers. In Du Bois's estimation, Griggs's strident racialism "spoke
primarily to the Negro race."[9]

One would think that in the past decade's flurry of activity in the
setting up of Black Studies departments, and in the search for methods
and discipline to determine the distinctively "Black" elements of Afro-
American art, Sutton Griggs might have been "discovered" and reex-
amined. Nothing of the sort has happened. Black Studies specialists have

continued to focus upon those writers who meet orthodox criteria of literary excellence, rather than turning their attention to neglected writers like Griggs. Authors like Jean Toomer, Ralph Ellison, Amiri Baraka, and Ishmael Reed have had widespread appeal to the literary establishments, white and black. Their stylistic accomplishments are of the sort that scholars are taught to recognize. One does not wish to ignore the accomplishments of the foregoing authors, nor to demean the critical insights of those who have appreciated them. Still, it would seem that if Afro-American literature specialists are to justify themselves and their professional existence as specialists—with singular insights and privy knowledge that are not shared by non-specialists—then they will have to attempt to adopt methods that will aid them in the analysis of novelists like Griggs, who have so far been avoided by perplexed conventional critics.

Since Griggs has commonly been assumed by such knowledgeable black contemporaries as Du Bois, Logan, and Charles Alexander[10] to have been reasonably influential among the literate black working class, he seems to have appealed to the same audience as Marcus Garvey, and like Garvey, Griggs was a successful orator before black audiences. His literary theory may indeed be seen as literary Garveyism, for it was strongly nationalistic. The purpose of literature was, he felt, to serve the masses of black people. It was to provide a basis for racial unity and at the same time to create channels of legitimate leadership. He recognized that the political potential of black Americans was severely limited by illiteracy, and he issued a call that was understandable enough for a novelist who did not wish to restrict his appeal to white readers, but hoped to find an audience among Afro-Americans.

> To succeed as a race we must move up out of the age of the voice, the age of the direct personal appeal, and live in an age where an idea can influence to action by whatever route it drifts one's way.

> When the time arrives that the Negroes are capable of being moved to action on a large scale by what they read, a marked change in the condition of the race will begin instantly and will be marvelous in its proportions.[11]

Griggs saw the need for the creation of a "Negro Literature," not only for the creation of particular works whose authors happened incidentally to be black, but for an integral body of literary tradition that would be readily identifiable as belonging to Afro-Americans. "Not a single race that has no literature is classified as great in the eyes of the world," he said. A nation's leaders could not "foster the patriotic spirit" without preserving their insights for future generations, "and those races that have no literature are devoid of a method of embalming."[12]

That Griggs's writing on the purposes of literature seems to neglect artistic concerns in favor of considerations chiefly political should not mislead us into thinking that his novels are without their aesthetic delights. His writing style is splendidly primitive, clear, forceful, and colorful. Primitive writing has never achieved the same degree of respectability as "primitive" music or sculpture, for example. We have no concept such as *folk novel* in the critical vocabulary, and such a term might be useful to describe certain aspects of Griggs's work, because in order to appreciate Griggs, one must either overlook or else learn to enjoy his stylistic "imperfections," just as one willingly overlooks the often flawed plots and characterizations in Shakespeare's plays or the flat characterizations of Bunyan. To say that great art is flawed is not to say that it lacks beauty; one can learn to appreciate the beauty of Griggs's style, if one can learn to appreciate such untrained painters as Edward Hicks and Henri Rousseau. Good art does not have to be "lifelike," and indeed Griggs's often is not. But if his characters have a pasteboard quality, perhaps there is a reason.

Edward Bland, a black critic, once observed that black literature of the late nineteenth century falls into a "pre-individualistic" mode.

> In the pre-individualistic thinking of the Negro, the stress is on the group. Instead of seeing in terms of the individual, the Negro sees in terms of "races," masses of peoples separated from other masses according to color. Hence, an act rarely bears intent against him as a Negro individual. He is singled out not as a person but as a specimen of an ostracized group. He knows that he never exists in his own right but only to the extent that others hope to make the race suffer vicariously through him.[13]

Clearly this holds certain implications for the way in which characters are drawn, for indeed in many black novels of the nineteenth century — including those of Martin Delany, Sutton Griggs, and William Wells Brown — one feels that the characters are not individuals but personifications of ideas common in Afro-American nonfiction such as racial ambivalence, or the "two-souls" motif, and black nationalistic themes.

The two-souls motif is prominent in all five of Griggs's novels, which give fictional form to an idea stated in Du Bois's *The Souls of Black Folk,* that the black American individual experiences a sense of "two-ness":

> An American, a Negro; two souls, two thoughts, two unreconciled strivings; two warring ideals in one dark body, whose dogged strength alone keeps it from being torn asunder.[14]

Several of Griggs's major characters display this "two-ness." Dorlan Warthell in *Unfettered* (1902) is a Negro American, committed to the advancement of the black cause in the United States. At the same time, he has a commitment to the elevation of the entire black race throughout the world. His goal of advancement for black Americans is inextricably bound up with the cause of universal Negro improvement. Ensal Ellwood in *The Hindered Hand* (1905) struggles manfully to realize his American nationality throughout the novel, but finally decides that he cannot continue to live as an American and still discharge his duties to his race. Bernard Belgrave in *Imperium in Imperio* (1899) is probably the most striking example of the two souls theme illustrated in an individual character. Bernard, a mulatto, combines the supposed emotionalism of the African personality with all the cruel intellectual cunning and insatiable spirit of the European. Also noteworthy, however, is Belton Piedmont in the same novel, who is torn between his desire to be a loyal and patriotic American and his need to fight for racial survival by the use of un-American tactics.[15]

At the climax of *Imperium in Imperio,* Bernard and Belton address a congress of black leaders in America, assembled in a huge subterranean chamber. Bernard calls for war against the United States, arguing that only by acts of violence can blacks prove themselves equal to or worthy of association with whites.

> To the martyr, who perished in freedom's cause, death comes with a beauteous smile and with most tender touch . . . if we die on the mountain side, we shall be shrouded in sheets of whitest snow, and all generations of men yet to come upon the earth will have to gaze upward in order to see our whitened forms.[16]

The symbolism of the foregoing cannot be ignored. Bernard desires to have his fallen form "whitened," if only in death. The frustration of Bernard in his half-caste status symbolized the frustration of all black Americans in their ambiguous status — both Negro and American.

Belton's response to Bernard's bloodthirsty cry is that black people cannot force whites to accept them and that there is no point in suicide. Blacks must make one final attempt to persuade whites to grant them justice. If that should fail, then and only then, Afro-Americans must seek a separate destiny and whites must face the consequences of having created an *Imperium in Imperio.* In such a spirit, Belton introduces the following resolution to the black congress:

> Resolved: That we spend four years in endeavors to impress the Anglo-Saxon that he has a New Negro on his hands and must surrender what

belongs to him. In case we fail by these means to secure our rights and privileges we shall all, at once, abandon our several homes in the various other states and emigrate in a body to the State of Texas, broad in domain, rich in soil and salubrious in climate. Having an unquestioned majority of votes we shall secure possession of the State Government.[17]

But Belton's proposed alternatives are not radical enough for Bernard. He insists upon either the total intermixture or the total separation of the black and the white nations in America. Thus he rebels against the ambiguous role of blacks in America, which is symbolized in his own schizophrenic personality and half-caste station. Bernard proposes full-scale revolutionary black nationalism.

> . . . Encourage all Negroes who can possibly do so to enter the United States Navy. . . .
> Enter into secret negotiations with all of the foreign enemies of the United States, acquainting them of our military strength and men aboard the United States war ships. . . .
> We can then, if need be, wreck the entire Navy of the United States in a night; the United States will then be prostrate before us and our allies. . . .
> We will demand the surrender of Texas and Louisiana to the Imperium. Texas, we will retain. Louisiana, we will cede to our foreign allies in return for their aid. Thus will the Negro have an empire of his own, fertile in soil, capable of sustaining a population of fifty million people.[18]

The novel ends with the execution of Belton, unable to reconcile his black nationalism with his love for America, and with the madness of Bernard, unable to live with the cruel ambivalence of white America.

Aside from the "two-ness" experienced by the characters in *Imperium in Imperio,* another duality is present. This is manifested in Griggs's use of dual protagonists to represent a conflict of ideas within the race. Belton and Bernard represent two antagonistic sets of traits commonly associated with the personalities of Afro-Americans. Belton represents the heroic Uncle Tom personality in the best sense. He is quietly courageous, loyal, enduring, and he possesses the Christian virtue of transcending hatred and revenge and desiring the salvation of his oppressor. The wrathful, vindictive Bernard is a no less common stereotype and a no less valid characterization of black American attitudes. The mounting tension between the two characters represents the warring opposites within the soul of each individual black American and the conflicting goals of leadership within the race.

The Hindered Hand is also concerned with this variation on the "so light of complexion that he could easily have passed for white," and Ensal Ellwood, "a fine looking fellow" of dark complexion. As an *Impe-*

rium in Imperio, the black protagonist is used to symbolize the virtues of classical Negro conservatism. He has a frank and dignified manner, a calm fortitude, and an instinctive sense of Christian virtue. The mulatto is bitter and vengeful. He gathers about himself a "Spartan band . . . five hundred men who are not afraid to die," and with these he plans to seize the state capitol and "when the city awakes tomorrow morning it will find itself at our mercy" (p. 144). Ensal attempts to dissuade Earl from his mad plan, but when he fails to do so, the novel is forced to a crisis. Ensal and Earl meet to wrestle at midnight on a bridge above a river that divides their city.

Black nationalist themes are given greater prominence in *Imperium in Imperio* than in any of Griggs's other novels, but this is not the only one in which they are present. Black nationalism and two of its variant forms known as pan-Africanism and "Ethiopianism" are present in several of Griggs's works. Pan-Africanism is a philosophy that emphasizes the spiritual unity of all black people. It is based on the idea that all blacks are victimized to some extent by the doctrine of white supremacy and that none of us are free till all are free. The liberation of the African continent from all manifestations of colonialism is its chief goal. Pan-Africanists believe that the uplift of Africa is an essential step in the uplifting of blacks in the United States. Griggs was among the group of pan-Africanists that included Du Bois, who believed that a concern for the uplift of Africa did not mean any lessening of concern for problems in the United States. For this group, pan-Africanism meant what the Zionist movement meant to American Jews, "the centralization of race effort and the recognition of a racial front."[19] Such a variety of pan-Africanism makes its appearance in *Unfettered* (1902), Griggs's third novel.

Unfettered is the story of Dorlan Warthell, who is in love with Morlene Dalton, a beautiful mulatto, widowed during the course of the novel. Morlene refuses to marry Dorlan until he can create a plan for organizing the political efforts of Afro-Americans and improving their position in the United States. Dorlan is able to come up with such a plan, partly due to his own intellectual ability and hard work and partly due to help from an unexpected source. One morning, while standing in his own front yard, Dorlan observes a motley procession of lower-class blacks following a parade of Negro musicians down the street. They present a rather untidy and boisterous appearance and Dorlan muses,

> Now those Negroes are moulding sentiment against the entire race. . . . Be the requirement just or unjust the polished Negro is told to return and bring his people with him, before coming into possession of that to which his

attainments would seem to entitle him. It is my opinion that there must be developed within the race a stronger altruistic tie before it can push forward at a proper gait. The classes must love the masses. . . . [20]

It is in the midst of this altruistic reverie that Dorlan's vision encounters a fantastic sight.

> Dorlan's eye now wandered from the people to the band. In the midst of the musicians he saw a cart pulled by five dogs hitched abreast. In the cart stood a man holding aloft a banner which bore a peculiar inscription.
> Dorlan read the inscription on the banner and looked puzzled. Coming out of his gate he kept pace with the procession, never withdrawing his eye from the banner. He read it the second, third, and fourth and fifth times. At length he called out, "Hold! Here am I." The occupant of the cart leapt up and gazed wildly over the throng, endeavoring to see the person that had spoken.[21]

As it turns out, the cart's occupant is an emissary from Africa, and the inscription on the banner is the motto of a princely African family, which is comprehensible to Dorlan because he is the descendant of an African king, sold into slavery as the result of an ancient feud. Furthermore, as Kumi, the African emissary, reveals, there is a long-hidden treasure and Dorlan's family lore is the only key to its whereabouts. Dorlan is not expected to return to Africa in order to reclaim the treasure, for as Kumi tells him,

> "In the event that the government of the tropics is to be conducted from the temperate zones, we tropical people will desire Negroes to remain in the temperate zones, to advocate such policies and form such alliances as shall be for our highest good.
> So, it may turn out to be the best for you, our king, to remain here, for our welfare, owing to our peculiar environments, depends, just now, as much upon what others think of us as upon what we ourselves may do."[22]

The speech of Kumi is not so improbable as it may seem. We must remember that pan-Africanists from Africa—Alfred C. Sam, Orishatukeh Faduma, and Edward Wilmot Blyden—proselytized among the less educated classes of black Americans during the period of Griggs's career as a novelist, a fact noted with ridicule by Joel Chandler Harris.[23] Griggs, however, seems to have found the activities of such sojourners worthy of serious regard. It would therefore seem impossible to achieve a full appreciation of him without some understanding of pan-Africanism in its literary and political manifestations, especially as these are expressed in the writing of other black men and women of letters. One such literary manifestation of pan-Africanism is the Ethiopian theme.

Ethiopianism, an important tradition in black literary and intellectual history, has been described by numerous students of the black religious experience.[24] It derives its name from a biblical verse often referred to by black preachers and writers: "Princes shall come out of Egypt; Ethiopia shall soon stretch forth her hands unto God" (Psalms 68:31). Like most Biblical quotations, the verse is subject to a number of interpretations limited only by the exegetical powers of the interpreter. Since the late eighteenth century, however, it has usually been interpreted to mean that Africa and her scattered peoples have a divine mission to fulfill in the course of history. Ethiopianism is essentially a view of history, then, and it consists of more than the mere reference to Ethiopia as a literary allusion. One of the best descriptions of Ethiopianism comes to us from the racist author Daniel Thwaite in his paranoid book, *The Seething African Pot* (1936). He attributes the rise of Ethiopianism to the sojourn of the African Methodist Episcopal bishop Henry McNeal Turner in South Africa during 1898. Thwaite saw Turner as inaugurating Ethiopianism on the basis of his speeches throughout the land and cited him in a typical passage:

> "Africa," roared the bishop, "is a new land, a new world; she needs new men, and we are the men she needs. Arise, Africa! For Ethiopia is holding out her arms, not as a suppliant, as the white men call her, but to incite us to throw out our arms like boxers, seize the enemy, chuck him out and conquer the first place among peoples."[25]

Ethiopianism, as defined by Thwaite and other observers, is clearly more than vague allusions to Ethiopia, but rather a cry for world revolution and universal elevation of the status of African peoples.

The title of *The Hindered Hand* signals the Ethiopian theme of Griggs's fourth novel, the struggle of races and nations for world dominance. It is concerned with the black perception of this world struggle and characterizes Anglo-Saxon dominance as a cosmic disorder that "circles the globe in an iron grasp."[26] This iron grip of Anglo-Saxon dominance that denies to Negroes their political rights "more than all other factors, causes the Ethiopian in America to feel that his is indeed "The Hindered Hand."[27]

The Hindered Hand is, like *Imperium in Imperio,* a novel of conspiracy. In its pages Griggs is concerned with racial politics in America, but no less concerned with the struggle of racial forces on an intercontinental scale. One of the novel's most interesting and prophetic characters is Mr. A. Hostility, who is "the incarnation of hostility to that

[Anglo-Saxon] race, or to that branch of the human family claiming the dominance of that strain of blood."[28] Mr. Hostility is a pan-Slavist who hopes to enlist the aid of Afro-Americans in his struggle against Anglo-Saxon power. Griggs's work is prophetic, for he anticipates the theory of Oswald Spengler that Russia would fuel the revolutionary struggles of colored races in the twentieth century.[29] But *The Hindered Hand* was written in 1905, when the Russian revolution was still only a gleam in Lenin's eye.

   The Hindered Hand is not a cheerful book. It ends with most of its main characters either dead or driven insane; and two of them sail for Africa,

> to provide a home for the American Negro . . . should the good people of America, North and South grow busy, confused or irresolute and fail, to the subversion of their ideals, to firmly entrench the Negro in his political rights, the denial of which and the blight incident there to, more than all other factors cause the Ethiopian in America to feel that his is indeed "The Hindered Hand."[30]

Griggs was, as we have seen, interested in pan-Africanism. He had ties to such proponents of the movement as W. E. B. Du Bois and Charles Alexander. In an addendum to *The Hindered Hand,* Griggs admitted to an interest in the Back to Africa movement, an interest not necessarily shared by all Afro-Americans.

> The overwhelmingly predominant sentiment of the American Negroes is to fight out their battles on these shores. The assigning of the thoughts of the race to the uplift of Africa, as affecting the situation in America, must be taken more as the dream of the author rather than as representing any considerable responsible sentiment within the race, which, as has been stated, seems at present thoroughly and unqualifiedly American, a fact that must never be overlooked by those seeking to deal with the grave question in a practical manner.[31]

The presentation of such sentiments as these gives credence to the statement of Rayford Logan that Griggs was a literary black nationalist and that his philosophy presaged that of Marcus Garvey.

   Sutton Griggs's interest in folklore should not go ignored in this discussion of nationalism in art. A concern with folkloristic themes is characteristic of much nationalistic art in the nineteenth century. Earlier black writers like Frederick Douglass, Martin R. Delany, and William Wells Brown had shown occasional interest in folklore or had used folk songs and folktales in their writings. Griggs seems, however, to have been the first black writer to have laced his novels thoroughly with the flavoring of Afro-American "jokelore" and folksy humor. In this respect, at least, he was a novelist of the "New Negro," and he even rivalled the writers of the Harlem Renaissance in his concern for capturing the thought and feeling of the black masses—both urban and rural. Griggs's concern for black folklore did not focus upon animal stories of the sort that Joel Chandler Harris popularized, however. He was more interested in the folk mythologizing of sociological and historical experiences that had actually occurred in the patterns of black life in the South.[32]

The fact that Griggs was a preacher gave him an intimate knowledge of the lives of the masses of the black working poor. He came to know them, not only through the practice of his ministerial duties, but also because of his efforts to disseminate his writings, which he sold from door to door, distributed on the campuses of the black schools, and peddled to workers at their places of employment during lunch hours.[33] Griggs had a keen sense of irony and bitter humor and seems to have taken seriously—but not too seriously—his role as a moral leader and man of letters. He was able, therefore, to laugh at stereotypes of the black preacher, which he included in two of his novels. In *Imperium in Imperio,* he relates a well-known story of a preacher who is invited to dine at the home of a poor woman and her several children. Two of the children, having been promised biscuits and chicken after the minister is done, watch from the loft as he makes his progress through the meal. As he reaches for the last biscuit they are so overcome with dismay that they lose their balance and topple out, dropping to the floor.[34] In *Overshadowed,* a more sinister type is described. Reverend Josiah Nerve, ridiculous and pompous, burns down his church in order to collect the insurance.[35]

Griggs's novels are also concerned with political folk mythologies. For example, *The Hindered Hand* is often discussed as a countermyth or as a response to Thomas Dixon's racist novel, *The Leopard's Spots.*[36] Griggs's last novel, *Pointing the Way,* introduces the memorable character of Uncle Jack, who is a sophisticated countermyth to Uncle Remus. Joel Chandler Harris, creator of Uncle Remus, clearly felt that both his own work and that of Harriet Beecher Stowe had defended slavery as a civilizing agency and as a favorable portrayal of the childlike and "feminine" virtues of the black race, as well as the nobility of the master class.

> I trust I have been successful in presenting what must be, at least to a large portion of American readers, a new and by no means unattractive phase of negro character—a phase which may be considered a curiously sympathetic

supplement to Mrs. Stowe's wonderful defense of slavery as it existed in the South.[37]

Both Uncle Remus and Uncle Jack represent what Du Bois once referred to as "the faithful, courteous slave of older days, with his incorruptible honesty and dignified humility."[38] Like Uncle Remus, Uncle Jack tells his story of the Civil War years and of how he stayed on the plantation and "looked atter de wimmins wid er eagle eye."[39] Griggs, however, has endowed his faithful old negro with complexity that Uncle Remus lacks. Uncle Jack, like Uncle Remus, remains loyal to his white folks after the Civil War, but unlike Uncle Remus, he develops a sense of social responsibility. Uncle Jack is sympathetic to the newer generation of black leaders, who "wants things to move 'cordin' ter some principull,"[40] while Uncle Remus considers them to be audacious upstarts. "I kin take a bar'l stave an' fling mo' sense inter a nigger in one minnit dan all de schoolhouses betwixt dis en de State er Midgigin."[41]

Of course it would be wrong to assert that any and all uses of folkish elements constitute literary nationalism. At the same time, folk themes are an important component of nationalistic art. The folksy and socially perceptive humor of Uncle Jack is perhaps the strongest element of Griggs's last novel. Indeed, he is hardly the minor character that Bone would have us believe he is.[42] Uncle Jack is the missing link between the "Old" and the "New" Negro. He dies forgiving his white oppressors and expressing his enduring love for them, but he dies defending his right and the right of even the most illiterate class of black people to vote. Griggs's Uncle Jack, then, like Harris's Uncle Remus and Stowe's Uncle Tom, has his political functions. While Uncle Jack is not portrayed as a black nationalist, he does represent ideals of grass roots political consciousness and black political unity that often characterize nationalistic rhetoric. Finally, Griggs's decision to transform the traditional stereotype of the contented plantation darky into a vehicle for progressive political thought is consistent with his nationalistic belief that the strength of black Americans must rise up out of the hearts of the people rather than descending from a superior Washingtonian technocracy or a Du Boisean talented tenth.[43]

With respect to the literary merit of Sutton Griggs, I feel that he deserves a more patient hearing than he has received. He is a forceful, colorful, and entertaining writer. He is capable of moving his readers—especially his black readers—very deeply. Griggs has a particular relevance for today, for he wrote in a time of white backlash, a time when white America was forcibly retracting those rights and privileges that had been ceded to black people during Reconstruction.

The pleasure to be derived form the novels of Sutton Griggs can be enhanced for those who have some understanding of the intellectual tradition in which he wrote and of some of the other figures who wrote in that tradition. This naturally implies understanding those writers who have already gained a modicum of respectability, like Charles W. Chestnutt and Paul Laurence Dunbar, but an understanding of the black nationalistic ministers who were writers, like Henry McNeal Turner and Orishatukeh Faduma, is also very helpful. These writers, like Griggs, were educated black clergymen, fueling the fires of the black nationalism of the working classes. I have identified several characteristically black American motifs in the novels of Sutton Griggs and have tried to demonstrate the usefulness of analyzing Griggs in connection with pan-Africanism, Ethiopianism, and the two-souls theme. There is no denying that Griggs was profoundly influenced by traditions outside the black world, as well. After all, he was a well-educated cosmopolitan man. His writing is full of allusions (and direct references) to Thomas Huxley, Benjamin Kidd, Prince Kropotkin, Herbert Spencer, and other social theorists of the day.[44] In better times, Griggs might have taught social anthropology in a university — but no such opportunities were present at the turn of the century, so Griggs wrote sociology in the form of the sentimental novel. He also wrote books on social theory and race relations that were not fictional.[45] Griggs was a serious thinker and an entertaining writer. If he has not been fully appreciated, it is not because his writing lacks depth.

Rayford Logan's assessment of Sutton Griggs as a literary black nationalist and precursor of Marcus Garvey seems insightful. The hostility of earlier generations of black scholars towards black nationalism and Garveyism probably accounts in part for their failure to perceive his literary merits. If I may speak for the younger generation of black scholars, I will assert that many of us are inclined to look at Garveyism and at black nationalism as phenomena to be studied objectively — neither to be ignored nor responded to in purely emotional terms.[46] When we turn to the question of evaluating his contribution to literature, we must compare Griggs to other Christian polemical writers. British critics have long defended the crude yet vivid beauty of works like *Pilgrim's Progress* and *Everyman* with the argument that these works enshrine the essential values of the societies that produced them as well as the eternal verities that have dominated life on this planet.[47] One might argue in the same vein that Griggs — with his understanding of laughter in the face of suffering, gentility amidst squalor, and toughness behind a mask of subservience — has managed to filter universal truth through the prism of Afro-American nationalism. Griggs gave us five novels, each of which is worth more than one reading. Taken together, they provide us with a more insightful picture of life in the black South at the dawn of this century than social science alone is capable of providing.

N O T E S

1. Bontemps's objections were expressed during an institute on Afro-American culture at the University of Iowa during the summer of 1970. Griggs is conspicuous by his absence from standard anthologies of black literature published since the late 1960s. An exception is the excellent text by Arthur P. Davis and Saunders Redding, *Cavalcade: Negro American Writing from 1760 to the Present* (Boston, 1971). Robert Bone has done a lazy job on Griggs in *The Negro Novel in America* (New Haven, 1958). He mistakenly refers to Uncle Jack in *Pointing the Way* (Nashville, 1908) as a minor character, and falsely states that "the term 'New Negro' was coined by Alain Locke during the 1920s. . . . " Griggs, of course, had already used the term in *Imperium in Imperio* (Cincinnati, 1899). The earliest occurrence of the term that I have thus far been able to locate is in the title of an address, "The New Negro," delivered on January 21, 1896, by John M. Henderson at the Bethel Literary Association, mentioned in John W. Cromwell, *History of the Bethel Literary and Historical Association* (Washington, D.C., 1896), p. 30. Also see William Pickens, *The New Negro* (New York, 1916), and Booker T. Washington, *A New Negro for a New Century* (Chicago, 1900). Hugh Gloster is correct in dating the New Negro Movement from the late nineteenth century, and it is Bone who is incorrect when he attempts to fault Gloster for so doing. See Gloster, "Sutton Griggs, Novelist of the New Negro," *Phylon* (1943): 335–45, and *Negro Voices in American Fiction* (Chapel Hill, 1948). August Meier in *Negro Thought in America* (Ann Arbor, 1963), p. 258, traces the term *New Negro* to circa 1895.

2. Logan comments on Griggs's popularity and proto-Garveyism in *The Betrayal of the Negro* (New York, 1965), pp. 357–58.

3. Sterling Brown, *The Negro in American Fiction* (Washington, D.C., 1937), pp. 100–101.

4. Gloster, "Novelist of the New Negro," p. 345.

5. Bone, *Negro Novel,* p. 33.

6. David M. Tucker, *Black Pastors and Leaders* (Memphis, 1975), pp. 71–72. Tucker's book involves some serious misreadings of some of Griggs's critics, and his interpretation of Griggs as a disgruntled intellectual who became an Uncle Tom is based upon hearsay.

7. Davis and Redding, *Cavalcade,* p. 163.

8. S. P. Fullinwider, *The Mind and Mood of Black America* (Homewood, Ill., 1969), p. 74.

9. Du Bois mentions Griggs's appeal to black readers in "The Negro in Literature and Art." *Annals of the American Academy of Political and Social Science* 49 (September 1913): 236.

10. Charles Alexander was the publisher of *Alexander's Magazine,* funded by Booker T. Washington and published in Boston as a counter agent to William Monroe Trotter's *Guardian. Alexander's Magazine* was ironically notable for its sympathy for Back-to-Africanism, which Washington tended to disparage. Alexander published two reviews of Griggs's *The Hindered Hand,* one on October 15, 1905, the other on August 15, 1906. A photograph of Griggs was published with each article.

11. Griggs, *Life's Demands, or, According to Law* (Memphis, 1916), pp. 51–52.

12. Ibid., p. 98.

13. Quoted in Ralph Ellison, *Shadow and Act* (New York, 1966), p. 95.

14. W. E. B. Du Bois, *The Souls of Black Folk* (Chicago, 1903), p. 3.

15. In addition to *Imperium in Imperio,* already mentioned, Griggs wrote four other novels: *Overshadowed* (Nashville, 1901); *Unfettered* (Nashville, 1902); *The Hindered Hand* (Nashville, 1905); *Pointing the Way* (Nashville, 1908). Reprints are available from Books for Libraries and AMS Press.

16. *Imperium in Imperio,* pp. 220–21.

17. Ibid., p. 245.

18. Ibid., pp. 251–52.

19. Du Bois, "Reconstruction and Africa," *Crisis,* no. 4 (February 1919), 166.

20. *Unfettered,* pp. 160–61.

21. Ibid., p. 161.

22. Ibid., pp. 167–68.

23. Joel Chandler Harris describes Uncle Remus's total lack of interest in "dat Liberious country" in *Uncle Remus Returns* (New York, 1918), pp. 158–65. Alfred C. Sam is discussed in William E. Bittle and Gilbert Geis, *The Longest Way Home* (Detroit, 1964). Mention is also made of Faduma. Blyden's American tours are mentioned in Edwin S. Redkey, *Black Exodus* (New Haven, 1969).

24. See George Shepperson, "Ethiopianism and African Nationalism," *Phylon* 14, no. 1 (1953): 9–18; St. Clair Drake, *The Redemption of Africa and Black Religion* (Chicago, 1970); Jomo Kenyatta, *Facing Mt. Kenya* (London, 1938); Daniel Thwaite, *The Seething African Pot* (London, 1936); F. Nnabuenzi Ugonna, Introduction to J. E. Casely Hayford, *Ethiopia Unbound* (London, 1969); Wilson J. Moses, "The Poetics of Ethiopianism: W. E. B. Du Bois and Literary Black Nationalism," *American Literature* (November 1975): 411–26.

25. Thwaite, *Seething African Pot,* p. 38.

26. *The Hindered Hand,* p. 243.

27. Ibid., p. 298.

28. Ibid., p. 202.

29. Oswald Spengler, *The Hour of Decision,* translated from the German by Charles Francis Atkinson (New York, 1934). See especially pp. 208–9: "Russia has removed its 'white mask' . . . has again become Asiatic with all its soul, and is filled with a burning hatred of Europe."

30. *The Hindered Hand,* p. 298.

31. Ibid., p. 303.

32. It should be remembered that Harris dealt with two varieties of folklore in his tales of Uncle Remus. The animal lore was no more important than the lore of the contented darky, unconcerned about his political and economic welfare.

33. Griggs tells of his attempts to market his works privately in *The Story of My Struggles* (Memphis, 1914), p. 14.

34. *Imperium in Imperio,* pp. 20–22. As a child, I heard my father tell this same story. After I became acquainted with Griggs's version of it, I showed the passage to my father, who could remember hearing it from his mother.

35. *Overshadowed,* pp. 73–81.

36. See, for example, Sterling Brown's discussion of *The Hindered Hand* as "counter-propaganda." *Negro in American Fiction,* pp. 100–101. Also see John Daniels, "A Negro's Answer to 'The Leopard's Spots,'" *Alexander's Magazine* 1, no. 6 (October 1905): 31–33.

37. Joel Chandler Harris, *Uncle Remus: His Songs and His Sayings* (New York, 1908), p. viii.

38. W. E. B. Du Bois, *Souls of Black Folk*, p. 80.

39. *Pointing the Way*, p. 59; cf., Harris, *Uncle Remus*, pp. 201–14.

40. *Pointing the Way*, p. 150; cf., Harris, *Uncle Remus*, pp. 231–33.

41. Harris, *Uncle Remus*, pp. 255–56.

42. Bone's misinterpretation of Uncle Jack, one of the dominant figures of *Pointing the Way* and one of Griggs's most memorable creations, can only be attributed to Bone's not having read the book; see *The Negro Novel*, p. 33.

43. Martin Delany, in his novel *Blake* (Boston, 1970), endows the plantation slaves with subtlety, wit, and the ability to deceive their masters while wearing a mask of subservience; see pp. 12 and 44–48. Also see William Wells Brown, *Clotel, or, The President's Daughter* (London, 1853), pp. 99–100.

44. To chart all of the influences of the social sciences upon Sutton Griggs would be a mammoth task, far outside the scope of this paper, which is concerned with his contributions as a novelist. Within the novels, however, he does allude to Benjamin Kidd, *Unfettered*, pp. 244, 167; *The Hindered Hand*, p. 147, utilizes some of Kidd's theories concerning climatological influences upon racial temperament, but no direct reference to Kidd is made. The evolutionists Charles Darwin and Prince Kropotkin are mentioned in *Unfettered*, p. 235. Darwin is also discussed in *Overshadowed*, p. 168. Most of Griggs's references to social Darwinists and other social theorists are to be found in his social studies, however.

45. The following works by Griggs are concerned with social theories: *The One Great Question: A Study of Southern Conditions at Close Range* (Nashville, 1907); *Wisdom's Call* (Nashville, 1911), which alludes to the work of Thomas Henry Huxley, p. 117, and Ray Stannard Baker, p. 122, and demonstrates a fair knowledge of the opinions of contemporary political leaders. *Lie's Demands, or, According to Law* attempts to work out an exact scientific approach to race relations. In this work, Griggs works out an exact ideology based on the writings of Kropotkin and Darwin, pp. 34–35, and elsewhere. *Guide to Racial Greatness, or, The Science of Collective Efficiency* (Memphis, 1923) makes copious references to theories in the social sciences and the biological sciences.

46. My own article, "Marcus Garvey: A Reapprasial," *The Black Scholar* 4, no. 3 (November/December 1972), is a poor example of this spirit of objectivity. It was indeed a step along the way to my becoming appreciative of Garvey's importance, but an extreme rejection of the uncritical adulation of him. An example of the more sophisticated treatment of Garvey and black nationalism that is becoming widespread is Tony Martin, *Race First* (Westport, Conn., 1976). Also of high quality is Robert Hill's essay in John Henrik Clarke, ed., *Marcus Garvey and the Vision of Africa* (New York, 1974).

47. The grand old work on John Bunyan, and a classic in its own right, is John Brown, *John Bunyan: His Life, Times and Work* (Boston and New York, 1886). See especially pages 282–300. British literary historians have long justified works within their own tradition on moral, political, or historical grounds. An application of such methodology might well be justified for proponents of Black Studies who wish to secure a fair hearing for Griggs.

Literary Myth
and Ethnic Assimilation

Israel Zangwill and Sutton Griggs

Israel Zangwill (1864–1926) was a man of two souls. As one biographer contends, "He was passionately devoted to the values of the Jewish past as enshrined in the ghetto, but at the same time, he sought to escape from what he felt to be the ghetto's restrictiveness." He was born in London of a poor Russian immigrant family, educated at the Jews' Free School in the East End of London, where he later became a teacher. He published prolifically, essays, stories, and plays, becoming known for his "Dickensian" portrayals of types of London Jewry. But the best known contribution that Israel Zangwill made to the thought of the modern world was a phrase that he donated to American culture. It is a phrase taken from the title of his now almost forgotten play, *The Melting Pot*. It is with the theme of this play that I am concerned here. Stated succinctly, and in its author's words, the central idea is that "America is God's crucible, the great melting pot, where all the races of Europe are melting and reforming." The plot is as follows: It is 1908, and young David Quixano, a Russian Jewish violinist, has recently arrived in America to live with his Uncle Mendel, a piano teacher, and Mendel's aged mother, who finds it hard to give up her old-country ways and speaks no English. They have a good-hearted, though sporadically ethnocentric, servant girl named Kathleen. She is Irish, of course, and provides much amusement with her attempts to speak

239

Yiddish and to remember the family's orthodox rituals and customs. At one point, Kathleen exclaims in exasperation that the Pope himself could not remember so many religious rules and dietary laws. One evening the family is visited by Vera Revendal, an idealistic young woman, who has recently emigrated from Russia. Her English is perfect because her parents, Czarist aristocrats (though of modest means), were able to provide her with an English governess. Vera asks David to play his violin at her settlement house, although, as she explains apologetically, she will not be able to offer a fee. But David responds with passion,

> A fee! I'd pay a fee to see all those happy immigrants you gather together—Dutchmen and Greeks, Poles and Norwegians, Welsh and Armenians. If you only had Jews, it would be as good as going to Ellis Island.

Ellis Island in New York is, of course, the symbolic gateway through which so many turn-of-the-century immigrants were herded before being officially admitted as residents. It was on Ellis Island that they often had their first contact with industrial bureaucracy, as they were issued their papers, and sometimes even, due to the carelessness or callousness of petty officialdom, new names. Once ashore, they usually found homes in immigrant neighborhoods. There they came into contact with the settlement house movement. This was an urban reform idea, originating among the educated classes to alleviate the cultural and spiritual poverty of the communities in which the immigrants often resided. Settlement houses existed for the purposes of assisting the immigrants in finding health, education, and social welfare services. They also provided artistic, political, and intellectual activities for the neighborhoods they served. As an idealistic, upper-class young woman, Vera Revendal would have been a typical settlement house type. As an immigrant from a Russian aristocratic family, she would have been extraordinary.

David, as we soon realize, is quite certain that she is the very "Spirit of the Settlement." He shares with her—because he is certain that she will understand—a rhapsody on the meaning of America as he sees it.

> "Here you stand, good folk," think I when I see them at Ellis Island, here you stand in your fifty groups with your fifty languages and histories, and your fifty blood hatreds and rivalries. But you won't be long like that, brothers, for these are the fires of God you've come to—these are the fires of God. A fig for your feuds and vendettas! Germans and Frenchmen, Irishmen and Englishmen, Jews and Russians—into the Crucible with you all! God is making the American. . . . The real American has not yet arrived. He is only in the Crucible, I tell you—he will be the fusion of all races, perhaps the coming superman.

David and Vera begin to fall in love, despite the fact that he knows she is from his native town of Kishineff and a member of that class who murdered his mother, his father, and his sister in a pogrom. Needless to say, his Uncle Mendel does not approve of the romance, but, says David, "The ideals of the fathers shall not be foisted on the children. Each generation must live and die for its own dream." Just as the young lovers have vowed "to throw off the coils of the centuries" and harken to the voice of "the living present," Vera's father enters. He is Baron Revendal, a stubborn and narrow man, who carries a pistol to defend himself from the anarchists, whom he believes to lurk behind every lamppost. David recognizes the Baron as the commander of the soldiers who stood coldly looking on while a mob hacked his mother and sister to bits. David staggers out the door; Vera collapses in tears, but the drama is to have a happy ending.

Herr Pappelmeister, an intelligent and sympathetic German conductor, peruses the score of the symphony that David has been composing. He recognizes, naturally, that David's composition is a work of genius and performs it before an admiring audience, who responds with half an hour of frenzied applause. David is overcome by the ideals represented in his "New World Symphony," and his heart is softened towards Vera. The curtain falls as the lovers turn their backs on the European past and pledge themselves to the future symbolized by an America that is not so much a nation as a negation of all traditional nationalisms.

There were others who found it more difficult to harbor such optimistic hopes for the future of America. Sutton Elbert Griggs was a black American Baptist minister, who between 1899 and 1908 wrote and published five novels. In all of them he is concerned with the barriers between the races and is pessimistic concerning any possibility of the black and white populations ever successfully merging into a united and happy people. Thus, in his first novel, *Imperium in Imperio,* Griggs describes the black population as a nation within a nation. He sees the only hope for survival among blacks as the creation of an invisible government with war-making powers and a sense of steadfast unity in the face of white America. At the end of the story, all the main characters, save one, have been lynched, murdered, or driven to suicide. The sole survivor, now quite mad, stands beside the grave of a fallen compatriot, plotting revenge upon the United States with the aid of European allies, and delivers the following soliloquy:

> Float on, proud flag, while yet you may. Rejoice, oh ye Anglo-Saxons, yet a little while. Make my father ashamed to own me, his lawful son; call me a bastard child; look upon my pure mother as a harlot; laugh at Viola in

the grave of a self-murderer; exhume Belton's body, if you like, and tear your flag from around him to keep him from polluting it! Yes, stuff your vile stomachs full of all these horrors. You shall be richer food for the buzzards to whom I have solemnly vowed to give your flesh.

In his second novel, *Overshadowed,* Griggs has his protagonist completely renounce all ties to the United States. As he boards a ship in New York harbor, his friends inquire of him where he is bound.

"Are you returning to your fatherland?" anxious friends, gathered at the pier, inquired.
Astral replied, "It, too, is overshadowed. Aliens possess it."

When the ship is in mid-ocean, Astral finally makes a declaration of his plans.

"I, Astral Herndon, hereby and forever renounce all citizenship in all lands whatsoever, and constitute myself A CITIZEN OF THE OCEAN, and ordain that this title shall be entailed upon my progeny unto all generations, until such time as the shadows which now envelope the darker races in all lands shall have passed away, away, and away.

In Sutton Griggs's third novel, *Unfettered,* the hero is brought into an international plot, led by members of his long lost tribe in Africa. In his fourth novel, *The Hindered Hand,* Griggs's black hero is invited to join in a conspiracy of the Slavic world against the Anglo-Saxon. A cadaverous white man in a brown derby presents himself at his front door and announces that he is the incarnation of hostility to those who identify with the Anglo-Saxon race.

"The world, you see, will soon contain but two colossal figures, the Anglo-Saxon and the Slav. The inevitable battle for world supremacy will be between these giants. Without going into the question as to why I am a Pro-Slav in this matter, I hereby declare unto you that it is the one dream of my life to so weaken the Anglo-Saxon that he will be easy prey for the Slav in the coming momentous world struggle."

The hero successfully resists the temptation to throw in with America's enemies, but nonetheless becomes increasingly alienated and spends the last several chapters of the book travelling to and from Africa. He finally decides to take his family to the Fatherland for good, in order "to provide a home for the American Negro."
In all of Sutton Griggs's novels, the theme of permanent separation of the races finally wins out in the end. Only in death do the black and

the white people ever meet, for in several instances Griggs mentions that
a faithful Negro retainer is sometimes buried at the foot of his master's
grave. This is indeed the final note of his last novel, *Pointing the Way.*
The best that could be hoped for in Griggs's novelistic America was a
spirit of mutual respectful avoidance between white and black.

The contrast between the two views, presented by Israel Zangwill
and Sutton Griggs, will perhaps provide us with some insights into the
theme of this conference, "Origins and Originality of American Culture." For Israel Zangwill, American culture represented a break with
the past, something completely new. It is clear that Zangwill identified
deeply with the mass experience of the 1,500,000 Jews who left Eastern
Europe between 1900 and 1914. Some 90 percent of this group settled in
the United States, where, despite the many hardships they encountered,
they nonetheless found conditions better than in Czarist Russia. But for
the Afro-Americans of whom Sutton Griggs wrote, conditions in the
United States were far different. For them, the American South was just
as brutal as the tyranny of the czars. The environment in which the vast
majority of black American peasants lived closely resembled the environment known to Russia's Jews.

The biases of Zangwill's point of view did not allow him to see this.
To be sure, he did have Baron Revendal defend the Jew-baiting of Russia
by asking of an American, "Don't you lynch and roast your niggers?"
And David Quixano, in one of his speeches, throws both "black and
yellow" into the crucible along with his assortment of Europeans. Yet, if
one examines the appendices to the 1913 edition of *The Melting Pot,* one
finds that Zangwill gives his approval to such traditional Anglo-Saxon
ideas as the following:

> . . . the prognathous face is an ugly and undesirable type of coun-
> tenance . . . it connotes a lower average of intellect and ethics . . . white
> and black are as yet too far apart for profitable fusion. Melanophobia, or
> fear of the black, may be pragmatically as valuable a racial defence for the
> white as the counter-instinct of philoeucosis, or love of the white, is a force
> of racial uplifting of the black.

The comments appended to *The Melting Pot* are clearly intended to
disassociate its author from the charge that he advocates contamination
of the white race. It is possible for Zangwill to advocate the cultural and
genetic assimilation of Jews into the rest of America, so long as the
Jews, like David Quixano, are willing to give up their memories of the
Old World and abandon the faith of their fathers. But Zangwill knew
full well that a play advocating interracial marriage could never have
been produced in Washington, D.C., in 1908, where *The Melting Pot*

had its very successful premier and was dedicated, by permission, to President Theodore Roosevelt. This same President Roosevelt had once been severely criticized as an advocate of race mixing because he had eaten at the same table with Booker T. Washington. From the perspective of the black American writer, America has never appeared so unique as Zangwill believed it to be. And even white American writers contemporary to Zangwill had some reservations concerning the myth of the Melting Pot. Upton Sinclair believed that assimilation into American life was a painful, even an unhealthy process. His novel *The Jungle* is said to have turned Theodore Roosevelt's stomach, with its description of the filthy conditions under which Eastern European immigrants worked in Chicago meat-packing houses. Sinclair showed how the healthy, robust customs of Slavic peasants soon were obliterated in the dehumanizing industrial slums of Chicago. He showed how the family disintegrated under the stresses of poverty, hunger, and unfamiliarity with urban conditions. The descriptions painted by Upton Sinclair and other writers, who came to be known as "muckrakers," led to health, education, and welfare reforms that benefited all Americans.

Settlement house workers, far from encouraging the complete eradication of all European ethnic traits, realized the importance of encouraging the immigrants to retain the essence of their ethnic heritages. Jane Addams, the dean of settlement house organizers, told in her minor literary classic, *Twenty Years at Hull House,* of her efforts to assist the children of immigrants in learning to appreciate the skills, crafts, arts, and ways of life brought to America by their parents and grandparents. She also praised Jewish and German immigrants for their intellectual interests and felt that all Americans might learn from their habits of political and literary discussion. Rather than assuming that all European traits must be eradicated, the best of the settlement workers encouraged immigrants to preserve the nurturing elements of their European cultures.

In all fairness to the Melting Pot school, they too believed that America benefited from the cultural influx of various nations. Even the Negroes had contributed a "comic spirit" or a sort of "spiritual miscegenation," which had led to "rag time" and the sexy dances that go with it. But the essential importance of genetic mixing to the Melting Pot theory cannot be denied. Zangwill articulated a belief that many Americans found acceptable at the time and that the majority of Americans still find acceptable. The American ideal is to forget the European past and become fully American. This implies intermarrying with other Americans. When an Irishman named John F. Kennedy marries a French woman named Jacqueline Bouvier, this is seen as the storybook wedding that logically fulfills the American dream. The Melting Pot ideal works as well for the Jews as for others, with the passing of years, as they become more and more removed form the ghettoes of New York's lower East Side. The increasing secularization of society aids the process. At present some 30 percent of American Jews marry outside their faith. The proportion increases the farther we are from the East Coast.

The miniscule occurrence of intermarriage between black Americans and other ethnic groups is not much affected by the passage of generations or internal migration. Intermixture between blacks and whites has diminished to almost nothing since the emancipation of the slaves, because white men are no longer able to have their way with black women.

The statistics do not lie. Although it has become fashionable among some American sociologists and ethnologists to deny that the Melting Pot ideal still predominates in America, the fact is that among fourth-generation Americans, religion and national origin seem to matter very little, if at all, in the selection of one's mate. But America, like every other culture, has its inassimilable ethnics. It is only when race is added to ethnicity that the melting process is considered undesirable. And even Israel Zangwill, during the heyday of his ideal, subscribed to the view that the black population would be better off founding its own separate state, or perhaps setting sail for Liberia, as did the hero of Sutton Griggs's novel, *The Hindered Hand.*

Sexual Anxieties
of the Black Bourgeoisie
in Victorian America

The Cultural Context of W. E. B. Du Bois's First Novel

I was not a prig," asserted Du Bois somewhat stiffly in his *Autobiography*. "I was a lusty man with all normal appetites. I loved 'Wine, Women and Song.' "[1] By his own admission, however, the youthful Du Bois found sexuality "a thing of temptation and horror," which attitude he later blamed on his New England schooling. When he went South to Fisk University at age seventeen, he recalled, "I actually did not know the physical difference between men and women."[2] He looked upon the South as a "region of loose sexual customs" and was jeered by his fellow students, who found it difficult to accept his claims of sexual innocence and regarded him as a "liar or freak." One summer, while working as a rural schoolteacher in Tennessee, he was "literally raped by the unhappy wife who was my landlady." In Paris during the 1890s, he experimented with prostitutes, but this, he insisted, "affronted my sense of decency."[3] His instructions to the black community of Philadelphia in 1899 are revealing. He advised not only a war on prostitution and adultery but "keeping little girls off the street at night [and] stopping the escorting of unchaperoned young ladies to church and elsewhere."[4]

Du Bois was disturbed by the alleged sexual delinquency of the black family, which he explained in the following way:

> Without doubt the point where the Negro American is furthest behind modern civilization is in his sexual *mores*. This does not mean that he is more criminal in this respect than his neighbors. Probably he is not. It does mean that he is more primitive, less civilized, in this respect than his surroundings demand, and that thus his family life is less efficient for its onerous social duties, his womanhood less protected, his children more poorly trained. All this, however, is to be expected. This is what slavery meant, and no amount of kindness in individual owners could save the system from its deadly work of disintegrating the ancient negro home and putting but a poor substitute in its place. The point is, however, now, what has been the effect of emancipation on the *mores* of the Negro family.[5]

Du Bois saw the development of a stratified black society, "successive classes with higher and higher sexual morals," as the important post–Civil War development. It was the special responsibility of the "talented tenth" to assume a missionary function with respect to the rest of the population.[6]

The idea was not new with Du Bois; this was an age in which bourgeois elites searched for new fields of endeavor for the uplift of the masses. It was the heyday of the settlement house worker, and the tradition of Yankee teachers going to work among the children of the freedmen was not yet dead. As John Blassingame has noted, Northern reformers undertook a campaign to offset the effects of "more than one hundred years of slavery and oppression" that had left black people with "a heavy burden of sexual immorality, ignorance, broken families, fear, and improvidence." Scholars who have viewed black family life in this way have been challenged recently by a group of social scientists who feel that slavery had no negative effects on black sexual morality, or at least none of lasting significance. The conclusions of these scholars are based largely on records kept by slaveholders or on statistics compiled in nineteenth-century censuses widely condemned for their bias.[7]

It has never been denied that the sexual morality of black sharecroppers was different from that of urban middle-class whites. Disputes have raged, however, as to how the difference was to be interpreted. Black middle-class intellectuals in the early years of this century revealed some embarrassment when discussing the sexual values of the masses, as is seen in their attempts to apologize for what they perceived as inferior organization in marital and familial life. Hence they explained all of the shortcomings that they saw in the black family as the inevitable consequences of slavery.

Charles S. Johnson, writing some thirty years after the Du Bois study, felt that the sexual customs of the black peasants (customs that survived well into the twentieth century) persisted because the economic conditions that produced them persisted. Like others, he was inclined to support the view that a change of values would be desirable, but he felt that such change could not occur except as the result of economic changes in the South and "comprehensive planning, which affects not merely the South but the nation." In describing the culture of isolated black agricultural workers, Johnson observed that in some communities there was "no such thing as illegitimacy." Premarital sex was generally accepted in practice, although not openly advocated as an ideal form of behavior. Although there were, of course, many families with stable organization and "conventional" sexual mores, Johnson was able to note the occurrence of certain common features of rural black life that were not conventional. These were "the unevenness of life, the amount of sexual freedom, the frequency of separation and realignment of families, the number of children born out of wedlock." But it would be wrong to say that these people lived without morality, that they had no concept of respectability, or that they had no "codes or conventions consistent with the essential routine of their lives."[8]

. In fairness to Du Bois, it must be observed that he toyed with ideas similar to those expressed by Johnson, both in his study of the black family and in his later essay, "The Damnation of Women." His ambivalence concerning Victorian sexual morality is evident in his novel of 1911, *The Quest of the Silver Fleece,* although it is also certainly evident that in 1911 Du Bois still looked upon the sexual values of the black peasantry as uncivilized. Despite his later disavowals of a belief in Christian philosophy, Du Bois's attitudes were consistent with those of the middle-class black clergy.[9] He was bitter and resentful at what he viewed as the degradation of black womanhood. On one occasion, he quoted extensively from the writings of his mentor, the Reverend Alexander Crummell, who wrote in 1883:

> From her childhood [the slave woman] was the doomed victim of the grossest passions. All the virtues of her sex were utterly ignored. If the instinct of chastity asserted itself, then she had to fight like a tigress for the ownership and possession of her own person. . . . This year she had one husband; and next year, through some auction sale, she might be separated from him and mated to another. There was no sanctity of family, no binding tie of marriage, none of the fine felicities and the endearing affection of home. None of these things were the lot of Southern black women. Instead thereof a gross barbarism which tended to blunt the tender sensibilities, to obliterate feminine delicacy and womanly shame, came down as her heritage from generation to generation; and it seems a miracle of providence and grace

that, notwithstanding these terrible circumstances, so much struggling virtue lingered amid those rude cabins, that so much womanly worth and sweetness abided in their bosoms, as slaveholders themselves have borne witness to.[10]

It was Crummell's view, passed down by W. E. B. Du Bois, that later formed the basis of E. Franklin Frazier's study, *The Negro Family,* and through that the so-called "Moynihan Report."[11] Recent scholars, attempting to de-emphasize the negative images that have predominated in past interpretations of black history, have attacked the so-called "pejorative tradition."[12] Nonetheless, most black leaders of the early twentieth century subscribed to the belief that black sexual morality had been damaged by the slavery experience.

Mary Church Terrell, first president of the National Association of Colored Women, endorsed this view in her article, "Club Work of Colored Women," when she wrote of "the fateful heritage of slavery . . ., the manifold pitfalls and peculiar temptations to which our girls are subjected." Terrell reported the determined effort of her Association "to have heart to heart talks with our women, that we may strike at the root of evils, many of which lie at the fireside." It was necessary that a special effort be made for women whose "shackles were stricken but yesterday."[13] Margaret Murray (Mrs. Booker T.) Washington said, "Our girls need social purity talks. They must be warned of evil company. They must be brought in closer contact with more that is good and pure."[14] Fannie Barrier Williams described the club movement as "organized anxiety" on the part of women who realized that "the consciousness of being fully free has not yet come to the great masses of the colored women in this country."[15] Josephine St. Pierre Ruffin, who called for a nationally coordinated effort on the part of black women's clubs to improve public images, warned against indifference to "temperance, morality, the higher education, hygenic and domestic questions."[16] The National Association of Colored Women (NACW) worked to promote Victorian bourgeois morality both in rural areas and in the emerging ghettoes of the North.

The defense of black males from sexual racism was also a concern of reform-oriented middle-class blacks. The lynching statistics for the years 1889–1919 are a useful index of sexual oppression, indicating that for whatever reasons, black males were lynched more than any other group in American society.[17] Among the most often cited reasons offered in justification of lynching was alleged rape or "attacks upon women."[18]

Many social scientists following in the tradition of Count Arthur de Gobineau looked upon blacks as a mentally inferior race with correspondingly powerful animal drives. John S. Haller has shown that such an attitude was widespread among late nineteenth-century physicians and anthropologists.[19] William T. English, a physician teaching at the University of Pittsburgh, argued that the Negro was a bestial moral delinquent and that proximity to a superior race aggravated his "innate tendency to sex appetite." The asserted tendency of Negro males to attack white females was seen as resulting from an uncontrollable instinct; as one scholarly writer observed, "the *furor sexualis* in the Negro resembles similar sexual attacks in the bull and elephant."[20] Another wrote of "the African birthright to sexual madness."[21]

The feeling of the slaves and subsequent attempts to educate them only brought out the worst of their antisocial instincts, it was argued. Charles Carroll, an amateur pseudo-Darwinist, insisted that the Negro was a beast and not a human being at all. "The screams of the ravished daughters of the Sunny South have placed the Negro in the lowest rank of the Beast Kingdom."[22] The mixed bloods (whose very existence would have seemed to disprove his theory) were just as bad, if not worse, and education had made them more of a menace. "To-day our wives and our daughters are not safe from their brutal assaults beyond the range of our shot guns."[23] In a similar vein, Claude Bowers attributed sex crimes by black males to their incapacity to understand freedom and the preaching of social equality by carpetbaggers. "Rape," he claimed, "is the foul daughter of Reconstruction."[24]

"The moral as well as the physical characteristics of a race are to a greater or less degree indelible," wrote Nathaniel Southgate Shaler, a Harvard professor and the son of a slaveholder.[25] Philip Alexander Bruce, a Virginia historian, defined as characteristic of the black race an "indifference to chastity in the females, [and] lewdness of the males."[26] The tendency to rape was innate and not societal in origin, proclaimed Lester Ward. The Negro was instinctively attracted to the white woman, he posited, for "the men of any race will greatly prefer the women of a race which they regard as higher than their own. . . . And when the man of an inferior race strives to perpetuate his existence through a woman of a superior race, it is something more than mere bestial lust that drives him to such a dangerous act. It is the same unheard but imperious voice of nature commanding him at the risk of 'lynch law' to raise his race to a little higher level."[27]

But while so many voices were raised in proclaiming the inevitability of Negro rape, a curious countermyth was simultaneously developing. This was the myth of the contented Negro slave, who was loyal throughout the war and would have remained perpetually faithful if it had not been for the evil promptings of carpetbaggers and scalawags. Frederick

Douglass, Ida B. Wells-Barnett, and other black spokespersons attempted to reverse this myth, to strip it of its Uncle Tom connotations
and exploit it for the benefit of black people.[28] If, as Joel Chandler
Harris had maintained, the typical "good darky" had stood behind "ole
Missus" with an axe in his hand, daring any Yankee to touch a hair on
her head, was it not shameful to pretend that this same faithful servant
had suddenly become a rapist due to the irresistible bestial instinct?[29]
Booker T. Washington also contributed to this myth in the Atlantic Exposition Address, where he referred sentimentally and yet pointedly to
the faithful law-abiding Negroes, "whose loyalty and love you have
tested in days when to have proved treacherous meant the ruin of your
firesides."[30] The report of Col. Thomas Wentworth Higginson, concerning the deportment of the first slave regiment mustered into the service
of the United States, is consistent with the foregoing observations. Higginson commented upon the natural gentility of his men, "an average
tone of propriety which all visitors noticed, and which was not created,
but only preserved by discipline." He noted the courtesy, decency, and
decorum of the freedmen in action and in bearing, calling special attention to the fact that ladies were able to move about the camp "without
the slightest fear of annoyance":

> I do not mean direct annoyance or insult, for no man who valued his life
> would have ventured that in the presence of others, but I mean the annoy-
> ance of accidentally seeing or hearing improprieties not intended for them.
> They both [the wives of two officers] declared that they would not have
> moved about with anything like the same freedom in any white camp they
> had ever entered, and it always roused their indignation to hear the negro
> race called brutal or depraved.[31]

Responses to the malignment of black men were often direct. Washington himself observed in February 1896 that "within the last fortnight
three members of my race have been burned at the stake; of these one
was a woman. Not one of the three was charged with any crime even
remotely connected with the abuse of a white woman."[32] And in 1912, he
remarked that in roughly seventy cases of lynching occurring in the past
year in which blacks were victims, "Only seventeen were charged with
the crime of rape."[33] Ida B. Wells offered more detailed statistics. These
she presented in a pamphlet published in 1892, *A Red Record*. Having
narrowly escaped lynching for her activities as a newspaper editor in
Memphis, Wells was aware that lynching had little to do with sex crimes,
as was often maintained. Her statistics demonstrated this fact for only in
a fraction of instances was there even an accusation of rape—much less
the proof of it.[34] Innocent men and women could be lynched for any-

thing or for nothing, she asserted. Victoria Earle Mathews, a fair-skinned "Afro-American" woman (she insisted on the term) had travelled extensively in the South to investigate race relations. She stoutly resisted any attempts to link together in the minds of the public black men, lynching, and the crime of rape. When some members of the women's club movement attempted at their meeting in Atlanta (1895) to issue a statement denouncing lynching and the "crime that provokes lynching," Mathews became indignant and justified the resolutions committee's rejection of the provision. She argued that there was "no tenable ground for the acceptance even of the injurer's apology, much less a condemnatory resolution based on no other evidence than the word or report of those who support by non-interference crimes against law, humanity, and god."[35]

Du Bois's first and perhaps best novel, *The Quest of the Silver Fleece*, published in 1911, may be seen as a counterbalance to the myth of black sexual depravity.[36] In fashioning his tale, Du Bois drew on the myth of Jason and the Golden Fleece, an idea that he had conceived a decade earlier, and sketched out in Chapter 8 of *The Souls of Black Folk*. He substituted the silver of a cotton field for the gold of the winged ram Chrysomallus, and endowed the fleece with a subtle sexual symbolism. The wanderings of Bles Alwyn and Zora Cresswell in their quest for Puritan respectability are analogous to the quest for the argonauts, who "went vaguely wandering into the shadowy East three thousand years ago."[37]

Early in the story, Bles Alwyn — a callow, idealistic boy of fifteen — explains to Zora — a half-wild, fourteen-year-old swamp child — that white folks' books "give them power and wealth and make them rule." In the course of the novel, the two gain maturity through suffering and achieve greater knowledge of life, as well as books. Throughout the novel, Bles subconsciously compares Zora to Mary Taylor and Miss Sarah Smith, the Yankee schoolmarms. The novel reaches its crisis when Mary leads Bles to believe that Zora is not "pure." Zora is an untamed creature of the swamp; Mary and Miss Smith represent civilization and propriety. There is no indication that Bles is attracted by their paleness, but he is fascinated by their bourgeois femininity, their book-learning, and their New England reserve. Thus he experiences confusing and contradictory emotions when he encounters Carolyn Wynn, a beautiful quadroon [mulatto], and mistakes her for a white woman.

> While Bles Alwyn in the outer office was waiting and musing, a lady came in. Out of the corner of his eye, he caught the curve of her gown, and as she seated herself beside him, the suggestion of a faint perfume. A vague resent-

ment rose in him. Colored women would look as well as that, he argued, with the clothes and wealth and training. He paused, however, in his thought: he did not want them like the whites—so cold and formal and precise, without heart or marrow. (235)

These are interesting musings. Bles is obviously attracted to the image presented by Carolyn Wynn. It is for this reason that he eventually becomes obsessed with marrying her. And yet he is uneasy in the presence of this woman:

her voice, her bearing, the set of her gown, her gloves and shoes, the whole impression was—Bles hesitated for a word—well "white."

Where has Bles formed his impressions of white women? The only two he has really come to know are Mary and Miss Smith—neither of them exactly cold. Miss Smith is laconic and formal, but motherly as well, and hardly "without heart or marrow." As for Mary, she constantly projects intense and confused emotions—intentionally and unintentionally. She has a way of inadvertently forcing acknowledgment of her sexuality. Her emotional naiveté continually places Bles in compromising situations. On their first meeting, she approaches him while he works in the field. Her manner is relaxed and intimate and her physical posture reminiscent of Zora's in an earlier scene, as she sits on the ground "clasping her hands about her knees."

"Have you never heard of the Golden Fleece, Bles?"
"No, ma'am," he said eagerly; then glancing up toward the Cresswell fields, he saw two white men watching them. He grasped his hoe and started briskly to work. (31)

Bles's manner towards white women is as respectful as that of the black troops described by Thomas Wentworth Higginson in *Army Life in a Black Regiment.* Nonetheless, the situation is fraught with sexual overtones, as Bles is dimly aware, or as he is suddenly reminded when the white men appear on the horizon. Such situations are a recurrent theme in the relationship between Bles and Mary. On another occasion, Bles and Mary are observed with some hostility by two white men, when he is ordered to drive her into town on a business trip.

"Who's that nigger with?"
"One of them nigger teachers."
"Well we'll stop this damn riding around or they'll hear something . . . "
(42)

As they continue homeward, they hear the approaching sound of galloping hoofbeats.

> "Who's this?" asked Miss Taylor.
> "The Cresswells, I think. . . . "
> "Good gracious!" she thought. "The Cresswells!" And with it came a sudden desire not to meet them—just then. . . . "Let's see the sunset in the swamp," she said suddenly. On came the galloping horses. Bles looked up in surprise, then silently turned into the swamp. The horses flew by, their hoofbeats dying in the distance. A dark green silence lay about them lit by mighty crimson glories beyond. Miss Taylor leaned back and watched it dreamily till a sense of oppression grew upon her. The sun was sinking fast.
> "Where does this road come out?" she asked at last.
> "It doesn't come out."
> "Where does it go?"
> "It goes to Elspeth's."
> "Why, we must turn back immediately. I thought—." But Bles was already turning. (42)

The sexually and socially naive Mary is too insensitive to think that by suggesting to Bles that they drive into the swamp she is placing him in a dangerous situation. What business does a young and attractive white woman have sitting in a buggy with a black boy in the middle of a swamp, leaning back and dreamily watching the sunset? The fact that the road goes to Elspeth's shack, from which "we must turn back immediately," is also interesting. Elspeth's shack in the swamp is the dominant symbol of sexual degradation throughout the novel. In the relationship between Bles and Mary, the road to Elspeth's always lies open, but of course their awareness of this fact is only semiconscious. Zora, who is at once sexually naive and sexually precocious, readily perceives the sexual potential of the relationship and looks upon Mary as a rival when she encounters them on Elspeth's road. Her reaction, like that of the white males, is sullen.

> At the sight of the lady, she suddenly drew back and stood motionless regarding Miss Taylor, searching her with wide black liquid eyes. Miss Taylor was a little startled.
> "Good—good—evening," she said, straightening herself.
> The girl was still silent and the horses stopped. One tense moment pulsed through all the swamp. Then the girl, still motionless—still looking Miss Taylor through and through—said with slow deliberateness:
> "I hates you." (43)

Zora is portrayed as a "child of the swamp . . . a heathen hoyden," who is one with the swamp "in all its moods; mischievous, secretive, brooding; full of great and awful visions, steeped body and soul in wood-lore." She is indeed the half-devil and half-child of Kipling's poem, and she constitutes a white man's or white woman's burden, particularly difficult for the sexual missionaries who attempt to uplift her before they have worked out their own salvation. She is constantly associated with sexual imagery, "great shadowy oaks and limpid pools, lone, naked trees and sweet flowers; the whispering and flitting of wild things, and the winging of furtive birds."[38] Twice she is depicted as taking Bles's hand and leading him into the swamp. The second of these instances is reproduced below with italics added to indicate words and phrases with traditional sexual connotations.

> In a moment she had slipped her hand away and was *scrambling upon the tree trunk*. The waters yawned murkily below.
> "Careful! Careful!" he warned, struggling after her until she disappeared amid the leaves. He followed eagerly, but cautiously; and all at once found himself *confronting a paradise*.
> Before them lay a long island, opening to the south the black lake, but sheltered north and east by the dense undergrowth of the black swamp and the rampart of dead and living trees. *The soil was virgin and black,* thickly covered over with a tangle of bushes, vines, and smaller growth all brilliant with early leaves and wild flowers. (77)

The author did not wish to suggest an actual sexual encounter in this scene, only to re-emphasize the sexual themes of the novel. When Bles and Zora emerge from the swamp, they are confronted by Mary, who does not overlook the sexual implications of the situation. Her righteous anger is brought on by more than her suspicion that Zora has stolen a piece of jewelry from her desk.

> Soon she saw, with a certain grim satisfaction, Zora and Bles emerging from the swamp engaged in earnest conversation. Here was an opportunity to overwhelm both with an unforgettable reprimand. She rose before them like a spectral vengeance.
> "Zora, I want my pin." (78)

This scene is reminiscent of an earlier confrontation—the one occurring when Zora sees Bles and Mary coming from the swamp. The basis of the feminine anger in each instance is sexual rivalry over the emotions of the unwitting Bles. Mary's pin is suspiciously phallic, symbolizing the "stolen" Bles, of whom she is jealously possessive throughout the novel, although she is too emotionally weak to deal with her feelings. Zora, far from being overwhelmed, debates the ownership of the pin with Marxist logic and with an exasperating sophistication that would do justice to a devil or a child.

One important fact to note about Zora is that she remains chaste, if not virginal, throughout the novel. Whether she has actually been the victim of defloration at the tender age of twelve is not artistically important. She is both sexually sophisticated and sexually naive at the beginning of the story, and although she learns the meaning of guilt under Bles's probing, she still must learn the concept of chastity. Since she is depicted as an earth sprite or a little animal, one finds it difficult to think of the concept of purity as applicable to her. But Zora's chastity by the end of the novel is of a monumental order. She has become, as Bles tells her, "more than pure."[39] Indeed, she is more than a woman. She has progressed from chthonic spirit to Olympian deity. Terms such as "purity" and "chastity" are irrelevant equally to wood nymphs and to goddesses.

All this is not to suggest that Zora never reveals any human qualities. On the contrary, she is always capable of feeling pain and defeat. She is vulnerable to the slights and insults that are the peculiar burden of a colored woman in a white world. But there is no denying that she undergoes a steady transformation throughout the story. In the early pages, she is surrounded by nature imagery — forests, birds, and wild flowers, symbolic of her own untamed spirit. By the end of the book she is referred to as a regal person. At her first meeting with Zora, Mrs. Vanderpool sees herself as "white, frail, and fettered . . . before the magnificence of some bejewelled barbarian queen. . . ."[40] And in a later confrontation with Zora, Mrs. Vanderpool is haunted by that same vision.

> She did not seem to see her maid, nor the white and satin morning room. She saw, with some long inner sight, a vast hall with mighty pillars; a smooth marbled floor and a great throng whose silent eyes looked curiously upon her. Strange carven beasts gazed on from a setting of rich barbaric splendor and she herself — the Liar — lay in rags before the gold and ivory of that lofty throne whereon sat Zora. (326)

From the earliest pages of the story, Zora has the ability to stare through people, unnerving them, making them feel "the uncomfortable sense of being judged, of being weighed. . . . " Although this is quite unconscious on Zora's part, she makes people feel that she is more than just a person; to Mary Taylor, she is downright "inhuman."

As for Mary, alas, she is all too human. She is neither a wicked person nor a stupid one. She is weak, but no weaker than most of us. Her character is portrayed with skill and not without sympathy, although her fate is cruel. Mary is well-meaning. She has a sense of duty, a naive idealism, and an awareness of the distinction between right and wrong. She has little self-awareness, however, and she therefore has little ability to cope with her own emotions. This becomes evident in Chapter VII, when she is shocked to discover the implications of her relationship with Bles.

> "Isn't Bles developing splendidly?" she said to Miss Smith one afternoon. There was an unmistakable note of enthusiasm in her voice. Miss Smith slowly closed her letter-file but did not look up.
> "Yes," she said crisply. "He's eighteen now — quite a man."
> "And most interesting to talk with."
> "H'm — very" — drily. Mary was busy with her own thoughts, and she did not notice the older woman's manner.
> "Do you know," she pursued, "I'm a little afraid of one thing."
> "So am I."
> "Oh, you've noted it too — his friendship for that impossible girl, Zora."
> (67)

Mary has always treated Bles in ways that bespeak social equality, but she tends to forget the fact that he is masculine — as Miss Smith reminds her — though he has never thought of her as anything but a teacher. "But," the senior teacher warns, "he's a man, and human one, and if you keep on making much over him, and talking to him and petting him, he'll have the right to interpret your manner in his own way — the same way that any young man would." Mary flares angrily, "But — but, he's a — a — ." Mrs. Smith speaks the word for her: "A Negro. To be sure, he is; and a man in addition. . . ." Mary retires to her room where she spends a restless night, tossing uneasily in her bed and muttering, "There must be a difference, always, always! That impudent Negro."[41] Her reaction is rather violent and excessive, as she projects onto Bles the guilt that she suddenly feels as a result of her own unconscious sexual advances. It is interesting to note, in this connection, that this emotion-laden scene begins with Mary's expressing disapproval of Zora.

Whether the German-educated Du Bois was yet aware of Freud is open to speculation. If he was not aware of Freud, then he anticipated him, as so many pre-Freudian authors, ancient and modern, seem to have done. The fact is that Mary is intentionally portrayed as a person who is unaware of her sexual emotions and who reacts with outrage and guilt when she is forced to confront them. Mary's conversation with Miss Smith, and her agonized thrashings later in bed, are interspersed with images of black male sexuality and are indications of her own erotic sensibilities:

She slowly undressed in the dark, and heard the rumbling of cotton wagons as they swayed toward town. The cry of the Naked was sweeping the world, and yonder in the night black men were answering the call. They knew not what or why they answered, but obeyed the irresistible call, with hearts light and song upon their lips — the Song of Service. They lashed their mules and drank their whiskey, and all night the piled fleece swept by Mary Taylor's window, flying — flying to that far cry. Miss Taylor turned uneasily in her bed and jerked the bedclothes about her ears. (69)

Should one see this passage only as a rhapsody on labor, interwoven with themes of supply and demand, after the manner of Frank Norris? Or should one attach a double significance to such phrases as "cry of the Naked" and "irresistible call?" What sorts of songs do whiskey-drinking black men sing in the night? Is the "Song of Service" one of those carnal work songs in which sexual rhythms and ribald lyrics lighten the burden of labor?

The unbidden and only partially acknowledged attraction that Mary feels for Bles is not wholly a sexual feeling, but something much deeper. As the story progresses, one realizes that her loneliness and lack of fulfillment are not only sexual but spiritual. Mary is looking for a companion who can help her to develop her nobler impulses. She does not possess the Puritan toughness and independence of Miss Smith, nor the intelligence and tenacity of Zora. Like Bles, she tends to look to others for inspiration. The white men surrounding her are all corrupt. Her husband is a moral degenerate who is guilty of an almost incestuous child molestation and finally infects her and her unborn child with syphilis.[42] Bles is the only real man she has ever known, and her attempts to manipulate his love life, to shield him from the threatening Zora, reveal an interest that is more than pedagogical. She continually places him in compromising situations with sexual overtones, finally inviting him to her boudoir, innocently enough, but under circumstances that might have cost him his life. The implications of her behavior are obvious to Zora and Miss Smith, but not to Bles and Mary, who are too inhibited to recognize their sexual feelings.

The pain of Bles and Zora as they strive towards the goal of bourgeois Victorian sexual respectability is symbolic of the pain experienced by many Blacks during the period under consideration. Bles must struggle against the stereotyping of himself as a "supermasculine menial," constantly viewed as a sexual threat by the white male characters, forced into compromising situations and yet expected to suppress completely his sexuality.[43] He seethes with rage when he must confront the reality of his powerlessness to force white males to show deference to black women.[44] Bles's emotional experiences are typical for black male characters in turn-of-the-century fiction, and he has counterparts in the novels of Paul Laurence Dunbar, Charles Chestnutt, and Sutton Griggs. Zora's fall from grace occurs not in Elspeth's cabin, but in Bles's mind. As the story progresses, she and Bles are forced to recognize that the basis of black sexual degradation is in their exploitation as a labor force. It is symbolically important that Elspeth's cabin is finally destroyed by intelligent and organized black labor.

Du Bois is also concerned with showing how middle class-marriage is sometimes only respectable prostitution. John Taylor and Harry Cresswell both prostitute their sisters to their business interests. Miss Carolyn Wynn marries the man who can offer her the most in terms of wealth, status, and political power. She is reminiscent of another character who appears in *Dark Princess,* Du Bois's second novel, written seventeen years later.[45] In this work sexual themes are also present, but not dominant as in *The Quest of the Silver Fleece.* Du Bois's developing ability to question bourgeois sexual conventions is revealed by involving the principals of *Dark Princess* in an extramarital affair, which the author views approvingly. Still, Du Bois's continuing ambivalence — indeed hostility — towards the sexual mores of the black masses can be seen in his review of Claude McKay's *Home to Harlem* in 1928, the same year that *Dark Princess* was published.[46] In 1957 Du Bois returned to the themes of the 1890s in his novel *The Ordeal of Mansart,* where a minor character plots the violation of a white girl whom he has known since childhood. His musings anticipate the rationalizations of Eldridge Cleaver, whose book *Soul on Ice* apologizes for rape as a liberating act of social protest. Du Bois's character is morally and emotionally incapable of perpetrating the dastardly act. Thus *The Ordeal of Mansart* is a protest against sexual racism rather than a plea for mindless retaliatory violence of the sort that Cleaver tries to justify in *Soul on Ice.*[47]

The Quest of the Silver Fleece is neither a protest against, nor a celebration of, white, middle-class, turn-of-the-century morality. It is neither a naive defense of peasant sexuality nor a condemnation of it. Placed within the context of what other black writers were saying in the early 1900s, it represents a questioning of the black middle class's quest for sexual respectability. That such a quest was undertaken is undeniable. The concern is present in the publications of the NACW and in the fiction written by black authors and "friend of the Negro" Mary White Ovington.[48] James McPherson has detailed the missionary concerns of white carpetbaggers and those blacks who represented the "Talented Tenth." Du Bois obviously shared such concerns, but he also seemed to be saying in 1911 that when one lifts the veil of middle-class respectability, one may find behind it horrors beyond the capacity of the black world to conceive or the white world to acknowledge. Zora, and the millions of poor women whom she represents, black and white alike, have been placed figuratively in Elspeth's cabin by cosmic manipulations, far beyond their comprehension. The most vicious rapists in Du Bois's cosmology were the men whose economic and social policies reduced women to a level where their spirits were broken and their bodies no longer their own. This rape of the soul was the crime that Du Bois could never forgive.[49] Although he viewed black people, from his own late Victorian perspective, as earthy, ribald peasants, who lagged behind the modern world with respect to sexual morality, he did not see them as hopelessly degraded. For, if the black peasantry had not yet learned to cherish the virtues of Anglo-American civilization, they had not yet assimilated all of its vices.

NOTES

1. W. E. B. Du Bois, *The Autobiography of W. E. B. Du Bois* (New York: International, 1968), p. 283.

2. Du Bois, *Autobiography,* p. 280.

3. Du Bois, *Autobiography,* p. 280. See also the scene of confrontation with a prostitute in Du Bois's *Dark Princess* (New York: Harcourt, Brace, 1928), p. 7.

4. W. E. B. Du Bois, *The Philadelphia Negro* (New York: Schocken, 1969), p. 391.

5. W. E. B. Du Bois, ed., *The Negro Family* (Atlanta: Atlanta University, 1909), p. 37.

6. Du Bois, *Negro Family,* p. 37; Du Bois, *Philadelphia Negro,* p. 392; W. E. B. Du Bois, "The Talented Tenth," in *The Negro Problem,* ed. Booker T. Washington et al. (New York: James Pott, 1903), pp. 31–75.

7. The anxieties of blacks resulting from sexual exploitation during and after slavery are discussed by Earl E. Thorpe in *The Mind of the Negro* (Westport, Conn.: Negro University Press, 1970), pp. 138–44. In *The Golden Age of Black Nationalism, 1850–1925* (Hamden, Conn.: Archon, 1978), I discuss the admiration of black clergymen William H. Ferris, Sutton Griggs, and Theophilus G. Stewart for middle-class, Anglo-American sex role ideals, pp. 183–89, 193. The concerns of middle-class black women are discussed in Chapter 5 of *The Golden Age.* John Blassingame mentions these concerns in *The Slave Community* (New York: Oxford University Press), pp. 82–83, and in *Black New Orleans, 1860–1880* (Chicago: University of Chicago Press, 1973), pp. 1, 84–87. James McPherson, *The Abolitionist Legacy: From Reconstruction to the NAACP* (Princeton: Princeton University, 1975), describes attempts to inculcate middle-class values among the freedmen, pp. 184–202. Also see McPherson's references to black ministers, Francis J. Grimke, Sutton Griggs, and National League for the Protection of Colored Women. Robert W. Fogel and Stanley L. Engerman in *Time on the Cross* (New York: Little, Brown, 1974) deny sexual exploitation of black women under slavery. Their study is based largely on testimony of plantation owners themselves. Leon Litwack in *North of Slavery* (Chicago: University of Chicago Press, 1961) discusses the unreliability of the variety of statistical data utilized by Engerman and Fogel. Herbert G. Gutman is concerned with family and structure rather

than with sexual mores in *The Black Family in Slavery and Freedom, 1750–1925* (New York: Vintage, 1976). He does provide new data on incest taboos, pp. 88–91, 561, but generally his interpretations of sexual morality follow after Charles S. Johnson, whose work is discussed herein.

8. Charles S. Johnson, *Shadow of the Plantation* (Chicago: University of Chicago Press, 1934), pp. 49, 58, 80–83, 89–90, 208.

9. Du Bois, *Autobiography,* pp. 284–86.

10. Alexander Crummell, "The Black Women of the South: Her Neglects and Her Needs," in his *Africa and America: Addresses and Discourses* (Springfield, Mass.: Wiley, 1891), pp. 64–66. Du Bois quotes numerous black clergymen in *The Negro Family.*

11. W. E. B. Du Bois, *Darkwater: Voices From Within the Veil* (New York: Harcourt, Brace, 1920), especially p. 171, where Crummell is quoted. Frazier alludes to *Darkwater* twice in *The Negro Family* (Chicago: University of Chicago Press, 1939), but makes no direct reference to the passage by Crummell. There is no question, however, of the consistency of his views with those of Du Bois and Crummell. Daniel P. Moynihan, however, alludes directly to the researches of Frazier. See Lee Rainwater and William L. Yancey, eds., *The Moynihan Report and the Politics of Controversy* (Cambridge: M.I.T. Press, 1967), p. 97. Also consult index references to Frazier.

12. The pejorative tradition is described in Charles A. Valentine, *Culture and Poverty: Critique and Counter-Proposals* (Chicago: University of Chicago Press, 1968). Two recent interpretations of slavery based on the extensive use of autobiographies of former slaves are Thomas L. Webber, *Deep Like the Rivers: Education in the Slave Quarter Community, 1831–1865* (New York: Norton, 1978), and Paul D. Escott, *Slavery Remembered: A Record of Twentieth Century Slave Narratives* (Chapel Hill: University of North Carolina Press, 1979).

13. Mary Church Terrell, "Club Work of Colored Women," *Southern Workman* (August 1901): 435–38; reprinted in *The Afro-Americans: Selected Documents,* ed. John H. Bracey, Jr., et al. (Boston: Allyn and Bacon, 1972)), pp. 391–92.

14. Mrs. Booker T. Washington, editorial, *The Woman's Era* 2, no. 7 (1895): 2.

15. Fannie Barrier Williams, "The Club Movement Among Colored Women of America," in Booker T. Washington et al., *A New Negro for a New Century* (Chicago: American Publishing House, 1900), p. 383.

16. Josephine St. Pierre Ruffin, "Address of Josephine St. Pierre Ruffin, President of the Conference," in *A History of the Club Movement Among the Colored Women of the United States of America* (Boston, 1902), p. 10.

17. *Thirty Years of Lynching in the United States, 1889–1918* (New York: National Association for the Advancement of Colored People, 1919), pp. 43–103.

18. *Thirty Years of Lynching,* p. 10, claims that 35.8 percent were accused of murder and 28.4 percent for sexual offenses.

19. John S. Haller, Jr., *Outcasts from Evolution: Scientific Attitudes of Racial Inferiority, 1859–1900* (Urbana: University of Illinois Press, 1971), pp. 51–57.

20. Haller, *Outcasts,* pp. 51–57.

21. Haller, *Outcasts,* pp. 51–57.

22. Charles Carroll, *The Negro a Beast* (N.p., n.d.), p. 50.

23. Carroll, *Negro a Beast,* p. 51.

24. Claude Bowers, *The Tragic Era* (New York: Houghton Mifflin, 1929). Quoted in *The Development of Segregationist Thought,* ed. I. A. Newby, (Homewood, Ill.: Dorsey Press, 1968), p. 88.

25. Nathaniel Southgate Shaler, "The Nature of the Negro," *Arena* 3 (Dec. 1980): 23–35; reprinted in Newby, *Segregationist Thought,* p. 55.

26. Philip Alexander Bruce, "Evolution of the Negro Problem," *Sewanee Review* 19 (October 1911): 285–99; reprinted in Newby, *Segregationist Thought,* p. 76.

27. Lester Ward, *Pure Sociology* (New York: Macmillan, 1925), pp. 258–59.

28. See the editorial in *The Woman's Era* (June 1894). See also Frederick Douglass, *The Reason Why the Colored Man Is Not Represented at the World's Columbian Exposition* (Chicago, 1892); reprinted in *The Life and Writings of Frederick Douglass,* ed. Philip S. Foner (New York: International, 1955), 4:478–90.

29. Joel Chandler Harris, *Uncle Remus: His Songs and His Sayings* (New York: Appleton, 1908), pp. 208–10.

30. Booker T. Washington, "The Atlanta Exposition Address," in *The Booker T. Washington Papers,* ed. Louis Harlan (Urbana: University of Illinois Press, 1972–1989), 3:585.

31. Thomas Wentworth Higginson, *Army Life in a Black Regiment* (New York: Collier Books, 1962). See the introduction by Howard N. Meyer, p. 23; see also 239–40.

32. Booker T. Washington, statement in *Minneapolis Journal,* 2 February 1896; reprinted in *Booker T. Washington,* ed. Emma L. Thornbrough (Englewood Cliffs, N.J.: Prentice-Hall, 1969), p. 72.

33. The antilynching writings of Ida B. Wells-Barnett have been collected with a new preface by August Meier in Ida Wells-Barnett, *On Lynching* (New York: Arno Press, 1969). See also Alfreda M. Duster, ed., *Crusade For Justice: The Autobiography of Ida B. Wells* (Chicago: University of Chicago Press, 1970), pp. 61–68.

34. Wells-Barnett, *On Lynchings.*

35. Quoted in Moses, *Golden Age,* pp. 122–23; from *The Woman's Era* 2, no. 10: 9.

36. W. E. B. Du Bois, *The Quest of the Silver Fleece* (Chicago: McClurg, 1911). All extended quotations from this novel will be cited parenthetically in the text.

37. W. E. B. Du Bois, *Souls of Black Folk* (Chicago: McClurg, 1903), pp. 135–36.

38. *Quest,* pp. 44–45.

39. *Quest,* pp. 44–45, 76.

40. *Quest,* p. 223.

41. *Quest,* pp. 68–69.

42. Zora is after all a Cresswell (p. 414) but Mary does not know or want to know the extent of sexual intimacy that has existed between the Negroes and the family into which she has married. Nor is she aware of the source of her husband's hostility towards Zora.

43. Eldridge Cleaver, *Soul on Ice* (New York: McGraw-Hill, 1968), pp. 179–80.

44. *Quest,* pp. 167–68, describes Bles's rage and dismay.

45. Du Bois, *Dark Princess,* pp. 109–19, introduces the character of Sara Andrews.

46. Du Bois's reactions to McKay's treatment of sexuality are described in Arnold Rampersad, *The Art and Literary Imagination of W. E. B. Du Bois* (Cambridge: Harvard University Press, 1976) and my *Golden Age,* p. 258. Du Bois's review of *Home to Harlem* is in *Crisis* (June 1928): 202.

47. *The Ordeal of Mansart* (New York: Mainstream, 1957); Cleaver, *Soul on Ice,* pp. 13–14.

48. The reader may familiarize himself with the novels of Paul Laurence Dunbar, Charles Chesnutt, and Sutton Griggs. For Ovington's bizarre little piece, see Mary White Ovington, *The Wall Come Tumbling Down* (New York: Harcourt, Brace, 1947), pp. 88–99.

49. See Du Bois's essay, "The Damnation of Women," in *Darkwater,* pp. 163–86.

More Stately Mansions

New Negro Movements and
Langston Hughes's Literary Theory

One of the perennial problems in discussions of the Harlem Renaissance has to do with its black nationalist elements. George Schuyler criticized it as pseudonationalistic. Alain Locke tried to straddle the fence. Du Bois emphasized different positions at different times. More recently, Robert Hayden described it as "clearly integrationist." The fact is that the Renaissance was both simultaneously nationalistic and assimilationistic.[1] It utilized, as Locke admitted in *The New Negro,* black particularism and a rhetoric of racial pride to demonstrate to any potential sympathizers that black people were indeed ready for integration. The peculiar manifestations of black culture associated with the Renaissance were successful, largely because of the fashionableness of cultural relativism between 1900 and 1930. Cultural relativism made it possible for stylish whites to think of black urbanites as culturally interesting. It made the form and content of the new black writing intellectually respectable in a society where art could be respected only if it struck at bourgeois convention. The concern for respectability predated cultural relativism; black nationalism has always been moved by cultural currents in the white world.[2]

It is difficult to conceive of a Harlem Renaissance without the fashionable celebration of "primitivism" that occurred during the first quarter of this century. Would there really have been an audience of trendy white patrons and sponsors without the counterculturalism that had been intellectually chic ever since the publication of T. S. Eliot's *The Waste Land* and Oswald Spengler's *The Decline of the West?* Albert Einstein's relativity theory and Bertrand Russell's logical positivism had provided a metaphysical open door through which the world of the primitive could be viewed with newly appreciative vision. Franz Boas's cultural relativism was the realization of that vision in the social sciences. Picasso and Stravinsky realized it in the arts, and the urban sophisticates of Paris and New York were prepared to view the "world of the primitive" within the framework of what might be called "modernistic primitivism."

There had been "New Negroes" at the turn of the century, of course.[3] It appeared with the rise of Booker T. Washington and the desire of many leaders and spokespersons to put forward the idea that the role of black people in the American economy would no longer be confined to plantation labor and domestic service. Black people were now to be an industrial force. They were literate, efficient, and progressive. To demonstrate this, Washington compiled the volume *A New Negro for a New Century* in 1900. The "new" New Negro of 1925 was a repudiation of the previous model and rejected the absolutist civilizing, industrial values that Booker T. Washington symbolized. The "new" New Negroes represented a pagan holiday spirit and an easy adjustment to life.

This new trend must be distinguished from the wistful presentations of heathen innocence that had been known in preceding centuries. It was no longer necessary, or even desirable to present the Negro as a "noble savage" or a "captive king" or a saintly "Uncle Tom." It was not even necessary to present Negroes as splendid heathens with tom-toms throbbing in their voices, although it is clear that many black artists and intellectuals were eager enough to exploit such images. The New Negroes often perceived themselves and their people as urban sophisticates. They always celebrated the wisdom of the urban working class, whose honest, simple folkways endowed them with the ability to see through the sham of Western civilization. Thus the New Negro represented not only an exotic "modern primitivism" but a "proletarian folk wisdom."

While many black American artists and intellectuals embraced this new synthesis of black culture with enthusiasm, others retained a loyalty to the older Victorian values of "classical black nationalism." This was the black nationalism that flourished from the 1850s to the 1920s, originating in the ideological writings of such nineteenth-century pan-Africanists as Henry Highland Garnet, Martin Delany, Alexander Crummell, and Edward Wilmot Blyden. Many of their ideas were still preserved in the Harlem of 1920 by W. E. B. Du Bois and Marcus Garvey, who ironically hated one another.[4]

The "old" New Negro movement, with which Garvey and Du Bois were familiar, existed in a blandly congenial détente with the artistic romanticization of Africa, which emphasized the exotic warmth and color associated with the mother continent. Garvey and Du Bois were not unaffected by this tendency, but their ties to the nineteenth-century tradition in black nationalism led them to portray Africa in terms of its potential as a modern nation and to emphasize the past glories of Ethiopia and Egypt. This led to a variety of Harlem Renaissance style that was somewhat at odds with the celebration of "modernistic primitivism," a style that may be called "monumentalism." An illustration of this style can be found in Aaron Douglass's painting, "More Stately Mansions," which depicts ancient Egyptians with strongly Negroid features building the pyramids. Although the style is influenced by "cubism," the content is clearly in the tradition of nineteenth-century black nationalists, who enjoyed portraying black Americans as heirs to the glories of ancient Egypt.[5] This monumentalism was an expression of the desire to associate black Americans with symbols of wealth, intelligence, stability, and power. It is to be glimpsed in the writings of J. A. Rogers, one of the most influential of the Renaissance nationalists, who tirelessly sought to link the black past with the greatness of empires and dynasties and "high culture." It was to be seen in the structuring of semiotic events by Marcus Garvey, who called on the black race to rise up and produce its army and navy and "men of big affairs." It was evident in the concern of Du Bois and Carter G. Woodson for discovering the heritage of great African kings. It was exemplified in the almost single-handed attempt of William H. Ferris to chronicle an intellectual history of Africans and Afro-Americans.[6]

In this tradition, both integrationists and separatists grasped the rhetoric of stoicism with determination, proclaiming values that the Anglo-America bourgeoisie would have liked to monopolize for themselves. Black leaders of the early century, like Mary Church Terrell and Booker T. Washington, had agreed on the necessity of "Negro Improvement," and both Garvey and Du Bois carried on that tradition. Nightlife, cafe-sitting, smoking, drinking, and sexual progressivism might be allowed in their black heaven, but one should remember that Garvey did not drink or smoke and that Du Bois felt that one could have more fun at a church social than at a cabaret.[7]

It is important to mention, however, that the primitivistic and the classical black nationalist elements were sometimes interwoven, as when

Alain Locke averred that the African tradition in art was "rigid, controlled, disciplined, abstract, heavily conventionalized," in contrast to the usual stereotypes about the Negro character. "What we have thought primitive in the American Negro—his naivete, his sentimentalism, his exuberance and his improvising spontaneity are then neither characteristically African, nor to be explained as ancestral heritage."[8] Primitivism was again linked to the classical black-nationalist ethos when Carter G. Woodson proclaimed that the striving work ethic of Afro-Americans came from West Africa, not from the Protestant tradition.[9] The pathways of Africanity did not necessarily pass through the Harlem cabaret.

Langston Hughes usually saw things differently than the monumentalists, although he was clearly on their wavelength when he wrote "The Negro Speaks of Rivers" and dedicated it to W. E. B. Du Bois. For the most part, however, he was less concerned than many of his contemporaries with being "dignified" or creating a "dignified" art. On the contrary, he identified with the urban primitivism, which saw the African heritage in the Harlem cabaret, and personified proletarian folk wisdom in Jess B. Semple. He readily embraced the counterculturalism of the twenties, and he rejected "civilizationism," not only in word but in spirit. Langston Hughes, in "The Negro Artist and the Racial Mountain," advised young black artists to look to their own class and ethnic backgrounds for the materials of their art. And, like Du Bois, he saw the ingredients of genuine classical tragedy in much black bourgeois experience. But at times, like most artists, Hughes did not heed his own advice. Like the very artists he had criticized, Hughes could stumble into some of the pitfalls of Western artistic consciousness. The cult of novelty, the myth of progress, and the necessity felt by Western artists to view themselves as *avant-garde* were some of the conventions that he assimilated. What this meant for Hughes, as it has for most black male authors, was a tendency to reject in the name of artistic creativity many of the insights of the generation preceding him. Thus, although Hughes demonstrated appropriate reverence for Du Bois and expressed his admiration for the "warm, rambunctious, [and] sassy" elements of Garveyism, he was essentially unsympathetic to the monumental fantasies of either man. Indeed, one finds little interest among any of the principal figures of the Harlem Renaissance in a novelist like Sutton Griggs, whose chronicles of black urban folklore and bitter sense of humor could have helped black artists to establish a sense of literary tradition. Nor was there any real desire to master the symbolic systems generated by Garvey, Carter Woodson, or J. A. Rogers. Rare are the moments, such as those in Claude McKay's *Home to Harlem*, where an awareness of the heroic tradition intrudes into the world of proletarian wisdom and primitive exoticism, as when Ray introduces Jake to the monumental tradition in black letters and folklore. The impatient young rebels of the Harlem Renaissance neglected much of the richness of black life that flourished within walking distance of where they sat at their typewriters.

Where else in the Harlem of the twenties, more than among Garvey-ites, can one find the exaltation of those traits whose absence from black writing Hughes lamented? And where else but in the novels of Sutton Griggs — which, according to Rayford Logan, "had little literary merit and presaged the black chauvinism of Marcus Garvey" — does one find the original "Novelist of the New Negro"?[10] The fact is that the Harlem intellectuals, despite their own caveats, were often so fascinated with the counterculturalism symbolized by the mythical "New Negro," that they missed many of the interesting and important characteristics of the ac-tual "New Negro." This was most clear in their failure to appreciate Garveyism as a source of artistic symbol and literary rhetoric. The tight sexual ethnic; the quest for refinement, grandeur, and pomp; the desire to erect more stately mansions, although clearly present in Garveyism, were impatiently dismissed by the artistic lights.

Perhaps the reason why the Harlem Renaissance paid so little hom-age to the monumental works of the past was that the older literature — represented by the works of Paul Laurence Dunbar, Pauline Hopkins, Sutton Griggs, and the earlier W. E. B. Du Bois — had been so hostile to the emerging new value system. *Home to Harlem* represented to both Du Bois and to Garvey the very epitome of "insult to the race," but it was nonetheless the quintessential novel of the "Harlem Renaissance," in ways that a novel like *Cane,* with its Southern rural setting, could not be.

The new generation, of which Hughes was a member, revelled in the very things that the "old" New Negroes had rejected. It is clear that they viewed themselves and their art in connection with twentieth-century modernism. They rejected the out-of-hand, heavy academic romanticism and empire-building fantasies of the nineteenth century. But this was exactly the universe of Du Bois and Garvey, who wanted to create a sphinx-like and majestic black nationalism. Much of what they admired, Hughes considered stuffy, dry, artificial, and ridiculously old-fashioned. The grandeur that Du Bois strained after in his novels and pageants was similar to what Garvey staged in his street demonstrations. On a sym-bolic level, they were almost identical, despite their mutual hatred. And these monumental symbols of civilization that they exalted were, in their view, the truest expression of what black people should be striving for — dignity, stability, formality, a princely hierarchy, and a cult of respecta-bility. The presentation of this mythology dominates the last pages of Du

Bois's *Dark Princess*. It is also to be seen in the Garveyite practice of conferring princely titles.

Hughes was an interested observer, but no active participant, in this "metanomaniac" pageantry. To him it was clear that the black American experience must be symbolized by the working-class rejection of bourgeois pretentiousness. If it may be said that the values of Josephine St. Pierre Ruffin and Alexander Crummell had been corrupted by the ethics of Victorian gentility, it may be said that Langston Hughes and Claude McKay were caught up in the 1920s fashions of cultural relativism, proletarianism, and modern primitivism. To Hughes, Harlem was "like a Picasso painting in his cubistic period."[11] Indeed, he shared at least one thing with the white jazz musician Mezz Mezzrow, who viewed black culture as "a collective nose thumbing . . . one big Bronx cheer for the righteous squares everywhere."[12] I doubt, however, that Hughes ever forgot, even if the Carl Van Vechtens and the Mezz Mezzrows sometimes did, that the backbone of the black community is the righteous square, the plain ol' workin' stiff like Jess B. Semple.

It is against the background of the "New Negro Renaissance" of the 1920s that Hughes's development as a literary theorist over the next forty years is to be understood. He viewed the role of the black artist in terms of the escape from formalism and stuffy traditionalism that he associated with both Washington and Du Bios. Black literature must be proletarian, but it must not become rigidly Marxist. He had no patience with the black Bolsheviks who were determined to reconstruct the Afro-American in the pattern of communist poster art. Jess B. Semple represented the commitment to unpretentious, commonsense values and a rejection of elitist silliness. Hughes once expressed his disgust for Haile Selassie, King of Kings and Conquering Lion of Judah, with the comment, "I expect black people to have more sense!"[13]

With the coming of the next New Negro Renaissance of the 1960s, Hughes continued to insist on common sense. Based on the experience of the twenties, he advised black writers not to rely on the fashionability of blackness. He adhered to the old Harlem Renaissance principle that artists must be committed first of all to their craft. No one was going to get very far by attempting to exploit sensationalist distortions of black life and culture. The debate with Amiri Baraka must be perceived in this context. Hughes stood by the position that all artists must be true to their cultural and class heritage, but he saw no contradiction between race and individuality, no more than he saw any contradiction between race and universality. In the opening essay of *The New Negro*, Alain Locke had stated that the racialism of the Negro "is no limitation or reservation with respect to American life." Hughes's writing a year later in "The Negro Artist and the Racial Mountain" had declared the intention of younger artists "to express our individual dark-skinned selves." The Harlem Renaissance had attempted to blend individuality, Americanism, and pan-Africanism.

The movement of the 1960s, as represented by Amiri Baraka, conceived itself as requiring only the last of these. Furthermore, it lacked historical consciousness, so that its advocates were not aware of the fact that many of its issues had been addressed, not only by the New Negroes of 1925 but by the New Negroes of 1900. Hughes found himself, by 1965, in the fatiguing and unrewarding position of having to warn the newer writers against becoming "black imitators of neurotic white writers." This was reminiscent of the misunderstood position of W. E. B. Du Bois with respect to Rudolph Fisher and Claude McKay.

Try as they might, the radical writers could not escape the charge of assimilationism of accommodation to white manners and morals. LeRoi Jones was just as inconceivable without the "beatniks" as Du Bois would have been without the "genteel tradition," or Hughes without "primitivism" and "proletarianism." The lesson to be learned from this is that every generation of black Americans, radically impatient with the irrelevancies of past ideology, is doomed to create a "New Negro." Despite the progress assumedly made by each consecutive generation, the knowledge gained never seems sufficient to force the insight that black nationalism and black culturalism to some degree is assimilationistic. Ideology adapts to the shape of its container and takes on the qualities of the environment in which it thrives. Hughes was ready enough to desert the stately Victorian mansion of nineteenth-century black nationalism and find his soul-world in the Harlem cabaret. He was not prepared to follow LeRoi Jones into the toilet.

N O T E S

1. George Schuyler, "The Negro Art Hokum," *The Nation* 16 June 1926. Also see the response of Langston Hughes in "The Negro Artist and the Racial Mountain," *The Nation* 13 June 1926. Alain Locke treated the issue with consummate skill in the title essay of *The New Negro* (New York: Albert & Charles Boni, 1925), where he compared the Harlem Renaissance to Zionism and other nationalist movements, nonetheless insisting that the Negro mind reached out "to nothing but American wants, American ideas," pp. 11–16. W. E. B. Du Bois emphasized the success, the failure, the universality, the particularism of New Negro art in *The Gift of Black Folk* (Boston: Stratford, 1924); "Mencken," *Crisis* (October 1927); and "The Negro College," *Crisis* (August 1933).

2. The adaptation of black nationalist rhetoric to the Victorian "worldview" is the central theme of Wilson J. Moses, *The Golden Age of Black Nationalism, 1850–1925* (Hamden, Conn.: Archon Books, 1978), in which it is argued that political separatism was

almost invariably accompanied by cultural assimilationism. Cultural assimilation in the 1920s was of a different character, reflecting the decline of Victorian manners and morals.

3. August Meier in *Negro Thought in America, 1880–1915* (Ann Arbor: University of Michigan Press, 1963), p. 258, traces the term "New Negro" to 1895. Sutton Griggs uses it in *Imperium in Imperio* (Cincinnati, 1899), p. 244. There were numerous other occurrences of the term before Alain Locke employed it in 1925; for example, William Pickens, *The New Negro* (New York: Neal, 1916).

4. Henry Highland Garnet and other black leaders founded the African Civilization Society in 1858. Its purpose was to establish "a Grand Center of Negro Nationality" and to work for the elevation of all black people throughout the world. See Earl Ofari, *"Let Your Motto be Resistance"* (Boston: Beacon, 1972). See also Joel Schorr, *Henry Highland Garnet* (Westport, Conn.: Greenwood, 1977). Martin Delany advocated establishing a modern black nation in Nigeria. See Cyril Griffith, *The African Dream* (University Park: Pennsylvania State University Press, 1975). Alexander Crummell, a school comrade of Garnet, spent eighteen years in Liberia as an advocate of pan-Africanism. See Wilson J. Moses, "Civilizing Missionary," *Journal of Negro History* (April 1975). Edward Wilmot Blyden was Crummell's compatriot during the late nineteenth century and is generally regarded as the most important pan-African theorist of his day. See Hollis Lynch, *Edward Wilmot Blyden: Pan-Negro Patriot, 1832–1912.* (New York: Oxford, 1967) The best short introduction to Marcus Garvey is John Henrik Clarke, ed., *Marcus Garvey and the Vision of Africa* (New York: Vintage Books, 1974). One of the many handy introductions to Du Bois is Meier Weinberg, ed., *W. E. B. Du Bois: A Reader* (New York: Harper and Row, 1970).

5. See William Wells Brown, *The Black Man, His Antecedents., His Genius, and His Achievements* (New York: Thomas Hamilton, 1863), p. 32.

6. Joel A. Rogers and William H. Ferris were among the numerous bourgeois intellectuals who flocked to the Garvey movement. For Rogers, see Earl E. Thorpe, *Black Historians: A Critique* (New York: Morrow, 1971), pp. 152–53. For Ferris, see Robert A. Hill, *The Marcus Garvey and Universal Negro Improvement Association Papers* (Berkeley: University of California Press, 1983), 1:75–76, n.3.

7. Garvey's personal habits are described in Amy Jacques Garvey, *Garvey and Garveyism* (New York: Collier, 1970), p. 70. Du Bois on church socials and cabarets is gratuitously presented in his *Dark Princess* (New York: Harcourt, Brace, 1928), pp. 66–67. In these pages Du Bois also expresses his distaste for "vulgar blues." But Du Bois spoke admiringly of W. C. Handy in "Mencken." Robert Hill commented on Marcus Garvey's suppression of "stride music" in a luncheon presentation at Brown University, 18 October 1984.

8. Locke, *New Negro*, p. 254.

9. See Carter G. Woodson, *The African Background Outlined* (Washington, D.C.: Association for the Study of Negro Life and History, 1936), p. 171: "The Negro is born a worker."

10. See Hugh M. Gloster, "Sutton Griggs: Novelist of the New Negro," in *Phylon* (1943): 335–45.

11. Langston Hughes, "My Early Days in Harlem," in *Harlem: A Community in Transition,* ed. John Henrik Clarke (New York: Citadel, 1969), p. 64.

12. Mezz Mezzrow is quoted in Lawrence W. Levine's *Black Culture and Black Consciousness* (New York: Oxford, 1977).

13. Interview by author with George H. Bass, Autumn 1982.

The Wings of Ethiopia

**Consensus History and Literary Allusion
in Ralph Ellison's *Invisible Man***

Tew Criticism and some of the more recently developing schools of American literary theory are often contemptuous of intellectual history, and can justify their contempt with an overwhelming array of reasons often expressed in an intimidating jargon. Rightly or wrongly, they have expressed concern with respect to the employment of instructional techniques and modes of literary analysis that they consider outmoded. Robert Stepto, in the lead essay of his *Afro-American Literature: The Reconstruction of Instruction,* rightly criticizes that style of teaching that indiscriminately utilizes such "embarrassingly antiquated" techniques as Freudian psychology or that concentrates on historical context and social-scientific analysis, and tends to ignore the text. Stepto's point is well-taken; certainly the study of literature is worthwhile in itself. Critics ought not to subordinate their craft to social science, history, or philosophy, and they should not think that they can make criticism more respectable by giving it the appearance of some other discipline.[1]

The present essay argues the legitimacy of lecturing on intellectual history when teaching Ralph Ellison's *Invisible Man,* not because criticism is inadequate to its own work, but because the novel is so rich in allusion. It provides such an encyclopedic approach to Afro-American life and values that I, for one, simply cannot teach it without either lecturing on its historical context or at least providing students with supplementary readings so that they can perceive the full richness of the text. It is a product of the consensus period in American literary and intellectual history. It should not be separated from the literary context of works produced during the 1940s and 1950s by scholars like F. O. Matthiessen and Louis Hartz. Nor can its richness be appreciated outside the spheres of Booker T. Washington, W. E. B. Du Bois, and Marcus Garvey. The visual imagery of the period will become more vivid for students who have seen photographs of Tuskegee or who have glanced at such pictorial volumes as *Twelve Million Black Voices* or *The Sweet Flypaper of Life*.[2]

Ellison clearly has a sense of literary and intellectual history, but like most of us, he is capable of feigning both knowledge and ignorance, and I suspect that he consciously dissembles when, in discussing the influences on his work, he skips over Richard Wright, Booker T. Washington, Marcus Garvey, and other well-known Afro-American writers who obviously influenced him profoundly. On the other hand, he acknowledges the influences of Afro-American blues and folklore, and pays frequent homage to such authors as Dostoevsky and Mark Twain. Of course, *Invisible Man* should not be represented in terms of a self-contained Afro-American literary tradition, but that does not mean that the reader should ideally come to it without any knowledge of traditions in Afro-American intellectual life or Western intellectual traditions in general. To do so would be about as meaningful as reading Milton without any knowledge of the biblical account of creation.[3]

That intellectual history bears some relation to literary instruction cannot be seriously questioned. The prefaces and footnotes, as well as the bibliographies, of such stately volumes as *The Norton Anthology of English Literature* make it clear that orthodox literary scholarship still seeks to place the work of art in its intellectual environment. Students of Afro-American literature have sometimes been inordinately sensitive to the accusation that what they are doing is not really literary scholarship but sociology. I have never been much impressed by such charges. Aside from the fact that good sociological criticism is better than half-digested anthropology or pseudo-philosophy, it seems silly to me to use the name of any academic discipline purely as a term of opprobrium. In any case, intellectual history is not sociology; it is not even *Wissenssoziologie*. Nor is it social history or "history of ideas" or any of the other disciplines with which some members of the profession obstinately confuse it. The preceding terms have their specific meanings, exemplified in the works of A. O. Lovejoy, Karl Mannheim, Robert K. Merton, Mary Berry, and other authors, from whom literary critics can learn a great deal. Intellectual history is not a rigid concept. It refers simply to the field of scholarship that seeks to understand the relationship between the evolution of ideas and the changing material environments that produce changes in people's thinking. Intellectual history is not inhospitable to the proposition that ideas affect environments; that is why its practitioners speak of influential books.[4]

I am not certain there is any such thing as an American intellectual history, although I am convinced that intellectual history is a valid concept and that many Americans, including black Americans, have participated in it. I refer, in this case, not to intellectual history as an academic discipline but to the mental activities of literate persons, who are influenced not only by class origins and ethnic or racial experiences but by ideas they have heard discussed and books they have read. Ralph Ellison has a great deal to share with us, in his observations on what he has read and in his debates and discussions with critics and interviewers. It is almost superfluous to add that he has much to share with us by the example of his creative practice. Both in *Invisible Man* and in the articles and interviews collected in *Shadow and Act,* he demonstrates that the concrete intellectual experiences of Afro-Americans are important as specific manifestations of universal human experiences. He shows this by having the protagonist of *Invisible Man* scramble spiderlike over a web of themes that, like a spider's web is the product of heritage, environment, and the individual activities of the spinner. If Ellison had been unacquainted with *Up from Slavery* or *Portrait of the Artist as a Young Man,* he probably could not have written this book. But it does not follow that the best way to teach Ralph Ellison's novel is to lecture about other books to the neglect of his.

During the 1960s, Ellison's attempts to disassociate himself from the fatuous dogmas of the "black aesthetic" led him to an unnecessary and unconvincing repudiation of his ties to all black literary traditions. I don't want to get involved in the old *ut pictura poesis* business, but I am reminded of Piotr Ilich Tschaikowsky's attempt to disassociate himself from the nationalistic movement in Russian music. In spite of his disclaimers, Tschaikowsky, with his borrowings from folk music and his splendid mazurkas, remains a "classic" illustration of what we mean by a "Russian spirit" in music. Ellison may claim that he is not a part of an Afro-American literary and intellectual tradition, but the evidence of our senses does not support his contention.[5]

Ralph Ellison was once an impatient young man. Born in Oklahoma in 1914, not only in the same state as John Hope Franklin but less than a year in advance of him, he had some of the same biases. Booker T. Washington died in 1915, and black intellectuals born around that time—I include Thurgood Marshall and Kenneth Clark in that category — grew up with an understandable hostility to any talk of separatism. When they began their careers, they had little time for the older generation, except for those they could mythologize as monumental figures that were somehow, like W. E. B. Du Bois, "ahead of their times." They thus failed to take advantage of a whole generation of black art and scholarship. If the new writers were interested in Oscar Micheaux or Sutton Griggs, they were amazingly secretive about it. The historians had read only superficially, if at all, in J. A. Rogers or Benjamin Brawley. Because of the integrationist bias of the black writers of this generation, once respected members of the black literary pantheon like Martin Delany and Alexander Crummell, if not exactly purged from the textbooks, were barely mentioned. Such lapses in historical reporting have been referred to as "social amnesia," but literary amnesia would better describe the antihistorical biases that dominated American letters in the form of New Criticism and "consensus history" at the time of Ellison's coming of age.[6] Although the idea of a black intellectual tradition was never completely wiped out, the tragic fact is that neither the Ellison-Franklin generation nor the younger generation, who in turn challenged them, were as aware of the history of black intellectual and literary traditions as they should have been. It is, therefore, remarkable that when Ellison set out to write a *Bildungsroman,* he happened, somehow, to produce something that was quite distinctly black.

In the tradition of Henry Adams, Ellison gave us a book about education; but for some cryptic reason, obscure beyond the understanding of anyone but himself, Ellison chose not to write about an Anglo-American from New England going to a school like Harvard but about an Afro-American from the South going to a school like Tuskegee. Ellison denies vehemently that the places and characters in his novel are meant to be symbols or analogues of actualities.[7] Curious, because the novel is filled with unmistakable allusions, literary and otherwise. It may or may not be important for students to be informed, early in a reading of *Invisible man,* that Ellison spent some time at Tuskegee Institute or that the statue of the Founder, lifting the veil from the face of a kneeling slave, is reminiscent of the Booker T. Washington statue at Tuskegee. On the other hand, because the themes of blindness and veiled vision are so important, it might be useful to call attention to these themes as they are introduced, both here and in the "battle royal" of Chapter One. Perhaps seeing a picture of Booker T. Washington's statue might be of interest to students, but it is certainly important for them to understand who Booker T. Washington was. And they should know that the Founder is not Booker T. Washington; nor is Ellison's description of the college intended to be a caricature of Tuskegee.

Invisible Man is the story of a Jonah, cursed with the gift of prophecy, cast overboard into the maw of a "white leviathan," vomited up in the streets of a sinful Nineveh. College students do not know much about the Bible these days. Nor should they be expected to recognize Ellison's allusion to the scene at the beginning of *Moby Dick* in which Ishmael stumbles into a black church with its dismal sermon on the blackness of darkness. Father Mapple's sermon will be as alien to them as Du Bois's use of the term "White Leviathan" in *Dark Princess.*[8] They are not likely to be aware that Ellison has compared his protagonist to Captain Ahab.[9] The student who is particularly interested in Afro-American literature may be interested in the observation that Rudolph Fisher makes use of the Jonah myth in his short story, "The City of Refuge," which appears in *The New Negro.* Exiting from the subway on his first day in Harlem, Fisher's character is a "Jonah emerging from the whale." Ellison's hero, arriving in New York for the first time, also takes the subway straight to Harlem and emerges feeling like "something regurgitated from the belly of a frantic whale." This, of course, may be coincidence, as may the fact that both Fisher's character and Ellison's hero have the shock of seeing a black policeman directing traffic immediately after emerging from the A-Train's belly. But the question of whether there are in the story, or elsewhere in Fisher's "Harlem Sketches," any sources or analogues for scenes in *Invisible Man* is a topic for a class discussion rather than a lecture.[10]

Invisible Man is the story of a young man's fight for individuality and personal responsibility. Ellison says in *Shadow and Act* that he considers the fight for individuality a particularly American theme because "the nature of our society is such that we are prevented from knowing who we are."[11] Certainly the Emersonian themes of self-reliance and self-trust have been central to his essays and interviews as well as to his novel. In one of his meditations, the protagonist of *Invisible Man* reflects on Woodridge, his college literature professor, who lectured on Joyce:

> Stephen's problem, like ours, was not actually one of creating the uncreated conscience of his race, but of creating the uncreated features of his face. . . . We create the race by creating ourselves. . . .[12]

One of the problems that led to misinterpretations of Ellison by many young black students and writers during the late 1960s was their having skimmed too hastily the message of Woodridge.[13] When Stephen Daedalus describes Ireland as the old sow that eats her young, he is issuing a warning against the one-dimensional vision of the nationalist. Ellison's hero, not to mention Ellison himself, recoils from what Frantz

Fanon calls "the pitfalls of national consciousness."[14] Just as Joyce had
to come to grips with Irish nationalism and Thomas Mann had to decide
where he stood with respect to Nazism, so too was Ellison forced to an
artistic confrontation with the nationalism of Harlem. The typical student, and of course the professor of American literature, will certainly
be better equipped to place Ellison's position in context if he or she
knows Richard B. Moore's article, "Africa Conscious Harlem." I am not
suggesting that it is necessary to wade through the voluminous bibliography on black nationalism and pan-Africanism. Ellison does not know it
himself. I do think, however, the knowledge of E. U. Essien-Udom's
"The Nationalist Movements of Harlem" or Roi Ottley's very readable
New World A-Coming will be helpful to those who do not know much
about black history.[15] I find these useful because they reveal the nexus
between black intellectual life and mass political fantasies. They cover
not only Garveyism but several other "pan-Negro" revivals and awaken-
ings, such as the movement of the 1930s in support of Ras Tafari, a.k.a.
Haile Selassie.[16]

It has mattered little to the black masses that the historical Marcus
Garvey held the historical Ras Tafari in profoundest contempt because
the latter lost his war with Mussolini, and even more, because Haile had
snubbed Garvey on a visit to England. Black mass movements, from
Capetown to Kingston, have merged the personalities of the two men to
create the Rastafarian myth, an illusion of black supremacy that meets
their emotional needs, that are sometimes far removed from social-scientific realities.

Ellison is doubtless aware of the role that Ethiopia has played in
Harlem streetcorner mythology and storefront sermons. Like Langston
Hughes, he had certainly heard the preachers and soapbox orators
prophesying that Ethiopia would stretch forth her hand. The Ethiopian
tradition of Africa, America, and the West Indies—as defined by St.
Clair Drake, George Shepperson, and others—is certainly important
here.[17] Ethiopianism is the idea that "The world moves in a circle like a
roulette wheel. In the beginning, black is on top, in the middle epochs,
white holds the odds, but soon Ethiopia shall stretch forth her noble
wings. Then place your money on the black!" (p. 75).

Ellison's protagonist and the more sophisticated Tod Clifton see
only the tip of the pyramid during their confrontation with Ras. They
give it a wide berth, even though they can only guess at its depth and
extent in religious and literary experience. The narrator is "glad to be out
of the dark and away from that exhorting voice." And Clifton says, "It's
a wonder he didn't say something about Ethiopia stretching forth her
wings" (pp. 326–27).

An interesting topic for class discussion might be: "Why do Ellison's characters speak of Ethiopia's wings, instead of her hands?" A little effort with a Bible concordance and the aforementioned works might even lead to a good seminar paper. Ellison has been so emphatic in denying that his novel is derived from a self-contained system of black literary influences and tradition that I think we had better listen to him and believe he means what he is saying. At the same time, we cannot ignore the fact that this book functions in terms of specific references to black institutional life, folklore, and intellectual tradition. It is no accident that Ellison created Dr. Bledsoe around the same time that E. Franklin Frazier was formulating his criticism of black education in *Black Bourgeoisie*.[18] And that was around the same time that Thurgood Marshall was arguing before the Supreme Court that separation in education must inevitably imply inequality. He used a sociological argument based on the work of E. Franklin Frazier and John Hope Franklin. We cannot ignore the fact that Ellison wrote about the ambiguous functions of black leaders at the same time that Oliver C. Cox and Ira De A. Reid were making observations on black leaders and messiahs similar to Ellison's. It is not surprising that Ellison created Rinehart within a decade of Arthur Huff Fauset's treatise *Black Gods of the Metropolis*.[19]

Ellison's relationship to American folklore as well as to European myths and epics, to Popeye the Sailor Man as well as Ulysses, has never been questioned. What has not been much explored is the fact that Ellison was early exposed to the depth and complexity of black bourgeois life. He grew up in the proximity of black college communities and had been to Tuskegee. He was, as he says in an interview with Harper and Stepto, more sympathetic to black intellectuals than Richard Wright was capable of being.[20] Ellison's obsession with individuality of expression is, of course, a characteristic concern of black artists and intellectuals. The tradition of extemporaneous improvisation and solo riffs is no more the property of jazz musicians than of highly educated orators like Martin Luther King, Jr.

What Ellison seems to be trying to avoid (and teachers of *Invisible Man* should strive to make this clear) is the reduction of his art to a system of stereotypes and clichés that pass for folklore. In any case, folklore is only a part of black literary tradition in America. There is a tradition of the printed word and a tradition of discussion and debate, rooted in an acquaintance with the works of Homer, Shakespeare, Austen, Dickens, Washington, Du Bois, and Ayn Rand.

Ellison has rightly refused to be strapped to the Procrustean bed of a naive black aesthetic. Of course, it is interesting and useful to know that Ellison discovered and utilized black literary themes such as the

Ethiopian allusion. But it is also important to note that, like most other black authors, Ellison is acquainted with the Anglo-American tradition of the "New England Renaissance." Too often, we seem to forget that Ellison is not the only black author to have read *Civil Disobedience* as well as *Up from Slavery.* To separate Ellison or his work from the world of educated Afro-Americans can be just as misleading as to remove him from the world of blues and folklore.

Finally, we ought to bear in mind that when Ellison attempts to place *Invisible Man* within the context of American literary tradition, he subjects his reading of his work to a reading of American literature that prevailed in the middle years of the twentieth century. This was a period during which Louis Hartz was arguing that the values of American culture were essentially libertarian and individualistic. It was a period during which the New Critics were touting ambiguity as among the highest literary values. It was a period during which F. O. Matthiessen's definition of the *American Renaissance* dominated all discussions of what was important in American literature. It should not be surprising that Ellison in his interviews of the fifties and early sixties compared his work to the very authors and themes that were considered, during that period of alleged "consensus," to have the greatest "universal" significance.

Like most bourgeois Afro-American artists, Ellison seems determined to assert his ties to the culture of the black masses, but, to his credit, he has never denied that this culture is woven into the fabric of American life as a whole. The novel is clearly consistent with both the Afro-American and the Anglo-American traditions of self-help and self-definition. It is no less related to Andrew Carnegie than to Dale Carnegie. It is, as he admits, a staging of "the black rite of Horatio Alger" (p. 101). This is a story about learning to insist on one's own individuality and personal responsibility. After reading *Shadow and Act* and being introduced to some of the literary and intellectual background, students may begin to wonder whether Ellison has not displayed some of the same arrogance that many "American Scholars" in the tradition of Emerson have displayed and whether he has always been fully open and honest about acknowledging his intellectual debts. He may see his roots in the underground of Dostoevsky, but why does he find it necessary to repugn the underground influences of Wright?

Is it really true that all trains go to the Golden Day? It might be useful for present-day students to examine Lewis Mumford's *The Golden Day* and to subject it and its premises to some probing analysis. I believe that Ralph Ellison's novel really is a product of consensus history, but it could also have been influenced by Mumford's earlier work, and the possibility should be investigated by skillful teachers. Such an approach may assist them in seeing not only the ways in which Ellison was a prisoner of his times and a participant in the very traditions that he sought to deconstruct. It will assist us in recognizing the ways in which writers, critics, and intellectual historians are all part of the same rhetorical universe, and to some inescapable extent, always victims and beneficiaries of one another's intellectual schemes.[21]

NOTES

1. Robert B. Stepto, "Teaching Afro-American Literature: Survey or Tradition, The Reconstruction of Instruction," in *Afro-American Literature: The Reconstruction of Instruction,* ed. Dexter Fisher and Robert Stepto, (New York: Modern Language Association, 1979), pp. 7–24.

2. F. O. Matthiessen, *American Renaissance: Art and Experience in the Age of Emerson and Whitman* (New York: Oxford, 1941). Louis Hartz, *The Liberal Tradition in America* (New York: Viking, 1941). Langston Hughes and Roy De Carava, *The Sweet Flypaper of Life* (New York: Simon and Schuster, 1955).

3. Ellison repudiated certain Freudian ties to Richard Wright in an interview with Robert B. Stepto and Michael Harper, "Study and Experience: An Interview with Ralph Ellison," in *Chant of Saints: A Gathering of Afro-American Literature, Art, and Scholarship,* ed. Michael Harper and Robert B. Stepto (Urbana: University of Illinois Press, 1979), pp. 451–69. He pays homage to Mark Twain, Dostoevsky, and the folklore/blues tradition in an interview published in *The Paris Review* (Spring 1955), reprinted in Ralph Ellison, *Shadow and Act* (New York: Signet, 1966), pp. 169–83.

4. For sociology of knowledge, see Karl Mannheim, *Ideology and Utopia: An Introduction to the Sociology of Knowledge,* trans. Louis Wirth (New York: Harcourt, Brace, 1936), and Robert K. Merton, *Social Theory and Social Structure* (Glencoe, Ill.: Free Press, 1957). For social history, see William G. McLoughlin, *Revivals, Awakening and Reform* (Chicago: University of Chicago Press, 1978).

5. Tschaikowsky's opposition to the aims of the Russian nationalist composers is summarized succinctly in *The New Columbia Encyclopedia* (New York: Columbia University Press, 1975).

6. Russell Jacoby, *Social Amnesia* (Boston: Beacon, 1979).

7. *Shadow and Act,* pp. 179–81.

8. W. E. B. Du Bois, *Dark Princess* (New York: Harcourt, Brace, 1928), p. 7.

9. Ellison compares the heroes of *Invisible Man* and *Moby Dick* in "An Interview with Ralph Ellison, by Allen Geller," in *The Black American Writer, Vol. 1: Fiction,* ed. C. W. E. Bigsby (New York: Penguin, 1971), pp. 153–68. Bigsby says the interview was originally published in *Tamarack Review,* but does not give details.

10. *Invisible Man* (New York: Signet, 1952), p. 141. Rudolph Fisher, "The City of Refuge," in *The New Negro,* ed. Alain Locke (New York: Albert & Charles Boni, 1925), pp. 57–58.

11. *Shadow and Act,* p. 177.

12. *Invisible Man,* p. 307.

13. Naive criticism of Ellison from a black aesthetic perspective is in Larry Neal, "And Shine Swam On," in *Black Fire: An Anthology of Afro-American Writing,* ed. Le Roi Jones and Larry Neal (New York: William Morrow, 1968), p. 652.

14. Frantz Fanon, "The Pitfalls of National Consciousness," in his *The Wretched of the Earth* (New York: Grove Press, 1963), pp. 119–65.

15. Richard B. Moore, "Africa Conscious Harlem," in *Harlem: A Community in Transition,* ed. John Henrik Clarke (New York: Citadel Press, 1964), pp. 77–96. E. U. Essien-Udom, "The Nationalist Movements of Harlem," in Clarke, *Harlem: A Community in Transition,* pp. 97–104. Roi Ottley, *New World A-Coming* (New York: Houghton Mifflin, 1943).

16. Afro-American reactions to the Italian invasion of Ethiopia are described in William R. Scott, "Black Nationalism and the Italo-Ethiopian Conflict, 1934–1936," *Journal of Negro History* 63 (April 1978): 124–35. See also Ottley, *New World A-Coming,* pp. 196–12; Rod Ross, "Black Americans and the Italo-Ethiopian Relief, 1935–36," *Ethiopia Observer* 15 (1972): 123–31; Robert G. Weisbord, *Ebony Kinship* (Westport, Conn.: Greenwood Press, 1973), pp. 89–114.

17. St. Clair Drake, *The Redemption of Africa and Black Religion* (Chicago: Third World Press, 1970); George Shepperson, "Ethiopianism and African Nationalism," *Phylon* 14 (1953): 9–18; Wilson J. Moses, "The Poetics of Ethiopianism: W. E. B. Du Bois and Literary Black Nationalism," *American Literature* 47 (1975): 411–26.

18. E. Franklin Frazier, *Black Bourgeoisie* (New York: Collier, 1962).

19. Oliver C. Cox, *Caste, Class, and Race* (Garden City, N.Y.: Doubleday, 1948), p. 572. Ira De A. Reid, "Negro Movements and Messiahs, 1900–1949," *Phylon* 9 (1949): 362. Arthur H. Fauset, *Black Gods of the Metropolis* (1944; reprint, Philadelphia: University of Pennsylvania Press, 1971).

20. Stepto and Harper, "Study and Experience," p. 357.

21. Lewis Mumford, *The Golden Day: A Study in American Experience and Culture* (New York: Boni and Liveright, 1929).

INDEX

Washington, D. C., 204
Webber, Thomas L., 54–55
Wells, H. G., 127
Wells, Ida B., 49, 213, 252
Wheatley, Phyllis, 103, 144–45, 147–48, 150
Wheeler, Edward L., 188
Whewell, William, 81, 82
Wilberforce University, 208
Williams, Chancellor, 80
Williams, Fannie Barrier, 212, 250
Williams, Henry Sylvester, 166, 170, 210
Williams, Peter, Jr., 167, 209
Williams, Samuel, 68–69, 72–73
Wilmore, Gayraud, 191
Wilson, William Julius, 32, 119–20

Winthrop, John, 162
Woman's Era, The, 212
Women: and black nationalism, 132–33; education of, 125; and sexual morality, 100; *See also* National Association of Colored Women
Wood, Peter, 54
Woodson, Carter G., 205, 210, 267
Woodson, Grandville B., 76
Woodson, Louis, 66
Wright, Richard, 103, 274, 279
Wright, Richard R., Jr., 166

Young, Alexander, 60

Zangwill, Israel, 239, 243–44, 245